The Vestry Book of Southam Parish Cumberland County, Virginia 1745-1792

Ann K. Blomquist

HERITAGE BOOKS
2006

HERITAGE BOOKS
AN IMPRINT OF HERITAGE BOOKS, INC.

Books, CDs, and more—Worldwide

For our listing of thousands of titles see our website
at
www.HeritageBooks.com

Published 2006 by
HERITAGE BOOKS, INC.
Publishing Division
65 East Main Street
Westminster, Maryland 21157-5026

Copyright © 2004 Ann K. Blomquist

Other books by the author:
Goochland County, Virginia Court Order Book 3, 1731-1735
*Southam Parish Land Processioning, 1747-1784
Goochland, Cumberland, and Powhatan Counties, Virginia*
The Vestry Book of South Farnham Parish, Essex County, Virginia, 1739-1779

All rights reserved. No part of this book may be reproduced or transmitted in any form or by any means, electronic or mechanical, including photocopying, recording or by any information storage and retrieval system without written permission from the author, except for the inclusion of brief quotations in a review.

International Standard Book Number: 978-1-58549-808-4

Table of Contents

Introduction
History of the Parish ... i
The Parish Officials ... iv
The Parish Properties ... v
The Ministers ... x
The Vestry Records ... xi
Editorial Notes and Methods ... xiv

Maps
The 1777 Map ... xvi
Parish Map 1745-1772 ... xviii
Parish Map 1772-1792 ... xix

Illustrations ... xxii

The Vestry Book ... 1

Appendices
A. Vestry Officials ... 268
B. Vestry Meetings ... 272
C. Vestry Levy ... 274
D. Glossary and Abbreviations ... 275

Bibliography ... 276

Index ... 278

INTRODUCTION

The Vestry Book of Southam Parish contains the proceedings of parish business from 1745 to 1792. Through these detailed entries, we witness the building of a community, the establishing of authority, and the handling of diversity in a new land. Though similar to other vestry books, this particular one is especially valuable because of its historical and genealogical records.

History of the Parish

When the first English settlers arrived in Virginia, they established various governing bodies. County government was the civil arm of colonial management while parishes served religious needs. These two institutions did not always coincide in geography. In 1720, Henrico Parish was divided into two parts with the upper part taking the name of St. James Parish. Goochland County was formed in 1728 from Henrico County and was intended to coincide with St. James Parish.[1] Both the county and the parish extended westward with no definite boundary.

Goochland County and St. James Parish continued together until 1745 when both were confined on their western edge by the formation of Albemarle County and St. Anne's Parish. In one act by the Virginia Assembly, St. James Parish was separated into St. James-Northam, St. James-Southam, and St. Anne's.[2] St. James-Northam was the part of the parish north of the James River while St. James-Southam was the part of the parish on the south side of the James River.

Southam Parish came into being on the first day of January 1745. The vestrymen had to create a functioning parish with officials and properties, services and taxes. Southam Parish served its community with the building of churches, the provision of a regular minister, the dependability of the vestry committee, and the annual payments of parish debts.

Within a few years, in 1749, the residents south of the James River requested a separate county, so Cumberland County was formed.[3] Cumberland County included all of Southam Parish and part of King William Parish. The arrangement stood until 1772 when Littleton Parish was taken from the western part of Southam Parish. The intent was to divide Southam so that there would be an equal number of tithes in Littleton and in Southam.[4] From 1777 until its demise, Southam Parish remained in this form.

The following chart summarizes the changes:

Year	Parish	County
1634	Henrico Parish	Henrico County
1720	St. James Parish	Henrico County
1728	St. James Parish	Goochland County
1745	Southam Parish	Goochland County
1749	Southam Parish	Cumberland County
1772	Southam Parish (Littleton removed)	Cumberland County
1777	Southam Parish	Powhatan County

For the period of 1745 through 1772, Southam Parish had the general shape of present day Cumberland and Powhatan counties combined. For 1772 through 1792, Southam Parish looked like present day Powhatan County. There are some minor exceptions to these two descriptions.

Throughout the Southam Parish Vestry Book, references to King William Parish and the "French line" appear. Even before St. James Parish or Southam Parish were formed, a different parish existed in the area. Protestant Huguenot refugees from Catholic France fled Europe and, in July 1700, some of them settled in Virginia at Manakintown in Henrico County. In December 1700, King William Parish was officially created to provide a separate parish for the French Protestant refugees.[5] The act which exempted the refugees from paying any county or parish levies for seven years also allowed the Huguenots to have their own minister and church and to collect their own tithes. In October 1705, the exemption was extended through December 25, 1708.[6]

Though the King William Parish boundaries were not clearly stated in the legislation, the Huguenots and other local residents understood the location of the lines. A portion of the land given to them was south of the James River, straddling what is now the county line between Powhatan and Chesterfield counties. A survey of the 10,000 acres was completed in 1704.[7] Even fifty years later at mid-century, county records mention the area as being part of the land surveyed for the French refugees.[8]

The other differences between the modern county lines and historic Southam Parish are two small pieces of land that belonged to other counties during this time period. Originally the line between Goochland

and Albemarle counties was completely straight from the Appomattox River to the James River. In 1778, this small piece of Buckingham County was added to Cumberland County which now forms the short segment of the county line from Randolph's Creek to the James River.[9]

In a similar manner, the original county line between Goochland and Henrico (later Cumberland and Chesterfield) was a straight line from the James River to the Appomattox River.[10] In 1850, Skinquarter Creek became the boundary between the counties, shifting a small area into Powhatan County.[11]

During the colonial era in Virginia, the Church of England was the official church which all residents were required to support with yearly taxes called tithes. However, at least one dissident congregation was tolerated in the parish. By July 1755, a group of Presbyterians had an official minister, Rev. John Wright, and by 1759, had purchased a site for their own church.[12] Charles Anderson, who had been a Southam Parish vestryman, sold the land to the Presbyterians. The deed indicates that a church building was already on the site.[13] Anderson had resigned his vestry seat in December 1749, perhaps because he had converted to Presbyterianism.

For over thirty years, Southam Parish contributed to the lives of its residents. But revolution brought changes. The parish attempted to continue with business as usual through the chaos of the American Revolution and until 1785. However, the records become less complete and briefer. After 1785, freedom of worship was demanded by Virginians, resulting in the disestablishment of the Episcopal Church and the end of mandatory public financial support. In Southam Parish, an inventory was made of the few possessions of the parish and recorded in the vestry book. Included were the glebe land valued at £300, a worn surplice worth 20 shillings, a worn altar cloth, a prayer book, a table and chest, and a damaged Bible. After 1792, Southam Parish officially ceased to exist.

For the years covered by this vestry book, Southam Parish was bounded as follows: on the north by the James River, on the east by the county line with Henrico County (until 1749 when the line became the Chesterfield County line) and King William Parish, on the south by the Appomattox River, and on the west by Albemarle County. The parish encompassed about 560 square miles until it was divided. When Littleton Parish was removed from Southam Parish, their mutual boundary became the western boundary for Southam and the parish was reduced to about 260 square miles.

The Parish Officials

The parish officials were the vestrymen, the minister, the churchwardens, the clerk of the vestry, the clerks (also called readers), the sextons, and the tax collector. The law directed that twelve responsible men be selected as vestrymen for the parish and that they subscribe to the beliefs and discipline of the Church of England. Their duties included care of the parish property, promoting religious life, keeping the parish accounts, having the parish processioned, ordering the care of the poor and needy, employing the minister, keeping records, and tending to all other parish business. The churchwardens were the chief executive officers of the vestry. There were usually two churchwardens, though for a few years only one is identified clearly in the vestry book.

The clerk of the vestry was responsible for recording the parish business in the vestry book. The handwriting in this book clearly changes each time the clerk changed. After the death of clerk Robert Walton in 1749, the vestry had some difficulty obtaining the record book from his family. Churchwarden Stephen Bedford reported to the vestry that "he hath demanded the parish book of the executors of Robert Walton deceased who refused to deliver the same." The vestry then ordered the churchwardens to "again demand the said books of the said executors & on their refusal to deliver them that they bring sute [suit] for the same."

The clerks were employed to conduct services when the minister was not able to attend the chapels or churches. The sextons were employees who were responsible for taking regular care of the church property as well as sometimes ringing the church bell for services or digging graves. Frequently, the parish provided employment to poor people by paying them to serve as sextons.

The parish tax collector was charged with collecting the tithe levied on the parish and paying creditors from the proceeds. The minutes usually direct the collector to post a bond with churchwardens. In the early years, the name of the collector was not recorded. The tithe collector was usually allowed a fee of six percent of the total levy.

At the beginning of the minutes of the vestry meetings, the list of attendees was usually written in the order of the minister, the two churchwardens, the vestrymen. The tax collector was usually listed at the end of the levy account.

See Appendix A for a list of the parish officials.

The Parish Properties

The primary church for the parish was Peterville Church. It had been built about 1730-1735 at a location which had been used as a meeting place as early as 1723.[14] By tradition, the church was named Peterville for Pierre LeGrand who selected the first site.[15] The church was located on the northeast corner of the intersection of Chapel Road (now U.S. Highway 60) and Askew's Path (now Bell Road).

Throughout the vestry book are records of periodic repairs and improvements to the church building. In June 1747, the vestry directed the churchwardens to "employ some person to tare [tar] Peterville Church all over." The following month, Thomas Harvey was chosen to install shutters on the five windows of the church. In November 1756, Wade Netherland was paid £5 for 150 panes of glass for the church and Joseph Epperson was paid £6.10.0 for installing and glazing the windows. In December 1759, Roger Hill was paid to remove old glass from Peterville.

Some changes were made to the structure when John Mayo and Benjamin Mosby were given permission in 1761 to install galleries in the southeast and northwest corners. The vestry advised that the galleries could not "prejudice" the building and further stipulated that the galleries could actually be removed at the discretion of the vestry. Just a year later, the vestry expanded Peterville by adding a section thirty feet by twenty-four feet to the center of the north side. During this addition, the entire roof was reshingled. In September 1763, the vestry budgeted £78 to pay Walter Keeble for this construction, however, nearly a year and a half passed before the payment was imminent in February 1765. Three porches were approved in 1766 for which Benjamin Mosby was paid £20.9.9 in March 1767. That sum also included payment for other work as well as supplying bread and wine for church services. Some leaks had developed by 1769, so necessary repairs were approved.

Nearly a decade passed before additional work was done to the building. In August 1778, John Netherland was chosen to "make new shutters to Peterville Church windows, put in glass where it is missing and make new steps to the doors and other necessary repairs that are wanting to the said Church." For a church that was nearing 50 years old, it is remarkable that so little was needed to keep it in repair.

After the Revolutionary War when the Episcopal Church was disestablished, several congregations shared the church. Later, it served a Baptist congregation until it was abandoned. The building burned in

1850.[16] Traces of the foundation and some gravestones in the cemetery are all that remain today. The site can be reached by walking over a pond dam north into the woods about .1 mile east of the intersection and about .1 mile north of the highway.

Peterville was Southam's only church when the parish was formed. Not surprisingly, the vestry's first items of business were the building of two chapels. For this, the vestry set a levy of £65 and 26000 pounds of tobacco and selected two sites.

The land of Daniel Coleman was chosen as the most convenient location for a chapel to serve the residents of the southwestern area of the parish.[17] The rather distinctive name of Tar Wallet for the new chapel derived from an incident involving a hog drover who stopped to rest under a tree. While he napped, a hog tore into the drover's wallet, a bag for holding food or clothing. Upon awakening, the drover chased away the hog, vowing he would teach that hog to "tear his wallet."[18] Other versions of the story include a dog tearing into the lunch wallets of men building an arbor and hogs getting into the feed wallets of horses.[19] In any case, the area took the name of Tear Wallet, with a creek and several churches bearing that name. Tear Wallet evolved into Tar Wallet, with the community making a distinction between the two names.[20]

Tar Wallet Chapel was ordered to be 40 feet by 20 feet with detailed specifications for the roof, windows, shutters, benches, and floor. These directions also provide an accurate description of Peterville Church because the chapel was directed to be built to the "same Dimentions of Peterville." Thomas Harvey was contracted to build Tar Wallet Chapel which was located near the current location of the Tar Wallet Baptist Church on Tar Wallet Road southwest of the village of Cumberland Courthouse.

Expenses were incurred for the construction and maintenance of Tar Wallet Chapel. Final payment of £16.16.9 was made to Thomas Harvey in September 1748. In January 1750, Daniel Coleman Jr. was paid for some repairs to Tar Wallet. In December 1754, the recent work at Tar Wallet was accepted. In November 1756, Humphrey Keeble was paid for 4 sets of horse blocks and two steps at the church. A gallery was added in 1757 and a variety of repairs were made through the years. Windows were fixed, horse blocks were installed, and a communion table was built.

When Littleton Parish was formed in 1772, this chapel left the jurisdiction of Southam Parish. After the Revolutionary War, the church was a "free" building which all denominations could use it. Presbyterians,

Methodists, and Baptists all shared expenses. The building underwent a variety of changes and was eventually demolished.[21]

The first vestry also hired Abraham Martin to construct a chapel in the northwestern area of the parish along Pruett's Path and Widow Dillon's Path of 1747. In the Vestry Book, this chapel name appeared as Willis' twice, but thereafter the name was always Ham Chapel. The current location would be approximately at Ashby, north of U.S. Highway 60 along Road 45 at the intersection with Deep Run Road.

It took some time to complete the two chapels. In February 1746, the vestrymen were directed to inspect the chapels when they were finished and to report to the next vestry. It was not until June 1747 that Abraham Martin was paid £33.18.6 as a partial payment for Ham Chapel and Thomas Harvey was paid £34.19.6½. Harvey also built the rails and banisters for the pulpit areas in both chapels, installed horse blocks, and cleared an acre around Tar Wallet Chapel. In July 1747, the vestry directed the churchwardens to pay John Blevings £2 for three acres of land which included Ham Chapel.

Additional modifications and repairs continued. In November 1747, "pieces" were put under the Chapel and an acre of land was cleared around the building. In January 1748, horse blocks were installed at the Chapel by Michael Johnson. In December 1754, recent work done at Ham Chapel was accepted. In February 1755, a gallery was to be added to the building. £13.6 was paid for the gallery in November 1756. In December 1757, Joseph Epperson was paid for work.. Other changes were made to the Chapel as needed. The pulpit was moved, benches added, shutters changed. In order to obtain a clear title to the property, the vestry paid for a survey of the tract.

Like Tar Wallet Chapel, Ham Chapel fell into Littleton Parish in 1772. There is no church building of any kind at the original location of Ham Chapel and even its name has passed out of the memory of local residents.

While the two new chapels were under construction, the vestry eagerly decided in 1746 to build yet another one. South Chapel, also called Lower Chapel and Worley's, was located in the southeast area of the parish, off Buckingham Road near present day Flat Rock. This location had been a "reading place" for many years prior to the construction of this chapel, so the location was a natural choice.

James Anderson won the bid in June 1747 and, in September 1748, with the chapel nearing completion, the building was inspected. However, finishing touches were not made until December 1749.

Fortunately, South Chapel still survives today. The church was Protestant Episcopal from 1784-1791, then reopened in 1794 as a Methodist Episcopal church. It was formally deeded as Rocky Oak Methodist Church in 1814 by Elisha Maxey. It survives today as a house of worship for a Holiness congregation.[22]

It was the responsibility of the vestry to provide a residence for the minister called the glebe. At the formation of Southam Parish in 1745, the current glebe land was determined "to be very inconvenient by Reason of its Remoteness from the Centre of the Parish," so the vestry petitioned the Virginia General Assembly to purchase a different piece of property.[23] William Randolph and George Carrington, as churchwardens, patented 340 acres for a glebe on June 3, 1745.[24] However, for some reason, the patent did not take effect. Meanwhile, the petition to the Assembly was granted and the old glebe land of 340 acres which was located southwest of Peterville Church was sold to William Smith by January 1747 for £53.10.0.[25]

Since there was not a suitable glebe for the minister, Rev. Robertson was allowed 2000 pounds of tobacco for his housing in 1747. Meanwhile the vestry decided to tax the parish 12000 pounds of tobacco to pay for land for a new glebe. They selected the land of John Lightfoot, paying him £90 for 270 acres in November 1747. He was allowed to continue his crop that year as long as he did not interfere with the construction of the new glebe buildings. The glebe land was bounded by Chapel Road and Askew's Path.

In July 1748, the original patent for 340 acres was granted again to the current churchwardens, Nicholas Davies and Thomas Turpin.[26] Public notice was given for bidders to build a house 42 feet by 20 feet with 2 brick chimneys. To pay for the new glebe and its outbuildings, 15000 pounds of tobacco were levied in the parish in January 1748. In May 1748, vestryman Nicholas Davies was awarded the contract to build the glebe house. The specifications are very detailed, down to the nails to be used and a "good spring lock" on the front door.

Davies did not comply with the contract. In both 1749 and 1750, Rev. Robertson was again allowed 2000 pounds of tobacco for lack of a glebe house. Finally, the vestrymen decided to bring a suit against Davies for damages for having to provide the minister with payment for lack of a glebe. Perhaps the threat of the suit spurred Davies to complete the glebe house because the vestry ordered that the house be accepted and payment made. Nicholas Davies was paid £190.6.4 for the glebe house by the May 1752 vestry.

In April 1750, several buildings were ordered for the glebe land. An old building that already existed on the property was ordered to be moved and renovated for a kitchen. Other buildings to be constructed on the glebe land included a smoke house, dairy, stable, henhouse, and an office, along with a fenced garden. In September 1751, a corn house was ordered for which Abraham Salley was paid £4.17.6 in May 1752. Rev. Robertson left Southam Parish before the glebe was completed, so the first minister to live there was Rev. McLaurine beginning in 1752.

In January 1754, a building 16 feet square with an exterior chimney was ordered, probably intended for slave quarters, to be built by John Baskerville. Then work was done to repair the cellar of the glebe in December 1754. In August 1755, the glebe buildings were to be tarred, and the main house was to be whitewashed and painted. The garden was repaired in April 1756. An additional garden the same size was ordered in November 1756. Work done on the glebe is mentioned again in December 1757. In 1759, a new kitchen was built. Repairs and minor improvements continued periodically. The record shows that the vestry invested in keeping the glebe property in good condition.

In 1807, John Hyde Saunders bought the glebe and 200 acres for $1000 to adjoin his 512-acre tract. Over the next century, the tract was sold numerous times and fell into disrepair. In 1954, the property was renovated by the Mason family.[27] Today, the glebe is a beautifully maintained private residence at the end of a drive, north of U. S. Highway 60 opposite County Road 627. It is one of the very few colonial glebes to survive and is much cherished by the community.[28] Considering that all of these early parish buildings were constructed of wood in the damp climate of Virginia's woodlands, it remarkable that two of these colonial structures are still in use today.

The Ministers

The ministers who served Southam Parish during the period of this vestry book were Rev. John Robertson, Rev. Robert McLaurine, and Rev. John Hyde Saunders. Rev. William Stith preached on a temporary basis in 1745.

The first minister of the new parish was John Robertson. He was licensed to preach in January 1746, and received a bounty of £20 for migrating to the colony in February 1746.[29] At the vestry meeting on 30 June 1746, Robertson was recommended to the parish Governor William Gooch and the Reverend William Dawson, Commissary of Virginia. He had been ordained by the Bishop of London one year earlier.[30] Robertson served Southam Parish from 1746 through 11 November 1751. He then moved to King William County were he served as the minister for St. John's Parish from 1752 until 1758.[31]

At the December 1751 vestry, Rev. Robert McLaurine (recorded as Mcklearing) was received on a probationary basis. Licensed by the Bishop of London in August 1750, he had received a bounty the following month.[32] In May 1752, the vestry accepted Robertson, beginning a tenure which lasted over twenty years. Born in Scotland about 1717, McLaurine married Elizabeth Blaikley (Blakeley), a daughter of William Blaikley and Catherine Weldon about 1753 in Cumberland County. At his death in July 1773, McLaurine was buried beneath the chancel floor of Peterville Church. Pioneer historian Bishop William Mead noted McLaurine for his piety and benevolence.[33]

After Rev. McLaurine's death, several ministers applied for the position. Jesse Carter, James Oglesby, and John Hyde Saunders all preached on a trial basis during 1773. Saunders became the parish minister and was paid for 1773 through 1776. No minister was paid after 1776. A son of John Hyde Saunders, he was born about 1746 in Cumberland County, and attended the College of William and Mary but was asked to leave the college in 1762.[34] He journeyed to England but returned to Virginia. Saunders married Rachel Bentley in May 1775 in Amelia County, Virginia. He served Southam Parish intermittently from 1773 through at least 1791. During the American Revolution, he took the side of the patriots and served on the county Committee of Safety. He died in Powhatan County in 1817.[35]

The Vestry Records

Upon the formation of Southam Parish, the vestry met every year for 40 years from 1745 through 1785 except the four years of 1753, 1764, 1768, and 1784. However, payments to the creditors were made for every year through 1784, except 1774, though occasionally a little late. Exactly seventy meetings are recorded here. After 1785, the vestry did not meet again until 1791. After 1792, the Episcopal Church was disestablished, so no further vestry records were kept. More than half of the vestry meetings took place at the county courthouse, but some were held at Peterville Church. The other meeting places were the glebe and the homes of Benjamin Childrey, Robert Murray, and William Prosser, while nine meeting places were not stated.

Parish business was conducted at the vestry meetings in four general categories. The vestry paid creditors by laying a levy on the parish tithables, they issued a variety of orders, they divided the parish into precincts for processioning, and they recorded the processioning returns. The records of the meetings were made by the clerk of the vestry. For each vestry meeting, several dates are applicable: the current date of the meeting, the past accounts which are being settled, and the future appointments for positions. See Appendix B for a list of meeting dates and the business of the meetings.

Most parish positions were salaried. Though vestrymen and churchwardens were not paid, the minister, clerk of the vestry, church clerks, sextons, and tax collector were paid in tobacco. The minister's salary of 16,000 pounds of tobacco (plus 640 pounds for the casks) was the largest expense of the parish other than the church buildings. The minister's salary was mandated by law in 1696 and remained fixed during most of the time period of this record.[36] It increased to 17,280 pounds of tobacco about 1773. At one of the highest levies of 52,836 pounds of tobacco in 1749, the minister's salary comprised over 31% of the parish budget; and at one of the lowest levies of 31,152 pounds in 1755, the minister received over 50% of the parish levy.

The parish was responsible for taking care of the poor and disabled, so payments were made to the poor or to local residents who cared for the needy. Construction and repairs of the chapels and glebe buildings all cost the parish.

In order to pay the vestry bills, the vestrymen "laid a levy" on every taxable person in the parish. The levy was collected in tobacco which was then sold for cash. An analysis of the Southam Parish levy for the years 1745 through 1784 is enlightening. Beginning in 1745, the number of tithables in the parish was 1207. Through the next twenty-five years, the number of tithables steadily increased to 3288 in 1771. In 1772, Littleton Parish was removed from Southam with the goal of equally dividing the tax base. They were successful. In 1772, the Southam levy was laid on only 1638 tithables. Through 1784, the number increased very little to 1800 tithables.

As the tax base more than doubled, levies decreased accordingly; the 1745 levy was set at 33 of tobacco, but by 1771 had dropped to 15 pounds. At the same time, the levy for the county government was between 6 and 10 pounds.[37] So, it is obvious that this religious tax was burdensome to the taxpayers.

After the division with Littleton Parish, the levy remained between 20 and 33 pounds of tobacco. However, significant changes occurred with revolutionary times. After the war started, the levy plummeted to 3 pounds of tobacco per levy because no minister was being paid. The next few levies of 2 through 6 pounds of tobacco were quite reduced from pre-Revolutionary years. See Appendix C for the yearly number of tithes, the levy per tithe, and the total levy.

Cash money during colonial times was in British pounds sterling (£). One pound was worth 20 shillings, and one shilling was worth 12 pence. For example, £6.15.4 meant 6 pounds sterling, 15 shillings, and 4 pence. The notation 15/4 means 15 shillings and 4 pence. Throughout this volume, the price of tobacco varied, probably depending on the quality. One hundred pounds of tobacco was priced between 11 and 15 shillings. £100 was worth 15000 pounds of tobacco. The tobacco levied on the parish was collected, shipped to a warehouse, and sold for cash.

Accounts were generally settled by the vestry at the end of each calendar year in November or December or in the first two months of the next year in January or February (33 times). A few times, the accounts were settled in other months: September (1 time), March (4 times), and May (1 time).

A second type of parish business recorded in the vestry meetings was the issuing of orders. Orders included positions of authority or responsibility, construction and repair orders, care of the poor or needy, and so forth.

However, the two remaining types of parish records, processioning orders and processioning returns, make up more than 60% of this book.

Processioning was a procedure to formally determine and agree on the boundaries between property owners. The vestry assigned leaders in each precinct to walk the property lines with all the landowners and to report back to the vestry with agreements and disagreements duly included. Following the law, the vestry ordered processioning of the property lines every four years beginning in 1747, except 1767. The processioning years were 1747, 1751, 1755, 1759, 1763, 1771, 1775, 1779, and 1783. The returns from the precincts were recorded in 1748, 1756, 1760, 1765, 1772, and 1780. No returns were recorded for 1752, 1776, or 1784.

The development of the parish is evident in the processioning orders. In 1747, the vestrymen divided the parish into 34 precincts of various sizes, from small to rather large. The number of precincts slightly increased during the next five processionings: 35 in 1751, 40 in 1755, 41 in 1759, 41 in 1763, and 43 in 1771. When the parish was divided to form Littleton Parish, the number of precincts dropped to 19 for all the remaining processionings.

The value of the processioning returns lies in the detailed naming of the property owners. Since each person's property could be bounded by several other people, the names of adjoining landowners and neighbors should appear in accurate processioning returns. Unfortunately, the processioners did not fully comply with their orders. While some returns do indeed contain complete lists of names, others report none, simply stating that all was performed "in peace and quietness." The process of processioning appears to have been quite successful; only twice were disputes mentioned in the vestry book, and those were quickly resolved.

Additionally, the rate of returns varied widely through the years. For example, in 1747, 62% of the precincts are properly reported, falling to 54% in 1775, and dropping further in 1759 to a mere 34%. The rate reached its highest at 80% in 1763 and then fell to its lowest at 14% in 1771. After the separation with Littleton, two of the three processionings had no returns while the one set of returns only reported back 47% of the precincts.

On the whole, the vestry proceedings are ordinary and repetitive. However, some unusual entries are found. At the January 27, 1766, vestry, Thomas Fretwell Freeman, longtime clerk for Ham Chapel, was ordered to appear at the next vestry as a "person of disorder" and to answer to the vestry. No disposition to this charge was recorded and Freeman continued to be paid until his death in 1769. Thomas Hall, the clerk of South Chapel, was also charged in August 1775 with neglecting his duty, so he was summoned to appear before the vestry. There is no further mention made of this charge.

The December 22nd 1762 vestry authorized the payment of 112 pounds of tobacco to purchase copies of the acts of the Virginia Assembly to be read in the churches. In January 1776, John Watts was paid £4.0.6 for "removing Judith May, a poor person, to Antrim Parish, Halifax County." Some other interesting entries are sums paid to Francis Amoss for sundries "supplied his father's family in the time they had the smallpox." Thomas Strange was paid for several years for the support of his two "unfortunate" children. Dr. William Cable was paid the extraordinary sum of £36.9.4 for "keeping and trying to cure Stephen Holland for a cancer in his mouth." The vestry also collected a few fines for swearing. In 1765 and 1766, the Tax Collector collected 15 shillings for "several oaths," 10 shillings for 2 oaths, and £1 for 4 oaths.

In 1770, in order to address the continuing issue of care of the poor, the vestry decided to purchase some land to build a poorhouse. Littleberry Mosby, William Fleming, and George Carrington Jr. were directed to buy no more than 100 acres for this purpose. However, no further mention was made of a poorhouse.

When Littleton Parish was created in 1772, Southam was required to pay the new parish their portion of the tithes.

Editorial Notes and Method

For this transcription of the Southam Parish Vestry Book, I used a microfilm copy of the photostat copy of the original book prepared by the Library of Virginia. The location of the original vestry book is not currently known though it has been thought to be in the Powhatan County Courthouse. After 1792, the book was used for nonparish processioning records for 1803 through 1838. The Powhatan County Courthouse has a different photocopy of the vestry book. The Library's copy is probably close to the size of the original, a large bound volume about 9.5 inches by 14.625 inches. For unknown reasons, the first 20 pages are slightly smaller at 8.75 by 13.875 inches. The first leaf of the vestry book is missing from both copies, so this transcription begins with page three.

For the researcher who wishes to refer to the original book, the page numbers have been denoted in brackets [ ]. Unfortunately, the pages were renumbered at some later time and there are now two different page numbers on most of the pages. The number on the outside edge of the page has been used here. The microfilm is available for patrons as Miscellaneous Record 2288.

Throughout this book, the handwriting of the vestry clerks is wonderfully legible. Style decisions, however, were needed for the printed transcription. My overall philosophy has been to change as little of the original record as possible. Attempting to preserve the flavor of colonial writing, I have retained superscripts, capital letters, and spelling. To aid in reading the names of individuals, commas and capitalization have been added. Punctuation has been modernized. Flourishes, long dashes, and decorative marks have been omitted. Spelling in the original book is, not surprisingly, haphazard. Vestry clerk Robert Walton is notably the worst speller in recording the 1747 processioning returns.

This vestry book covers the time period when the method of recording dates was changed. Through 1751, the first day of the year was considered to be March 25 with January and February as the last months of the year. So, January and February were written in a different style, for example, January 13, 1750/1 would mean January 13, 1751 to modern readers. Calendar reform finally reached the colonies in September 1752 when 11 days were removed from the calendar and the first day of the year was set at January 1. Prior to September 1752, the vestry meetings dated for the months of January and February may appear to be out of order, but the reader should realize that those meetings actually should be numbered with the next year. Dates after September 1752 are in the modern form.

This vestry book holds a special interest for me because three of my Virginia ancestors are included in its pages. What a marvel to find familiar names and allied families going about their lives not knowing that a granddaughter many generations removed would put their names into print two and a half centuries later.

This project would only be possible with the help of many people. The editor wishes to make grateful acknowledgment to the Library of Virginia for their contributions to this book; to John Blomquist for his computer wizardry; and to Tate Blomquist for her patient proofreading.

August, 2002   Ann Kicker Blomquist
Orlando, Florida

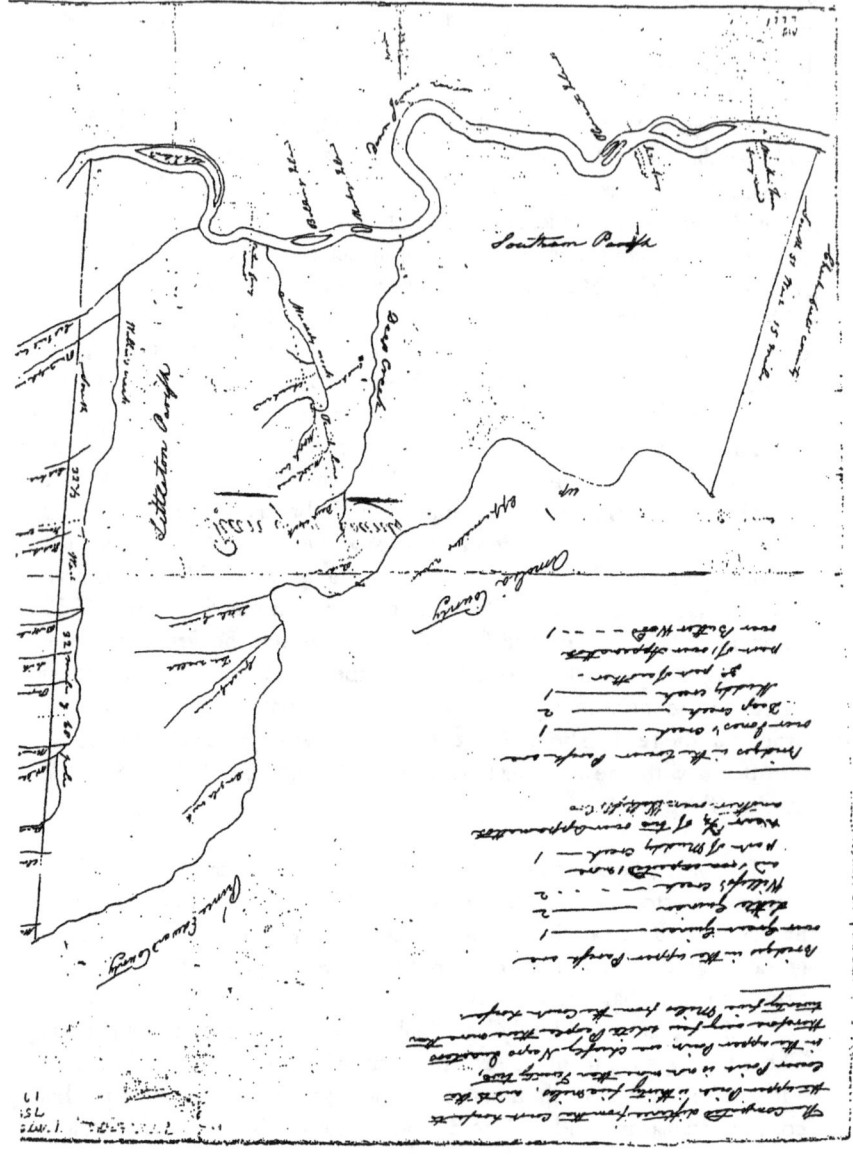

The 1777 Map

In 1777, the residents of the eastern half of Cumberland County petitioned the Virginia General Assembly for a new county to be called Powhatan. Since the dividing line between Southam Parish and Littleton Parish had been a successful separation in 1772, the same line was used to divide the counties.

Probably as part of the petition to the Assembly, a map of Cumberland County was drawn in 1777, showing the proposed dividing line and some landmarks.[38] This map is a very early county map in the collection of the Library of Virginia. Interestingly, the map is drawn "upside down" with north at the bottom of the page and south at the top. This map clearly shows the original shape of Cumberland County with completely straight eastern and western county boundaries. The following is written on the map:

The computed diffrance from the court house to the upper point is thirty five miles, and to the lesser point is now more than Twenty two, in the upper Point are chiefly Negro Quarters there very few white People there more than twenty five Miles from the Court house.

Bridges in the upper Parish are over
Great Guinea	1
Little Guinea	2
Willies's Creek	2
and soon accepted 1 more part of Muddy Creek	1
near 3/4 of two over Appamattox another over Willis's Cr	

Bridges in the lower Parish are over
Jones's Creek	1
Deep Creek	2
Muddy Creek	1
D°. part of another	1
part of 1 over Appamattox over Butter Wood	1

SOUTHAM PARISH 1745-1772

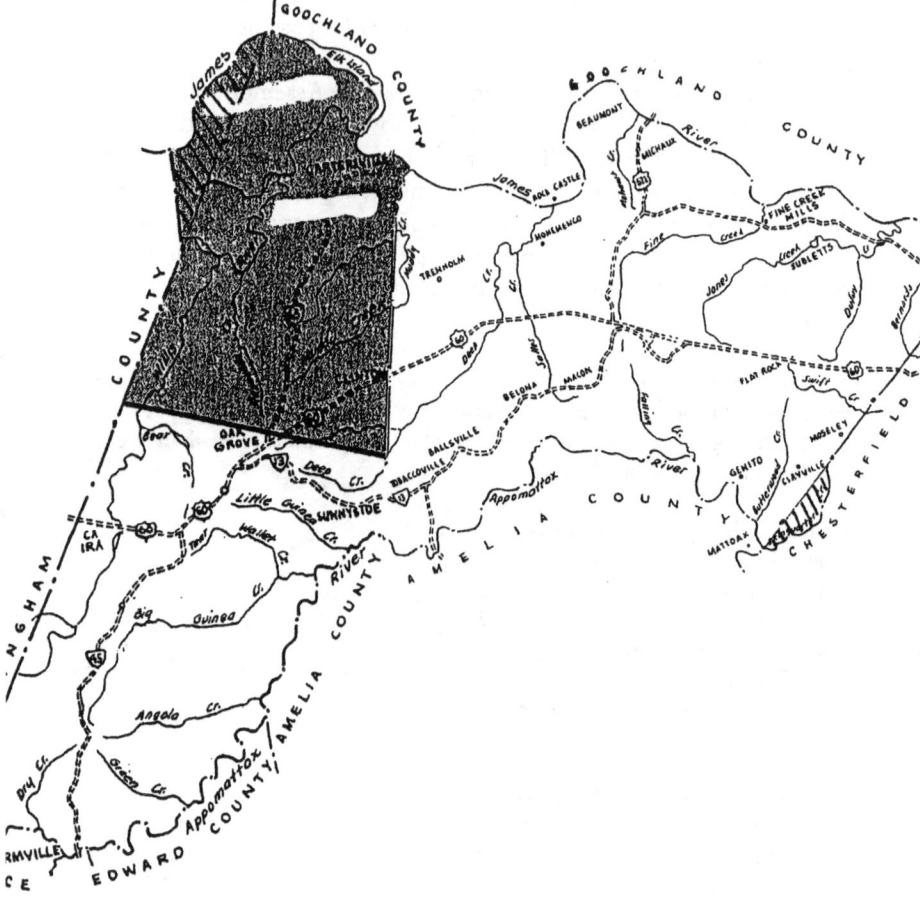

Map adapted from
Charles Cocke
Parish Lines of the Diocese of Southern Virginia

SOUTHAM PARISH 1772-1792

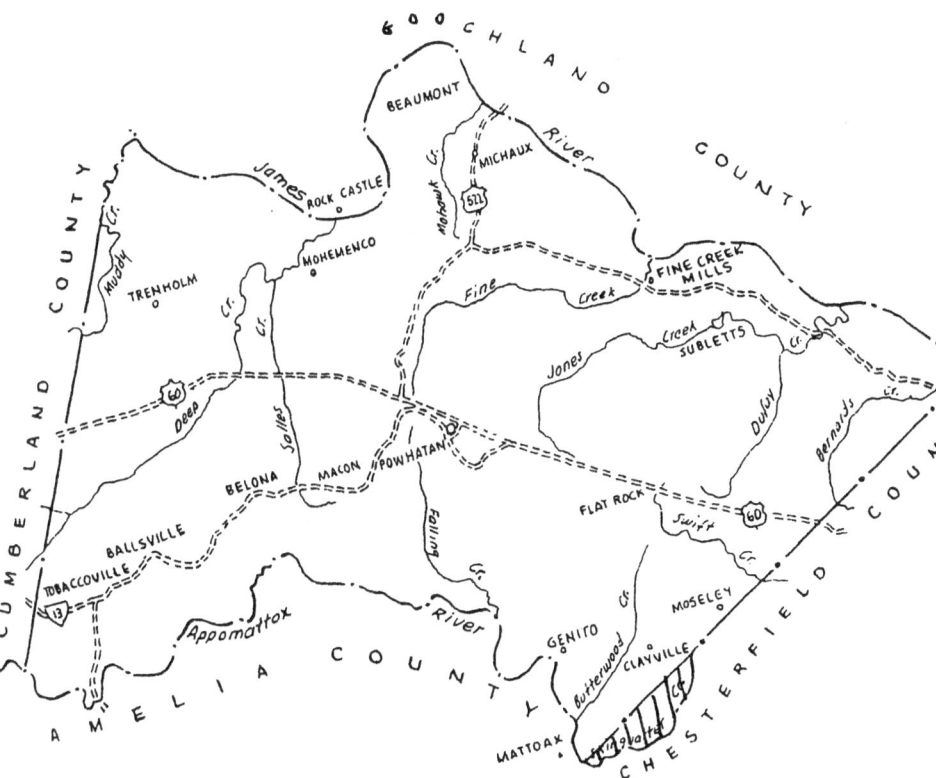

Map adapted from
Charles Cocke
Parish Lines of the Diocese of Southern Virginia

Notes

1. Cocke, p 28.
2. Cocke, p 134; Hening 5:266-267.
3. Hening 6:12.
4. Cocke, p 135; Hening 8:603.
5. Hening 3:201.
6. Hening 3:478-479.
7. Cabell, p 10.
8. Cumberland County, Virginia, Deed Book 2, page 19 (deed between Thomas Porter and Daniel Scott, dated November 27, 1752); page 69 (deed between Daniel Perro and William Harris, dated September 24, 1753); page 239 (deed between William Mosley and Robert Chandler, dated August 2, 1755).
9. Hening 5:267; 9:559.
10. Hening 4:240; Winfree p 321.
11. Acts of the General Assembly 1849-1850, Chapter 28, p 26.
12. Cumberland County, Virginia, Deed Book 2, page 515.
13. The Farmville Herald, *Today and Yesterday in the Heart of Virginia*, p 322.
14. Powhatan County Independence Bicentennial Commission, *Powhatan's Strength*, 1977, p 3.
15. "Peterville Church and the Glebe," *Powhatan Today*, March 3 1994. Section B.
16. "Restoration Hopes High for Old Peterville Church," *Richmond News Leader*, May 12, 1953; "Peterville Church and the Glebe," *Powhatan Today*, March 3, 1994, Section B.
17. Meade, Vol 2., p 34.
18. Hopkins, p 25; Vaughan, p 69.
19. *Cumberland County Virginia and Its People*, p 30; "Excerpts of the History of Tar-Wallet Baptist Church," *Farmville Herald*, August 3, 1930.
20. *Cumberland County and Its People.* p 30.
21. Putney, Dorothy R. *Tar Wallet Church, A History.* p 7.
22. Powhatan County Independence Bicentennial Committee. *Powhatan's Heritage 1700-1978*. Powhatan, Virginia, 1978. p 3.
23. Winfree, Waverly. *The Laws of Virginia, Being A Supplement to Hening's.* p 396-397.
24. Nugent, Patent Book 23, p 130.
25. Vestry Book, p [24, 46]; Goochland County VA Deed Book 5, page 473-474, dated Sep 16, 1748.
26. Nugent, Patent Book 26, p 259-260.
27. "Peterville Church and the Glebe," *Powhatan Today*, March 3, 1994, Section B.

28. Davis and Rawlings, p 104.
29. Goodwin, p 302.
30. Meade, Vol. 2, p 33.
31. Meade, II, 380; Goodwin, p 302.
32. Goodwin, p 289-290.
33. Meade, Vol 2., p 33.
34. William and Mary Quarterly, 1st Series, Vol XIV, 1906, p 145-150; *Genealogies of Virginia Families*, Vol IV N-T, p 346.
35. Goodwin, p 304.
36. 3 Hening p 152.
37. Cumberland County Court Order Books.
38. Original map is in the collection of the Library of Virginia. The locator card states "This plan which indicates the present county of Powhatan probably accompanied a petition for the division of the county." Call number 755.572.

January 1748

1748. Southam Parish

Description		
To the Reverend John Robertson his Salary Due the 15th this Instant	16.000	Cash 640
To John Cardwell Clk Peterville Church	1000	40
To Thomas Freeman Fretwell Clk Ham Chapel	1000	40
To Sylvanus Witt Reader at Worley's	1000	40
To John Hubbard Clk Tear Wallet Chapel	1000	40
To Robert Walton Clk of the Vestry	500	20
To John Legrand Sexton	500	
To William Easley Sexton	500	
To Michael Johnson Sexton	500	
To Judith Bradshaw for keeping George Dobbins 'til the 27th of November last	708	
To John Taylor for keeping Robert Saunders's Child till the first day of this Instant January	900	
To Danl Witmore for keeping Eliza Howle	300	
To John Hatch for himself and his Wife	600	
To John Worley for serving as Sexton at the Reading place	250	
To Michl Johnson for putting up two House Blocks at Ham Chapel	60	
To Edward Yarbour	500	
To Henry Wood for Clks fees	119	
To Samuel Bridgwater for keeping Johannah Parish	600	
To Tobo Levied to raise £100 towards paying for the Glebe House	15.000	
To John Smith Junr for 13 Insolvent Tithables	455	
To Bowker Smith for 32 Insolvent Tithables	1120	
To Paul Michaux for two Levies overlisted in 1747	70	
To William Taylor for keeping Alxr Blunt 4 Months	266	
	42940	
Cash Added	1870	
	43760	

August 11th 1755

Ordered That Joseph Baugh Israel Winfrey and John Watkins on the 10th Day of November Next Begin and Procession all the Lands and Renew and mark the several Lines Between Buckingame Road the New Road Peneto Road and the County Line and make their Return according to Law —

Ordered That George Hancock Richard Moseley and William Moseley on the 10th Day of November next Begin and Procession all the Lands and Renew and Mark the several Lines Between the County Line Appamattox River and Peneto Road and make their Return according to Law —

Ordered That Williams Daniel William Mills and William Frigg on the 10th Day of November next Begin and Procession all the Lands and Renew And mark the several lines Between Bollings Road Buckingame Road The main Road and the County line and make their Return according to Law —

Ordered That Samuell Allen Alexander Trent and Thomas Putterey on the 10th Day Of November next Begin and Procession all the Lands and Renew and mark The several lines Between Buckingame Road the County line Harrisons Road And the Road from Murrays to John Burtons and make their Return according to Law —

Ordered That John Hopson William Hopson Field Robertson and George Winnefrod on the 10th Day of November next Begin and Procession all the Lands and Renew And mark the several lines Between Buckingame Road the Road from John Burtons To Murreys the Courthouse Road and Mayos old mill Path to Benjamin Harris's And make their Return according to Law —

Ordered That Poindexter Mosby John Scruggs and John Hughes on the 10th Day of November Next Begin and Procession all the Lands and Renew and mark the several Lines Between the middle Road Mr Salleys Path Buckingame Road Mr Harris's Path to Mayo Old mill and Deep Creek and make their Return according to Law —

Ordered That Sanborn Wooten George Owen George Cardwell and Frances Macraw on the 10th Day of November next Begin and Procession all the Lands and Renew and mark the Several Lines Between the middle Road Randolphs Church Road Buckingame Road and Mr Salleys Path And make their Return according to Law —

Page 80 from the Vestry Book
showing 1755 processioning orders

The Vestry Book

The Vestry Book of Southam Parish

[pages 1 and 2 are missing]

[3]   [1745]
[this page is inserted backwards in the microfilm copy]
[the right hand edge of this page is missing]
[torn, words missing] if not the Church [torn, words missing]
other Clergiman for the said Tobacco.   [torn] usa [torn]
    William Randolph Church Warden   [torn] Balle [torn]
    George Carrington Ch. W^d.   [torn] or [torn]
    Alexander Trent   C[harles] Ander[son]
    James Barnes   Samuel Scott
    James Terry   Stephen Bedford

****

At a Vestry held at Peterville Church the 22^d August 1745. Present William Randolph, Thomas Turpin, Alexa[nder Trent], George Carrington, James Barnes, Benjamin Harrison, [James] Terry, Samuel Scott, and Nicholas Davies, and Creed Hask[ins] Vestrymen.

Pursuant to the order of Vestry in May last James Terry a[nd Alex]ander Trent Report that the most Convenient place to set the [torn] Chapel will be on Tear Wallet Hill on the Land of Daniel [Coleman] whereupon the Vestry order that the Hull of a Chapel be B[uilt on] Said Hill Forty foot long and Twenty four foot wide with [torn] with Summers and girders Fifteen feet Pitch in the [torn] Pulpit and Desk and Communion Table Five sash W[indows] the same Dimentions of Peterville with wooden Shutters [torn] with feather Edge Plank with Benches set up within the C[torn] Seats. The said Chapel is to have a girt Roof with Principal [rafters] Braced and covered with heart Shingles nailed on with [torn] nails to be done workmanlike to be set upon Lightwoods [torn] Stone Eighteen Inches from the ground to be Delivered up and [torn] October 1746.

Pursuant to an order of Vestry in May last George Carring[ton, Ben]jamin Harrison, and Samuel Scott Report that the most con[venient] place for the other Chapel on James River will be at a Spring [on Thomas] Carter's Land between John Blevings and William Salmon upon the Vestry order that a Chapel be Built at the said p[torn, letters and word missing] as the other. Thomas Harvy having given [security.]

[4]
[left and right edges of this page are missing]
[illegible line]
[torn] the Building the other Chapel for the sum of [torn] Current Money.
    [William] Randolph Church Warden   Samuel Scott
    [George] Carrington Church Warden   Creed Haskins
    [Alexander] Trent   James Barnes
    [Thomas] Turpin   Benjamin Harrison
    [James Ter]ry
    [Nicholas] Davies

****

At a vestry held for Southam Parish at Peterville Church 3^d day of November 1745 in order to Lay the Parish Levy. William Randolph, Alexander Trent, James Terry, James [Barnes], [Benja]min Harrison, Nicholas Davies, Stephen Bedford, [Creed Has]kins Gent. Vestrymen.

Southam Parish D^r.	Tobacco	Cask
To Levy'd to Raise £65 for Thomas Harvy and [Abraham] Martin for Building two Chapels	26000	
[To Mr.] William Stith for preaching three Sermons [torn] and for Six Sermons Pursuant to order of [torn]ay of May last 1500. Twice coming	2250	90
To James Terry Reader at Tear Wallet	1000	40
[To Thomas Fr]eeman Fretwell Reader at Willis's	1000	40
[To Robert Wal]ton Clk Peterville Church & D°. of the vestry	1500	60
[To Sylvanus] Witt Reader at Worley's from June 1st to [torn]	500	20
[To John Leg]rand Sexton	500	

[To George Do]bbins	500
[To] John Taylor for Keeping Robert Saunders's Child 'till [torn]st	800
[To Samuel Sco]tt for keeping Hendrick Scales from May 12	600
[To] Netherland Gent. For keeping & Burying the Wid°. Scales	600
[To Alexander] Trent for 21 lb sugar for the Widow Kent	150
[torn]ence Turpin for Burying &c of Anne [Kent] [torn]tertaining and Nursing of her two Months	600
[torn]s for 47 Insolvents at 17 lb p Poll	799
	36799
Cask	250
	370[49]
Sal[ary] at 6 p Cent	22[23]
	392[72]

[5]

	Contra C' Tobacco	
[torn] proportional part of 1240 lb Tobacco due from [torn] Collector last year		414
By 1207 Titheables at 33 lb p Poll		39831
		4024[5]
By Depositum in the hands of the Collector		973
		39272

Robert Walton took the Oaths appointed by Act of Parliament and Subscribed the Test and then also took the Oath of a Clerk of the Vestry.

Ordered that Joseph Terry be paid at the Laying the next Parish Levy one thousand Pounds of Tobacco for keeping the Widow Kent 'till the 17th day of next August or in proportion in Case she dies within that Time.

Ordered that the Church Warden's Provide necessary Apparel for the said Anne Kent and bring in their account thereof which also be allowed them at the Laying the next Parish Levy.

   William Randolph James Terry
   Benjamin Harrison Stephen Bedford
   James Barnes   Creed Haskins

Alexander Trent   Nicholas Davies

****

At a Vestry held for Southam Parish at Peterville Church June 30th 1746. Present William Randolph, Thomas Turpin, Alexander Trent, George Carrington, James Barnes, James Te[rry], Benjamin Harrison, Samuel Scott, and Creed Haskins Gent. [Vest]rymen.

Ordered that the Reverend John Robertson being Recommended [to] this Parish by His Honour William Gooch Esq and the Reverend William Dawson Commissary of Virginia be Received as Minister for the Parish of Southam.

Ordered that William Roberts do keep Ezekiel Turner untill the [la]ying the next Parish Levy and that he be allowed at the Rate of [on]e thousand pounds of Tobacco p year from the Middle of [torn]

[l]ast untill then.

Ordered that Samuel Scott be allowed at the Rate of [one thousand] pounds of Tobacco p year from this Time for keeping William [Ballew] untill the Church Wardens provide for him some other way [torn] in Health.

Ordered that a Chapel be Built at or near the Reading place at Worley's as soon as Conveniently may be done.

Ordered that the Vestry do Levy for Richard Henderson Three Hundred pounds of Tobacco at the Laying the next Parish Levy.

William Randolph	James Barnes
George Carrington	Samuel Scott
Thomas Turpin	Creed Haskins
Alexander Trent	Benjamin Harrison
James Terry	

****

At a Vestry held for Southam Parish at Peterville Church in order to Lay the Parish Levy the 12th Day of January 1746. Present the Reverend John Robertson Minister, Alexander Trent, George Carrington, James Terry, Nicholas Davies, Benjamin Ha[rri]son and Samuel Scott Gent. Vestrymen.

1746 Southam Parish	D^r. Tobacco	C[ask]
To the Reverend John Robertson Minister from the 30th of June 'till the 15th day of January at 16000 p An.	9333	37[4]
To James Terry Reader at Tear Wallet	1000	[40]
To Thomas Freeman Fretwell D^o. At Willis's	1000	[40]
To Sylvanus Witt D^o. At Worleys	1000	[40]
To Robert Walton Clerk of Peterville Church D^o. of the Vestry	1500	[60]
To John Legrand Sexton	500	
To George Dobbins	500	
To John Taylor for keeping Robert Saunders's Child	800	
To Samuel Scott for keeping Hendrick Scales till this day	1066	
To Samuel Scott for keeping William Ballew at 1000 lb Tob. p year from June 30th 'till the 3^d of October last	255	
To William Roberts for keeping Ezekiel Turner at 1000 lb p year from the Middle of May 'till the 12th January	666	
[errors, sum should be 17620, cask 554]	17320	

[7] [J]anuary 12 1746	Tobacco	Cask
To Brought from the other side	17320	574
Present James Barnes		
To Richard Henderson 300 due & 500 for the Ensuing year	800	
To Joseph Terry For keeping the Widow Kent from the 17th day of August 1745 'till the 17 day of Augst. 1746 at the Rate of One Thousand pounds Tobacco p An.	1000	
To Isaac Bates Sherif for 20 Insolvents at 33 p Poll	660	
To Joseph Terry for his account of 17 shillings in Tobacco	136	
To the Reverend William Stith for Preaching four Sermons in April Last	1000	
To John Hatch for himself and his Wife	600	

To William Easley for work done at Tear Wallet	80	
To Tobacco Levy'd for the use of the Parish to be left in the Church Wardens hands 'till it is Wanted	10000	
To William Wamack for feeding and Cloathing the Widow Kent untill the 17th day of August 1747	800	
[this total is correct]	32696	574
	574	Cask
	33270	
Salary at 6 p Cent	1997	
	35267	

[17]46 P   Contra   C^r

	Tobacco
By a Depositum left in the hands of the Collector last year	973
By 1267 Titheables at 27 p Poll	34209
By a Ballance arising by this Collection due to the Collector	85
	35267

Ordered that John Taylor Keep Robert Saunders's Child at the Rate of One thousand pounds of Tobacco p year from the 1st January 1746 'till the Laying the next Parish Levy.

Ordered that George Carrington, Nicholas Davies, Benjamin Harrison, Alexander Trent, and Samuel Scott or any three of

[8]   February 25, 1746
them do View Ham Chapel when Finished and make Report thereof to the next Vestry.

Ordered that Alexander Trent, James Terry, Benjamin Harrison and Charles Anderson or any three of them do View Tear Wallet Chapel and make Report to the next Vestry.

Thomas Turpin and Nicholas Davies is appointed Church Warden in the Room of William Randolph and George Carrington.

Nicholas Davies took the Oath of a Church Warden.

John Cardwell is appointed Clerk of Peterville Church at the Rate of one thousand Pounds of Tobacco and Cask pr Annum.

Ordered that the Former Church Wardens pay Thomas Harvy £3.

John Robertson	George Carrington
Nich^s Davies Church Warden	James Barnes
Alexander Trent	James Terry
Samuel Scott	Benjamin Harrison

****

At a Vestry held at Benjamin Childrey's the 25th day of February 1746. Present the Reverend John Robertson Minister, William Randolph, Thomas Turpin, George Carrington, James Barnes, Nicholas Davies, Samuel Scott, Stephen Bedford and Creed Haskins Gent. Vestrymen.

The Vestry met according to appointment upon the Glebe Land and find it to be very Inconvenient by Reason of its Remoteness from the Centre of the Parish and thereupon agree that a Petition be Preferr'd to the Assembly to grant an Act to Impower the Vestry to make Sale of the said Land and to apply the Money arising from the Sale thereof to the purchase of other Lands more conv.

Thomas Turpin took the Oath of a Church Warden.

Ordered that the Church Wardens do give Notice that a Chapel a[t] Worley's be Let to the Lowest Bidder at the next Vestry.

John Robertson	James Barnes
Nicholas Davies Church Warden	Stephen Bedford
Thomas Turpin Church Warden	Samuel Scott
William Randolph	Creed Haskins
George Carrington	

****

[9]   June 15, 1747

At a Vestry held for Southam Parish at Peterville Church the 15th day of June 1747. Present The Reverend John Robertson Minister, William Randolph, Thomas Turpin, Alexander Trent, George Carrington, James

Barnes, James Terry, Nicholas Davies, Stephen Bedford, and Creed Haskins, Gent. Vestrymen.

Ordered that the Late Church Wardens pay Abraham Martin Thirty-three pounds Eighteen shillings and Six pence in part of payment for Building Ham Chapel.

Ordered that the Late Church Wardens pay Thomas Harvy Thirty Four pounds Nineteen shillings and Six pence half penny being the Ballance due to him agreed by the Vestry for Building the Chapel at Tear Wallet, for the Cornish Horse Blocks, Steps to the Doors and Clearing half an Acre of Ground Round the Chapel.

Ordered that the Remainder of the Money which will be (when Ham Chapel be Finished) due to Abram Martin by [be] paid to him by the Church Wardens after it is Received by the Gentlemen appointed to Receive the same.

Ordered that William Easley Serve as Sexton of Tear Wallet Chapel at Five Hundred pounds of Tobacco p Annum from the first day of this Ins^t. June.

Ordered that Michael Johnson Serve as Sexton of Ham Chapel at Five Hundred pounds of Tobacco p annum from the first day of this Ins^t. June.

Ordered that William Randolph, Thomas Turpin, George Carrington, Alexander Trent, James Barnes, Samuel Scott, James Terry, Stephen Bedford, and Creed Haskins or any three of them do meet at M^r. John Lightfoots on Saturday the 27th of Instant in order to View the Lands that is offered for Sale to the Vestry, for a Glebe, and make Report to the next Vestry.

Ordered that William Randolph, Thomas Turpin, and Creed Haskins or any two of them do View and appoint a place to Set the Lower Chapel which is to be Built by James Anderson.

The Vestry agree to give Thomas Harvy £3.12 for to Rail and Ban[is]ter Round the Communion Tables at Tear Wallet and Ham Chapels' and to give him £3. To put up Shutters to the five Windows at Peterville Church with H L Hinges the Shutter in one piece.

Ordered that one of the Church Wardens Employ some Person to Tare [tar] Peterville Church all over.

[10] July 27, 1747
Ordered that Nicholas Davies as Church Warden pay John Blevings two pounds Current Money and take a Deed from said Blevings for three Acres of Land Including Ham Chapel to be Invested to the Parish of Southam.

  John Robertson   James Barnes
  Thomas Turpin Church Warden Stephen Bedford
  Nicholas Davies Church Warden Creed Haskins
  Alexander Trent
  George Carrington

****

At a Vestry held for Southam Parish the xxvii [27] day of July mdccxlvii [1747] Present the Reverend John Robertson Minister, Thomas Turpin, Alexander Trent, George Carrington, James Barnes, James Terry, Benjamin Harrison, Nicholas Davies, Stephen Bedford and Creed Haskins Gent^n Vestrymen.

Pursuant to an Order of Goochland Court bearing date July the xxi mdccxlvii for processioning the several Lands in Southam Parish the Church Wardens have laid off the said Parish into the precincts hereafter mentioned (vizt).

Ordered that William Marshall, Arthur Moseley and William Moseley on the 10th of November next begin at the County line on Appamattox River thence along the line to Jeneto Road up the Road to the River and down the River to the beginning do Procession the several Lands and renew and mark the respective lines and make return to the Vestry by the last of March of every persons Land they shall procession of what persons are present at the same of what Lands in the said precinct they shall fail to procession and the particular reasons of such failure.

Ordered that Richard Moseley, Francis Marshall and Thomas Locket, on the 11th of November next begin at Jeneto Road at Butterwood Creek thence up the Road to the River up the River to Fighting Creek up the Creek to William Clay's thence down Clay's Path by

[11]   July 27, 1747
Edward Watkins's to the beginning do procession the several Lands and renew and mark the respective lines and make return to the Vestry by the last of March of every persons Land they shall Procession of what persons are present at the same, of what Lands in the said precinct they shall fail to procession and the particular reasons of such Failure.

Ordered that Henry Clay, William Clay and John Moseley on the 12th of November next begin at William Clays on Fighting Creek thence up the Creek to Buckingham Road at the Reading place down the Road to Thomas Watkins's and down Butterwood Creek, to the Main Road thence up by Edward Watkins's to William Clays do procession the several Lands and renew and mark the respective lines and make return to the Vestry by the last of March of every persons Land they shall procession of what persons are present at the same of what Lands in the said precinct they shall fail to procession and the particular reasons of such Failure.

Ordered that John Watkins, Joseph Baugh and Israel Winfree on the 13th of November next begin at Buckingham Road at the head of Butterwood Creek thence down the Road to the County line along the line to the main Jeneto Road up the Road to Butterwood Creek and up the Creek to the beginning do procession the several Lands and renew and mark the respective lines and make return to the Vestry by the Last of March of every persons Land they shall procession of what persons are present at the same of what Lands in the said precinct they shall fail to procession and the particular reasons of such Failure.

Ordered Richard Povall, George Williamson and John Mossom, on the 14th of November next begin at the Fork of Fighting Creek thence up Randolphs Fork to Buckingham Road down the Road to the Reading place, and down Clays fork to the beginning do procession the several

[12] July 27, 1747
Lands and renew and mark the respective lines and make return to the Vestry by the last of March of every persons Land they shall procession of what persons are present at the same of what Lands in the said precinct they shall fail to procession and the particular reasons of such Failure.

Ordered that Benjamin Childrey, Henry Brazeal and Philip Thomas on the 15th of November next begin at the mouth of Fighting Creek thence up the River to Liles's Ford along Liles's Road to Benjamin Childreys down Buckingham Road to Fighting Creek and down the Creek to the beginning do Procession the several Lands and renew and mark the respective lines and make return to the Vestry by the Last of March of every persons Land they shall procession of what persons are present at the same of what Lands in the said precinct they shall fail to precession and the particular reasons of such Failure.

Ordered that John Cannifax, Nathanael Maxey and Bennet Goode on the 12th of October next begin at the Mouth of Fine Creek thence down the River to the French line thence along their lines to Jones's Creek up the same to the head and from thence the nearest Course to Buckingham Road up the same to Stratton's House thence down Fine Creek to the beginning do Procession the several Lands and renew and mark the respective lines and make return to the Vestry by the last of March of every persons Land they shall procession of what persons are present at the same of what lands in the said precinct they shall fail to procession and the particular reasons of such Failure.

Ordered that John Radford, William Maxey and Sylvanus Maxey on the 13th of October next begin on the South side Jones's Creek at the French line thence up the Creek to the head then the nearest Course to Buckingham Road down the Road to the Road to the French line and along their lines to the beginning do precession the several Lands and renew and mark the

[13] July 27, 1747
respective lines and make return to the Vestry by the last of March of every persons Land they shall Procession of what persons are present at the same of what Lands in the said precinct they shall fail to Procession and the particular reasons of such Failure.

Ordered that John Baskorville, William Chandler and Anthony Hughes on the 14th of October next begin at Strattons plantation thence up Buckingham Road to Benjamin Childrey's along the Courthouse Road to Chandler down the Chapel Road to Fine Creek at the three Bridges and up the Creek to the beginning do procession the Several Lands and renew and mark the respective lines and make return to the Vestry by the last of March of every persons Lands they shall procession of what person are present at the same of what Lands in the said precinct they shall fail to procession and the particular reasons of such Failure.

Ordered that Thomas Walker, Thomas Stovall and John Legrand on the 15th of October next begin at Benjamin Childrey's thence along the Court House Road to Lax's up the Chapel Road to the Ridge Path between Little Deep Creek and Great Deep Creek along the Path to Buckingham Road and down the Road to the beginning do procession the several Lands and renew and mark the respective lines and make return to the Vestry by the last of March of every person Land they shall procession of what persons are present at the same of what Lands in the said precinct they shall fail to procession and the particular reasons of such Failure.

Ordered that Joel Chandler, John Taylor and William Taylor on the 16th of October next begin at Deep Creek Bridge then up the Main fork to the Chapel Road down the Road to the new Road at Walton's along the new Road to Askews Path up the Path to the River Road and up the Road to the beginning do procession the several Lands and renew and mark the respective lines and make return to the Vestry by the last of March of every persons Land they shall procession of what persons are present at the same

[14]   July 27, 1747
of what Lands in the said precinct they shall fail to procession and the particular reasons of such Failure.

Ordered that John Hyde Saunders, William Lax and Daniel Johnson on the 19th of November next begin at the Mouth of Deep Creek up the same to the Bridge down the Road to Askew's Path down the same to the new Road along the same to Walton's down the Chapel Road to Lax's along the Courthouse to Bates's House up the River Road to Solomons

Creek down the same to the River and up the River to the beginning do procession the several Lands and renew and mark the respective lines and make return to the Vestry by the Last of March of every persons Land they shall procession of what persons are present at the same of what Lands in the said precinct they shall fail to procession and the particular reasons of such Failure.

Ordered that Paul Michaux, Daniel Coleman and Frederick Cox on the 20th of October next begin at the mouth of Solomon's Creek thence down the River to Jacob Michaux's Ferry along the Ferry Road to Bates's House up the Road to Solomons Creek and down the same to the beginning do procession the Several Lands and renew and mark the respective lines and make return to the Vestry by the last of March of every persons Land they shall procession of what persons are present at the same of what Lands in the said precinct they shall fail to procession and the particular reasons of such Failure.

Ordered that Robert Hughes, Charles Railey and Joseph Johnson the 21st of October begin at Jacob Michaux's Ferry along the Ferry Road to Bates's House down the Road to Fine Creek down the Creek to the River and up the River to the beginning do procession the several Lands and renew and mark the respective lines and make return to the Vestry by the Last of March of every person Land they shall procession of what persons are present at the same of what Lands in the said precinct

[15] July 27, 1747
they shall fail to procession and the particular reasons of such Failure.

Ordered that John Bates, Bartholomew Stovall and Daniel Wilmore on the 22[d] of October next begin at the Road where it crosses Fine Creek at Scotts Mill thence up the Road to Bates's House along the Road to Lax's down the Chapel Road to Fine Creek at the three Bridges and down the Creek to the beginning do procession the several Lands and renew and mark the respective lines and make return to the Vestry by the last of March every persons Land they shall procession of what persons are present at the same of what Lands in the said precinct they shall fail to procession and the particular reasons of such Failure.

Ordered that Alexander Moss, Abraham Wamack Junr and John Alexander on the 2^d of November begin at Deep Creek Bridge down the Creek to the River up the River to Muddy Creek up the Creek to the Bridge and down the Main Road to the beginning do procession the several Lands and renew and mark the respective lines and make return to the Vestry by the last of March of every person's Land they shall procession of what persons are present at the same of what Lands in the said precinct they shall fail to procession and the particular reasons for such Failure.

Ordered that Robert Carter, Isaac Hughes and William Dillon on the 4th of November next begin at Muddy Creek Bridge thence down the Creek to the River up James River to Willises River up the same to the Bridge and down the Main Road to the beginning do procession the several Lands and renew and mark the respective lines and make return to the Vestry by the Last of March of every persons Land they shall procession of what persons are present at the same and what Lands in the said precinct they shall fail to procession and the particular reasons of such Failure.

[16]   July 27, 1747
Ordered that William Moss Senr. Miles Gathwrite and Abraham Womack Senr on the 4th of November next begin at Deep Creek Bridge thence up the Creek to the Chapel Road up the Road and Scotts Path to Muddy Creek down the same to the River Road and down the River Road to the beginning do procession the several Lands and renew and mark the respective lines and make return to the Vestry by the last of March of every persons Land they shall procession of what persons are present at the same of what Lands in the said precinct they shall fail to procession and the particular reasons of such Failure.

Ordered that Thomas Walton, John Creasy and William Palmer on the 2^d of November next begin at Muddy Creek Bridge thence up the River Road to the Widow Dillon's Path thence by Salmon's to Ham Chapel thence by the new Chapel Road near M^r. Scotts to Muddy Creek and down the said Creek to the beginning do procession the several Lands and renew and mark the respective lines and make return to the Vestry by the last of March of every persons Land they shall procession of what persons are present at the same of what Lands in the said precinct they shall fail to procession and the particular reasons of such Failure.

Ordered that James Cunningham, Merry Webb and John Salmon on the 4th of November next begin at the Widow Dillons Path thence by Salmon's to Ham Chapel thence by Pruet's Path to Barnets Road thence by the said Road to Willis's River down the said River to the Bridge and down the River Road to the beginning do procession the several Lands and renew and mark the respective lines and make return to the Vestry by the last of March of every persons Land they shall procession of what persons are present at the same of what Lands in the said precinct they shall fail to precession and the particular reasons of such Failure.

[17]   July 27, 1747
Ordered that Samuel Bridgwater, Joseph Price and Valentine Martin on the 5th of November next begin at Willis's Bridge thence up Willis's River to Randolph's Creek, up the same to the County line along the line to the River Road and down the Road to the beginning do procession the several Lands and renew and mark the respective lines and make return to the Vestry by the last of March of every persons Land they shall procession of what persons are present at the same of what Lands in the said precinct they shall fail to procession and the particular reasons of such Failure.

Ordered that Joseph Hooper, Samuel Taylor and Phineas Glover on the 3d of November next begin at Willis's Bridge thence down Willis's River to James River up James River to the County line along the line to the River Road and down the said Road to the beginning do procession the several Lands and renew and mark the respective lines and make return to the Vestry by the last of March of every persons Land they shall procession of what persons are present at the same of what Lands in the said precinct they shall fail to procession and the particular reasons of such Failure.

Ordered that John Merriman, William Bond and Thomas Watts on the 2d of November next begin at Ham Chapel thence by the new Road near Mr Scotts to Muddy Creek up the same to Barnets Road up Barnet's Road to Pruet's Path along the same to Ham Chapel do procession the several Lands and renew and mark the respective lines and make return to the

Vestry by the last of March of every persons Land they shall procession of what persons are present at the same of what Lands in the said precinct they shall fail to procession and the particular reasons of such Failure.

Ordered that George Stovall, Hezekiah Mosby and William [Roberts] on the 5th of November next begin at Great Deep Creek Bridge at [Chapel]

[18]   July 27, 1747

Road up the said Creek to M^{rs}. Mayo's Mill thence by her Chair Road to the Chapel Road and down the same to the beginning do procession the several Lands and renew and mark the respective lines and make return to the Vestry by the Last of March of every persons Land they shall procession of what persons are present at the same of what Lands in the said precinct they shall fail to procession and the particular reason of such Failure.

Ordered that Philip Poindexter, William Smith and John Cardwell on the 2^d of November next begin at Great Deep Creek Bridge at the Chapel Road thence down the Road to the Ridge Path along the said Path to Buckingham Road up the said Road to M^r. Benjamin Harris's thence by his Path to M^{rs}. Mayo's upper Mill & down the Creek to the beginning do procession the several Lands and renew and mark the respective lines and make return to the Vestry by the last of March of every persons Land they shall procession of what persons are present at the same of what Lands in the said precinct they shall fail to procession and the particular reasons of such Failure.

Ordered that William Stone, Joseph Woodson and Samuel Burton on the 6th of November next begin at Lile's Ford thence along the Courthouse Road to Benjamin Childreys up Buckingham Road to the Two Blazed Path along the Path to the River and down the River to the beginning do procession the several Lands and renew and mark the respective lines and make return to the Vestry by the last of March of every persons Land they shall procession of what persons are present at the same of what Lands in the said precinct they shall fail to procession and the particular reason of such Failure.

Ordered that Robert Burton, Hutchins Burton and William Spiers on the 3^d of November next begin at the mouth of Randolph's

[19] July 27, 1747
Creek thence up the same to the County line along the same to Brooks's Mill and down Willis's River to the beginning do procession the several Lands and renew and mark the respective lines and make return to the Vestry by the last of March of every persons Land they shall procession of what persons are present at the same of what Lands in the said precinct they shall fail to procession and the particular reasons of such Failure.

Ordered that Richard Burton, Josiah Burton, Samuel Allen jun^r. and William Johns on the 6th of November next begin at Quarter thence up Willis's River to Buckingham Road down the same to Daniels down Daniels new Road to Johns's up Hornquarter Road to Barnet's Fork and up Barnets Road to the beginning do procession the several Lands and renew and mark the respective lines and make return to the Vestry by the Last of March of every persons Land they shall procession of what persons are present at the same of what Lands in the said precinct they shall fail to procession and the particular reasons of such Failure.

Ordered that John Robinson, John Hopson and John Scruggs on the 3^d of November next begin at Johns's thence up the new Road to Buckingham Road down the same to M^r. Benjamin Harris's thence by his Path to M^{rs}. Mayo's upper Mill thence by her Chair Road to the Chapel Road and up the same to the beginning do procession the several Lands and renew and mark the respective lines and make return to the Vestry by the last of March of every persons Land they shall procession of what persons are present at the same of what Lands in the said precinct they shall fail to procession and the particular reason of such Failure.

Ordered that Stephen Cox, Richard Parker and Adolphus Hendrick on the 7th of November next begin at the Two Blazed Path on Appamattox River thence up the same to McCoy's thence by Burton's Path to Buckingham

[20] July 27, 1747
Road thence down the same to the Two Blazed Path and along the same to the beginning do precession the several Lands and renew and mark the

respective lines and make return to the Vestry by the last of March of every persons Land they shall procession of what persons are present at the same of what Lands in the said precinct they shall fail to procession and the particular reasons of such Failure.

Ordered that John Woodson, Joseph Terry and Thomas Devonport on the 2^d of November next begin at McCoy's on Appamattox River thence by Burton's Path to Buckingham Road up the same to Daniels and up Randolph's Road to Tear Wallet [Creek] down the same and Great Guiney to the River and down the River to the beginning do procession the several Lands and renew and mark the respective lines and make return to the Vestry by the last of March of every persons Land they shall procession of what persons are present at the same of what Lands in the said precinct they shall fail to procession and the particular reasons of such Failure.

Ordered that Thomas Harvy, Williams Daniel and William Trigg on the 5th of November next begin at Daniels thence up Buckingham Road to Willis's River up the same to Brooks's Mill and down the Road to the beginning do procession the several Lands and renew and mark the respective lines and make return to the Vestry by the last of March of every persons Land they shall procession of what persons are present at the same of what Lands in the said precinct they shall fail to procession and the particular reasons of such Failure.

Ordered that John Cooke, John Brown and Richard Ward on the 8th of November next begin at Brook's Mill thence along the County line to Appamattox River down the River to Green Creek up the said Creek to Randolph's Road down the same to Brooks's Road

[21]   July 27, 1747
and up the same to the beginning do procession the several Lands and renew and mark the respective lines and make return to the Vestry by the last of March of every persons Land they shall procession of what persons are present at the same of what Lands in the said precinct they shall fail to procession and the particular reasons of such Failure.

Ordered that William Womack, Daniel Coleman jun^r. Charles Bostick and Gideon Glen on the 3^d of November next begin at Tear Wallet Bridge thence down the same and Great Guiney to Appamattox River up the same to Green Creek up the said Creek to Randolphs Road and down the said Road to the beginning do procession the several Lands and renew and mark the respective lines and make return to the Vestry by the Last of March of every persons Land they shall procession of what persons are present at the same of what Lands in the said precinct they shall fail to procession and the particular reasons of such Failure.

Ordered that William Randolph, Thomas Turpin and Creed Haskins Gent or any two of them do Purchase a place convenient to set the Lower Chapel which is to be Built by James Anderson if the places formerly appointed are found inconvenient.

Jno. Robertson	Geo Carrington
Thos Turpin	Benj^a Harrison
Nicho^s Davies Church Warden	James Barnes
Alexd^r Trent	Step^n Bedford
J Terry	Creed Haskins

****

[22]   November 27, 1747
At a Vestry held for Southam Parish at Peterville Church for laying the Parish Levy the xxvii day of November mdccxlvii Present the Reverend John Robertson Minister, Thomas Turpin, Alexander Trent, George Carrington, Benjamin Harrison, Samuel Scott, Nicholas Davies, Stephen Bedford, and Creed Haskins Gent^n. Vestrymen.

1747 Southam Parish is	D^r.	Tobco	Cask
To the Reverend John Robertson Minister his Salary due the 15th of January next		16000	640
To James Terry Clk Tear Wallet Chapel		1000	40
To John Cardwell Clk Peterville Church		1000	40
To Thos Freeman Fretwell Clk Ham Chapel		1000	40
To Sylvanus Witt reader at Worleys		1000	40
To Robert Walton Clk of the Vestry		500	20
To John LeGrand Sexton		500	
To D^o for setting up a sett of Horse Blocks		30	

To William Easley Sexton	500	
To Michael Johnson Sexton	500	
To D°. for putting pieces under Ham Chapel and Clearing near an Acre of Ground Round the same	300	
To Judith Bradshaw for keeping George Dobbins 15 months	625	
To John Taylor for keeping Robert Saunders's Child 'till the first day of January next	1000	
To Samuel Scott for keeping Hendrick Scales 'till Janry 12	1000	
To Richard Henderson	800	
To William Womack for feeding and Cloathing the Widow Kent from the 17th day of Last August 'till this day	200	
To Anne Kent for a Year yet to come	800	
Carried forward	26755	820

[23]   November 27, 1747

Brought forward	26755	820
To John Hatch for himself and his Wife	600	
To John Woodson Sub Sherif for 12 Insolvent Titheables at 27	324	
To John Smith Junr Sub Sherif for 10 Insolvent Titheables at 27	270	
To Samuel Burton for 4 Levy's Double listed in 1745 at 33	132	
To D° for 1 Levy overlisted in 1746 at 27	27	
To Robert Thompson for 4 Levys overlisted in 1746 at 27	108	
To William Moss for Burying Thomas Laffoon deceased	300	
To Henry Wood for Clks Fees	336	
To Thomas Turpin Gent. for his expenses in a General Suit in the time of his being Church Warden of S^t. James's Parish	900	
To the Reverend John Robertson in Lieu of a Glebe	2000	
To Tobacco Levied to Raise Money towards a Glebe	12000	
To John Smith Collector a Ballance due to him last Year	65	
	44637	

	Salary	2680
		47317

D°	C^r	
By 1360 Titheables at 35^{lb} p Poll		47600
Due to the Parish		283
		47317

Judith Bradshaw agrees to keep George Dobbins a Year from this time for 680^{lb} of Tobacco and Cask.

Daniel Wilmore agrees to keep Elizabeth Owle a Year from this Time for 300^{lb} of Tobacco.

The Vestry agree with M^r. John Lightfoot for to give him ninety pounds Current Money for two hundred and seventy Acres of Land where he now lives allowing the said Lightfoot Liberty to make a Crop on the

[24]   Janry 26, 1747
said Land he not interrupting the Vestry in making necessary Buildings for a Glebe.

John Robertson	Alexd^r Trent
Thomas Turpin	Step^n Bedford
Nicho^s Davies	Creed Haskins
Geo Carrington	Sam^{ll} Scott

****

At a Vestry held for Southam Parish at Benjamin Childrey's Janry 26, 1747. Present The Rever^d John Robertson Minister, Nicholas Davies, Thomas Turpin, Samuel Scott, Stephen Bedford, Creed Haskins, William Randolph Gent. Vestrymen.

Pursuant to an Act of the General Assembly made in the twentieth Year of His Majesties Reign Impowering the Vestry of the Parish of Southam to sell the Glebe Land of the said Parish the Church Wardens having given Notice according to the directions of the said Act, met and put up the Land at Publick A[u]ction which was Sold at Fifty three pounds ten shillings.

Ordered that the Church Wardens take a Sufficient Bond to Secure the said Fifty three pounds ten shillings to be paid by the tenth day of January next.

John Hubbard is appointed Clerk of Tear Wallet Chapel in the Room of Ja^s. Terry.

Ordered that the Church Wardens give Publick Notice that a Dwelling House Forty two by twenty and Eleven foot Pitch in the Clear two Outside Brick Chimneys, is to be Lett to the lowest Bidder on the tenth day of March next at the Plantation of Doctor Lightfoot near upper Deep Creek Bridge.

      John Robertson   Thomas Turpin CH W^{dn}
      William Randolph   Nicho^s Davies Chwd
                            Sam^{ll} Scott
                            Stephen Bedford
                            Creed Haskins

****

At a Vestry held at the Glebe in Southam Parish the xxi Day of May mdccxlviii. Present The Rever^d. John Robertson Minister, Thomas Turpin, Nicholas Davies,

[25]   Processioners returns May 21, 1748
James Barnes, Stephen Bedford, George Carrington, Creed Haskins Gent. Vestrymen.

The Church Wardens of Southam Parish make the returns of the processioners which are as follows.

In Goochland County and Southam Parish We the Subscribers have procission'd the Several Lands and renew'd and mark't the Respective lines in our precincts Beginning at Muddy Creek Viz^t. Richd Fains Land mark't himself & Ralf Flipping Present, Thos Flippings Land mark't himself & Thos Walton Present, part of Ralph Flippings Land mark't himself and Thos Walton Present, part of Tho Walton's Land markt himself and Thos Flipping present, part of Watson's Land mark't Thos

Walton & Ralph Flipping present, part of Pendletons land mark't Eleander Hughes present, part of John Hudgins Land mark't Phillip Hudgins present, John Hudsons Land mark't David Roberts & Robt Walton present, part of Thos Carters Land mark't Wm Sammons Present, part of Sylvanus Witts Land mark't Wm Cox present, Robt Duglass's land mark't himself & Philip Hudgins present, Philip Hudgins's Land mark't himself & Rich. Fain present, Wm Mullins's Land mark't Richd Fain and Phillip Hudgins present, Sampson Flemings Land mark't himself & Jacob Winfrey present, part of Jacob Winfreys Land mark't himself & Samson present, part of George Owens Land mark't Jacob Winfrey present, part of Philip Poindexters Land mark't Jacob Winfrey present, part of Peter Hollands Land mark't Samson Fleming present, part of Joel Meadowes Land mark't Sampson Fleming present, part of Wm Bond's Land mark't himself Joel Meadow & Peter Holland present, part of John Merriman's Land mark't himself Wm Bond & Joel Fain present, part of Ashford Hughes Land mark't Philip Hudgins present p[er] us.

William Bond
&
John Merriman

November y^c 12, 1747. We don a lin betwen Will Clay and Timson, Timson not ther, A lin betwin Will Clay and Henry Cley, A lin betwin John Mosely & Henry Clay, A lin betwen Edward Watkin & Timson t s n t[?], A lin betwin Edard Watkins & John Moseley, A lin between John Moseley & John Farmer, A lin between John Fermer & Eard Wadkins, A lin between Thomas Wadkins & Steven Mallet, A lin betwin Thomas Wadkins & Henry Clay, A lin betwin Steven Mallit & Henry Clay, A lin betwin John Mosley & Timson tsnt[?], A lin betwin Will Clay & John Mosley, A lin betwin J Mosley & Thomas Wadkins, A lin betwin

[26]   Processioners returns May 21, 1748
Thomas Wadkins & John Worley, Alin betwin John Worley & Henry Clay, Alin betwin John Worley & William Worley, Alin betwin John Worley & William Rigen, Alin betwin John Mosley & John Worley, Alin betwin John Mosley & William Rigen, Alin betwen Edard Wadkins & Franses Chactune, alin betwin Fransses Cheatone & Morris Robards, per us dun by us, Henry Clay, William Clay, John Moseley. All the Land has bin prosesond In pees [peace] only wone [one] line betwin Merry Roberts

& Timson narrow wone there the parttys by or agreed that We Should do it all the rest.

The within named processioners have renewed the lines of the within Limmets as followeth Viz^t. Begining at Scotts Mill on John Pleasants and Samuel Manksfields line James Glass being present, Plesents and Daniel Wilmores line renewed Samuel Manksfield and James Glass being present, Thomas Bassett refuses to meat to have his lines renewed, Major Stoner and Elizabeth Woodsons line renewed Christopher Nordin being present, Major Stoner and Charles Bates line renued Christopher Nordin being present, & Stoner & John Bates's line the above Nordin being present, Wm Chandler & Charles Woodson line renewed Wm Chandler being present, Major Stoner & Ann Mayo line not renewed, no one apeared to Shoe the line Ann Mayo & Charles Woodsons the same.

John Bates

March 31st 1748. According to the Directions given us We have diligently prosesioned y^e. Several lines in our Precinct Viz^t. Begining at Stratons on Coln^l. Wm Randolph^s Line, Rich^d. Ligon Matt. Ligon & James Ligon present, Philip Thomas for Col^o. Randolph. The line between Coln^l W^m. Randolph and Col^o. Wm Randolph dec^d. Estate, Philip Thomas James Davis for the Estate. The line between Col^o. Wm Randolph Estate dec^d. & M^r. Matthew Ligon, James Davis the other present. The line between Col^o. Wm Randolph & y^e. Land formerly called y^e. Glebe & the line between Benj^a. Childreys & y^e. s^d. Glebe, Ph^p. Thomas for Randolph, Benj Childrey. The line between Col^o. Wm Randolph & Miss Mayo, Philip Thomas for Randolph, Danl. Mayo. 2 lines between Col^o Wm Randolphs Estate decd & Miss Mayo, Danl. Mayo & James Davis for the Estate.

The line betwen Col^o. Wm Randolph dec^d. & Char[l]es Woodson, James Davis &

[27]   Processioners returns May 21, 1748
Chandler. The line betwen Miss Mayo W^m. Chandler & Joseph Chandler, Danl. Mayo & others present. The line betwen Charles Woodson & W^m. Chandler, Wm Chandler p^r. Woodsons Desire. The line betwen Anthony Hughse & W^m. Chandler, both present. The line betwen Wm Chandler & Joseph Chandler, b[o]th present. The line betwen Col^o. Wm Randolph

dec^d. & John Baskervile & a small line betwen M^r. Matt Ligon & the s^d. Baskervile, James Davis for Estate others present.

To the Vestry of Southam Parish according to your Order Dated the 27th day of July 1747. We have possesioned y^e. Following Lands To Wit, Begining at the Two Blazed Path on Appomattox River thence Round Patrick Adams. a line to y^e. Two Blazed Path, Samuel Burton, George Cox, David Hadaway, Willm Shees [Shays] present. thence round Stephen Coxes line, Samuel Burton, George Cox, David Hadhaway present. Thence Round Henry Coxes line, Samuel Burton, George Cox, David Hadhaway present. thence round George Coxes line, George Cox, David Hadhaway, Samuel Burton present. thence round Daniel Terys line, David Hadhaway, George Cox, Samuel Burton present. thence round David Hadhaways line, Samuel Burton David Hadhaway & George Cox present. thence round Isaac Hughes line, David Hadhaway, George Cox present. thence round James Murreys line, Benjamin Harris Joyning David Hadhaway present. thence round Richard Parkers line, Henry Hatcher adjoyning Henry Hatcher present. thence round Robt. Tomsons line, Saml. Burton present. thence round Holman Freemans line, Henry Hatcher present. thence round Richard Parkers line, Samuel Burton present. thence round Hutchins Burtons line, David Hadhaway, Samuel Burton, George Cox present. thence round Samuel Burtons line, W^m. Parker present. No persons failing to possession.

March 30th day 1748   Stephen Cox
                                      Richard Parker

November 12th day 1747
Possioned the lines betwen Joseph Baugh and Israel Winfree, James Baugh present. allso betwen Joseph Baugh & Thomas Baugh, Jeams Baugh present. allso the lines betwen Thomas Watkins and John Farmer, John Mosley and Henry Clay present. allso the lines betwen John Watkins and John Farmer, Stephen Russel present. allso the lines betwen Arthur Mosley and Joel Locket, Lodwick Ealum present. allso the lines b^{tw}. Lodwick Ealum and Arthur Mosley, Joel Locket present. allso the line betwen John Watkins and Matthew Chitwood, Jeams Chitwood present. allso the line betwen Mathew Chitwood and

[28]   Precessioners returns May 21, 1748
William Acin, Jeams Chitwood present. allso the lines Between Mathew

Chitwood and William Bass, James Chitwood present. allso the line betwen Joseph Baugh and Mathew Chitwood, Jeams Baugh present. allso between Thomas Baugh and Mathew Chitwood, Mathew Chitwood present, allso betwen John Watkins and William Acin. allso betwen Joseph Baugh and John Watkins, James Baugh present. allso between Thomas Baugh and Joseph Baugh, Jeams Baugh present. allso the lines betwen Thomas Baugh & John Watkins, Jeams Baugh present. allso the lines betwen Thomas Watkins and Thos Wooldridge, both parties present. allso between Thomas Wooldredge and Thomas Russel, William Worley present. allso between Thomas Wooldredge and Henry Hatcher, William Worley present. also betwen John Wooldredge and Henry Hatcher, both parties present. allso betwen Henry Hatcher and Israel Winfrey, Josiah Hatcher present. allso between Morris Roberts and Thomas Cheetum, Edward Watkins present. allso betwen Edward Watkins and Thomas Cheetum, Edward Watkins present. allso betwen Benjamin Mosley and William Bass, Arthur Mosley present. allso betwen Benjamin Mosley and William Acin, Arthur Moseley present. allso between Benjamin Moseley and Thomas Cheetum, Arthur Mosley present. allso between Edward Watkins and Frances Cheetum, William Acin present. allso between Morris Roberts and Frances Cheetum, William Acin present. allso betwen Thomas Cheetum and Frances Cheetum, William Acin present. allso betwen Thomas Cheetum and William Acin, William Acin present.

       Joseph Baugh
       Israel Winfrey
       John Watkins

October the 13 day 1747. Then we began to presion in our precink Begaining at the French Line and Capt Turpin, John Bondrunt presant for M^r. Turpin. thence along the French [Line] to Peter Bondrants line. Presiond Betwn M^r. Thos. Turpin and Nat Maxey, John Bondrant pst for Capt Turpin. thence presisoned the lines of John Smith and Nat Maxey, Both present. thence pressioned the line of Jacob Tribeu and Nat Maxey Lines, John Smith presant for Tribeu. thence to W^m. Maxey and Tribeu, John Smith presant for Tribeu. thence to pressioned the lines Easter Lansdon and Matthew Age, both present. then prissoned of Easter Lansdon and John Worley, both presant. then betwen John Worley and Will Wriggin to Buckingham Road, W^m. Maxey presant for Riggin. then presioned the line between Wm Wriggin and Samuel Hatcher to the Road, both presant. then presioned the lins of John Maxey and Samuel Hatcher, W^m. Maxey present for Hatcher. then presioned the lines betwen W^m. Maxey and John Maxey both

[29]   Processioners returns May 21, 1748
Present. Presioned betwen W^m. Maxey and John Smith, both presant. Then presioned the line betwend Richard Epperson and John Radford, both Presant. then presioned the line betwend Radford Maxey & John Radford, presant for both. then presioned the line of Sill Maxey and Radford Maxey, John Radford present for both. then presioned the line betwend Nat Maxey & Radford Maxey, John Radford present. then presioned the lines o[f] Thomas Bradley and Radford Maxey, John Radford present for Maxey. Then presioned the line of Nat Maxey and Thomas B[r]adley, Borth presant. February the 2^d Day 1747. Presioned the line betwend Sill and Walter Maxey, borth presant. then presioned the line betwend John Mossom and Thos. Basset, John Maxey presant for Mr Bassett. then presioned the line betwend John Mossom and Samuel Hatcher, John Maxey present for Hatcher. presioned the lin betwent Sill Maxey & Thos Bassett, John Maxey present for Bassett. prsioned betwend Thos Bassett and Joseph Suinne, John Maxey p[r]esant for borth Bassett & Suinne. Presioned the line betwent John Maxey & Thomas Bassett, John Maxey presant. presioned the line betwend John Maxey and Joseph Suinne, John Maxey presant for borth. presioned the lines betwend Capt Thos. Turpin and Capt James Cocke, John Radford presant for Capt. Cock. presisoned the line of Capt James Cock and Nat Maxey, John Radford for Cock. presioned the line betwend Capt James Cock and Radford Maxey, John Radford present for both. presioned the line betwend Capt James Cock and John Radford, present for Cock and himself. presisoned the line betwend Capt James Cock and Richd Epperson, John Radford for Cock. presioned the line betwend Sill Maxey and John Radford, present for both. presioned the line betwend William Maxey and Nat Maxey, borth presant.

W^m. Maxey
John Radford

1747 November the feift and Sixt^d
We begoon to possiesion a part between Bartho^w Stoval and John Hyde Sanders agreed, a part beteen John Hyde Sanders and Thomas Dickens not their, Bartho^w Stoval and John Bates their bey, a part beteen Bartho^w

Stoval and Thomas Dickens not their, John Bates and John Franklin their bey, a part between John Bates and John Franklin agreed, a part beteen John Bates and Thomas Dickens not their and Bartho^w Stoval their bey, a part beteen John Bates and James Bates not their and Bartho^w. Stoval their bey, apart beteen John Bates and Dudley Diggs not their and Bartho^w Stoval their bey, A part beteen Bartho^w Stoval and Edmond Toney agreed, a part between Edmond Toney and Joel Chandler agreed, a part beteen Joel Chandler and

[30]   Processioners returns May 21, 1748

Robert Walton not their, Willm. Chandler and Anthony Heughs their bey, A part beteen Robert Walton and Anthony Hughes and Joel Chandler and Willm. Chandler their bey, A part beteen Antoeny Heughs and Joel Chandler agreed, a part beteen Willm. Chandler and Joel Chandler, a part beteen Willm. Chandler and Charles Woodson not their and Joel Chandler their bey, a part beteen Willm. Cha[n]dler and Charles Woodson not their Joel Chandler their bey, a part beteen Dudley Diggs not their and Charles Woodson not their and Willm. Chandler their bey and Joel Chandler their bey. Daniel DI his mark Johnson Novr 20. A part beteen Edmond Toney and Ma^m. Mayo agreed, a part beteen Barth^o. Stoval and Ma^m. Mayo agreed, a part beteen Barth^o. Stoval and Maj^r. Howard agreed, a part beteen Ma^m. Mayo and Maj^r. Howard Joel Chandler and Majo^r. Charton. Janry 20. Apainted to Sho[w] his lines that day, a part beteen Maj^r. Howard and John Hyde Sanders agreed John Leak bey, a part beteen Maj^r. Howard John Leak bey, and Ma^m. Randolph agreed Willm. Hount bey, a part beteen Maj^r. Howard John Chsot Joel Chandler and John Taylor agreed Willm. Taylor William Hount bey, a part beteen Ma^m. Randolph and she apainted John Chsot and John Taylor agreed and John Hyde Sanders to Seall the lines don heir mensoned Willm. Hount by, a part beteen Ma^m. Randolph and John Pleasant not their William Hount John Chsot and John Taylor their bey, a part beteen John Taylor and John Pleasant not their Willm. Hount and John Shsot bey, a part beteen Capt Bedford and John Pleasant not their and John Taylor Shod the line Willm. Hount John Shsot their bey.

John Hyde Sanders
W^m. Lax

To the Honerable Vesterry of Southam Parish We the Subscribers Have possessioned the Lands in our precincts hereafter mentioned Begining at William Triggs line, then Daniel Colemans present Daniel Coleman, then Adolphas Hendricks present Benj^a. Hendrick, Williams Daniels Land Thomas Harveys line, Henry Terrys present Henry Terry, Ralph Flipings present James Doudy, John Martins present Robert Kent, Thos. Johnses present Thos. Johns, Josiah Payns present Josiah Payn, Elex^r. Spearses present William Still, Elex^r Trents present Elex^r Trent, Arch Carys present Arch Cary, William Easleys present Worum Easley, & James Daniels Lands no Attendance to Shoe the lines, Colquits no Attendance given to Shoe the lines, William Millses no Attendance, John Archers no Attendance, William Chumles patent not out, Robert Kents patent not out, John Reterfords patent not out, Errors Excepted p Thomas Harvey.

William Trigg

[31]   Processioners returns May 21, 1748

We the Subscribers have possessioned all the Lands mentioned in the precinct of the within order Except a line or lines Dividing the Lands of James Bates & the Lands of the Late Thomas Dickins which it is said he in his life time sold to M^r. Dudley Digges nobody on either part attending to Shew the lines Given under our hands this 31st day of March 1748.

Paul Michaux
Frederick Cox

In obedience to an Order of the Vestry of Southam Parish We have processioned the lines in our precinct as followeth, a line between James Cock and Nathaniel Maxey not done, a line between Cock and George Baskervile not done for want of Cock Attendance, all the rest of the lines procession^d in presants of Benjamin Childrey, Philip Thomas, George Baskervile, John Woodson, Hutchins Burton, John Wright, Stephen Cox and William Sheys processioned by us.

March y^e. last day 1748   William Stone
                                         Jos: Woodson

The lines of the Land procission'd by Arthur Mosley W^m. Marshall & W^m. Mosley Viz quiet procission betwen M^r. Creed Haskins & Margret Hancock parties preasant Also betwen y^e. s^d. Haskins & Richard Moseley prasant also betwen the s^d. Haskins & W^m. Marshall preasant also betwen the s^d. Marshal and Rich^d. Mosely present also betwen the s^d. Marshal and

Francis Marshal present also betwen Francis Marshal and George Tod dec^d. W^m. Marshall present for the same also betwen G^o. Tod dec^d. & Geo: Williamson W^m. Marshall present for both parties the lines of Francis Marshall & Geo Tod dec^d. & Thos. Lokitt Joyning to M^r. John Timson dec^d. not procession'd there being no owner to be found as we know of to the said Timsons Land, Quiet procission betwen Richard Mosely & William Mosely Arthur Mosely preasant for boath parties also betwen Arthur Mosely & W^m. Mosely preasant also betwen Thos. Lokitt & Joel Lokitt Boath present also betwen Lodwich Elam and Arthur Mosely also betwene the s^d. Elam & Gideon Lokitt also betwene the s^d. Lokitt & Arthur Mosely also betwene Lodwich Elam & Perrin Allday also betwene the s^d. Alday & Bengemen Mosely also betwen W^m. Bass & John Northcote Witness our hands March ye 9, 1747/8.

W^m. Marshall
Arthur Mosely
W^m. Mosley

[32]   Procissioners returns May 21, 1748

In obedience to an Order of the Vestry of Southam Parish Appointing us processioners We have processioned in the following manner, to wit, January the Eleventh processiond the lines between George Carrington & Joseph Price present George Carrington Phineas Glover & Gideon Martin, the same day procession'd the lines between George Carrington & Phineas Glover, between Phineas Glover & Valentine Martin, between Phineas Glover and Joseph Price the same persons present as above between Joseph Price & Valentine Martin, between George Carrington & Thomas Bassett Present George Carrington, between George Carrington & John Reynolds Present George Carrington & John Reynolds, between John Reynolds & James Cunningham, between John Reynolds & Thomas Bassett present John Reynolds, between James Cunningham & Thomas Bassett John Rennels and William Cunningham present. January y^e. twelfth processon'd betwen Vallentine Martin & Thomas Bassett between Joseph Price & Thomas Bassett between Stephen Hughes and Thomas Bassett betwen Stephen Hughes and Edward Hambleton, between Joseph Price and Edward Hambleton, between Joseph Price and Vallentine Martin Gideon Martin present.   Samuel Bridgwater
Joseph Price
Vallentine Martin

Goochland County
We the Subscribers in Obedience to an Order of Vestry bearing Date July 27, 1747 Requiring us to possesion the Lands within the precinct in the said Order mentioned have duly complied theirwith and the bounds of all Lands within Such precinct have view'd and the Several Land marks renew'd in presence of the persons mentioned Robt. Hughes, Nicholas Davies, William Dellon, Thomas Bracket, Henry Dellon, Robert Carter Junr, Major Bolling, and George Carrington Witness our hands this 27 Day of Febry 1747.

                         Isaac Hughes
                         Robert Carter

In pursuant of the within Order We have prossessioned all the Lands in our precinct Except Nicholis Giles is his reson is that he has not his Complement he thinks March 30, 1748.

                         Philip Thomas
                         Henry Breazeale
                         Benj^a. Childrey

[33]   Processioners returns May 21, 1748
December 7, 1747. In obedience to an Order of Vestry We Hutchins Burton, W^m. Spears, Robert Burton have possesioned the lines of Thos. Bassett, of Drury Scruggs & Robert Wooding & Isaac Bates, Robert Burton, Hutchins Burton, W^m. Finney, W^m. Spears, Wolter Daniel, Benj^a. Harrison, Joseph Farrar & M^r. Bells & should have gone farther if Sickness had not prevented us.

Southam Parrish pursusant to an Order of Vesterry baring Dait 27th July 1747 y^e. following lands possessiond October 21 y^e. lines between Cor^l John Fleming & Stephen Hughes present John Robinson & John Fleming Junr. between John Fleming & Joseph Johns John Robusson, John Fleming Junr. James Riley pres. between John Fleming & John Plesant Present the afoar named parsons, Octo^r. 22 possession ye lines between John Plasent & Joseph Johns & John Plesant and Susanna Gasper between Gasper & Daniel Wilmare between Daniel Wilmore & y^e. Oalfins [orphans] of Stephen Woodson Deceast between Danil Wilmoar & John Riley present Danil Wilmoar & Joseph Hughes Oct^o. 26. possessioned ye lines between Cor^l. John Fleming & Daniel Wilmoar & Joseph Johns & Salvater Alford William Rinalds, John Spurlock, John Riley Charles Riley and Daniel Wilmoar & the lines between Steph Hughes & y^e. afoar Named persons & between Stephen Hughes & Daniel Stoner present John Spauldin and Joseph Hughes & W^m. Dudley. November 26. Possen'd the [lines] between Stephen Hughes & Robert Hughes & Robert Hughes & John Pleasant & Robert Hughes & John Cannon & John Cannon & Francis James & Robt. Hughes & Francis James & bettwen Francis James & Nicholas Wilkinson & Francis James & the Alfins of Jacob Michaux, March 19. Possoss^d. y^e. lines between Nicholas Wilkinson & Robert Hughes & Nicolas Wilkinson & Frederick Cox & Robert Hughes & Fredrick Cox & Fredrick Cox & Henry Bagby & between Henry Bagby & John Plesant [illegible name] & John Cox & Henry Bagby & John Cox & John Plesant & between John Cox & Daniel Stoaner & James Bates & Daniel Stoaner a line between John Plesant & Daniel Stoaner left undon nither party being preasant Sartified by us.

       Robert Hughes
       Charles Raley
       Joseph I his mark Johns

Prosessioned the line between Col^o. W^m. Randolph & Richard Povall present Philup Thom[a]s for Randolph, the line between Col^o. Richard Randolph & Richard Povall Thomas Hall present Poval & Hall for Randolph the line betwen Col^o Wm Randolph & Col^o. Ric^d. Randolph Philup Thomas for W Randolph

[34] Processioners returns May 21 1748
& Thomas Hall for R Randolph, the line between Col^o. Ric^d. Randolph & John Hales Thomas Hall for R. Randolph & John Radford for Hales. The line betwen Col^o. W^m. Randolph & John Hales Philip Thomas for Randolph & John Radford for Hales, the line betwen John Hales & Ric^d. Ligon John Radford Ordered to Attend for both parties the line betwen Richard Ligon & Abraham Womack ye parties present. The line betwen John Hales & Abraham Womack John Radford Ordered to Attend for both parties, the line betwen James Davis & Abraham Womack John Dunkin ordered to Attend for both parties, The line betwen Col^o. Ric^d. Randolph & James Davis Thomas Hall for Randolph & John Dunkin for Davis, The lin betwen James Davis & John Mossom John Dunkin present John Dunkin for both parties. The line betwen Col^o. Ric^d. Randolph & John Mossom present Thos. Hall for ye parties, The line betwen Col^o. Ric^d.

Randolph & Henry Clay present Thomas Hall for Randolph, The line betwen John Moseley & Henry Clay both present, The line betwen Col^o. Richard Randolph & John Moseley Thomas Hall for both Parties, The line betwen Samuel Hatcher & John Moseley John Mossom for both parties, The line betwen John Moseley & William Riggin the Parties present, The line betwen Samuel Hatcher & William Riggin John Mossom, The line betwen Col^o. Ric^d. Randolph & Samuel Hatcher Thos. Hall for Randolph & John Mossom for Hatcher, The line betwen John Mossom & Samuel Hatcher parties present, all agreed.

March 4th 1747/8 Richard Povall
George Williamson
John Mossom

Pursusant to an Order of the Vestry for Southam Parish in Goochland County Land poscession'd by we the Subscribers as follows Viz^t. Poscessioned the line betwen Abraham Womack and Richd Legon parties present. D^o. the line between Jno. Baskervile and Abraham Womack Jno. Baskervile present and Rich^d. Ligon and Abraham Womack, D^o. the line between Jno. Radford and John Baskervile parties present & Jos: Bundrant, D^o. the line between Joseph Bundrant and Jno. Baskervile parties present & Jno. Radford D^o. the line between Col^o. W^m. Randolph decd and Jno. Baskervile present Jno. Baskervile and James Davis, D^o. the line between Ja^s Davis and John Radford present John Radford, D^o. the line between Abraham Womack and John Radford present John Radford, D^o. the line between Jno. Mossom & Walter Maxey John Radford present.

[35]   Processioners returns May 21, 1748
The line between Walter Maxey and John Radford not poscessioned by reason they cant agree, The line between M^{rs}. Mayo and John Archer not found, the line between M^{rs}. Mayo and Col^o. Peter Jefferson not found. Decemb^r. the 7th. The line between Jn . Archer and Tho . Turpin poscessioned present Thos. Turpin & James Robinson, D^o. the line between Col^o. Jefferson and Jno. Archer present Tho . Turpin and Ja . ^{s} Robinson, D^o. the line between Thos. Turpin and John Cannifax present Thos. Turpin and James Robinson, D^o. the line between Thos. Turpin and Jno. Archer, D^o. the line between Thos. Turpin and Col^o. Peter Jefferson, present Thos. Turpin and James Robinson. March the 18th. Poscessioned the line between M^{rs}. Mayo and Jo^s. Bondrant present George Carington and John Radford, D^o. the line between M^{rs}. Mayo and John Baskervile

Jo^s. Bondrant and Jno. Radford present, D^o. the line between Col^o. W^m. Randolph decd and M^{rs}. Mayo present Geo: Carington and Ja^s. Davis, D^o. the line between Col^o. Peter Jefferson and John Cannifax present Daniel Mayo, D^o. the line between Col^o. Jefferson and M^{rs}. Mayo present Daniel Mayo, None of the Lands belonging to Jno. Pleasant in our precinct Poscessiond by the Reason he refuseth.

Bennet Goode
John Cannifax
Nathl. M his mark Maxey

November 3, 1747

Joseph Hooper Samuel Taylor and Phinehas Glover precessions begun betwen Maj^r. Gorge Carrinton and Phinehas Glover and run along the line to Glover Corner Tree then betwen Phinehas Glover & Isaac Bates Joyning To the County line then betwen Maj^r. Gorge Carrinton & David Priyo along the Line to Priyo Corner tree then betwen Maj Gorge Carrinton and Richard Tayler along the line to Tayler Corner Tree then between Capt James Nevil and Philip Mayo along the line to Mayo Corner Tree Maj^r. George Carrinton and Cornelus Nevil prasant, then we begun at Maj^r. Gorge Carrinton Corner Tree on Willis's River along the line to Philip Mayo Corner Tree thence Down Mayo Line to Robert Carter then down Skelton line to Skelton Corner Tree on James River Then on Cor^l. Baj^n. Harrison along his line down to his Corner Tree on Willises River then at the Corner Tree between Phillip Mayo And Skelton along the line down the Skelton Corner Tree on James River Maj^r. Gorge Carrinton Thomas Bracket Robert Carter and John Burnet Present Then we begun at the Corner Tree between Joseph Hooper and Phillip Mayo along the line to the Corner tree between Phillip Mayo Joseph Hoper and James Nevil then along the line betwen Hooper and Nevil to the Corner betwen Joseph Hooper James Nevil & Phillip Mayo

[36]   Processioners returns May 21, 1748

Henry Trent Robert Duglis and Cournelus Nevil present Then We begun at the County line on David Priyo Line and Richard Taylor down the line to Priyo Corner Tree then one [on] the County line betwen James Daniel and Richard Tayler along the line to James Daniel Corner Tree Thence along Richard Tayler line Joyning of Phillip Mayo Line Richard Tayler prasant.

Joseph Hooper
Samuel Tayler
Phinehas Glover

Lines betwene Gorg Willemson & Temson Gorg Willemson present lines betwen Curnel Richeard Randolp and Curnel Baneley John Patson & Thomas Hall precind lines betwen Edweard Watkins & Temson Edweard Watkins precinct line betwext Edward Watkins & Joel Locket both precinct lines betwene Joel Locket & Temson Jacob Locket precinct lines betwene Curnel Banley & Temson John Patson prescinct lines betwen John Stourt and Curnel Randalp Stort ont atend Pesashand by.
Richard Mosley
Francis Marshall
Thomas Locket

We the Subscribers Alex^r. Moss Abra^m. Womack & John Alexander have processioned all the lines of Lands in our precincts of Such persons as would meet us at the Days Appointed after haveing Publick Notice the Perticulers of which is as followeth Viz^t. First precessioned between Robt. Hughes & John Alexander Robt. Hughes Junr. & Jno. Alexander present, Second, between John Alexander & Robt. Hughes & M^{rs}. Jane Randolph John Alexander & Robt. Hughes Junr. & Drury Scruggs for Randolph present, Third between M^{rs}. Randolph & Thomas Moss of New Kent County the said Scruggs & Geo: Going for Thos. Moss preasant, fourth betwen Randolph & Micajah Mosby Scrugs & Micajah Mosby preasant the Land of Thos. Moss the Land of M^{rs}. Randolph and the Land of Micajah Mosby Joyning on the Land of John Bradley who is not to be found which Land is not precession'd, fifth between Micajah Mosby and M^r. John Pleasants of Henrico County Micajah Mosby and Geo Owen for Pleasants prasant the Land of Micajah Mosby and John Pleasants Joyning on the Land of Miles Gathwrite who refuseth to precession.
Alex^r. Moss
Abraham Womack
John Alexander

[37]   Processioners returns May 21, 1748
In Pursuance to the within Order of Vestry we have processioned and mark'd all the Lines in the said precincts present Benj Mosby, James Roberts, George Stovall, William Roberts, and Francis Steager as Witness

our hands this 10th March 1747/8.

William Roberts
Hez^c. Mosby

In obedience to an Order of the Vestry for Southam Parish appointing us processioners, we have procession'd all the lines within the Bounds of our precint, that we know to be patented, Except the lines hereafter mentioned which we did not procession for want of Attendance from the proprietors Viz; Part of Bowlar Cocks, Part of Nicholas Davies's, Part of Benjamin Harrisons, Part of Benjamin Dumas's, Rachel Ferres's, William Willis's, Part of Toliac Powers's and John Blevins, Given under our hands March 29, 1748.

William X his mark Palmore
Thomas Walton

March 9th 1747/8
According to an Order of Vestry Dated 27th of July 1747. We the Subscribers with Joseph Rediford, John Phelphs, Joseph Woodson, William Stone, Joel Chandler, Gervas Jackson, Capt Barnes, Benj^a. Harris, David Winifred, John Hughes, Francis Stegar in Company have marked and renewed all the respected lines in the precinct from the upper Bridg of Deep Creek & down the Road to the Ridge Path along the said Path to Buckingham Road up the s^d Road to Mr Harris Mill Path along the s^d Path to Mayo's Old Mill on Deep Creek down the s^d Creek to the Beginni'g.

Philip Poindexter
Willm. Smith
John Cardwel

We the Subscribers have new Remarked all the Several Land and old lines within the precint as the Vestrey Ordered the line between John Taylor & Allen Howard and between Allen Howard and Ann Mayo Line John Hyde Sanders, William Lax, Allin Howard, John Lake, John Scot & William Hunt presant, the Line between Stephen Bedford & John Tayler Stephen Bedford present, the line between Ann Mayo and Stephen Bedford Stephen Bedford present, the line between Ann Mayo & John Taylor by our Selves the line between Stephen Bedford and Nicholas Cox or Jacob Mosby and the line between Philip Cockerham and the said

[38]   Processioners returns May 21, 1748
Above mentioned Cox or Mosby, Stephen Bedford and Jacob Mosby present and Thos. Low present part of Cockaham Line the Line betwen Stephen Bedford and Cockaham & the line between Ann Mayo & Cockaham the line between Cockhaham & the Gleab Stephen Bedford and Thos. Low present the line between Ann Mayo and the Gleab the Line between Thos. Low and the Gleab the line between Salley and the Glebe Stephen Bedford and Thos. Low present, the line between Low and Selly the line between Low and Ann Mayo Thos. Low present the [line] between John Taylor and William [Taylor] nobody present but we that mark'd the line the line between Joel Chander and Ann Mayo the Line between Ann Mayo and Robt. Walton to the Chappel Road nobody presant between Robt. Walton and Joel Chander William Lax presant at the processioning of that line and there we finished Given under our hands this 4th Day of Feb^r. 1747/8.

W^m. Tayler
Joell Chandler

We do hereby Certifie that after giveing Publick Notis, We gave our Attendance in order to purcession according to order of Vestry and no person Attended us March y^e. 29th 1748.

Joseph Terry
Thos. Davenport
John W his mark Woodson

To the Honourable Vestry of Southam Parish, These. We the Subscribers being Appointed processioners by an Ord^r. of Vestry have Set up Advertisements for all persons within our precinkt to meet at the place & time Appointed by y^e. afores^d. ordr & we giving our Attendance at the same time no person appearing to Shew their Respective lines therefore we return no Land processioned March y^e. 26th 1748.

W Womack
Gideon Glen
Daniel Coleman
Charles Bostick

March 31, 1748. W^m. Moss he reports that he gave dew Attendance but Abr. Womack being decd and Miles Gathwrite being removed into Henrico therefore could not Comply with the w^{h}in Order. August 16th

1748. the Several Processioners returns before W^m. Moss Senr. mentioned as here recorded were this Day Examined by the present Church Wardens.

Test R. Walton Clk Vestry

[39]   May 21, 1748
George Carrington Late Church Warden being thereunto required doth this day return an Account to the Vestry by which Account there arises a Ballance of Thirty three pounds eight pence Curr^t. Money due to Southam Parish.

1746 Southam Parish	D^r	lb Tob.
To paid Sundry Parish Creditors		11032
To Tob^o Sold to M^r. William Gray at 13/p C^t		1352
To D^o Sold to M^r. Atchison at 13/ p C^t		13588
To D^o Bollings Point		115
To D^o Merrwethers Warehouse		70
To the Collectors List of Insolvents		660
Ball^c Due to C^r		<u>1023</u>
		37049

1746 Contra	C^r	
By Tobacco Levied by the Vestry Anno 1745		37049

Decr 18		
To Cash paid Henry May		£ 26. 1.6
Janry 17		
To D^o paid Thos. Harvy		35. 0.5
1747 June 20		
To D^o paid M^r. Stith in Lieu of the Tob^o Levied for him		15.13.6
To Cash paid Thos. Harvey		17. 0.8
To D^o paid Abraham Martin		33.18.6
Ballance due to the parish		<u>33. 0.8</u>
		£ 160.15.3

C^r.

By the above Ballance 10232 take off 6 p C^t 9618 one moiety at 13/6 p C^t being	32.17.6½
By the other Moiety 4809 at 15/ p C^t	36. 1.4
By Cash of Mr Atchison for the Tob^o Sold him	83. 0.7½
By D^o of Mr Wm Gray for the Tob^o Sold him	<u>8.15.9</u>
	£160.15.3

Errors and omissions are Excepted March 31, 1748.

P Geo Carrington

[40]   May 21, 1748

Ordered that Geo Carrington Gent pay Thos. Harvy Sixteen pounds Sixteen Shillings & nine pence half penny being the Ballance due to him for Building Tear Wallet Chapel.

Ordered that the Church Wardens pay James Terry three Hundred pounds of Tobacco for so much Expended for Richard Henderson together with his Cash Account when made out.

Ordered that the Vestry Levy for Samuel Bridgwater at the Laying the next Parish Levy Six hundred pounds of Tobacco for feeding and Cloathing Johannah Parish 'til the tenth day of next March.

Glebe House

Ordered that instead of the House ordered to be Lett Janry 26, 1747 A House forty two foot Long and thirty foot Wide ten foot Pitch in the Clear no Stair Case nor Rooms above Four Windows in the Front, Eighteen Lights Eight by ten Inches two in the backside the same bigness a Brick Cellar Sixteen foot Long and fourteen foot Wide with a ten foot Passage and one Room in the Front, Eighteen foot Square the other Eighteen foot Long and fourteen foot Wide One back Room fourteen foot Long and twelve foot Wide the other back Room Eighteen foot Long and twelve foot Wide taking off a Space for a Closet and Stairs to go into the Cellar of Twelve foot Long and four foot Wide two passage Doors, Six Pannel Doors Four Chamber Doors a Closet Door and a Cellar Door five Pannels Each under Pin'd with Brick two foot from the Ground Brick and half thick two inside Brick Chimneys two fire places in Each the floor framed and finished with Summers and Girders with full Inch Plank Quarter'd Nailed down with twenty Penny Nails or Bradds

Weatherboarded with Feather Edged Plank a Girt Roof with Principal Rafters braced and Covered with Heart Shingles Nailed on Laths with Six Penny Nails the Eves plain Box Cornish'd the Doors to be Hung with H L Hinges one good Spring Lock for the Front Door Iron Rim'd Eight Inches the other Seven Doors to have Locks five Inches, the Walls and Ceiling to be plaistered and White Washed a Porch outside to go into the Cellar with a Door and Strong Stock Lock.

Nicholas Davies gives Bond and Security for the Building the said House for the Sum of Two hundred pounds Current Money. Stephen Bedford enters himself Security.

[41]
John Taylor agrees to keep Robert Saunders's Child 'til the first day of January next for Nine hundred pounds of Tobacco.

     James Barnes   Jno. Robertson
     Step^n. Bedford   Thos. Turpin Chw^{dn}.
     J Terry   Nich^s. Davies Chwd^n.
     Creed Haskins   Ge^o. Carrington

****

At a Vestry held for Southam Parish at Peterville Church the Sixteenth Day of September Anno Dom' mdccxlviii [1748]. Present The Reverend John Robertson Minister, Thomas Turpin, Alexander Trent, George Carrington, James Barnes, Samuel Scott, Stephen Bedford, Nicholas Davies Gent. Vestrymen.

South Chap^l.
Thomas Turpin, James Barnes and Creed Haskins Gent. Or any two of them are appointed to View and receive South Chapel if Built according to Agreement and make Report to the Vestry.

John Worley (the Elder) is appointed Sexton of South Chapel at the Rate of 500^{lb} Tobacco p Year.

Michael Johnson (the Elder) is Exempted from Paying Parish Levies.

Ordered that Nicholas Davies (as Church Warden) bring Suit ag^t Edmund Gray on his promise for William Gray's Parish Levies for the Year 1746 in Southam Parish being 675^{lb} Tobacco.

John Baskerville is Elected Vestryman in the room of William Randolph Gent.

Benjamin Harris is Elected Vestrymen in the room of Benjamin Harrison who resigns, his resignation is Ordered to be recorded and is as

[42] January 1748
follows.

Sepr. 12, 1748 Gentlemen of the Vestry. I desire You'l Chuse another Vestrymen in my room for I am Determined not to Serve any longer I am Gent. Y^r. very Hum^{ble}. Servt.

Benj^a. Harrison

James Barnes and Stephen Bedford Gent. Are Elected Church Wardens for the Ensuing Year who take the Oath appointed by Law.

John Robertson
Step^n. Bedford
James Barnes Ch. W

****

At a Vestry held for Southam Parish at Peterville Church for Laying the Parish Levy the xxvi Day of January. mdccxlviii. 1748 Present. The Reverend John Robertson Minister, Thomas Turpin, George Carrington, James Barnes, Nicholas [Davies], Creed Haskins, Benjamin Harris, John Baskerville Gent. Vestrymen.

Benjamin Harris and John Baskerville Gent. Take the Oaths appointed by Act of Parliament to be taken instead of the Oaths of Allegience and Subscribe the Test.

George Carrington, James Barnes, Nicholas Davies, Creed Haskins, Benjamin Harris and John Baskerville Subscribe to be Conformable to the Doctrine and Discipline of the Church of England Pursuant to Law.

[43]   January 1748
Southam Parish   Dr Tob°.   Cask
To the Reverend John Robertson his Salary Due ⎫
    the 15th This Instant   ⎭   16000   640
To John Cardwell Clk Peterville Church   1000   40
To Thomas Freeman Fretwell Clk Ham Chapel   1000   40
To Sylvanus Witt Reader at Worley's   1000   40
To John Hubbard Clk Tear Wallet Chapel   1000   40
To Robert Walton Clk of the Vestry   500   20
To John Legrand Sexton   500
To William Easley Sexton   500
To Michael Johnson Sexton   500
To Judith Bradshaw for keeping George Dobbins 'til ⎫
    the 27th of November last   ⎭   708
To John Taylor for keeping Robert Saunders's Child ⎫
    'till the first day of this Instant January   ⎭   900
To Danl. Wilmore for keeping Eliz^a. Howle   300
To John Hatch for himself and his Wife   600
To John Worley for serving as Sexton at the   ⎫
    Reading place   ⎭   250
To Mich^l. Johnson for putting up two Horse Blocks ⎫
    at Ham Chapel   ⎭   60
To Edward Yarbour   500
To Henry Wood for Clks Fees   119
To Samuel Bridgwater for keeping Johannah Parish   600
To Tob°. Levied to raise £100. towards paying for ⎫
    the Glebe House   ⎭   15000
To John Smith Junr. for 13 Insolvent Tithables   455
To Bowker Smith for 32 Insolvent Tithables   1120
To Paul Michaux for two Levies overlisted in 1747   70
To William Taylor for keeping Alex^r. Blunt 4 Months 266
                                                      42948   820
                    Cask added   820
                                                      43768
Salary at 6 p C^t. on 43768 is   26[26]

[44]   January 1748

	46394
P Contra C^r	
By a Depositum left in the Hands of the Collector Last Year	283
By 1325 Tithables at 35^{lb} p Poll	46375
	46658
Due to the Parish	264
	46394

William Taylor is appointed to keep Alexander Blunt 'til the next Vestry at the Rate of 800^{lb} Tobacco p Year.

Ordered that Nicholas Davies pay James Meredith Forty five Shillings for Attorneys fees out of Maggehee's fine.

Ordered that the Church Wardens Borrow One hundred pounds for the use of the Parish and that the Gent. of the Vestry now Present pay the Interest on the same by Subscription.

Nicholas Davies late Church Warden renders an Account Debitor and Creditor which is Examined and Ordered to be Recorded. Ballance Due to the Parish £3.0.2.

Ben Harris	Jno Robertson
John Baskervile	James Barnes Ch W
Nicho^s Davies	Geo Carrington
	Thos Turpin
	Creed Haskins

1747 Southam Parish D^r.	
To paid John Blevins for Land to Build a Chapel on	2. 0.0
To paid William Parks for 2 Books for Records	2.10.0
To paid Charles Turnbull for two Table Cloths and two Napkins for Tear Wallet and Ham Chapels	2. 2.0

[45]   January 1748

To paid William Smith for a Chest for Peterville	0.15.0
Sep^r.	
To Bottles of Red Wine for Ham & Tear Wallet	0. 7.0

Dec.
To 1 Q^t. Madera Wine for Tear Wallet   0. 2.6
To 2 Earthen Bowls for Ham and Tear Wallet   0. 2.0
April
To 1 pint Wine for Ham Chapel   0. 1.3
To paid M^{rs}. Webb for a Surplice   5.15.9
To paid Andrew Barclay for 1 p^r Holland for Surplice   6.18.7
    20.14.1
To ½ oz Nunns thread for to make the Surplices   0. 1.6
To p^d Ann Rice for making D^o   1.10.0
To p^d M^r. Walthoe for an Order of Council for a New Patent for the Glebe Land   0.10.6
To paid the Clk of the Secretaries Office Patent fee   0.10.6
To Attending 2 Days on the Council to Obtain the said Patent and ferriage and a Day going and returning my Expenses the said four Days   0.15.0
To paid Nicholas Spiers for going to M^r. Woods for a Copy Of Lightfoots Mortgage to Moss   0.02.6
To Costs of two Folio Bibles and Prayer Books in London £7.17.2 at 37 p C^t Extra   10.16.0
    14.06.0
June 25, 1748
To paid M^r. Carrington for a Jugg   0. 3.0
To paid John Rowland for Carrying Books to Tear Wall^t   0. 2.6
Aug 30
To paid M^{rs}. Freeman for twice washing a Surplice   0. 2.6
Decem
To 1 pint Wine for Ham Chapel   0. 1.3
To Cash paid William Moss   90. 0.0
    90. 9.3
    £ 125. 9.4
         Due to Southam Parish in Cash   3. 0.2
    £ 128. 9.6

         Per Contra   C^r.
1747
By Cash of Charles Turnbul for 667^{lb} Tobacco at 11/10 p Ct   3.18.10
By 6000^{lb} Tob^o. at Shockoes to W^m. Randolph at 12/6   37.10.0

[46]   December the 16th 1749
By 3327^{lb} Tob^o. at Warwick to W^m. Randolph at 12/4   20. 9.11
1748   By Cash of William Smith for Land   53.10.0
By rec^d. of Maj^r. Carrington p Hands of William Moss   13. 0.0
By rec^d. of M^r. Robertson on Acco^t. of W. R. 6^{lb} Tob^o.   0. 0.9
                                                              £ 128 9.6

Errors Excepted Janry 25, 1748. p Nicho^s. Davies

****

1749 Decr. 16th
At a Vestry held for Southam parish at the Glebe of the said parish on Saterday the 16th of December 1749 Present the Rev^d. M. John Robertson Minister Stephen Bedford & James Barnes Chur. Wardens, James Terry, Alex^r. Trent, John Baskervil & Benjamin Harris Gent Vestrymen.

Ordered that Amy Loe to act as Sexton in Petervile Church in the Room of the widow Legrand who hath resigned the Same.

Stephen Bedford Gent one of the Church wardens for this parish haveing acquainted this Vestry that he hath Demanded the parish Book of the Executors of Robt. Walton Dec^d. who refused to Deliver the Same.

Ordered that one of the church wardens do again Demand the Said Books of the said Executors & on their Refusal to Deliver them that they bring sute for the same.

Alex. Trent   John Robertson M^r.
John Baskervile   Stephen Bedford ⎫
Benj Harris   James Barnes   ⎬ Ch W
                       J Terry   ⎭

****

At a Vestry held for Southam parish at the Glebe for Laying the levy this 20th Day of December [1749] Vizt Present The Rev^d. M^r. John Robertson Minister, Stephen Bedford & James Barnes Chur Wardens, Geo Carrington, Thomas Turpin, Nich^o. Davis, James Terry, Allex. Trent, John Baskervile, Creed Haskins & Benj Harris Gent. Vestry men.

	Tob°	Cask
D^r. Southam p[ari]sh		
To the Rev^d. M^r. Jn°. Robertson	16000	640
To John Cardwell Clk Petervil Chur	1000	40
To Thos. Freeman Fretwell Clk	1000	40
To Sylvanus Witt Clk South Chapel	1000	40
To John Hubbard Clk Tarewallet Chapil	1000	40
To Robt. Waltons Executors for his being Clk Vestry	500	20
To John Legrand Sexton	500	
To W^m. Easeley Sexton	500	
To Mical Johnson Sexton	500	
To Judith Bradshaw for keeping George Dobbins Till the 27th of November Last	708	
To John Taylor for keeping John [Robert] Sanderses Child Till the fifth Day of Jan^y.	900	
To Danl. Wilmore for keeping Eliz Howl	300	
To John Hatch and his wife	600	
To Edward Yarbrough	500	
To Joanna Parish	600	
To William Taylor for keeping Allex Blunt	800	
To Capt. W^m. Womack for keeping the widow Kent two year from the 27th Novr. 1747	1600	
	28828	820

[47]		
To brought up	28828	
To John Rowland Constable 1 Levy in 1748	35	
To John Whorley as Sexton of South Chapil	500	
To John Worley for Clearing round South Chapil	300	
To John Worley for three horse Blocks	90	
To John Worley for Setting up Tenn benches	100	
To John Worley for Pins for the Windows of South Chap^l.	20	
To Thos. Stovawl for making & mending benches at Petervil Church	60	
To Geo Nicholas for Eight Lists	112	
To Fra^s. Amoss for keeping Eliz Howl three months	200	
To Mich^l. Johnson for Clearing the Chur Yard	60	
To Mich^l. Johnson for fetching the bread & wine	40	

To the Rev^d. M^r. John Robertson for lack of the Glebe house for the year 1749	2000
To Booker Smith for 31 Insolvents for the year 1748	1085
To Thos. Bedford for 18 Insolvents for the year 1748	630
To Levied for the use of the parish toward paying for the Glebe & for other uses	16000
To Sallery at 6 p C^t on 50060	3004
	53064
Pr Contra Credit	
By 1428 Tithables at 37 pr pole	52836
By Ball. Due to the Colector	228
	53064

Charles Anderson haveing resign'd his place of Vestryman it is ordered that Archebald Cary be appointed in his room & that the said Andersons resignation be Recorded.

Ord^r. that an acc^t. Debtor & Credit of Maj^r. George Carringtons Be recorded & that the Ballance Eleven pounds thirteen Shillings & Seven pence half penny be paid to William Moss Senior.

Ord^r. that M^r. Nich^s. Davis be allowed five Shillings Curr^t. Money For bread & wine that he found when he was Church warden.

Ord^r. that Capt. Stephen Bedford & Capt. James Barnes be Church wardens for the Insuing year.

Ord^r. That William Smith be paid for making a Coffin for Dobbins Dec^d. Seven Shillings & Six pence Curr^t. Money.

Ord^r. That James Terry be Clerk of the Vestry for the Sallery as usual.

Ord^r. That Warham Easely be Sexton of Tarewallet Chapil.

Nichs Davis
Creed Haskins
John Baskervile
Benjamin Harris
J Terry

John Robertson Min^r.
Stephen Bedford }
James Barnes   } Chur Wardens
George Carrington
Thos Turpin

[48]   December the 20th 1749
1748   Dr. Southam parish   £   s   d
Sepr.   To Cash paid Thomas Harvy   16.16.9½
1749   To Do Paid Do Pr ordr. James Barnes   3.12.0
June 26th
To 10s omitted in the last account   0.10.0
To Ballance Due to Credit   _11.13.7½_
                                                    £ 32.12.5
1748
To George Carringtons Credit
By Balla. acct. Rendered   32.12.5

1749
Decr.   By the above Ballance   11.13.7½

Jany. 23, 1748 Sir I desire you'l acquaint the Vestry that I am Desirous they would appoint a Vestry Man in my Roome I live very Ilconvenient & many times the Vestrys held before I hear of it So that I Decline it your Humble Servt, Charles Anderson To Mr. James Terry These
Test J Terry Clk Vestry

****

1750. At a Vestry held at the Glebe for Southam parish The 24th day of April 1750 Present The Revd. Mr. John Robertson Minr. Stephen Bedford Chur. Warden, Geo. Carrington, Alex. Trent, Thos. Turpin, Nichs. Davies, John Baskervile, James Terry & Benj. Harris Gentn. Vestry men.

Ordr Kitchon   That the Chur wardens Thos. Turpin, John Baskervile, Alex. Trent & Nichs. Davies or any two of them do agree with workmen to Repair the Old Dwelling house on the Glebe for a Ketchen that is to Say line the Walls with Plank and after the sd house is moved to Some Convenient Place lay the under floor with good Brick Build an Inside Brick Chimney Eight foot in the Clear the wall of the Back & Jamms two brick thick with a broad step lather into the Loft together with a Dresser & other Convenient Shelves all which to be done workman like.

Smoak house   Also that they agree in like manner for the building of a Smoak house twelve foot by twelve nine foot Pitch to be Fraim'd & Covered with heart & weatherboarded with Featheredged Plank the foundation of the Said building to be Six Corses of Brick one & a half thick two of the Courses to be under the Surface of the Earth & the other four above the Same to be laid in good Lime morter also a Small place in the midst of the said house to contain the fire for Conveniency of Smoak all which to be done workman like.

[49]   April the 24th 1750
Dary   also A Dary twelve foot square nine foot Pitch Bricked underneath as the Smoak house & Covered & weatherboarded as the Same two Sides of the said house to Lo[?]ised Eighteen Inches Deep the Jetts to be two foot the same to be Plastered & White washed & Suted with Convenient Shelves & Dressers Round the house & the floors to be paved all which to be Done workman like.

Stable   Also A stable twenty eight by sixteen eight foot Pitch Framed Work weatherboarded & Cover'd as the Smoakhouse or Dary with an Appartment taken of[f] at One End Eight foot with a Convenient Door to receive Wheal Carriage the Said building to be underpin'd with Brick one foot from the Ground & Ceeld with Inch Plank two foot above the Sill all which to be done Workman like.

Henhouse   Also a hen house twelve feet by eight seven foot Pitch Fram'd weather Boarded & Cover'd as the other houses above mentioned the Same to be done workman like.

House of Office   Also A small house that is to Say eight foot by six seven foot Pitch Framed weatherboarded & Covered as the other houses with a Convenient Bench (for ease) raised as Usual the Same to be workman like Each & Every of the Said buildings to have Ballain Doors Coverings to be Nail'd on with Six penny Nails the weather Boarding With Tenn Penney Nails Doors to be hung with H L Hinges with good Locks on Each Door.

Garden   Ordered that the S^d Gent^m Do agree with workmen to make a Garden one hundred & Tenn foot Square with Sawed Rails & Posts of white oak or Light wood Each post to be fraimed Eight foot Distant the

Pails to be four foot & a half long got out of the heart of Pine to be Rove & Drawn with a Gate well Hung with Hook & Hinges the Same to be Done workman like.

Ord^r That the S^d Gent^m do agree to pay one half of the money at the Compleation of the work and the Other Moiety by the twenty forth Day of January Next.

On the Petition of the uper Inhabitants of this parish it is ordered That James Terry be Clerk of Tarewallet Chapel in the Room of John Hubbard & that the Said Hubbard be paid at the laying the next psh Levy for the time wch he hath Served in that office.

Ord^r that the Church wardens do Credit Margaret Arms to the Vallue of fifty Shillings Curr^t Money to be laid out in beding for the Said Arms.

Ord^r That James Terry do assist the widow Bell to Such Corn & meat as he Shall See Cause till her children can be bound out & that the S^d Terry bring in his Charge.

Mr Arch^d Carry haveing left this parish it is ord^r that Thomas Deavanport Junr Be appointed Vestry man in his Roome on the Motion of Nich^s Davies to Receive the Glebe house so far as is Done it is ordered that the Same be not received till compleetly finished.

        Thom^s Turpin   James Terry
        Geo Carrington   Jno. Robertson Min^r
        Benj Harris   Jno. Baskervile
        Alex Trent   Steph^n Bedford CW

****

[50]
Att a Vestry held for Southam parish at the Glebe for laying the parish levy & other parish bussness this 8th Day of Jany 1750 Present the Revd Mr John Robertson, Stephen Bedford, John Baskervile, Saml Scott, James Terry, Benj^a Harris & Thos Deavanport Gent^n.

Ord^r that the Revd Mr Jno Robertson have for his Sallary	16000
To 4 pr Cent on D^o	640
To John Cardwell Clk Petervil Church	1000
To 4 pr Cent on D^o	40
To Silvanus Witt Clk of South Chapel	1000
To 4 pr Cent on D^o	40
To James Terry for being Clk to the Vestry	500
To 4 pr Cent on D^o	20
To James Terry Clk Tare wallet at Chapel	1000
To 4 pr Cent. On D^o	40
To Amy Low as Sexton to Petervil Church	500
To Susanna Easeley as Sexton at Tarewallet Chapel	500
To Michael Johnson Sexton at Ham Chapel	500
To John Whirley Sexton at South Chapel	500
To James Terry for 18 lb of Bacon 1 bushel of Meat & 1 bottle of Wine	100
To Gideon Glenn for being twice listed in the year 1748	35
To Wm Taylor for keeping Alex Blunt one year	800
To John Taylor for keeping Wingfield Sanders	900
To Capt Wm Womack for keeping the Widow Kent one year	800
To Fran^s [A]Moss for keeping Eliz^a Howl	800
Ord^r that John Hatch & his wife have	1000
Ord^r that Daniel Coleman J^r have for making Seals & stoping under Tarewallet Chapel	100
Ord^r that there be left in the hands of the Church wardens For the use of the Clks of Ham Chapel	1040
Ord^r that Mr Thos Bedford have for 32 Insolvents	1184
Ord^r that the S^d Bedford have for 28 tithes Permiscuously listed	1036
Ord^r that the S^d Bedford have for his last Ballance	228
Ord^r that the Revd Mr John Robertson have for the want of the Glebe house	2000

Ord^r that the Church wardins bring Suit against Mr Nich ^{s}Davis for the Damages Sustain'd for his not Complying wth his Contract in building the Glebe house Except he will account with the Succeeding Church Wardins for 2000 ^{lb} of Tob^o wch the Vestry were forced to levy for the lack of the S^d. Building.

[51]
Ord^r that there be levied for the use of the parish   12000
Ord^r that the Colector pay Mr John Neatherland }
  £ 3.7.6 for building an Oven at the Glebe   }
Ord^r that there be left in the Church Wardins hands }
  for the use of the parish   }   1207
                                    Total D^r.   45510
Pr Contrary Credit
By 1517 tiths at 30 pr Pole. 45510 Which the Church wardins is Impowered to Receive of each respective Tithable they giveing bond & Security to the Vestry for the Same.

Ord^r that Capt. Bedford pay Mr John Neatherland 30£ in part of the work done at the Glebe.

Ord^r that Susannah Easely be Sexton at Tarewallet Chapel & that all Other Sextons in the S^d Parish be Continued in their Respective places & that John Hubbard be Clk of Ham Chapel & that all other Clks be continued in their Respective places.

Ord^r that Mr Benj Harris & Mr John Baskervile be Church wardins for this present year in Case Mr Creed Haskins refuses to Stand Church wardin at the next Vestry wch is appointed to be held at Benj Mosbys the 29th of this Instant.

Ord^r that the 500^{lb} Tob^o wch was Levied for William Easly be paid Warham Easly for the use of his mother Mary Easley.

   John Robertson
   Benjamin Harris   Step^n Bedford C Wardin
   James Terry   Saml. Scott
   Thomas Deavanport John Baskervile

****

[52]
Att a Vestry held at the Courthouse the 29th Day of Jany. 1750 Present the Rev^d. M^r. John Robertson, Creed Haskins & Benjamin Harris Chr Wardins Nicho^s. Davise, Saml Scott, James Terry, John Baskervile, Stephen Bedford, Thos Deavanport and George Carrington Gent^m.

Ord[r] that John Hubbard be paid out of what was left Levied for James Terry from the time he was made Clk of Tarewallet Chapil that is to say from Jan[y]. 1749 till the S[d] Terry Succeeded him in that office and also that the Church wardins pay the S[d] Hubard out of the 1040 left in their hands for the Clks of Ham Chapil from the first of July last till the last laying the levy & that the residue of the S[d] Sum be paid to Tho[s]. Freeman Fretwell.

Ord[r] that M[r]. Abra. Sally be Vestryman in the Room of M[r]. James Barns Dec[d]. and that M[r]. W[m]. Barnit be Elected in the Room of M[r]. Alex. Trent Dec[d].

Ord[r] that the Church Wardins be paid 6 percent for the Colecting the last parish propotion out of the Tob[a]. levied for the use of the parish & left in their hands.

M[r]. Abra. Sally haveing taken the Oaths by law Injoynd and Subscribed the Test is admitted accordingly.

On the Motion of M[r]. Nich[s]. Davise it is ord[r]. that the Glebe house be rec[d]. and that the Ballance of his Demand for the said house be paid by the former Church Wardins as far as Shall appear to be in their hands and the Rest (if any wanting) to be paid by the psent Church Wardins.

M[r]. Creed Haskins & M[r]. Benj Harris haveing taken the Oath of Church Wardins are admitted accordingly.

It is agreed that the ord[r] last made for 2000 pounds of Tob[o] for the use of the Rev[d]. M[r]. John Robertson for the want of the Glebe house be Null & also the ord[r] for Sueing M[r]. Davise & that the Said Tob[a]. be for C[r] use of the parish & that one half of 2000 [lb] Tob[o] be paid the S[d] Robertson by the S[d]. Davise & the other Moiety by the rest of the Vestry.

George Carrington	Nich[s]. Davis
Jn[o] Robertson	Tho[s] Davanport
Steph Bedford	Jn[o] Baskervile
Sam[l]. Scott	Creed Haskins ⎫
James Terry	Benj Harris ⎭ CW

[53]

Att a Vestry held at the Courthouse for Southam parish for laying off the S^d. parish in Small precincts & appointing processioners to procession the Same this 10th day of Sepr. 1751. Present George Carrington, the Revd Mr John Robertson, Thomas Tirpin, Creed Haskins, Jno Baskervile, Stephen Bedford & Ja^s Terry.

Persusant to an Ord^r. of Cumberland Court dated July 1751 the Church wardins have laid ofe [off] the s^d. parish into precincts Which is as followeth (Viz^t).

Ord^r that John Retterford William Retterford & Robt. Thomson on the 11th of Novr. Next begin at the County line on Brookes Road thence along the line to Bowlings Road Down the Same to the main Road & up the Same to the begining Do procesion the Several lands and renew & mark the Several lines and make return according to law.

Ord^r that George Wright Charles Anderson & John Richason on the 11th of November Next begin & procesion all the lands between Brookes & Randolphes Roads up to the County line & make their return according to Law.

Ord^r that Williams Daniel William Mills & William Trigg on the 11th Day of November next begin & procesion all the lands between the County Line Bowlings Buckingham & the main County Roads & make their Return according to Law.

Ord^r that Saml. Allin Allex. Trent & Thomas Coleman on the 11th Day of November Next Do begin & procession all the lands from the County line between Buckingham & Harrisons Roads down to Johnses Road & make their Return according to Law.

Ord^r that Daniel Coleman Junr William Womack William Arnald and John Woodson on the 11th Day of November next do begin & procesion all the Lands between Tarewallet & Great Gennia Creeks up to the main Road & make their return according to Law.

Ord^r that [smudged] Allin Joshua Doss Ambrose Ranson & William Angel [on the] 11th of November next do begin & procession all the [Lands] between the River & Great Ginnia Creek Including [Col°.] William Maconses land & Down Angola Creek & m[ake the]ir return according to Law.

[54]
Ord^r that Thomas Cock Edward Davidson Thos. Williams Edward M^ckgehee Nehemiah Glenn & John Cooke Do begin on the 11th Day of Novem^r next & procession all the lands above Col°. William Maconses uper line & Angola Creek between the River & Great Gennia Creek up to Randolphs Road and make their Return according to Law.

Order^d That John Bostick Humphry Kibble & William Watson on the 11th Day of November next do begin & procession all the lands between the main Road Tarewallet Creek and Ginnia Road & make their Return according to Law.

Ord^r. That Rich^d. Parker Daniel Terry & George Cox on the 11th Day of November Next do begin & procession all the lands below Ginnia Road between the River & the main Road Down to the Road that leads to Clementses Mill & make their Return According to Law.

Ord^r that William Marshal Richd Moseley & William Mosely on the 11th Day of November next do begin and procession all the lands from the County line up the River to Ginnito Bridge thence Down Ginnito Road to the County line and make their Return according to Law.

Ord^r that John Watkins Joseph Baugh & Abra. Baugh on the 11th of November Next do begin & procession all the lands from Ginnito Road up the Church Road to Buckingham Road Down the Said Road to the County line along the Said line to Gennito Road up the s^d Road to the Church Road and make their Return according to Law.

Ord^r that Henry Clay William Clay & George Williamson on the 11th of November next do begin & procession all the Land from Ginnito Bridge up the River to Fighting Creek up the lower Creek to Buckingham Road at the Church Down the Church Road to Ginnito Road up that Road to the bridge & make their Return according to Law.

[55]
Ordʳ That John Mosham Thoˢ. Hall & John Mosely on the 11ᵗʰ Day of November Next do begin & procession all the lands from the Church up Buckingham Road to Colᵒ Randolphs Down the Mill Creek to the fork then up the lower fork to the Church and make their Return according to Law.

Ordʳ That Benj Childers William Bayly & Henry Braseal on the 11ᵗʰ Day of November Next do begin & procession all the land from the mouth of Fighting Creek up the River to Lileses Ford along the Road to Buckingham Road by the sᵈ Childruses Down the Sᵈ Road to Colᵒ Randolphs then Down the Mill Creek to the River & make their return according to Law.

Ordʳ That William Stone Joseph Woodson Stephen Cox & Booker Smith on the 11ᵗʰ Day of November Next do begin & procession all the lands between Appamatox River Clementses Mill Path Buckingham Road & the Road from Benjamin Childruses to Lileses Ford & Make their return according to Law.

Ordʳ That Robᵗ. Hughs Junʳ. Michajah Mosby & Abra. Baker on the 11ᵗʰ Day of November next do begin & Procession all the lands between Deep Creek James River Muddy Creek & the River Road and make their return according to Law.

Ordʳ That Robᵗ. Carter Junʳ. John Carter & Henry Dillion on the 11ᵗʰ Day of November Next do begin & procession all the lands between Muddy Creek James River Willises Creek & the River Road and make their Return according to law.

Ordʳ That William Moss Junʳ William Stratton & Abra. Womack on the 11ᵗʰ Day of November next do begin & procession all the lands between Muddy Creek the River Road Deep Creek the Middle Road & Samˡ Scotts Road to Muddy Creek & make their return according to Law.

Ordʳ That Ralph Flipping William Terrill & Orlander Hughes on the 11ᵗʰ Day of November next do begin & procession all the lands between Muddy Creek the River Road the Path from the Widow Dillions by Thoˢ.

Potters & John Salmons to Ham Chapil & the Chapil Road & make their return according to Law.

[56]
Ord^r That James Cunningham Junr Jonathan Cunningham & Saml Bridgwater on the 11th Day of November Next do begin & procession all the land between the Widow Dillions Path by Thomas Potters & John Salmons to Ham Chapil Hugh Pruits Path from the Chapil to Barnards Road & the S^d Road to Willises Creek and the River Road and make their Return according to Law.

Ord^r That John Runald Job Thomas & Thomas Christan on the 11th Day of November Next do begin & procession all the lands between Willisses Creek Randolphs Creek the County line & the River Road & make their return according to Law.

Ord^r. That Saml Taylor Phineas Glover and Edward Daniel on the 11th Day of November Next do begin & Procession all the lands between Willises Creek James River the County line and the River Road and make their Return according to Law.

Ord^r That John Merryman Thomas Walton & Thomas Merryman on the 11th Day of November Next do begin & procession all the lands between Muddy Creek Barnards Road Hugh Pruits Path & the Chapel road and make their Return according to law.

Ord^r That George Chambers Jacob Mosby & Littleberry Mosby on the 11th Day of November Next do begin & procession all the Lands between Deep Creek Mrs Mayos Chair Road and the middle Road and make their Return according to Law.

Ord^r That Richd Cardwell John Cardwell & Saml Phelps on the 11th Day of November next do begin & procession all the lands between Deep Creek the Middle Road M^r. Sallys Path Buckingham up the Same to Harrisses Path along the Same to Mrs Mayos Old Mill on the S^d Creek Down the Same to the begining and make their Return according to Law.

Ord^r That Benjamin Harrison Thomas Tabb & John Bradley on the 11th Day of November next do begin & procession all the lands between

Willises Creek Buckingham Road the County line & Randolphs Creek & make their Return according to Law.

[57]
Ord^r. That John Hollaway William Hollaway & John Minter on the 11th. Day of November Next do begin & procession all the lands between Barnards Road Horn Quarter Road and Willises Creek and make their Return according to Law

Ord^r That John Taylor William Taylor & Joel Chandler John Hide Sanders Daniel Johnson & William Spiears on the 11th Day of November next do begin & procession all the land between Deep Creek James River the Chappel Road & the Road from Michaux to Speares along the Path from Howards Quarter to Solomans Creek Down the Same to the Said River and make their Return according to Law.

Ord^r That Paul Michaux Daniel Coleman & Frederick Cox on the 11th Day of November Next do begin & procession all the lands from James River the Road from Jacob Michaux Ferry to Paul Michaux the Court house Road to Solomons Creek & Make their return according to Law.

Ord^r That Robt Hughes Stephen Hughes & John Realy on the 11th Day of November next do begin & procession all the land between Michaux Ferry & Fine Creek up the Road to Paul Michaux and make their Return according to Law.

Ord^r that Fran^s. Epperson Robt. Bagby & Daniel Wilmore on the 11th Day of November next do begin & procession all the lands between Fine Creek the Middle road to Paul Michaux & Wm Speares & Fine Creek at the Three Bridges & make their Return according to Law.

Ord^r that John Cannafax Nathl. Maxey & Bennet Goode on the 11th Day of November Next do begin & procession all the Lands between Fine Creek Buckingham Road James River & Joneses Creek & make their Return according to Law.

Ord^r That John Radford William Maxey & Richd Epperson on the 11th Day of November next do begin & procession all the Lands between

Joneses Creek Buckingham Road and the French lines and make their Return according to Law.

[58]
Ord^r That James Davis James [Ligon] and Richd Liggon on the 11th day of November Next do begin & procession all the lands between Col^o Randolph Church Road the Middle [Road] & Buckingham Roads and the Negros Arm to Mrs Mayos Road and make their Return according to Law.

Ord^r That Sanburn Woodson George Cardwell & George Owen on the 11th Day of November Next do begin & procession all the lands between the Middle Road Randolph Church Road Buckingham Road & M^r. Sally (or the Ridge) Path & make their Return according to Law.

Ord^r that the Rev^d. M^r. John Robertson & M^r. Abra. Sally do agree with workmen to build a Corn house on the Glebe twelve foot by twelve Six foot Pitch.

Stephen Bedford	John Robertson
John Baskervile	Creed Haskins
J Terry	George Carrington
	Thos Tirpin

****

Att a vestry held for Southam Parish at the Court house for Laying the parish Levy the xvith Day of December 1751 Present Creed Haskins & Benj. Harris Church Wardins, George Carrington, Stephen Bedford, Abra. Sally, Saml. Scott, Thos. Deavanport, and John Baskervile Gent^m Vestrymen.

Southam Parish	D^r. Neet Tob^o	D^o for Cask
To the Rev^d. M^r. Jno. Robertson for Services till 11th Novr. 1751	14088½	
To Jno. Cardwell Clk Petervil Chur.	1000	40
To Thos. Freeman Fretwell D^o	1000	40
To Silvaster Witt for D^o	1000	40
To James Terry for D^o	1000	40
To the Same for acting as Clk Vestry	500	20
To Amy Low as Sexton &c	500	

To Mrs Easley as D^o	500
To Mich^l. Johnson D^o	500
To Mrs Judith Bradshaw for two years keeping of Geo Dobbins 27th 9^ber last	1416

[59]

To John Taylor for keeping Robt. Sanderses Child to the first Day of Jan^y	900
To Fran^s. Amoss for keeping Eliz. Howl 8 Months to the 26th of Augt. last	450
To Joseph Johns for keeping Eliz Howel four months to this Day	350
To Jno Hatch & his wife	1000
To Johannah Parish for two years Viz^t. Jno. Runals 600 Saml. Bridgwater 600	1200
To William Taylor for Alex: Blunt	800
To the widow Kent for two years to Novr. 27th	1600
N.B. here is levied 800 too much	
To Jno. Whirly as Sexton 500 & for the use of his Bible two year	550
To Jo^s. Terry for one levy twice listed	30

	£ s d
To Benj Harris for Eliz. Brown	1. 0.0
To Benj. Harris for wine for three Churches &c	0. 9.0
To Michajah Mossby for bur[y]ing Jno Brown	1.18.6
To Mr Haskins as p acc^t	4.12.4½
To Capt Thos Terpin as p acc^t	1.11.3¾
To Jno Woodson Q T R T S [quit rents] Glebe land	6.9
To Mich^l Johnson as pr acc^t	3.9
	10. 6.4

To D^o Cleaning Chur. yard 2 years	100
To Jno Woodson 9 Levies Insolvents	277
To Guy Smith for D^o. Insolvents	780
To be levied for the use of the parish to repair the Churches & Other uses	9000
To levied to Discharge the Cash acc^t. as above 10.6.4	1500

To Hannah Wood	250
To 6 p Ct. for Colecting 40291½ lb Tob°	2418
To M[rs] Easely for Extraordinary Services	50
To Ball. Due to the p[ari]sh	273½
Contrary Credit	43033
By 1579 at 27 p[r] Pole	43033

Ord[r] that the Church Wardins Pay M[r]. John Netherland 39.19.0 out of the money in their hands.

[60]
Ord[r] the Rev[d]. M[r]. Rob[t]. Mcklearing be rec[d]. as a probationer for this parish for a twelve month.

Ord[r] that there be an addition of 12 foot & a Gallary to the Churches of Tarewallet & South Chapil & that Ham Chapil be Sealed and Glazed & finished with Pews &c & that George Carrington wth the Church Wardins or Either of them do agree with workmen to Finish the S[d]. Chapil & that M[r]. Tho[s]. Deavanport wth Either of the Church Wardins do agree for the addition of Tarewallet & M[r]. Baskervile wth the S[d]. Church Wardins or Either of them do agree with workmen for the addition of South Chapel &c.

    Stephen Bedford   Creed Haskins ⎫
    Abra: Sally   Benj. Harris   ⎬ C W
    Jn[o]. Baskervile   Geo: Carrington ⎭
    Tho[s]. Davenport   Sam[ll]. Scott

****

Att a Vestry held for Southam parrish at the Court house The 16th May 1752 present Benj[a]. Harris, Creed Haskins Church Wardens, George Carrington, Stephen Bedford, Sam[ll]. Scott, Thomas Davenport, John Baskervile, and Abraham Salley Gent. Vestrymen.

Ordered that Thomas Davenport Ju[r]. is Elected Clark of the Vestrey in the Room of James Terry the Said Terry haveing Removed out of the parrish.

Ordered that the Reverend M^r. Robert McLaurine be Received as Minister for the parrish of Southam.

Wade Neatherland is Elected Vestryman in the Room of James Terry the Said Terry haveing Removed out of the parrish.

Ordered that Rachel Faris be Sexton of Ham Chappel in The Room of Michal Johnson.

[61]   May 16th 1752

Order that there be New buildings of 16 feet by 24 on the North Sides of Tarewallet and South Chappels and the pulpets to be Removed to the Other Sides and that there be a gallery of 10 feet in South Chappel, and that there be a Gallery of 12 feet in Tarewallet Chappel.

Order that the former orders for the addisions to the Said Chapels of 10 feet and a Gallery be null.

Order that the Collector pay Abraham Salley £4.17.6 Current money For building a Corn Creeb on the Gleab.

Order that Creed Haskins Church Warden and John Baskervile Do Let the work to be Done to South Chapel to the Lowest Bider, and that Benj^a Harris Church Warden and Thomas Davenport Do Let the New building at Tarwallet Church.

Stephen Bedford Late Church Warden for the year 1748 and 1749 Renders an accompt Debtor and Creditor, which is Examined and ordered to be Recor[d]ed, Ballance Due to the parrish 1/3.

				D^r
1748 Stephen Bedford is to Southam parrish				
To 15000 ^lb of Tobacco Sold t[o]wards the gleab house at 14/8				110. 0.0
1749	To 2462 ^lb of Tobacco	at 13/6		16.12.4
	To 2003 Ditto	at 14/6		14.10.5
	To 1309 Ditto	at 14/6		9. 9.9
	To 10089 Ditto	at 15/		<u>75.13.4</u>
				£ 226.5.10

Per Contra   C^r
By Cash paid M^r. Nicholas Davis towards the Gleabe   190. 6.4
By 11 bottles of wine at 3/ & Q[uit] Rents of
   270 acres Land 6/4½   1.19.4½

[62]   May 16th 1752
By Cash paid Marget Arms by order of Vestry   2.10.0
By Cash paid John Netherland   30. 0.0
By Cash paid William Smith   1. 2.6
By the Q Rents of 270 acres Land   0. 6.4½
                                            £ 226. 4.7
Bal^c. Due to the parrish   1.3
                                            £ 226. 5.10

Erro[r]s Excepted P Stephen Bedford

September 27th 1751 then Recev'd of Capt. Stephen Bedford on acco^t. of Southam parrish one hundred and ninety pounds Six shillings and four pence Curr^t.

                                          P Nicholas Davies
Test Matt. Whitinge

The Returns of the Several prosessioners hereafter mentioned.

Pursuant to this order of Vestry we the subscribers have marked the within mentioned bounds of Land saveing one Line between M^{rs}. Anne Mayo and Frances Steger and we Could not fine the Line.
                                       P Rich^d. Cardwell
                                       John Cardwell
                                       Sam^{ll}. Phelps

To the Vestry of Southam parrish Whereas this order Come two late to hand I hope the Gent. of the Vestry will Excuse their Hble Serv^{ts}.
                                       William Trigg & Company

[63]
According to Directions given we have processioned the several lines Within our precincts (Viz^t.) Beginning at W^m. Womacks Corner between Henry Harman & the Said Womack Henry Macon John Chafin present The line between W^m. Womack & Daniel Coleman Junr. parties present

The line between James Terry & Robert Lowry Henry Macon John Chafin Present, the line between Daniel Coleman Junr.& Henry Harman Henry Macon John Chafin present, the several lines between Henry Macon and John Chafin Henry Harman present, the lines between Henry Macon and James Allen Henry Harman & John Chafin present the line Between Henry Macon & the land formerly belonging to Charles Bostick Henry Harman & John Chafin present, the line between Paul Pigg and W^m. Arnald Henry Arnald present the several lines between W^m [Arnald] & John Woodson Henry Arnald present, the Several lines Between Martin Slaughter & W^m. Arnald Henry Arnald present The line between John Woodson & Martin Slaughter Henry Arnald present The line between Martin Slaughter & Isaac Allin John Chafin Henry Harman present, the line between John Chafin & John Woodson parties Present, the line between John Chafin & W^m. Chumley David Bradley present Between James Holland & John Chafin W^m. Chumley present, between John Chafin & Josiah Payne David Bradley present, between John Chafin & William Davis David Bradley present, between Wm Chumley & W^m. Davis John Chafin and David Bradley present, between James Allen & John Chafin, John Smith and W^m. Basham Junr present, between James Allen & Wm Basham Junr John Smith present, D^o. between Thos. Huckaby & W^m. Basham Senr. Jno. Smith Present, D^o. between W^m. Basham Senr. & Thos. Harris Jno. Smith W^m. Basham Junr Present, D^o. between James Holland & W^m. Basham Senr. Jno. Smith & Wm Basham Junr present, Witness our hands.

        Daniel Coleman Junr
        Wm Womack
        John Woodson
        William Arnald

[64] May 16th 1752
To the Gentlemen of the Vestry the Land that we have Done in the Year 1752, one line between Coll^o. Richard Randolph & William Randolph, Thos. Hall John Eggleston present, a line between William Clay & Henry Clay both present, a line between William Clay & Timson, Timson not present, a Line between Thos. Moseley and Timson, aline between John Moseley & Thos. Moseley both Present, a line between Henry Clay & John Moseley both present One line between John Steward & Coll^o. Richard Randolph not Done, nobody there one line between George Williamson

and Timson Williamson Denys to have it Done, one line between William
Randolph & Timson not Done nobody there to Do it.
> William Clay
> Henry Clay

We cartifie to the Vestrey that we have prosessioned & Renewed all the
Lines within our presincts mentioned in the order Except a peace Of Coll°
William Randolphs Line which we could not git any body To shew, that
had orders from Randolph.
> George Owen
> Sanbuarn Woodson
> George Cardwell

This is to Cartifie We the Said poscessioners have poscessiond and,
Renewed and mark'd all the Lands between James River, the Rhode from
Jacob Michaux Ferry to Paul Michaux & the Courthouse Rhoad to
Solomons Creek according to a order of Vestry granted The 10th Day of
September 1751 Witness our hands.
> Paul Michaux
> Frederick Cox
> Daniel Coleman

[65]   May 16th 1752
In obediance to the Vestry we possession'd one line between Col°.
William Randolph & Capt. Richd Pouvaul, Pouvaul & John Barkesdail
present, & one Line between Col°. Richd Randolph Deceas^d. Pouvaul &
Hall present, one line Between Richd Randolph & William Randolph,
Barks. & Hall present, one line Between Richd Randolph & John Hales
Deceas^d. Hall & Mossom for Halls, one Line between Col°. Will. & John
Hails Barks^d. & Mossom present, one line Between Richd Legon & John
Radford Legon & Mossom present, & one line between Radford & James
Davis Charles Davis & Mossom present, one line Between John Blackbon
& James Davis Mossom & Charles Davis present, One line between Col°.
Richard & James Davis Charles Davis & Hall present, One Line between
Col°. Richard & Black^r. Moss. & Hall present, one line Between Samuell
Hacher & Blackbon Moss & Bunn present, one line Between Col°.
Richard & Hacher Bag & Hall present, one line Between Col° Rich^d &
Edward Moseley present, one Line between Henry Clay Col°. Richd Clay
present, one line between Henry Clay & John Moseley Clay & Moseley

present, one line Between William Maxey & Edward Moseley present, one line between Hacher & Thomas Basset not Renewed Nobody to attend in Bassets Behalf. Gentlemen Your Most Hble Servants.

Thos. Hall
John Moseley
John Mossom

Gentlemen of the Vestry we the Subscrbers have vewed & new marked the Several lines within the Bounds perscribed according to the order you made at The Vestry held in September the tenth Day 1751 & all a peaceable possesion Given under our hands this 22nd Day of April 1752.

John Watkins
Joseph Baugh
Abraham Baugh

[66]   May 16th 1752
Pursuant to this order of Vestry We the Subscribers have Renewed And marked the within mentioned bounds of Land.

John Hidesanders	William Tayler
William Spears	Joel Chandler
Daniel Johnson	John Tayler

Pursuant to an order of Vestry Beginning at Muddy Creek Bridg We Abraham Womack & William Stratton have possescioned the line Between M^r. Nicholas Davies & Robert Hughs Absalom Jurden present and the Lines Between M^r. Davies & William Stratton & the lines Between M^r. Davies & Abraham Womack & the lines between M^r. Edward Tabb & Alexander Moss & the line between Jacob Mosby & Alexander Moss & the line between Thos. Moss & Henry Stratton and the line between William Stratton & Thos. Moss & the lines Between Abraham Womack & William Stratton & the lines Between Micajah Mosby & Nowel Wadel & the lines between Thos. Bedford & Thos. Moss & the line between Thos. Bedford and Nowel Wadel, & the line between Thos. Bedford & Micajah Mosby Joseph Mosby present & the line between M^r. Pleasent & Capt. Bedford Micajah Mosby & Jacob Mosby present, & the line Between M^r. John Pleasent & Micajah Mosby Jacob Mosby present and the line between Jacob Mosby & Micajah Mosby & the line between Jacob Mosby & Nowel Wadel & the Lines between Jacob Mosby & William Moss.

Micajah Mosby present & the line between Henry Stratton and Nowel Wadel & the line between Thos. Moss & Nowel Wadel Henry Stratton present, & the line between M^r. Edward Tabb & W^m. Moss and the Line Between Bowler Cock & Edward Tabb & part of a Line Between Bowler Cock & William Moss the Remainer Cant be found.

[67] May 16th 1752
Pursuant to an order of Vestry held for Southam parrish the 10 Day of September 1751 We the Subscribers have prosessioned all the Lines of Land in our precinct and peaceable and Quiet prosession is agreed on by all parties within our bounds Except George Williamson who Refuses to prosession the line between him and George Tod Dec^d. By Reason he Says he hath not his Complyment of Land.

William Marshall
Richard Moseley
William Moseley

In obediance to an order of Vestry of Southam parrish in the County of Cumberland we the Subscribers have Caused all the Lines to be new marked of all the land within the bounds as to us Directed Except part of one line between John Pleasents Fine Creek Land and the Land of Susanna Gasper which Cannot be Found Witness our hands.

Robert Hughes
John Railey
Stephen Hughes

In obedience to an order of vestry we have prosessioned the Lands and marked the Lines within our bounds Excepting John Salmon Rachel Farisses and part of Nicholas Davis part of Benjamen Harrisons part of John Blevens part of John Rowland part Of Michal Rowlands part of Benjamen Dumas, part of Stephen Hughes being Not Done For want of attendance.

Ralph Flippen
Orlando Hughes

[68] May 16th 1752
In obedience to this order of Vestry I should have procession But the other parties is Removed out of the precincts before The order Came to Hand P^r.

John Retterford

Pursuant to an order of Southam Vestry bareing Date the Tenth Day of September 1751 we that ware appointed have seen all the Lines New markt and peaceablely processioned (Vz) between Hughes & Allexander, Alexander & Thomas Bedford & Edward Scrugs pres[ent], Between Hughes and Mr Randolph the persons before mentioned Present, between Randolph and Stratton Wm Stratton Abraham Womack E^d. Scrugs Thomas Bedford present, Between Randolph and Stephenson Moss and Stephenson the above mention^d. persons prese[nt], Between Moss and Randolph Thomas Bedford E^d. Scrugs Geo. Going Present, Between Moss and Randolph and Moss and Bedford the Same Persons present, between Bedford and Randolph and Randolph and Mosby the same persons present, between Mosby and Bedford Thomas Bedford present, between Mosby and Pleasent Thomas Tucker present, The [w]hole processioned the 19th Day of February 1752.

Robert Hughes
Abram Baker
Micajah Mosby

[69]   May 16th 1752

Pursuant to an order of Vestry have prosessioned the Lines Between the Persons hereafter Named

Persons hereafter Named				Whom present	
Between James Holloway Senr.		& Richard Murry		John Allen	
James	D^o	D^o & Jonus Meadors		D^o	D^o
D^o	D^o	D^o & Jacob Mosby		D^o	D^o
James Halloway Junr.		& John Hallaway Senr.			
D^o D^o	D^o	& W^m D^o		John Bradley	
D^o D^o	D^o	& John Bradley			
John Bradley		& Wm Halloway		James Holloway	
John Holloway Junr.		& W^m D^o		John Bradley	
D^o	D^o	& John Bradley		James Holloway	
D^o	D^o	& Ambrose Wood		D^o	D^o
D^o	D^o	& James Anderson		D^o	D^o
D^o	D^o	& Alex^r. Trent		D^o	D^o
John Bradley		& D^o D^o		James Holloway	
Williams Daniel		& D^o D^o		John Bradley	
Nicholas Speirs		& D^o D^o		D^o	D^o
Daniel Coleman Senr.		& James Daniel			
D^o D^o	D^o	& Robert Lowry		D^o	D^o

Dº	Dº	Dº	& Robert Hudgens	Dº	Dº
Dº	Dº	Dº	& Thoˢ. Tilman	Dº	Dº
Robert Hudgens			& Robert Lowry	Dº	Dº
Dº	Dº		& Nicholas Speirs	Dº	Dº
Dº	Dº		& Alexʳ. Trent	Dº	Dº
Dº	Dº		& Samˡ. Allen	Dº	Dº
Samˡ Allen			& Alexʳ. Trent		
Joseph Woodson			& Dº Dº		
Thoˢ. Hughs			& Dº Dº		
Ambrose Wood			& Dº Dº		
Thoˢ Tabb			& Farrer		
Dº	Dº		& Benjᵃ. Harrison		
Benjᵃ Harrison			& Farrer	Thoˢ. Tabb	
Thoˢ. Tilman			& Alexʳ. Trent		
Alexʳ. Trent			& John Moore		
Alexʳ. Speirs			& Alexʳ. Trent	Benjᵃ. Harrison	
Dº	Dº		& Thoˢ. Guttery	Dº	Dº
David Bell			& Alexʳ Trent	Dº	Dº
Benjᵃ. Harrison			& Farrer		
Dº	Dº		& Archᵈ. Cary		

Thoˢ. Coleman
Samˡ. Allen
Alexʳ. Trent

[70]   May 16ᵗʰ 1752
Richard Cardwell, John Cardwell, Samˡ. Phelps, Wᵐˢ. Daniel, Wᵐ. Trigg, Wᵐ. Mills, Wᵐ Womack, John Woodson, Wᵐ. Arnald, Wᵐ. Clay & Henry Clay, Sambuarn Woodson, George Owan, George Cardwell, Paul Michaux, Fredrick Cox, Daniel Coleman, Thoˢ. Hall, John Moseley, John Mossom, John Watkins, Joseph Baugh, Abram Baugh, Wᵐ. Tayler, & others, Abraᵐ. Womack, Wᵐ Stratton, Wᵐ Marchal, Richard & Wᵐ. Moselseys, Robert Hughs, John Raley & Stepⁿ Hughs, Ralph Flippen, Orlander Hughs, John Retterford, Robert Hughes, Abraᵐ. Baker & Micajah Mosby, Thomas Coleman, Samuell Allen & Alexʳ. Trent Order that the above Returns Entered be Recorded

        Stephen Bedford   Robert McLaurine
        John Baskervile   Creed Haskins ⎫
        Thomas Davenport Benjamen Harris ⎬ C. Wˢ.

Abraham Salley   George Carrington
                      Samuell Scott

****

At the Vestry held for Laying the parrish Levy of Southam at the Court House December the 9th 1752   Present the Reverend Mr. Robert McLaurine, Creed Haskins Church Warden, George Carrington, Nicholas Davis, Stephen Bedford, John Baskervile, Thomas Davenport, Abraham Salley, and Wade Netherland Gent Vestrymen.

Southam Parrish	Debtor	Neet Tobacco
To the Reverend Mr. Robert McLaurine minister		16000
To John Cardwell Clark of Petervile Church		1000
To Thos. Freeman Fretwell Clark of Ham Chapel		1000
To Silvanus Wett Clark of South Chapel		1000
To Ame Loe Secton of Petervile Church		500
To Mary [Susannah] Easley Secton of Tarewallet Church		500
To the Reverend Mr. Robert McLaurine for Cask & pr Ct		1600
		21600

[71]   December 9th 1752

To the sum brought over	21600
To Rachel Fares Secton of Ham Chapel	416
To Judith Bradshaw for keeping George Dobings	513
To John Tayler for keeping Sanders's Child	1200
To John Hatch and his wife	1000
To Joannah Parrish	600
To William Tayler for keeping Alexr. Blunt	800
To the Widow Kent	800
To John Wherley Secton of South Chapel	500
To Ditto for makeing benches	200
To James Terry for services Done	625
To Michal Johnson for two months serving as secton	84
To Mery Webb for moveing Hatch & his wife	1200
To Paul Michaux pr accompt	100
To Joseph Price for burying Strange	300
To John Robertson for keeping George Dobings 3 months	177

To Daniel Wilmore for keeping Elizabeth Howl	600
To Ame Loe for makeing benches at the Church	75
To Ditto for makeing fiers in the Glebe house	25
To the Reverend M^r. Robert McLaurine for services Done	1466
To Thomas Davenport for being Clark of the Vestry	500
To John Woodson Shrf. for 14 Insolvents	378
To Frances Mackcraw for Ditto	459
To John Hubbard for acting as Clark at Tarewallet	500
To Levy^d. for the use of the parrish	10000
To the Collector for Collecting the above Tobacco	2617
	46753
To Ballance in the hands of the Collector	712½
	47465½
P Contra Credit	
By 1609 Tithables at. 29½ lb Tob°. p pole	47465½

[72]   December 9th. 1752

Ordered That John Baskervile and Abraham Salley be Church Wardens and that they Settle with the Former Church Wardens and Receive The ballences in their hands.

Ordered That Gidion Glen be Clark of Tarewallet Church.

Ordered That the Collector pay the several Clarks Casks with the Tobacco Levyed for them.

	Robert McLaurine Minister
Stephen Bedford	John Baskervile CW
Creed Haskins	Abraham Salley CW
Thomas Davenport	George Carrington
Wade Netherland	Nicholas Davis

****

At a Vestry held For Laying the Parrish Levy of Southam at The Courthouse January the 30th 1754. Present the Reverend M^r. Robert McLaurine minister, John Baskervile Ch. Warden, George Carrington, Nicholas Davies, Stephen Bedford, Thomas Turpin, Creed Haskins, Benjamin Harris, Wade Netherland, and Thomas Davenport Gent. Vestrymen.

Southam Parrish	Dr.	Neet Tobo.	Cask
To the Reverend Mr. Robert McLaurine minister		16000	640
and Six Percent for Scrinkage		960	
To John Cardwell Clk of Petervile Ch		1000	40
To Thos. Freeman Fretwell Clk. Ham Chapel		1000	40
To Gideon Glen Clk. Tarewallet Ch		1000	40
To Silvanus Witt Clk. South Chapel		1000	40
To Thomas Davenport for being Clk. Vestry		500	20
To Amy Loe Secton of Petervile Church		500	820
		21960	

[73]   January 30th 1754

Brought over the sum Levyd. is	21960
To Rachel Faris Sexton of Ham Chapil	500
To Susannah Easley Sexton Tarewallet Ch	500
To John Wherley Sexton South Chapil	500
To John Tayler for keeping Sanders's Child	1200
To John Rennals for keeping Joannah Parrish	600
To the Widow Kent	800
To John Robertson for keeping George Dobings	700
To Bartholomew Stovaul for being twice Listed 7. tithes at 29½	206½
To William Marchel 5 Levys at 29½ Twice listed	147½
To Jacob Mosby 5 Levys at 29½ Twice listed	147½
To John Holland 2 Levys at 29½ Twice listed	59
To Martin Slaughter 2 levys at 29½ Twice Listed	59
To Henry Davenport 1 Levy at 29½ Twice Listed	29½
To Nicholas Davies 7 Levys at 26 Twice Listed	182
To Rachel Faris for Servises Done	70
To Susannah Easley for Servises Done	70
To John Tayler for keeping Elizabeth Howl 4 months	200
To Joseph Woodson 3 Levys at 26 Twice Listed	78
To Francis Cannefax for keeping Elizabeth Howl 10 months	600
To Henry Farmer	250
To William Bosticks for keeping Mrs. Parker 4 months	100
Thomas Davvenport for goods Deliverd to Mrs. Parker	100
To Freaderick Hatcher for 21 Insolvents	619
To Frances Maccraw for 10 Insolvents	295
Levyed for the use of the Parrish	10000

To the Collector for Collecting the above Tobacco	2398
	42371
To ballance Due in the hands of the Collector	754
	43125

P Contra   C.ʳ
By tithables 1723   ⎫
By John Dickerson 2   ⎬ in all 1725 at 25 ᵇ Tob°. p pole   43125

Frances Cannefax Doth agree to keep Elizabeth Howl at the Rates of 800 lb Tob°. year William Bostick Doth agree to keep Mʳˢ. Parker at the Rates of 600 ᵇ Tob° p annom Joseph Woodson Doth agree to keep George Dobings from the ninth of December Last at the Rates of 500 ᵇ Tobacco p annom.

[74]   January 30ᵗʰ 1754
Ordered That Mʳ. John Baskervile Pay to Elenor Sutlief Two pounds Current money.

Ordered That Nicholas Davies, Thomas Turpin, Wade Netherland and George Carrington or any two of them Do Settle the Several accompts with Benjamin Harris and Creed Haskins Late Church Wardens. and John Woodson S. Shrf. [Sub Sheriff].

Ordered That John Baskervile agree with workmen for building a Quarter on The Glebe Sixteen feet square and a outside Chimney.

Ordered That George Carrington, Nicholas Davies, Benjamin Harris, and Thomas Davenport or any Two of them Do agree with workmen For the new building to Tarewallet Church as before mentioned in a Former order.

Alexander Trent is Elected Vestryman in the Rume of William Barnard who hath Refused to Quallefie.

Wade Netherland	Robert MᶜLaurine Minister
Stephen Bedford	John Baskervile Ch. W.
Creed Haskins	George Carrington
Benjamin Harris	Nicholas Davies
Thomas Davenport	Thomas Turpin

****

Att a Vestry Held For Laying the Parrish Levy of Southam Att the Courthouse the Second Day of December 1754 Present the Reverend M^r. Robert McLaurine Minister, John Baskervile Church Warden, George Carrington, Nicholas Davies, Stephen Bedford, Wade Netherland, and Thomas Davenport Gen^t. Vestrymen

[75] December 2nd 1754

Southam Parrish	D^r.	Neet Tob^o	Cask
To the Reverend M^r. Robert McLaurine minister		16000	640
and 6 pr cent for scrinkage		960	
To John Cardwell Clk Petervile Church		1000	40
To Gideon Glenn Clk. Tarewallet Church		1000	40
To Thos. Freeman Fretwell Clk. Ham Chppel		1000	40
To Silvanus Witt Clk. South Chappel		1000	40
To Thos. Davenport for Being Clk Vestry		500	20
The Cask aded		820	820
To Ame Loe Sexton Petervile Church		500	
To Susannah Easley Sexton Tarwallet Church		500	
To Rachel Faris Sexton Ham Chappel		500	
To John Wherley Sexton South Chappel		500	
To John Tayler For keeping Sanderses Child		1200	
To John Runnals For keeping Johannah Parrish		600	
To the Widow Kent		800	
To Thos. Davenport by order of William Bostick		529	
To William Bostick his Ballance For keeping the Widow Parker		71	
To Joseph Woodson For keeping George Dobings		500	
To Francis Cannafax for keeping Elizabeth Howl		800	
To John Wherley for makeing Benches at South Chappel		100	
To Frederick Hatcher for 15 Insolvents at 25 p pole		375	
To Francis Maccraw for 17 D^o. & for 5 Patrolers at D^o.		550	
To Edward Cannafax for Being Twice Listed in 1752		39	
To Henry Farmer		400	
Levyed For the use of the Parrish		10100	
		40344	

To the Church Wardens For Collecting the above Tob°. 2420
42764
To Ballance Due in the hands of the Church Wardens   292
43056

P. Contra   C^r.
By 1872 Tithables at 23^{lb}. Tob°. P. Pole   43056

Order^d That M^r. John Baskervile agree with Workmen to Repair the Seller at The Glebe the Brickwork Excepted.

[76]   December 2nd 1754
Order^d That M^r. John Baskervile and M^r. Wade Netherland be Church Wardens for this Present Year.

John Fleaming Ju^r. is Elected Vestryman in the Room of Abraham Salley.

Order^d. That the Church Wardens Give Elenor Sutlief and Jobe Walker C^r. For Fourty Shillings Each to Be Paid Next year.

Order^d. That M^r. George Carrington and M^r. Nicholas Davies Receive the Work Done at Ham Chappel and that M^r. Davies and Thos. Davenport Receive the work Done at Tarewallet Church
    John Baskervile   }   Robert McLaurine
    Wade Netherland } CW Stephen Bedford
    George Carrington   Nicholas Davies
    Thomas Davenport

****

Att a Vestry held this 8th Day of February 1755. For the Parrish Of Southam Present the Reverend M^r. Robert McLaurine minister, George Carrington, Thos. Turpin, Nicholas Davies, Creed Haskins, Stephen Bedford, and John Baskervile Gent^n Vestrymen.

John Baskervile Formerly appointed one of the Church Wardens for the Said Parrish hath this Day taken the Oath by Law Requiered of Church Wardens.

Order^d. That John Woodson Be appointed Collector of the Parrish Levy This Present year and that he when Requiered by the Church Wardens Do Give Bond and Security according to Law.

[77]   February 8th 1755

Order^d. That George Carrington and Nicholas Davies Do agree with Workmen To Build a Gallery in Ham Chappel in the land of the Building and in A Workm^n Like mannar of Such Dementions as shall be Directed by The Said Persons Impowered.

	Robert McLaurine Minister
John Baskervile CW	Nicholas Davies
Georg Carrington	Creed Haskins
Thomas Turpin	Stephen Bedford

****

Att a Vestry held for Southam Parrish at Petervile Church for Laying Off the said Parrish into small Precincts and appointing Processioners to Procession the same the 11th Day of August 1755 Present the Revend M^r. Robert McLaurine minister, John Baskervile & Wade Netherland Chu^ch. War^dn, Nicholas Davies, Creed Haskins, Stephen Bedford, and Thomas Davenport. Gent^n. Vestrymen.

Pursuant to an order of Cumberland Court Dated July the 29th Day 1755 the Church Wardens have Laid off the said Parrish into Precincts Which are as Followeth Viz.

Ordered That Charles Anderson John Woodson Thomas Williams and George Right on the 10th Day of November next Begin and Procession all the Lands and Renew and mark the several Lines Between Randolphs Road Brooks Road and the County Line and make their Return according to Law.

Ordered That James Anderson James Allen Thomas Cock and Charles Cotterell on the 10th Day of November Next Begin and Procession all the Lands and Renew and mark the several Lines Between Green Creek Appamattox River and Randolphs Road and make their Return according To Law.

[78]   August 11th 1755
Ordered That Thomas Merryman John Retterford Senr. and Higginson Barksdale on the 10th Day of November Next Begin and Procession all the Lands and Renew and mark the several Lines Betwen Brookss Road the County Line Bollings Road and the Main Road and make their Return according to Law.

Ordered That John Cook Phillip Holcomb Warren Walker and John Nelson on the 10th Day of November next Begin and Procession all the Lands and Renew and Mark The several Lines Between Angoler Creek Appamattox River Green Creek and Randolphs Road and make their Return according to Law.

Ordered That Isaac Allen Joshua Doss James Daniel and Frances Epperson on the 10th Day of November Next Begin and Procession all the Lands and Renew and mark the several Lines Between Great Guinea Creek Appamattox River Angoler Creek and Colo. Wm. Macons upper Lines and make their Return according to Law.

Ordered That Edward Mackgehe Charles Lee and Nehemiah Glen on the 10th Day of November Next Begin and Procession all the Lands and Renew and mark The several Lines Begining at Colo. Wm. Macons upper Line Thence on the said Line to Angoler up Angoler to Randolphs Road Down Randolphs Road to Glens Path on the same to Great Guinea Down the same to the Begining Do Procession all the Lands within the said Bounds and Renew and mark The several Lines and make their Return according to Law.

Ordered That Henry Macon William Womack and Daniel Coleman Jur. on the 10th Day of November Next Begin and Procession all the Lands and Renew and mark the several Lines Between Tarewallet Run Great Guinea Creek and the Main Road and make their Return according to Law.

Ordered That John Bostick Richard Weatherford Henry Davenport and Henry Harman on The 10th Day of November Next Begin and Procession all the Lands and Renew and Mark the several Lines Between Little Guinea Creek Appamattox River Great Guinea Tarewallet Run and the Main Road and make their Return according to Law.

[79]   August 11th. 1755

Ordered That Humphrey Keeble William Hambleton and William Watson on the 10th Day of November next Begin and Procession all the Lands and Renew and mark the several Lines Between Little Guinea Creek the Main Road and Guinea Road and make Their Return according to Law.

Ordered That Robert Thomson Richard Parker and Lawrence Smith on the 10th Day of November Next Begin and Procession all the Lands and Renew and mark the several lines Between Little Guinea [Creek] Guinea Road Appamattox River Buckingame Road and the Road to Clements's Mill and make their Return according to Law.

Ordered That Ackillis Bowker Joseph Woodson Bowker Smith and Nathaniel Ford on the 10th Day of November Next Begin and Procession all the Lands and Renew and mark the several Lines Between Appamattox River Lileses Road Buckingame Road and the Road To Clements's Mill and make their Return according to Law.

Ordered That Richard Pouvaul Benjamin Childrey and William Bailey on the 10th Day of November Next Begin and procession all the Lands and Renew and mark the several Lines Between Appamattox River Fighting Creek Buckingame Road and Lileses Road And make their Return according to Law.

Ordered That John Moseley Edward Moseley and Henry Clay on the 10th Day of November Next Begin and Procession all the Lands and Renew and mark the several Lines Between From the fork of Fighting Creek up Randolphs Mill Creek to Buckingame Road Down the Said Road to the Church Down the Creek to the fork and make their Return according to Law.

Ordered That Frances Marchal Thomas Locket and Joel Locket on the 10th Day of November Next Begin and Procession all the Lands and Renew and mark the several Lines Between Geneto Road the Church Road Fighting Creek and Appamattox River and make their Return according to Law.

Ordered That Edward Watkins Isham Ackins and Abraham Baugh on the 10th Day of November Next Begin and Procession all the Lands and Renew and mark the several lines Between the New Road Buckingame Road the Church Road and Geneto Road and make their Return according to Law.

[80]   August 11th 1755
Ordered That Joseph Baugh Israel Winfrey and John Watkins on the 10th. Day of November Next Begin and Procession all the Lands and Renew and marke the several Lines Between Buckingame Road the New Road Geneto Road and the County Line and make their Return according to Law.

Ordered That George Hancock Richard Moseley and William Moseley on the 10th Day of November next Begin and Procession all the Lands and Renew and Mark the several Lines Between the County Line Appamattox River and Geneto Road and make their Return according to Law.

Ordered That Williams Daniel William Mills and William Trigg on the 10th Day of November next Begin and Procession all the Lands and Renew and mark the several lines Between Bollings Road Buckingame Road the Main Road and the County line and make their Return according to Law.

Ordered That Samuell Allen Alexander Trent and Thomas Gutterey on the 10th Day of November next Begin and Procession all the lands and Renew and mark The several lines Between Buckingame Road the County line Harrosons Road and the Road from Murrays to John Burtons and make their Return according to law.

Ordered That John Hopson William Hopson Field Robertson and George Winneford on the 10th Day of November next Begin and Procession all the lands and Renew and mark the several lines Between Buckingame Road the Road from John Burtons to Murrays the Courthouse Road and Mayos Old Mill Path to Benjamin Harris's And make their Return according to law.

Ordered That Poindexter Mosby John Scrugs and John Hughes on the 10th. Day of November Next Begin and Procession all the lands and Renew and mark the several lines Between the Middle Road Mr. Salleys

Path Buckingham Road M^r. Harris's Path to Mayo Old Mill and Deep Creek and make their Return according to Law.

Ordered That Sanburn Woodson George Owen George Cardwell and Frances Macraw on the 10th Day of November next Begin and Procession all the lands and Renew and mark the Several Lines Between the Middle Road Randolph's Church Road Buckingame Road and M^r. Salleys Path and make their Return according to Law.

[81]   August 11th 1755
Ordered That James Davis Richard Ligon and James Ligon on the 10th Day of November Next Begin and Procession all the lands and Renew and mark the several lines Between the Middle Road Randolph's Church Road Buckingame Road and the Road from the Negros Arm to M^{rs}. Mayo's and make their Return according to Law.

Ordered That John Radford William Maxey and Joseph Bundurent on the 10th Day of November Next Begin and Procession all the lands and Renew and mark the several lines Between Jones's Creek the French lines and Buckingame Road and make their Return According to Law.

Ordered That Bennet Goode Nathaniel Maxey and Edward Parrott on the 10th Day of November next Begin and Procession all the lands and Renew and mark the several Lines Between Joneses Creek James River Fine Creek and Buckingame Road And make their Return according to Law.

Ordered That John Rayley Joseph Hughes and Daniel Wilmore on the 10th Day of November Next Begin and Procession all the lands and Renew and mark the several lines Between Michaux Ferrey Road James River Fine Creek and the Road to Paul Michaux and make their Return according to Law.

Ordered That Robert Bagby Henry Bagby and William Cox on the 10th Day of November Next Begin and Procession all the Lands and Renew and mark the several lines Between Fine Creek the Middle Road to Paul Michaux and from Michaux to William Spiers's and Fine Creek at the Three Bridges and make their Return According to law.

Ordered That Paul Michaux John Franklin and Robert Chandler on the 10th Day of November Next Begin and Procession all the lands and Renew and mark The several lines Between James River the Ferrey Road to Paul Michaux The Courthouse Road to Solomons Creek and make their Return according to Law.

Ordered That John Tayler William Tayler John Hidesanders Daniel Johnson William Speirs and Edmon Toney on the 10th Day of November Next Begin and Procession all the Lands and Renew and mark the several Lines Between Deep Creek the Church Road the Road from Speirses to Michaux Solomons Creek and James River and make their Return according To Law.

[82]   August 11th 1755
Ordered That Robert Hughes Micajah Mosby and Joseph Mosby on the 10th Day of November next Begin and Procession all the Lands and Renew and mark the several Lines Between Deep Creek James River Muddy Creek and the River Road and make their Return According to Law.

Ordered That Abraham Womack William Stratton and William Moss on the 10th Day of November Next Begin and Procession all the Lands and Renew and mark the several Lines Between Muddy Creek The River Road Deep Creek and the Middle Road and make their Return According to Law.

Ordered That George Chambers Littleberry Mosby and Jacob Mosby on the 10th Day of November next Begin and Procession all the Lands and Renew and Mark the several Lines Between Deep Creek Mrs Mayo's Chear Road and the Middle Road and make their Return according to Law.

Ordered That Robert Carter Junr. Henry Dillion and John Carter on the 10th. Day of Novembr. Next Begin and Procession all the Lands and Renew and mark the several Lines Between Muddy Creek James River Willisses Creek and the River Road and make their Return according to Law.

Ordered That Ralph Fliping William Terrell and Orlando Hughes on the 10th Day of November next Begin and Procession all the Lands and

Renew and Mark the several Lines Between Muddy Creek the River Road the Path from the Widow Dillions by Thos. Potters and John Salmons to Ham Chappel And the Chappel Road and make their Return according to Law.

Ordered That John Merryman Thomas Walton and Richard Murrey on the 10th Day of November next Begin and Procession all the Lands and Renew and mark The several lines Between Muddy Creek Barnards Road Hugh Prewits Path And the Chappel Road and make their Return according to Law.

[83]   August 11th 1755
Ordered That William Holland John Minter and Christopher Dickens on the 10th Day of November Next Begin and Procession all the Lands and Renew and mark the several lines Between Barnards Road Horn Quarter Road and Willises Creek and make their Return according to Law.

Ordered That James Cuningame Jonathan Cuningame and Samuel Bridgwater on the 10th Day of November next Begin and Procession all the lands and Renew and mark the several Lines Between the Widow Dillions Path by Thomas Potters and John Salmons to Ham Chappel Hugh Prewits Path to Barnards Road the said Road to Willises Creek the said Creek and the River Road and make their Return according to Law.

Ordered That Benjamin Harroson Thomas Tabb and Benjamin Wilson on the 10 Day of November Next Begin and Procession all the lands and Renew and mark the several lines Between Willises Creek Buckingame Road the County line and Randolphs Creek and make Their Return according to Law.

Ordered That Jobe Thomas John Runnals and Thomas Christian on the 10th. Day of November Next Begin and Procession all the Lands and Renew and mark the several lines Between Willises Creek Randolphs Creek the County line and the River Road and make their Return according to Law.

Ordered That Samuel Tayler Phenehas Glover and Benjamin Cannon on the 10th Day of November next Begin and Procession all the lands and

Renew and mark the several Lines Between Willises Creek James River the County Line and the River Road and make their Return according to Law.

Order That the Present Church wardens Do Receive the sum of Fifty two Pounds nineteen Shilling and five Pence Current money of Messers Benjamin Harris and Creed Haskins Late Church wardens which appears by auditors Report To be the Ballance Due from them to this Parrish.

Thompson Swann is Elected Vestryman in the Room of M^r. Samuel Scott. Deceased.

Ordered That the Churchwardens agree with workmen to Tare the Glebe houses and whitewash and Paint the Dweling house.

Stephen Bedford	Robert McLaurine minister
Creed Haskins	John Baskervile
Thomas Davenport	Wade Netherland } C. W^s
	Nicholas Davies

****

[84] December 2nd 1755

Att a vestry held for laying the Parrish Levy of Southam att the courthouse The 2nd Day of December 1755 Present the Reverend Robert McLaurine John Baskervile and Wade Netherland Church Wardens, George Carrington Nicholas Davies Stephen Bedford Benjamin Harris Thomas Davenport and John Fleming Gent. Vestrymen.

Southam Parrish Debtor	Neet Tob^o	Cask
To the Reverend Robert McLaurine minister	16000	640
and six P^r. Cent for scrinkage	960	
To John Cardwell Clark of Petervile Church	1000	40
To Gideon Glen Clark of Tarewallet Church	1000	40
To Thomas Freeman Fretwell Clark of Ham Chappel	1000	40
To Silvanus Witt Clark of South Chappel	1000	40
To Thomas Davenport for Being Clark of the Vestry and for Extraordinary services. it being Processioning year	1000	<u>40</u>

To Cask aded	840
To Ame Loe Sexton of Petervile Church	500
To Susannah Easley sexton of Tarewallet. Church	500
To Rachel Faris sexton of Ham Chappel	500
To John Wherley sexton of South Chappel	500
To John Tayler for keeping Sanderses Child	1200
To John Runnals for keeping Johannah Parrish	600
To the Widow Kent	800
To Thomas Davenport by order of W^m. Bostick	60
To William Bostick his Bal^c. for keeping M^{rs}. Parker	440
To Joseph Woodson for keeping George Dobings	500
To Francis Cannafax for keeping Elizabeth Howl	800
To John Woodson for 10 Insolvents at 23^{lb} Tob^o. p^r pole	230
To Frederick Hatcher for 36 Insolvents at 23^{lb} Tob^o p^r pole	828
To William Bond for being twice listed 23^{lb} Tob^o. for 1754	23
To William Basham Senr. for keeping Henry Farmer	600
To John Boles for Clothing the Widow Parker ⎫ William Bostick haveing failed to Cloth her ⎭	100
	30981
To the Collector for Collecting the above Tob^o	1858
	32839

Pr Contra	C^r.	
By 1947 tiths at 16^{lb} Tob^o. p pole		31152
By Cash in Part in the hands of M^r. Benja. Harris and the Present Church Wardens £14.1.2 it being For the Tob^o. Ballance Due to the Collector which at 2^d p lb		1687
		32839

[85]   December 2nd 1755
Southam Parrish Debtor in Cash

To Joseph Epperson for work when finnished	£ 24.18.9
To Orlando Hughes for work when finished	14. 4.0
To John Wherley for three setts of horse Blocks at South Chap^l	0.12.0
To Gideon Seay for one Chest at Tarewallet Church	0.12.0
To Col^o. Bedford for work Done at the Glebe	1. 3.0
To John Felps for Eleven weaks boarding a pore person	1.13.0

To Wm Taylor for two setts of horse blocks at Petervile Church	0.08.0
To Richard Murrey for wine for the use of Ham Chappel	0.14.0
To M^r. Wade Netherland for three Bottels of wine for Petervile Ch	0.07.6
To Adalphus Hendrick for the support of Lemmy Childreses Children	3.00.0
To Ballance Due from the Parrish in Tobacco on the other side 1687^{lb} which at 2^d p lb is	£ 47.12.3 14.01.2
	£ 61.13.5

P Contra   C^r.

By Cash in the hands of Mes^{rs} Benj^a. Harris & Creed Haskins	£ 52.19.5
By Ballance Due in the hands of Mr. Baskervile	41.17.0
	94.16.5

Ballance Due to the Parrish as above   £ 33. 3.0

Ordered That Every tithable Person in this Parrish Pay 16^{lb} Tob^o for their Propotion of the Present Levy.

Ordered That John Woodson be Collector for the Levy now assest and that he give Bond and Security to the Church Wardens when Requiered according to Law.

Ordered That John Baskervile and Wade Netherland be Church Wardens for this Ensuing year.

    Stephen Bedford   Robert McLaurine Minister
    Benjamin Harris   John Baskervile ⎫
    John Fleming   Wade Netherland ⎭ C W^s
    Thomas Davenport Ju^n. George Carrington
                                   Nicholas Davies

****

[86]   April 19th 1756

Att a vestry held for Southam parrish att the Court house the 19th Day of April 1756. Present the Reverend Robert McLaurine Minister, John Baskervile Church Warden, Nicholas Davies, Stephen Bedford, Benjamin

Harris, Alexander Trent, and Thomas Davenport Ju^r. Gent. Vestrymen.

The Returns of the several processioners are as followeth (to witt)
Charles Anderson Thomas Williams John Woodson
    & George Wright   makes Return
Edward Mackgeh Charles Lee and Nehemiah Glen   [dittos down]
Humphrey Keeble W^m. Hambleton & W^m. Watson   [the page]
Williams Daniel W^m. Trigg W^m. Mills
John Cook John Nelson and Warren Walker
Henry Davenport Henry Harman and Richard Weatherford
Benjamin Harrison and Thomas Tabb
Henry Macon W^m. Womack & Daniel Coleman Junr.
John Moseley Henry Clay & Edward Moseley
Robert Hughes Joseph Mosby & Micajah Mosby
William Holland John Minter & Christopher Dickens
Edward Watkins Abraham Baugh & Isham Akin
William Maxey and John Radford
Abraham Womack W^m. Stratton & William Moss
John Tayler. W^m. Tayler. John Hidesanders & others
Paul Michaux John Franklin & Robert Chandler
William Cox Harry Bagby & Robert Bagby
George Cardwell and George Owen
Bowker Smith Joseph Woodson & Ackillis Bowker
James Cunningame Jonathan Cunningame & Samuel Bridgwater
John Merryman Richard Murrey & Thomas Walton
Samuel Allen and Thomas Guttery
William Moseley Richard Moseley & George Hancock

[87]   April 19th 1756
Robert Thomson Richard Parker and Lawrance Smith
Thomas Lockett Joel Lockett and Francis Marshall
Poindexter Mosby and John Hughes
Joseph Baugh and Israel Winfree
Jobe Thomas and John Reynolds
Samuel Tayler and Benjamin Cannon
John Hopson William Hopson Field Robertson & George Winneford
Littleberry Mosby Jacob Mosby and George Chambers
Richard Povaull and Benjamin Childrey

Ordered that the several Returns be Recorded.

Ordered that the Church wardens or Either of them Do view the garden att the Glebe and make Repourt to the next Vestry what will Put the same in Tenantable Repair.

    John Baskervile CW   Robert M{c}Laurine Minister
    Stephen Bedford   Nicholas Davies
    Benjamin Harris   Alexander Trent
                                  Thomas Davenport Junr

In compliance to the within order we the subscribers have Processioned the within Mentioned Lands Except the Land belonging to the Estate of Thomas Hodges Deceased & a line Between the said Hodges & Henry Bell not to be found & a line between Trent & Bassit Not found & a line Betwixt Bassit and Isham Richardson not found.

                                  Charles Anderson
                                  Thomas Williams
                                  John Woodson
                                  George Wright

[88]   Processioners Returns April 19th 1756

We the subscribers according to an order of vestry made for Southam parrish Have peaceably and Quietly Processioned the following lines (Viz) Between Christopher Chafin and Francis Epperson Beginning at A corner Hickory on Scots line to a Corner Poine [Pine] on Angela then Between Christopher Chafin and William Angela Beginning at a Corner pine on Co{ll}. Macons to Francis Epperson and Christopher Chafins Corner Pine from thence Between William Angela and Francis Epperson to a corner pine on Pleasant. then between Charles Lee and John Brown Cooper from a Corner pine in the said Browns Cornfield to a corner Hickory on Edward Mackgehe from thence between Edward Mackgehe and John Brown Cooper to pointers on Scott thence Betwen John Brown Cooper And Pleasent to a corner pine from thence to a corner Red oak on Mayo Then Between John Brown Cooper and Charles Lee from a Lightwood Not Corner on Mayo to a corner Red oak. thence to a Corner white oak Then between Gideon Glenn and Thos. Arnald Beginning at Great Guinea To a corner pine on Thomas Merryman. then Between James Glenn and William Basham from Great Guinea to a corner white oak on Mackgehe From thence Between Edward Mackgehe and James Glenn to a Corner white oak on Scott.

>
> Edward Mackgehe
> Charles Lee
> Nehemiah Glenn

Pursuant to a Vestry held for Southam Parrish the 11th Day of August 1755. We have Processioned the lands as folers and Renewed the marks.

Persons Present

The Land of James Patterson	⎫	Capt. Thos. Davenport
D^o Christoper Chalton	⎪	Francis Allen
D^o Joseph Jinkins	⎬	Richard Sharp
D^o Mary Jinkins	⎪	John Hubburd
D^o Thos. Davenport Senr.	⎭	
D^o Richard Sharp	⎫	
D^o [blank] Freeman	⎪	Capt. Thos. Davenport
D^o Gideon Marr	⎬	Francis Allen
D^o Francis Allen	⎪	Richard Sharp
D^o John Woodson	⎭	
D^o Joseph Hubburd	⎫	
D^o Capt. Thos. Davenport	⎪	Capt. Thos. Davenport
D^o Harrison Jones	⎬	John Jones, Joseph Hubberd
D^o John Jones	⎪	Harrison Jones
D^o Humphrey Keeble	⎭	

Humphrey Keeble
W^m. Hambleton

Processioners Returns April 19th 1756

The Land of William Hambleton	⎱	Persons Present
D^o William Watson	⎰	Will Martin
D^o Samuel Meredith	⎫	
D^o John Farmer	⎪	Will Arnald
D^o James Daniel	⎬	John Farmer
D^o Susannah Martin	⎪	Thos. Whitton
D^o Thos Riddle	⎭	John Burton
D^o John Burton	⎫	
D^o William Arnald	⎬	Adalphus Hendrick
D^o Julius Allen	⎪	
D^o Adalphus Hendricks	⎭	

Humphrey Keeble
William Hambleton
William X his mark Watson

November 10th 1755
In obediance to an order of Vestry for Southam Parrish we the subscribers have procession'd all the lands Underneath mentioned and mark'd the several lines (Viz) William Triggs Land, Daniel Colemans Himself Present, Adolphus Hendricks himself Present, Williams Daniels himself Present, Tarewallet Church land Thomas Guttrys himself Present, James Browns himself Present, John Kendalls Present, John Harrelson Robert Kents himself Present, William Mills's Robert Hudgens's himself Present, Warham Easleys himself Present, Thomas Johns's Henry Gerratts himself Present, Alexander Speirs's Present, Mr. Thos. Tabb & John Harrelson, Alexander Trents James Wilkins's himself Present.

Anthony Levillions Decd. John Martins } Nobody to shew the lines
Ralph Flippins, John Bullocks, Zachr. Terrys } and Not Procesionsed
Williams Daniel
William Trigg
William Mills

We the appointed Persons have Processioned all the Lands in our precincts In manner and form to (Viz) Richard Wards in Presence of Wm. Baley and John Nelson, John Nelsons in Presents of the said Baley & John Hammon Senr, Matthew Nelsons in Presents of the same, Ambrose Hammons in Presence of James Walker & John Hamman, Warren Walkers in the Presence of the same, Joel Walkers in the Presence of the same, John Hammons in the Presence of Joel Walker & Warren Walker, Ambrose Ransones in the Presents of Ambrose Ransone Junr. and Joel Walker, Wm. Angles in Presence of the said Angle & Wm. Walker.

[90]   Processioners Returns April 19th 1756
Vallintine Corleys in Presence of the said Corley and Jonus Reynols Jonus Reynols's in the Presence of Wm. Walker & Jonus Reynols, James Walkers In the Presence of Jonus Reynols & James Walker, Wm. Walkers in the Presence of Wm. Walker & Jonus Reynols, David Davisons in the Presence of Wm. Davison and Wm. Walker, James Townses in the Presence of Wm. Walker & Wm. Davison, Richard Wards at Green Creek

Quarter in the Presence of the same, an Entrey Belonging to Wadk[i]ns in the Presents of John Brown & John Nelson, John Browns in the Presents of the same, James Browns in the Presence of James Brown and Richard Epperson, Zechariah Browns in Presence of the same, M^r. Pleasents in the Presents of Richard Epperson & James Brown, Col^o. Peter Randolphs in the Presence of Robert Tenham and James Brown, John Cooks in the Presence of John Cook & John Wright, Thos. Cocks in Presence of Thos. Cock & John Cook, John Wrights in the Presence of John Right & John Cook, George Wrights in the Presence of George Wright & John Wright, John Mayos in the Presence of John Cook and John Wright, which is all the Lands as we can find in our Precincts Given under our hands this the 24th Day of February 1756.

         John Cook
         John Nelson
         Warren Walker

Pursuant to an order of vestry we have Processioned the lines Between The Persons hereafter Named

Between		Whom Present
Richard Daniel	& Jinkins orphan	John Hubbard & Richd Daniel
Richard Weatherford	& D^o	D^o
D^o	& Richard Daniel	D^o
Jinkins's Orphan	& Mary Jinkins orphan	D^o
D^o	& John Boles	D^o
D^o	& William Hambleton	D^o
D^o	& Thomas Davenport Senr.	D^o
John Boles	& D^o	Thomas Davenport Senr.
D^o	& W^m. Hambleton	D^o & John Boles
Martin Slaughter	& D^o	D^o
D^o	& W^m. Arnald	D^o
Thomas Davenport Senr.	& John Jones	D^o & Harrison Jones
Thos. Davenport Ju^r.	& Harrison Jones	D^o

Processioners Returns April 19th. 1756

Between		
W^m. Hambleton	& D^o	D^o
Thos. Davenport Senr.	& W^m. Arnald	D^o & Wm Arnald
Gideon Marr	& D^o	D^o

D⁰	& Thoˢ. Davenport Senʳ.	D⁰
John Smith	& James Davenport	D⁰
Wᵐ. Watson	& D⁰	D⁰
D⁰	& Thoˢ. Davenport Junʳ.	D⁰
Wᵐ. Hambleton	& D⁰	D⁰
D⁰	& Wᵐ. Watson	D⁰
John Smith	& D⁰	D⁰
D⁰	& Samuel Meredith	D⁰
D⁰	& Hodges's orphan	D⁰
Samuel Meredith	& D⁰	D⁰
Gideon Marr	& D⁰	D⁰
Ackillis Bowker	& Samuel Meredith	Christopher Watson
Wᵐ. Womack	& D⁰	D⁰
Henry Harman	& Ackillis Bowker	
D⁰	& Daniel Coleman	
John Tayler	& D⁰	
D⁰	& Henry Harman	
Wᵐ. Trigg	& D⁰	
D⁰	& Ackillis Bowker	
Thoˢ. Davenport Senʳ.	& James Davenport	Thoˢ. Davenport Senʳ.
D⁰	& Henry Davenport	Thoˢ. Davenport Junʳ.
Thoˢ. Davenport Junʳ.	& D⁰	D⁰
D⁰	& James Davenport	D⁰
Henry Davenport	& D⁰	D⁰
Samuel Meredith	& Ackillis Bowker	Wᵐ. Trigg
D⁰	& John Fermer	D⁰
D⁰	& Wᵐ. Watson	D⁰
Wᵐ. Trigg	& John Fermer	D⁰

The line Between Joseph Jinkins orphan
and John Bostick in Dispute and not Processioned.

                                  Henry Davenport
                                  Henry Harman
                                  Richard Weatherford

[92]   Processioners Returns April 19th. 1756
Pursuant to an order of vestry held for Southam Parrish the 11th Day of August 1755. We the subscribers have Processioned the several Lines within our Precincts as followeth (Viz.)

The lines Between Job Thomas & Tucker Woodson
Also the lines Betwen Job Thos. & John Jude
Also the lines Between Job Thos. & Drury Scrugs.
   Present Job Thomas
   Present David Maccomack
As also the lines Between Robt. Burton & Job Thomas
   Present Benj^a. Wilson
As also the lines Between Thos. Tabb & Drury Scrugs
   Present David Maccomack
As also the lines Between Thos. Tabb [&] Lenard Keeling
   Present Benj^a. Wilson
As also the lines Between Benj^a. Harrison & Thos. Tabb
As also the lines Between Benj^a. Harrison & M^r. Cary.
As also the lines Between Benj^a. Harrison & Joseph Farror
   Present Field Trent & David Thomson
As also the lines Between Alex^r. Trent. & Joseph Farror
   Present Alex^r. Trent & John Bartee
As also the lines Between Alex^r. Speirs & Alex^r. Trent
   Present Field Trent
As also the line between M^r. Cary & Joseph Farror
   Present Field Trent & David Thomson

The lines Between Watt Daniel & Job Thos not Processioned not knowing the lines.

                              Benj^a. Harrison
                              Thomas Tabb

November 1755
In obedience to an order of vestry of Southam Parrish in Cumberland County we the Subscribers have Processioned and Renewed the lines within our Precinct (Viz) Wm Basham Senr, Edwd. Mcgehe, James Holland, W^m. Basham Senr, James Holland Present. Daniel Coleman, Wm Daniel, Rich^d. Bandy, Wm Womack, Doct^r Thos Forster, Wm Arnald, Jno Chafin, Henry Macon, James Allen Senr, Jno. Chafin, W^m· Arnald, W^m. Daniel Present.
                          Witness our hands
                          Henry Macon
                          W^m. Womack
                          Daniel Coleman Junr.

[93]   Processioners Returns April 19th. 1756
According to order we have Processioned the several lines mentioned in our Precinct and all Done in Peace and Quietness, and in the Presents of the owners. March 26th 1756

       John Moseley
       Henry Clay
       Edward Moseley

Pursuant to an order of Vestry we the subscribers has Possessioned the lines within Our Precincts as followeth. Between Alexander and Hughes, Alexander & Hughes Present. Between Alexander and Wamack, the Proprietors Present. Between Hughes and M^{rs}. Randolph, Hughes and Edward Scrugs Present. Between Randolph & Womack, Scrugs & Womack Present. Between Stratton and Randolph & Thos. Moss John Stephenson, Straton & Scrugs Present. Between Stephenson & Randolph, Scrugs & Stephenson Present. Between Stephenson & Moss, Stephenson Present. Between Pleasants & Mosby, W^m. Carr and Mosby present. Betwen Mosby & Bedford, Mosby Present. Between Moss and M^{rs}. Randolph. Moss & Bedford not Processioned for want of the Party being Present.

       Robert Hughes
       Joseph Mosby
       Micajah Mosby

In obediance to an order of Vestry held for Southam Parrish the 11. Day of August 1755. We the subscribers have Procession'd all the Lands by the lines that Is in our Precincts, as followeth (Viz). a line Between William Holland and John Holloway, also Between John Holloway & Joseph Butler, Between John Holloway & William Holloway, Between William Holloway & Joseph Butler, Between Joseph Butler & James Anderson, Between Joseph Butler & Job Thomas, Between Joseph Butler & W^m. Holland, Between Saml. Browne & James Brown, Between Saml. Brown & James Holloway Senior, Between Ja^s. Holloway & W^m. Holland, Between Saml. Browne & William Holland, Between William Holland and Andrew Edwards, Between Andrew Edwards & John Minter, Between John Minter & William Holland, Between John Minter & Job Thomas Between Job Thomas & John Holland, Between John Holland & James Anderson. The owners of these Lands Being Present.

pʳ William Holland &
John Minter
Christopher Dickens

[94]   Processioners Returns April 19ᵗʰ. 1756
Pursuant to an order of the Vestry Dated August 11ᵗʰ. Day 1755. wee the subscribers have Vewed and new marked all the several lines in the Bounds Mentioned in the said order.

Edward Watkins
Abraᵐ. Baugh
Isham Aken

We have marked all the within lines of the within order of Vestry According to order in Peace February the 10ᵗʰ Day 1756.

William Maxey
John Radford
Processioners

Pursuant to an order of the Vestry wee the Processioners Abraham Womack William Stratton & William Moss Beginning at Deep Creek have Processioned The lines Between Mʳ. John Pleasant Collº. Bedford & Micajah Mosby, Miajah Mosby Present. also the lines Betwen Micajah [Mosby] Noel Wadel & Thoˢ. Bedford, Micajah Mosby Present. also the lines Between Henry Stratton Noel Wadle & Thomas Moss, Charles Finch Present. also the lines Between Abraham Womack & William Stratton, Richard Womack Present. also the lines Between Mʳ. Nicholas Davies Robert Hughes & Jane Randolph, Mʳ. Davies Present. also the lines Between Mʳ. Davies William Stratton & Abraham Womack, Mʳ. Davies Present. also between Mʳ. Davies Nicholas Speirs & Bowler Cock, Mʳ. Davies Present. Also the lines Between Edward Tabb Alexander Moss & Jacob Mosby, Alexander Moss Present. also the lines Between Jacob Mosby James Moss. & William Moss. Also Between Bowler Cock & William Moss. Also Between Edward Tabb and James Moss, Nicholas Speirs Present. also Between Edward Tabb and Bowler Cock, Edward Tabb Present. also Between Edward Tabb Samuel Scott and Nicholas Speirs, Edward Tabb Present. also Between Bowler Cock and Nicholas Speirs, Nicholas Speirs Present.

Abraham Womack
William Stratton
William Moss

[95] Processioners Returns April 19th 1756
1755 November the 10th. John Tayler, [John] Hidesanders, Edward Scrugs & Daniel Johnson, James Crafford, John Meanley, & myself marked the line trees. Between Howard and Randolph then John Tayler left us and we marked the lines Between Howard and John Tayler to a corner white oak. and then we went thro the woods to Mayo Line & marked Between Howard & Mayo to Stobals & then Between Howard & Stovall To a corner in a Branch. November 11, John Tayler, Edward Scrugs Tom Scrug & myself Marked the lines Between Madam Randolph & John Tayler & Between Pleasent & John Tayler & the 12 Day Col°. Bedford and myself marked the line Between Bedford and Pleasent Down to the Creek. December the 8th. John Tayler Cor^{ll} Bed[ford] & myself Marked the lines Between John Tayler & Cor^{ll}. Bedford and so along James Tayler & Bedford & so along Mayo & Bedford line to a corner Between Cockaham & Bedford and Mayo. then along the lines of the Glebe & Loe, Loe Present with James Tayler, and along the line between Salley & the Glebe. & on the line Between Salley & Low. & on the line Between Low & Mayo then on the line Between the Glebe & Cockaham. then on the line Between Bedford & Cockaham. then Bedford & Jacob Mosby & James Tayler Present, then On the line Between Jacob Mosby & Cockaham, then on the line Between Jacob Mosby and Bedford Down to the Creek. 1756, January the 30. Edmon Toney James Tayler and myself Went to mark the lines between Daniel Mayo & James Tayler but Tayler would Not agree to mark the lines the Reason he gave was his Pattan Begun at a black oak and Mayo Begun at a white oak, then we went on Between Mayo & John Tayler and Howard and John Tayler, Edmon Toney James Tayler John Tayler & myself Present, then we went Between Bartholomew Stovall & Mayo & Edmon Toney & Mayo. and Chandler & Mayo, Timothy Chandler Present. and along Mayos and Walton line, John Tayler Edmon Toney & Myself Present. then Between Walton and Chandler we three. Between David Chandler and his mother, David Chandler Present. the line Between John Tayler & William Tayler was marked by William Tayler with John Taylers orders, all the with mentioned lines Is marked according to order Vestry. Mayo was Busie and Desired us to go Round his Lines without him. John Hydesanders Daniel

Johnson and W^m. Speirs marked The other Part of our Bounds by agreement made among ourselves and we All make this Return.

William Speirs and Daniel Johnson went In order to mark the lines of Bartholomew Stovall and he Refused to go with them and They was not Done.

> John Tayler
> William Tayler
> John Hidesanders
> William Speirs
> Daniel Johnson
> Edmon Toney
> all appointed Processioners

[96]   Processioners Returns April 19th. 1756
In complyance to an order of Southam Parrish the 11th. Day of August 1755. We Paul Michaux John Franklin and Robert Chandler have Processioned and marked all the lines Between James River the Ferry Road to Paul Michaux the Court house Road to Solomans Creek and so make Return 22nd. March 1756.

In complyance to an order of Southam Parrish 11th. Day of August 1755 we William Cox Harry Bagby Robert Bagby have processioned and marked all the lines Between Fine Creek and the River Road to Paul Michaux and to Speirses and To the Three Bridges and to make Return. Excepting a line Between Cor^l. Stoner and Madam Mayo which Could not be found 22nd. March 1756.

March 22nd 1756
Memorandon that at a Vestry held for Southam Parrish, the 11th. of August 1755 Ordered that Sanburn Woodson Deces^t. George Owen George Cardwell Frances Macraw to Procession the lands in the order mentioned Woodson being Dead and Francis Macraw Refusing to fulfil the order so that we George Owen and George Cardwell have Indeavoured to Comply with the order as followeth (Viz). Beginning at Sanburn Woodsons line Between him & Capt. Daniel Mayo, Charity Woodson widow Present. thence Between Woodson & Owen, Woodson Present. Procession Between Mayo & Owen, Procession Between Mayo

& John Hidesanders. Proct Between Owen and John Netherland, Netherland Present. Between Woodson and Netherland, both Present. Procession Between Woodson and W^m. Headspeth, Woodson and Benjamin Childrey Present. Proce^s. Between Headspeth and John Howlet, Headspeth and Samuel Oslen overseer Present. thence between Abraham Salley and William Smith, Smith Present. thence Between Salley and Duke Hix, Smith and Hix Present. thence Between Smith and Hix, Both Present. thence Between Hix and Widow Barns, both Present. thence Between Smith and Barns, both Present. Between Smith and John Pleasants, Smith and Daniel Carter overseer Present. thence Between Barns and Pleasents, Barns and Carter Present. thence Between Pleasants and John Phelps, Carter Present. thence Between Barnes and Coyller Basdale, Barns and Joseph Atkins Present. thence Between Phelps & Basdail, Atkins Present. Thence Between Basdail & George Cardwell, Atkins Present. thence Between Basdail & Frances Macraw, Atkins Present. thence Between Macraw & John Phelps, thence Between Phelps & John Netherland, thence Between Phelps and Headspeth, thence Between Phelps & Basdail, Joseph Atkins Present. thence Between Basdail & John Howlet, Joseph Atkins Present. thence Between Macraw & Netherland, Thence Between Netherland & Cardwell, thence Between Cardwell & Barns, Coll^o. William Randolph line between him and Mayo not Procession not attending To shew the line, also Between Ozbu[r]n formerly Thos. Walker and William Headspeth not any body appeared for Ozburn, also Between Ozburn & John Netherland for the same Reason, also betwen Netherland & John Hidesanders.

         George Owen
         George Cardwell

[97] Processioners Returns April 19th 1756
Pursuant to the within order we the subscribers have Procesionsed all the Lands and Have mark^d and renewed Every Line within the said Precincts alotted us.
         Bowker Smith
         Joseph Woodson
         Ackillis Bowker

In Pursuants of this order we have Processioned all the lands Belonging to such Persons as were Reaaday to give their attendance within our Bounds, George Carringtons line William Boling Present, John Carters line Frances Amos Present, Carter Harrysons line William Boling Present, Francis Amoses line William Bowling Present, William Dillins line Henry Dillin Present, John Armsteds Line John Salmon Present, Joseph Priceses line John Carter Present, Samuel Bridgwaters line John Armsted Present, Edwards Clements line Samuel Brown Present, Samuel Browns line Edwards Clements Present, Robert Smiths line William Bond Present, Job Thomases Line Present Thos Christian, William Clarks line John Hill Present, William Bonds line W^m. Clark Present, Thos. Christians line Job Thomas Present, Samuel Atkins line John Robertson Present, John Robertsons lines Samuel Atkinson Present, Andrew Edwards line John Tatum Present, Christopher Dickens line Jonus Medder Present, Jonus Medders line Christopher Dickens Present, Alexander Cuningames line John Mackguire Present, Jonathan Cuningames line John Mackguire Present, James Cuningames line Thomas Christian Present, Part of John Flemings line not processioned for want of attendance, Part of land Belonging to Jacob Mishshow not Processioned for want of attendance, Part of land Belonging John Cox not Processioned for want of attendance.

James Cuningame
Jonathan Cuningame
Samuel Bridgwater

We the Precessioners has Processioned all the Lands Between Muddy Creek Barnards Road Hugh Pruets Path and the Chapple Road according to Law Certified under our hands.

John Merryman
Richard Murrey
Thomas Walton

[98]   Processioners Returns April 19th 1756
Pursuant to an order of Vestry held at the Court house of the Parrish of Southam & County of Cumberland the 11th Day of August 1755 for Processioning of Land, we Samuel Allen and Thomas Guttrey being appointed Processioners of all the land Between Buckingame Road the County line Harrisons Road and the Road from Murrys to John Burtons. have in obedience To the said order of Vestry Processioned as Followeth to wit.

Richard Murrys line	Present	William Holland
James Holloway Sen[r]	Present	D[o]
John Bradley	Present	James Holloway
John Bolton	Present	William Hollond
James Holloway Jun[r].	Present	John Bolton
John Holloway Sen[r]	Present	James Holloway Ju[r].
Abraham Bayley	Present	W[m]. Holland
Sam[l]. Jones	Present	James Holloway Jun[r].
Jonas Meadors Sen[r].	Present	William Holland
Alexander Trents	Present	William Holland
Joseph Woodson	Present	David Thomson
Samuel Gladoe	Present	David Thomson
Ambrose Wood	Present	David Thomson
James Anderson	Present	David Thomson
Thomas Tabb	Present	David Thomson
Joseph Farrar	Present	David Thomson
Benjamin Harrison	Present	D[o] D[o]
Thomas Holland	Present	Williams Daniel
Nich[s]. Speirs	Present	Sam[l]. Melton
Samuel Melton	Present	William Rowton
William Routon	Present	Samuel Melton
Williams Daniel	Present	Thomas Holland
Daniel Coleman Sen[r].	Present	Thomas Coleman
William Hix Sen[r].	Present	Samuel Melton
Robert Lowery	Present	Thomas Coleman
Robert Hudgens	Present	Randolph Richerson
Thomas Tilman	Present	Daniel Coleman Sen[r].
Samuel Allen	Present	Randolph Richerson
John Burton	Present	William Hix Sen[r].
Thomas Guttrey	Present	Robert Moore
Alexander Speirs	Present	Robert Moore
		Samuel Allen
		Thomas Guttrey

[99] Processioners Returns April 19th 1756
Pursuant to an order of Vestry Dated the 11th of August 1755. We the subscribers Procession'd the lines as followeth (Viz).

The line Between Ch^r Bass & John Northcut agre^d Present John Northcut
Bet^n. Lodwick Elam & Gideon Lockett agre^d. Present Lodwick Elam &.
Gideon Lockett
Bet^n. Lodowick Ealam & John Northcut agre^d. Present Lodowick Elam
& John Northcut
Bet^n. Capt. Creed Haskins & William Marshall agre^d Present W^m. Marshall
Bet^n. Capt. Creed Haskins & Richard Moseley agre^d Present Richd Moseley
Bet^n. Capt. Haskins & George Hancock agre^d Present Geo. Hancock
Bet^n. Thos. Lockett & Timson agre^d Present Thos. Lockett
Bet^n. Thos. Lockett & Joel Lockett agre^d Present Thos Lockett & Joel Lockett
Bet^n Joel Lockett & Edward Watkins agre^d. Present Thos. Lockett & Joel Lockett
Betwe^n Richd Moseley & Wm Moseley agre^d Present Richd Moseley
Bet^n. Arther Moseley & W^m. Moseley agre^d. Present W^m. Moseley
Bet^n. Arther Moseley & Lodowick Elam agre^d. Present Lodowick Elam
Bet^n. Arther Moseley & Gideon Lockett agre^d. Present Gideon Lockett
Bet^n. Benj^a. Moseley & Mark Tayler agre^d. Present Mark Tayler
Bet^n. Francis Marshall & Timson agre^d. Present W^m. Marshall
Bet^n. W^m. Marshall & Richard Moseley agre^d. Present W^m. Marshall & Richd Moseley
Bet^n. Francis Marshall & Todd agre^d. Present W^m. Marshall & Fran.^s Marshall
Bet^n Francis Marshall & Wm Marshall agre^d Present Wm Marshall
Bet^n. Mark Tayler & Thos. Lockett agre^d. Present Mark Tayler
Bet^n. Mark Tayler & John Northcut agre^d. Present Mark Tayler
Bet^n. Todd & Timson agre^d. Present W^m. Marshall & Francis Marshall

The Line Between William Marshall and George Williamson Deces^d. Left Undon by Reason of a former Dispute & li[n]es yet undetermined.

William Moseley
Richard Moseley
George Hancock

[100]   Processioners Returns. April 19th 1756
Pursuant to an order of the vestry made the 11th. Day of August 1755. We the subscribers have Processioned and markt the lines within our Bounds Beginning at Hatchers line Running Down Murrys line To Thomsons

Corner, thence along Murrys line to Clements Mill Path Between Pringle Hall Cox & Isaac Hughs, thence along a line Between Thomson & Parker, Hall Cox & George Cox Present, Then Beginning a line Between Hall Cox & Murry to Pringles Corner then Between Pringle & Hall Cox to George Coxs & Burtons Corner, then Between George Cox & Burton to Smith's line, John Blan Horton, Hall Cox Present Then Between Burton & Smith to Thomsons line, Between Burton and Thomson to William Parkers line, then Between Burton & W^m. Parker Rich^d. Parkers line & Burtons to Thomsons. Corner on Buckingham Road, then Between W^m. Parker & Thomson to Appamattox River, then Between W^m. Parker & Richard Parker from the River to Burtons line, Then Between W^m. Parker & Rich^d. Parker Beginning on the Creek Runing To Hatchers line on Buckingham Road, then along Hatchers line to Freemans line, then along Freemans line Between W^m. Parker & Freman To a Corner, then from the Corner to the Creek Between Richd Parker & W^m. Parker, then a line Between Richard Parker & Freeman to Burtons Corner, Rich^d. Daniel Richd Parker Junr John Blan Horton Present, then Beginning on Appamattox River Runing Between Burton & Richard Parker to Burtons Corner before mentioned, then Between Freeman & Yarborough to the new Road, then Beginning at Burtons aforesaid Corner Between Yarborough & Burton to the new Road, then Between Citt. Chalton & Burton from the Road to the River, & then Between Cit Chalton & Rich^d. Daniel from the River to the Road to Little Guinea Bridg, W^m. Daniel W^m. Allen Sam Burton Present, then along between George Cox & Hall Cox to the River, & they Contented then Between George Cox & Smith and then Between Smith & Thomson to the River All Contemptted by us the subscribers April 17th 1756.

          Robert Thomson
          Richard Parker
          Lawrance Smith

[101] Processioners Returns. April 19th 1756
Pursuant to an order of vestry Dated the 11th of August 1755 We the subscribers Procession'd the lines as followeth Viz.
The line Between
John Moseley & Thos Moseley agre^d Present Thos Moseley
Bet^n Thos Moseley & Wm Clay agre^d Present Wm Clay
Bet^n Thos Moseley & Timson agre^d Present Thos Moseley
Bet^n Willm Clay & Timson agre^d Present Wm Clay

Bet^n Thos. Moseley & Henry Clay agre^d Thos Moseley Henry Clay
Bet^n Bret Randolph & Timson, overseer agre^d Present Larkin Chew
Bet^n Wm Randolph & Brit Randolph, overseer Present Thos Hamblet

John Storts line left undon the Reason it was he wodent [wouldn't] attend.

Thomas Lockett
Joel Lockett
Francis Marshall

Pursuant to the within order we the subscribers have Processioned all the Lands Except Part of Jacob Woodsons which said land we could gitt nobody to attend us.

Poindexter Mosby
John Hughes

Pursuant to an order of the vestry Dated 11th. Day of August 1755. We the Subscribers have viewed and new marked all the several lines in the bounds Mentioned in the said order.

Joseph Baugh
Israel Winfree

Pursuant to an order of the Vestry of Southam Parrish Dated 11th. Day of August 1755 to us Directed we have Processioned the following lines on the nineteenth Day of November Between Joseph Price & Vallintine Martin, Present the said Price & the said Martin, Between Joseph Price & Job Thomas Present the said Thomas & said Price, Between the said Thomas & Morris Langhorn Present Joseph Price & Wm Evans, Between the said Langhorn & Edward Hambleton Present Joseph Price & W^m. Evens, Between the said Hambleton and Joseph Price Present the said Price & Volletnine Martin, Between Joseph Price & Phenihas Glover Present the said Glover & the said Price.

[102]   Processioners Returns April 19th. 1756
Between Phenihas Glover & Vollentine Martin Present the said Glover & the said Martin, Between Job Thomas & Vollentine Martin Present the said Thomas & the said Martin, Between Col^o. George Carrington & Vollentine Martin Present Joseph Price & the said Martin. March the second, Between. Coll^o. George Carrington & David Reynolds Present

the said Carrington & Benj[a]. Cannon, Between the said Reynolds & Phenihas Glover Present. Benj[a]. Cannon For Reynolds, Between the said Glover & Benj[a]. Cannon Present the said Cannon, Between the said Cannon & the said Reynolds Present the said Cannon, Between Coll[o]. George Carrington & Phenihas Glover Present the said Carrington, Between the said Carrington and Joseph Price Present the said Price & the said Carrington, Between Coll[o]. George Carrington & Job Thomas Present the said Carrington & the said Thomas, Between the said Carrington & John Reynols Present the said Carrington & the said Reynolds, Between John Reynolds & Job Thomas Present the said Reynolds & the said Thomas, Between the said Reynolds & James Cuningam Present David Thomson, Between the said Cuningam & Job Thomas Present David Thomson, Certified by us this fourth Day of March 1756.

          Job Thomas
          John Reynolds

Pursuant to an order of the Vestry for Southam Parrish we the subscribers Have on the 5 Day of February 1756 Processiond the lines Between Col[o]. George Carrington and Benj[a]. Cannon and Carrington and David Prier, the said Carrington and Phillip Mayo and Carrington and Sam[ll]. Tayler, also Between the Estate of James Nevil Dec[d] and Elizabeth Hooper, the said Estate & Phillip Mayo, the said Estate and Sam[l]. Tayler, Present Col[o]. George Carrington. On the 7 Day of February, the lines Between Robert Carter & Phillip Mayo, Between Reuben Skelton and the said Mayo, Present Michal Rowland, John Burnet Robert Carter Jn[r]. On the 12 Day of February, The lines Between Sam[l]. Tayler & Daniel Jones, also Between the said Jones & David Prier Dec[d]. the other Parties Concern'd had Notice but Failed to appear.

          Samuel Tayler
          Benjamin Cannon

[103] Processioners Return. April 19th. 1756
We the Processioners have Done & markt the following Lines Beginning and Marked John Robertson lines, Field Bradshaw lines, Renew[d]. Charles Bradshaw Lines, Renewed Samuel Nuckels gave no attendance, Field Robertson line Renewed, Josiah & John Bradshaw lines Renewed, Richard Murrys lines Renewed, Jonus Medors lines Renewed, Edward Robertson line Renewed, Samuel Jones lines Renewed, Dolphis Hendrick Lines

Renewed, John Burton Lines Renewed, John Hubburd Lines Renewed, Humphrey Keeble Lines Renewed, Julius Allen no attendance, Stephen Mallet no attendance, Joseph Hubburd Lines Renewed, Nathaniel Fords Lines Renewed, William Hutsons Lines Renewed, George Evens Lines Renewed, William Matthiss Lines Renewed, Gideon Patteson Lines Renewed, William Bradshaw Lines Renewed, John Hopson Lines Renewed, Anthony Colquitt Lines Renewed, William Hopson Lines Renewed, Christopher Robertson Lines Renewed, Joseph Fuqua lines Renewed, William Clark Lines Renewed, Francis George Steger Lines Renewed, Nicholas Cox Lines Renewed, David Winneford Lines Renewed, John Wayles Lines Renewed, John Pleasants Line Renewed, Robert Thomson Lines Renewed, Frederick Hatcher Lines Renewed, William Hopson Lines Renewed, Henry Hatcher Lines Renewed, John Mayo Lines Renewed, George Winneford Lines Renewed, William Holloway Lines Renewed, Thomas Tabb no attendance, John Madock no attendance, Wm Battersby no attendance, John Brumskil no attendance, Holeman Freeman no attendance.

> John Hopson
> William Hopson
> Field Robertson
> George Winneford

Pursuant to the within order we have Processioned the within mentioned Land.

> George Chambers
> Jacob Mosby
> Littleberry Mosby

[104]   Processioners Return. April 19th. 1756
Pursuant to an order of the Vestry we have processioned the lines Between James Cock Dec^t. & Phillip Thomas, the line Between Phillip Thomas & Nath. Maxey, the line Between the said Thomas and Richard Williamson, Between the said Phillip Thomas & Henry Breazeal, Between William Hudspith & Natt Maxey, also Hudspith & Richard Williamson, also Hudspith & Maxey, also Hudspith and Williamson, Between Hudspith & William Smith, Between William Smith & Richard Williamson, Between William Baley & Nicholas Giles, Between Nicholas Giles & Henry Brazeal, Between William Eallom and William Baley,

Between Nicholas Giles & William Eallom, Between Coll°. William Randolph & Henry Brazeal, Between Randolph & Baley, Between Randolph & Eallom, Between Randolph and Pouvall.
March. the 10th. 1756   Richard Pouvall
           Benjamin Childrey

July 28 1756 the several Possessioners Returns Before Mentioned as here Recorded were this Day Examined By the Present Church wardens.
           Alex^r. Trent } C W
           Thos Davenport

****

Att a vestry held for Southam Parrish att the Court house of Cumberland County the 29th. Day of November one thousand seven hundred and Fifty six Present the Reverend M^r. Robert McLaurine Minister, John Baskervile and Wade Netherland Church Wardens, Thomas Turpin, Nicholas Davies, Stephen Bedford, Thomas Davenport, Thompson Swann and John Fleming, Gent. Vestrymen.

Southam Parrish Debtor	Neet. Tob°.	Cask
To the Reverend Robert McLaurine Minister	16000	640
To Ditto six percent for scrinkage	960	
To John Cardwell Clk. of Petervile Church	1000	40
To Gedion Glenn Clk of Tarewallitt Church	1000	40
Carry^d forward	18960	720

[105]   November. 29th 1756

Southam Parrish D^r.	Neet Tob°	Cask
To Tobacco brought Forward	18960	720
To Thomas Freeman Fretwell Clk of Ham Chappel	1000	40
To Silvanus Witt Clk of South Chappel	1000	40
To Thomas Davenport Clk of the vestry	500	20
To the Cask aded	820	820
To Ame Loe sexton of Petervile Church	500	
To Susannah Easley Sexton Tarewallet Church	500	
To Rachal Faris Sexton at Ham Chappel	500	
To John Whereley sexton a[t] South Chappel	500	
To John Tayler for keeping Sanderses Child	1200	

To John Reynonds [Reynolds] for keeping Johannah Parrish	600
To the Widow Kent	800
To Joseph Woodson for keeping George Dobbins	500
To Frances Cannefax for keeping Elizabeth Howl	800
To William Basham Senr. for Keeping Henry Farmer	600
To John Boles for Keeping the Widdow Parker	500
To F[r]ederick Hatcher for 36 Insolvents at 16 lb Tob^o Each	576
To Frances Epperson for keeping Reynoldes Child 9 months and the said Epperson agrees to keep the said Child for 500 lb Tob^o. per annum	400
To Charles Holland for four tithables of Hudgenses listed to Him by Mistake	64
To Sampson Fleming for 1 D^o. Dubble listed	16
To Tobacco Levyed to pay the Cash for the use of the Parrish	7500
	37836
To the Collectors Sallery on the above Tob^o. 6 p C^t.	2270
	40106
To Ballance Due in the hands of the Collector	170
	40276

P Contra Creditor

By 2013 tithables at 20 lb. Tobacco p pole	40260
By Levy Receiv^d. by John Woodson not in the former Levy	16
	40276

The Cash Carryed forward
John Welch for takeing Care of Catharine May and maintaining and Cloathing her Doth agree after the Rate of 1000 lb. Tob^o. p annum Commencing the 25th. of October Last.

[106]   November 29th. 1756
Southam Parrish Debtor in Cash

To Richard Murry for finding bread and wine Att Tarewallet and Ham Churches	£1. 1.0
Humphrey Keeble for four setts of horse blocks and two steps att Tarewallet Church	0.18.0
To Wade Netherland for 150 panes of glass 100/ 10 by 11. and Charges In bringing up the same for Petervile Church. 7/6 and for Finding two bottles of wine for Petervile Church 5/	5.12.6

To Cash to be Levyed for the parrish to make good £14.1.12 which Was to have bin Received by the Collector of Benja Harris in the last Levy which the Collector alledges has not bin paid	14. 1.2
To Cash to be levyed for the parrish to pay Joseph Epperson for Work att the Glebe agreed to be finished by the last of April next	18.14.9
To Ditto to pay Dito for sashes Glazing and puting in windows And finding puttey att Petervile Church when finished	6.10.0
To Ditto to pay Orlando Hughes for a gallery at Ham Church when finished	<u>13. 6.0</u>
	60. 3.5

P Contra Creditor
By Ballance Due to the parrish in the hands of John Baskervile Late Church warden   <u>9.12.0½</u>
                                                                                                                               50.11.4½

Thomas Davenport and Alexander Trent Gent. are appointed Church wardens For the Ensuing year in the Room of Wade Netherland and John Baskervile Late Church wardens.

Ordered that John Woodson be appointed Collector of the above levy and He is hereby appointed on his giveing bond and good security for the same according to Law to the Church wardens, and thereupon he is ordered To Collect of Every tithable person within this parrish Twenty pounds of nett Tobacco and pay the same according to Law.

Ordered that Stephen Bedford and Wade Netherland Gent. agree with a workman To Pale in at the Glebe of this parrish a garden the same size with the garden now paled There to be Done with good white oak well sawed posts and Rails to be sett two feet in The ground and that part of the posts that goes in the ground to be well burned.

[107]   November 29${th}$ 1756
The poles to be well sawed Pine or Poplar Inch thick Clear of the saw and to be nailed with Two ten penney nails Each at Least and the whole to be in a workmanlike manner.

Ordered that the Churchwardens Do Receive of Benj^a. Harris formerly a Church Warden of this Parrish the money Due from him to the Parrish and accompt for The same to the vestry.

<table>
<tr><td>John Baskervile</td><td>Robert McLaurine Minister</td></tr>
<tr><td>Wade Netherland</td><td>Thomas Davenport Ch: Warden</td></tr>
<tr><td>John Fleming</td><td>Thomas Turpin</td></tr>
<tr><td>Thompson Swann</td><td>Nicholas Davies</td></tr>
<tr><td></td><td>Stephen Bedford</td></tr>
</table>

****

Att a vestry for Southam Parrish att the court house of Cumberland County the 15th. Day of December 1757. Present Reverend Robert McLaurine Minister, Alex^r. Trent and Thos. Davenport Church Wardens, George Carrington, Thos. Turpin, Nicholas Davies, Stephen Bedford, Creed Haskins, Wade Netherland, And Thompson Swann Gen^t. Vestrymen.

Southam Parrish. Debtor	Neet Tobacco	Cask
To the Reverend Robert McLaurine Minister	16000	640
and six p cent for scrinkage	960	
To John Cardwell Clark of Petervile Church	1000	40
To Gideon Glen Clark of Tarewallet Church	1000	40
To Thomas Freeman Fretwell Clark of Ham Chappell	1000	40
To Silvanus Witt Clark of South Chappell	1000	40
To Thomas Davenport Clark of the Vestry	500	_20_
To Ame Loe sexton of Petervile Church	500	820
To Susannah Easley sexton of Tarewallet Church	500	
To Rachel Farris sexton of Ham Chappell	500	
To John Wherley sexton of South Chappell	500	
To the cask aded	820	
To John Tayler for keeping Sanderses Child	1200	
To John Reynolds for keeping Joannah Parrish	600	
To Joseph Woodson for keeping George Dobbins	500	
To Henry Farmer Ju^r. for keeping Henry Farmer	600	
To the Widow Kent	800	
To Silvater Alford for keeping Reynolses Child	_500_	
	28480	

[108]   December 15th. 1757
Southam Parrish Debtor   Neet Tobacco   Cash
To Tobacco brought from the other side   28480
To Frederick Hatcher for 13 Insolvents at
   20 lb. Tob° Each   260
To Nathaniel Ford for two Levys twice Listed   40
To Alex^r Trent for the support of Phillemon
   Childress family   400
To Anne Eaton a Pore Person   250
To M^{rs}. Baker for keeping Elizabeth Brown from
   this time six months   250
To Easter Wherley for her husband makeing & seting
   up 5 racks at South Chapel   100
To John Welch for keeping Catharine May without
   Clothing her   600
To Edward Parret for keeping Elizabeth Howl   700
To Daniel Wilmore for Clothing Elizabeth Howl   100
To M^r. John Pleasants for the use of Elenor Suttlef   £2. 0.0
To M^{rs}. Baker for keep Elizabeth Brown three months   3. 0.0
To Richard Murrey for Bread and wine at Tarewallet
   & Ham Churches   1.11.6
To M^r. McLaurine for four bottles of wine for the use
   of Peter^l. & Sou Ch^s 0.10.0
To John Woodson collector for Ballance Due p. accompt   0.17.1
To Joseph Epperson Ballance for work Done at the Glebe   5. 4.9
To Joseph Epperson for work Done at Ham Chappel   2. 1.0
To Joseph Epperson for building the garden at the Glebe   18. 0.0
To Orlander Hughes for work when Finnished   6. 4.0
To Gedion Seay for H L Hinge & fixing it to a Dore
   at Tarw^t Church   0. 2.6
To M^r. McLaurine for work Done at the Glebe   <u>3.11.8</u>
                                                                       43. 2.6

To Tob°. Levyed for the use of the parrish to pay }   6500
   the Cash Debt
To the collector for collecting the above Tob°. 6 p cent <u>2260</u>
                                                         39940

P Contra Creditor
By 2098 Tithables at 19 lb. Tob⁰ p pole   39862
By ballance Due to the Collector   78
                                                      39940

M^{rs}. Hannah Baker agrees to keep Elizabeth Brown for five hundred pounds of Tobacco p annum and two hundred and fifty of the same is now Levyed.

Daniel Wilmore agrees to keep Elizabeth Howl and cloth her after the Rates of Eight hundred Pounds of Tobacco p annun.

John Tayler agrees to keep Reynoldses child and cloth it after the Rate of five hundred pounds of Tobacco p annum.

John Woodson collector Renders an accompt Deb^r. & Cre^r. Bal^c. Due to the said Collector 17/1 Ordered that the said accompt be Recorded.

[109]   December 15th 1757

Thomas Davenport and Alexander Trent is appointed Church wardens for this Enusing year.

Ordered that John Woodson be appointed collector of the above Levy and he is hereby appointed on his giveing Bond and good security according to Law and thereupon He is ordered to collect of Every Tithable person within this parrish nineteen Pounds of Neet Tobacco and pay the same according to Law.

Esther Wherley is appointed sexton of South Chapel in the Room of John Wherley Deceased.

Ordered that George Carrington and Nicholas Davies gent. agree with workmen to glase Ham Chapell.

Ordered that Thomas Davenport and Alexander Trent Church wardens Do Examine the Returns of the several possessioners as they are Recorded.

Ordered that Thomas Davenport and Alexander Trent gen^t. agree with workmen to build a Gallery in Tarewallet Church and seal and Furnish the same with pews the sealing to Be as highe as the pews.

Ordered that Stephen Bedford and Nicholas Davies gen^t. agree with workmen to Build A Barn on the Glebe of this Parrish Twenty feet square.

Nicholas Davies	Robert McLaurine Minister
Stephen Bedford	Thomas Davenport Church warden
Wade Netherland	Alexander Trent Church warden
Creed Haskins	George Carrington
Thompson Swann	Thomas Turpin

1757. Southam Parrish in accompt with John Woodson D^r.

To cash paid Joseph Epperson	£ 20. 0.0
To ballance Due to me	14. 1.2
To M^r. Wade Netherland	5.12.6
To M^r. Richard Murrey	1. 1.0
To M^r. Humphrey Keeble	0.18.0
To Quitrents Glebe Land	0. 9.5
	42. 2.1

1757 Southam Parrish C^r	
By 7500 lb Tob^o. at 11/	£ 41. 5.0
By ballance Due to J[ohn]. W[oodson].	0.17.1
	42. 2.1

****

[110] December 21st 1758
Att a vestry held for Southam Parrish at the Courthouse of Cumberland County the 21st. Day of December 1758. Present the Reverend Robert McLaurine Minister, Thomas Davenport Church Warden, George Carrington, Creed Haskins, Wade Netherland, John Baskervile, John Fleming, and Thompson Swann Gent Vestrymen.

Southam Parrish Deb^r.	Neet Tob^o	Cask
To the Reverend Robert McLaurine Minister	16000	640
and six p cent for scrinkage	960	

To John Cardwell Clerk of Petervill Church	1000	40
To Gideon Glenn Clk of Tarwallet d°	1000	40
To Thos Freeman Fretwell Clk of Ham d°	1000	40
To Silvanus Witt Clk of South d°	1000	40
Thomas Davenport Clk of the Vestry	500	20
To the Cask aded	820	820
To Roger Hill sexton of Petervile Church	500	
To Susannah Easley sexton of Tarwallet Church	500	
To Rachal Farris sexton of Ham Church	500	
To Esther Wherley sexton of South Church	500	
To Avis Tayler for keeping Sanderses Child	1200	
To Francis Epperson for keeping & Cloathing Reynolds d°.	500	
To Vallintine Martin for keeping Joannah Parrish	600	
To Joseph Woodson for keeping George Dobbins	500	
To the Widow Kent a Poor Person	800	
To Daniel Wilmore for keeping & Cloathing Elizabeth Howl	800	
To Peter Bowker & Jn° Wright for keeping & Cloathing Cannefaxes 2 boys	800	
To Richd Parker for keeping the Widow Parker Ten months and Burying her	800	
To Thompson Swann for being Dubble Listed 14 Tithables to George Cox. 1 Tithable Abraham Womack 3.d°. William Stratton 6 d°. John Mayo 2 d°. at 19 lb Tob°. p pole to be Repaid on Their satisfying the Church wardens that they wer Dubble Listed	494	
To Alexr Trent for the support of Philn Childreses Family	400	
To Ellenor Sutlief a Pore Person	500	
To Anne Eaton a Pore Person	300	
To Tob°. to be Levyed and Sold for Raising the Cash Debt	6700	
	38674	
To the Collector for Collecting the Above Tob°.	2320	
Credr.	40994	
By Balc. Due to the Parrish on the state of the 2 foregoing Levys 92 & commissions on d° 5	97 40897	

By 2145 Tith^s. at 19 lb Tob^o p pole	40755
By Bal^c. Due to the Collector	142
	40897

[111] December 21st 1758
Southam Parrish in Cash   D^r.

To William Clarke for Bread & Wine at Tarwallet & Ham Churches	£ 3. 0.0
To Benj^a Mosby for bread and Wine at Petervile & South churches	0.15.0
To Mary Easley for Needle Work	0. 5.6
To Roger Hill for Eight Benches at Petervile Church	0.10.0
To Gideon Seay for work at Tarwallet church when Received	52. 0.0
To Joseph Epperson for work on the Glebe when Received	16. 9.4
Creditor	72.19.10
By Bal^c. Due in the collectors Hands upon his cash accompt this Day Rendered	17. 6.4½
	£55.13.5½

John Fleming and Thompson Swann are Elected Church warden for the Ensuing year.

Ordered that John Woodson late Collector Pay to Gideon Seay in Part for his Work on Tarwallet Church 17.6.4½ appearing on his accompt mentioned above.

Ordered that John Woodson be appointed collector of the Levy now assigned on Condition he give Bond with good security according to Law for Collecting and Paying the same as the Law Directs to the several Persons Entitled to Receive the same and for settling his accompt thereof with the vestry when Required etc.

Littleberry Mosby is Elected a Vestryman for this Parrish in the Room of Stephen Bedford Deceased.

Ordered that Nicholas Davies agree with a workman to glaze the windows of Ham Chappel and to Repair the wooden shetters.

Ordered that Littlebery Mosby and Thompson Swann view the kitchen at the Glebe and Employ a workman to make the Necessary Repairs thereon.

    John Baskervile   Robert McLaurine Minister
    Wade Netherland   John Fleming Ch Warden
    Creed Haskins   Thompson Swann Ch Warden
    Thomas Davenport   George Carrington

****

[112]   August 11th 1759

Att a vestry held for Southam Parrish at the courthouse of Cumberland County for Laying off the said Parrish into small Precincts and appointing Possessioners to Possession the same this 11th Day of August 1759. Present the Reverend Robert. McLaurine Minister, John Fleming and Thompson Swann Church wardens, George Carrington, Thomas Davenport, Nicholas Davies, Thomas Turpin, John Baskervile, Alexander Trent, And Littleberry Mosby. Gent. Vestrymen.

Pursuant to an order of Cumberland County Court Dated July 23rd 1759 The Church wardens have laid off the said Parrish into small Precincts Which are as Followeth (Viz).

Ordered that Charles Anderson John Woodson and Saymore Scott on the 10th Day of November Next Begin and Possession all the Lands and Renew and Marke the several Lines Between Randolphs Road the Clouver Forrest Road And the County Line and make their Return according to Law.

Ordered that George Wright Thomas Williams John Wright and Charles Lee on the 10th Day of November Next Begin and Possession all the Lands And Renew and marke the several lines Between Randolphs Road The Clouver Forrist Road the County Line and Brookses Road and Make their Return according to Law.

Ordered That Matthias Williams John Chambers Charles Cotterell and Aron Butler on the 10th Day of November Next Begin and Possession All the Lands and Renew and Marke the several Lines Between Appamattox

River Green Creek and Randolphs Road and make their Return according to Law.

Ordered that Higginson Barksdale Julius Davenport John Retterford Senr. And Thomas Jeffries on the 10th Day of November Next Begin and Possession All the Lands and Renew and marke the several Lines Between Brookses Road and County Line Bollings and the Main Road and make their Return according to Law.

Ordered that John Cook James Brown Warren Walker and William Bailey on the 10th of November Next Begin and Possession All the Lands and Renew and Marke the several Lines Between Angoler Creek Appomattox River Green Creek and Randolphs Road and make their Return according to Law.

Ordered that Culvarine Ford Dudley Rowntree and Frances Epperson on the 10th. Day of November Next Begin and Possession All the Lands and Renew and Marke the several Lines Between Great Guinea Creek Appamattox River Angoler Creek and Col^o. William Macons upper Lines and make their Return according to Law.

[113]   August 11 1759
Ordered that Edward Mackgehe Nathan Glen and William Anglea Ju^r. on the 10th. Day of November Next Begin and Possession all the Lands and Renew & Marke the several Lines Between: Beginning at Col^o. William Macons Upper lines on the same to Angoler Creek up the same to Randolphs Road Down the same to Glens Path on the same to Great Guinea Creek Down The same to the Beginning and make their Return according to Law.

Ordered That Henry Macon William Womack Daniel Coleman Junr. And John Noel on the 10th Day of November Next Begin and Possession All the Lands and Renew and Mark the several Lines Between Tarwallet Run Great Guinea Creek and the Main Road and make Their Return according to Law.

Ordered That Henry Davenport, Henry Harman, Richard Weatherford, And Richard Daniel on the 10th Day of November Next Begin and Possession all the Lands and Renew and Mark the several Lines Between

Littleguinea Creek Appamatox River Great Guinea Creek Tarewallet Run And the Ridge Road and Make their Return according to Law.

Ordered that William Watson Henry Farmer John Jonas & Francis Allen on the 10th Day of November Next Begin and Possession all the Lands And Renew and Mark the Several Lines Between Littleguinea Creek Buckingham Road and Guinea Road & make their Return according to Law.

Ordered That Lawrance Smith Robert Thomson Richard Parker & George Cox on the 10th Day of November Next Begin and Possession All the Lands and Renew and Mark the several Lines Between Appamattox River Littleguinea Creek Guinea Road Buckingham Road and the Road to Clementses Mill and make their Return according to Law.

Ordered That Richard Pouvaul William Smith Joiner & Phillip Thomas Junr. on the 10th Day of November Next Begin and Possession all the Lands and Renew and mark the several Lines Between Appamattox River Fighting Creek Buckingham Road & Lileses Road and make their Return according To Law.

Ordered That John Moseley Edward Moseley & Henry Clay on the 10th Day of November Next Begin and Possession all the Lands and Renew and marke the several Lines Between From the fork of Fighting Creek up Randolphs Mill Creek to Buckingham Road Down the Road To the Church Thence Down the Creek to the fork and make their Return According to Law.

[114]   August 11th 1759
Ordered That John Cox Thomas Locket and Joel Locket on the 10th Day of November Next Begin and Posession all the Lands and Renew And Marke the several lines Between Geneto Road the Church Road Fighting Creek & Appamattox River and make their Return according to Law.

Ordered That Edward Watkins Isham Aiken and Abraham Baugh on the 10th Day of November Next Begin and Possession all the Lands And Renew and Mark the several Lines Between the New Road Buckingham Road the Church Road and Geneto Road and make Their Return according to Law.

Ordered That Israel Winfry Joseph Baugh & John Watkins on The 10th Day of November Next Begin and Possession all the Lands And Renew and mark the several lines Between Buckingham the New Road Geneto Road and the County Line and make Their Return according to Law.

Ordered That George Hancock Richard Moseley & William Moseley on the 10th Day of November Next Begin and Possession all the Lands And Renew and mark the several Lines Between the county Line Appamattox River and Geneto Road and make their Return According to Law.

Order That Williams Daniel Robert Kent William Mills and John Seay on the 10th Day of November Next Begin and Posession All the Lands and Renew and mark the several Lines Between Bollings Road the Main Road Buckingham Road and the County Line and make their Return according to Law.

Ordered That Capt. Samuel Allen Thomas Guttery and Alexander Trent on the 10th Day of November Next Begin and Possession all the Lands And Renew and mark the several Lines Between Willises River Soakass Creek to Daniels old houses and Buckingham old Road and make their Return according to Law.

Ordered That James Holloway John Bowden Isaac Beacham And William Rowton on the 10th Day of November Next Begin And Possession all the Lands and Renew and mark the several Lines Between Harrisons Road the Road to John Burtons Buckingham Road to Daniels old houses and Soakass Creek And make their Return according to Law.

[115]   August 11th. 1759
Ordered That John Hobson Samuel Jones Field Robinson & William Hobson on the 10th Day of November Next Begin and Possession all the Lands and Renew and mark the several Lines Between Buckingham Road the Road from John Burtons to Murreys the Courthouse Road and Mayos Mill Path to Ben Harrises and make their Return according To Law.

Ordered That George Owen John Burch & John Netherland on The 10th Day of November Next Begin and Possession all the Lands and Renew and mark the several Lines Between the Middle Road Randolphs Church Road Buckingham Road and M^r. Salleys Path and make their Return according to Law.

Ordered That Richard Ligon John Baskervile & William Davis on The 10th Day of November Next Begin and Possession all the Lands and Renew and mark the several Lines Between the Middle Road Randolphs Church Road Buckingham Road and the Road from the Negros Arm to M^{rs}. Mayos and make their Return according to Law.

Ordered That Humphrey Smith John Maxey and Thomas Ballow on The 10th Day of November next Begin and Possession all the Lands and Renew and Mark the several Lines Between Joneses Creek King William Parrish Line and Buckingham Road and make their Return according to Law.

Ordered That Edward Parrott John Cannefax and George Radford on the 10th Day of November Next Begin and Possession all the Lands And Renew and Mark the several Lines Between Joneses Creek King William Parrish Lines James River Fine Creek to the Middle Road the Middle Road to M^{rs}. Mayos M^{rs}. Mayos Road to Buckingham Road and Make their Return according to Law.

Ordered That John Railey David Sceasor Bennet Goode and Henry Hobson on the 10th Day of November Next Begin and Possession all the Lands and Renew and Mark the several Lines Between the Road from Michaux Ferry as far as Speirses ordinary the Middle Road to Fine Creek Down Fine Creek to James River and up the River to the said Ferry And make their Return according to Law.

Ordered That William Prosser Robert Bagby and William Cox on The 10th Day of November next Begin and Possession all the Lands and Renew and Mark the several Lines Between James River the Ferry Road to Paul Michaux the River Road and Solomans Creek And Make their Return according to Law.

[116] August 11th. 1759
Ordered That Bartholomew Stovaul Ju^r. Edmon Toney David Chandler

& James Tayler Son of John Taylor Dec^d. on the 10th Day of November Next Begin and Possession all the Lands and Renew and Mark the several Lines Between Deep Creek the Middle Road the Road from Spierses to Paul Michaux the River Road to Solomans Creek Solomans Creek & James River And make their Return according to Law.

Ordered That Micajah Mosby Charles Finch & John Stephenson on the 10th Day of November Next Begin and Possession all the Lands And Renew and Mark the several Lines Between Deep Creek James River Muddy Creek and the River Road and Make their Return according to Law.

Ordered that James Moss Edward Tabb and Henry Stratton on The 10 Day of November Next Begin and Possession all the Lands and Renew and Marke the several Lines Between Muddy Creek as High As Scotts Mill thence Pattesons Road to the Middle Road the Middle Road [to] Deep Creek and the River Road and Make their Return according to Law.

Ordered That Littleberry Mosby Benjamin Mosby and Frances George Steger on the 10th Day of November Next Begin and Possession all The Lands and Renew and Mark the several Lines Between Deep Creek M^{rs}. Mayos Chear Road and the Middle Road and Make their Return according to Law.

Ordered That Stephen Moseby Hezekiah Mosby and George Chambers on the 10th Day of November Next Begin and Possession all the Lands And Renew and Mark the several Lines Between the Middle Road to Murrys ordinary Muddy Creek to Scotts Mill Pattesons Road to the Middle Road and Make their Return according to Law.

Ordered That Charles Carter William Dillion & Henry Dillion on The 10th Day of November Next Begin and Possession all the Lands And Renew and Mark the several Lines Between Muddy Creek James River Willises River and River Road and Make their Return according to Law.

[117]   August 11th 1759
Ordered That Orlando Hughes William Terrel and John Creacey on The 10th Day of November next Begin and Possession all the Lands & Renew and Mark the several Lines Between Muddy Creek the River Road Carters

Ferry Road and the Chappel Road to Scotts Mill and make Their Return according to Law.

Ordered That Ralph Flipping Jacob Winfrey and Robert Duglass on The 10th Day of November next Begin and Possession all the Lands and Renew and Mark the several Lines Between Muddy Creek Barnards Road Carters Ferry Road and the Chappel Road to Muddy Creek and Make their Return according to Law.

Ordered that William Holland Thomas Tabb and John Holland on the 10th Day of November next Begin and Possession all the Lands and Renew and Marke the several Lines Between Barnards Road Horn Quarter Road and Willises Creek and Make their Return according to Law.

Ordered That Samuel Oslen John Armsteed and John Salmons on the 10th Day of November next Begin and Possession all the Lands and Renew and Mark the several Lines Between Carters Ferry Road Barnards Road Willises River and the River Road and Make their Return according to Law.

Ordered That Benjamin Harrison Benjamin Wilson & Drury Scruggs on the 10th Day of November Next Begin and Possession all the Lands and Renew and Mark the several Lines Between Willises River Buckingham Road the County Line and Randolph's Creek and Make their Return according to Law.

Ordered that Phenehas Glover John Reynolds and Joseph Price on The 10th Day of November Next Begin and Possession all the Lands and Renew and mark the several Lines Between Willises River Randolphs Creek the County Line and the River Road and make their Return according to Law.

Ordered that Samuel Tayler and Benjamin Cannon on the 10th Day of November next Begin and Possession all the Lands and Renew and mark The several Lines Between Willises River James River the County Line and The River Road make their Return according to Law.

Ordered that Poindexter Mosby Rhoderick Easley Joseph Woodson & John Hughes on the 10th. Day of November next Begin and Possession all the Lands and Renew and mark the several lines Between Deep Creek the Middle Road to Salleys Path on That to Buckingham Road to Lileses Road on that to Appamattox River Appamattox River to Clementses Mill on Clements Mill Road to Buckingham Road Down the same to M^r. Harrises Mill Path on the same to Mayo Old Mill and make their Return according To Law.

[118]   August 11th 1759
Ordered that Alexander Trent have leave to build a gallery in Tarwallet Church at his own Expense Provided he doth not lesson the Room nor Pregudice The church.

Ordered that Alexander Trent and Thomas Davenport agree with workmen To make wooden Shetters and Fix them to the windows of Tarewallet Church.

Ordered that Thompson Swann and Littleberry Mosby agree with workmen to Build a kitchen at the Glebe of the same Size and on the Same Foundation and to the same Chimney to which the kitchen at the Glebe now stands. The same being found to be too far decayed for to be worth Repairing the Same to be Framed well Clapboarded Below and Shingled Roof.

Thomas Turpin	Robert McLaurine Minester
John Baskervile	John Fleming ⎫ Church Wardens
Alexander Trent	Thompson Swann ⎭
Littleberry Mosby	Nicholas Davies
Thomas Davenport	George Carrington

****

Att a vestry held for Southam Parish at the courthouse of Cumberland County the 15th day of December one thousand Seven hundred and fifty nine.

Present the Reverend Robert McLaurine Minister John Fleming Church Warden, George Carrington, John Baskervile, Creed Haskins, Wade Netherland, Alexander Trent and Littleberry Mosby Gent. Vestrymen.

Southam Parrish D^r.	Neet Tob^o	Cask
To the Reverend Robert McLaurine Minister	16000	640
and 6 p cent for scrinkage	960	
To John Cardweel Clk Petervile Church	1000	40
To Gideon Glen Clk Tarwallet d^o	1000	40
To Thos Freeman Fretwell Clk Ham d^o	1000	40
To Silvanus Witt Clk South d^o	1000	40
To Thos Davenport Clk Vestry	500	20
To d^o for Extraordinary servis as Possessioning Year.	500	20
To the cask aded	840	840
To Roger Hill Sexton of Petervile Church	500	
To Susannah Easley d^o of Tarwallet d^o	500	
To Rachal Faris d^o of Ham d^o	500	
To Hester Wherley d^o of South d^o	500	
	24800	

[119]   December 15th 1759

Southam Parrish D^r.	Neet Tob^o
To the Sum brought forward	24800
To Avis Tayler for keeping Sanderses Child	1200
To Francis Epperson for keeping Reynoldses Child	500
To Vallintine Martin for keeping Joannah Parrish	600
To Joseph Woodson for keeping George Dobbins	500
To Daniel Wilmore for keeping & cloathing Eliz. Howl	800
To Elenor Sutlieft a Pore Person	600
To Anne Eaton a Pore Person	500
To Richard Pringle for keepin Catharine May three months	200
To Edward Parrott for keeping Cathrine May two months	150
To Elizabeth Wright for keeping Cannefaxes two boys	800
To Col^o. Carrington to be applyed towards the support of Eliz Golliham	400
To Alex^r Trent to be apply^d towards the support of Phil^n Childress Ju^r family	600
To Rachal Farris for three benches at Ham Chappel	30
To Tobacco Levyed to Pay the Cash Debt	3320
To John Woodson Collector for his Ballanc in the former Levy	142
	35142

To the collector for collecting 39270 lb Tob°	2356
To a Depossetom in the Collectors Hands	1772
	39270
C^r	
By 2310 Tithes at 17^{lb} Tobacco p pole	39270

Debt^r in Cash	
To Nicholas Davies for assisting Mary Dillion	£ 1.00.0
To Edward Parrott for sundry good for Catharine May as p accompt	0.18.5
To Benjamin Mosby his accompt for Bread & wine for the Churches & Removing Catharine May	5.10.0
To Col° Carrington his accompt for Elizabeth Golleham	1.01.9
To Roger Hill for Removing the old Glass of Petervile Church	0.05.6
To Cash to be Paid for the kitchen at the Glebe when finish^d & Received	15.00.0
	£ 23.15.8

John Woodson is appointed [collector] of the above Levy for this parrish for the ensuing year he giving Bond and good security to the Church wardens according to Law.

Thomas Davenport a member of this vestry and also Clerk: in obedience to an Act of Assembly Disableing a member of the Vestry to serve as Clerk Doth therefore Resign his Trust as Vestryman and is thereupon continued Clerk of the said Vestry.

Mr Henry Macon is Elected a Vestryman in the Room of the said Thomas Davenport And M^r. Rhoderick Easley is Elected a Vestryman in the Room of Benjamin Harris Dec^d.

Poindexter Mosby Doth agree to keep and Cloath George Dobbings for 800^{lb} Tob° p anum.

[120] December 15th.1759.
Edward Parrott agrees to keep and Cloath Catharine May for 1000^{lb} Tob°. p annum.

Col⁰ George Carrington is appointed to agree with workmen to Repair Ham Chappel Windows.

M.ʳ Alexander Trent is appointed to agree with workmen to Repair the windows of Tarwallet Church.

Col⁰. John Fleming and Thompson Swann is Continued Church wardens For the Ensuing year.

Creed Haskins	Robert M.ᶜLaurine Minister
John Baskervile	John Fleming Church Warden
Alexander Trent	George Carrington
Littleberry Mosby	Wade Netherland

****

Att a vestry held for Southam Parrish at Cumberland Courthouse the Twenty second Day of August 1760 Present the Reverend M.ʳ Robert M.ᶜLaurine, John Fleming Churchwarden, Thompson Swann Churchwarden, George Carrington, Nicholas Davies, Alexander Trent, Littleberry Mosby, and Rhoderick Easley. Gent. Vestrymen.

George Carrington Ju.ʳ is appointed Clerk of this vestry.
The Returns of several Posessioners are as Followeth: (viz)

Edward Parrott John Cannefax & George Radford	to be Recorded
Richard Povaul & Phillip Thomas Ju.ʳ	d⁰
Henry Macon William Womach Daniel Coleman Ju.ʳ & John Noel	d⁰
Charles Anderson John Woodson & Saymore Scott	d⁰
George Wright Tho.ˢ Williams John Wright & Charles Lee	d⁰
Benjamin Harison Benjamin Wilson & Drury Scruggs	d⁰
Henry Davenport Henry Harmon Rich.ᵈ Daniel & Rich.ᵈ Weatherford	d⁰
Lawrance Smith George Cox & Rich.ᵈ Parker	d⁰
Isham Aiken Edward Watkins & Abraham Baugh	d⁰
John Reynolds & Joseph Price	d⁰
Micajah Mosby Charles Finch and John Stevenson	d⁰
Benjamin Cannon and Samuel Tayler	d⁰
Edward Tabb and James Moss	d⁰

[121]   August 22ⁿᵈ 1760

John Railey Bennet Goode Henry Hobson & David Sceasor to be Recorded Jurors Report on the Lines Between John Radford and Walter Maxey Certified By the Clerk of Cumberland Court Returned and to be Regestered. Jurors Report on the Lines Between Nathaniel Maxey and Thomas Cock Certified By the Clerk of Cumberland Court Returned and to be Recorded.

Jurors Report on the Lines Between Thomas Cock and Thomas Ballow Certified by the Clerk of Cumberland Court Returned and to be Regestred.

Rhoderick Easley and Poindexter Mosby Possessions Made Return to be Record.

Frances George Steger & Littleberry Mosby dº dº.

Ordered that the Parrish Collector Pay the Church wardens the Tobaco and Money of the Parrish in his hands and that Church warden Dispose of the Tobacco for Paying the Money Debts of the Parrish.

Ordered that Alexʳ. Trent Receive of Gideon Seay the work Done by him at Tarewallet Ch.

Ordered that Nicholas Davies Receive the Barn Built at the Glebe by Joseph Epperson.

Ordred that Ham Chappel be Enlarged by an addition of Twenty four feet at one End and Mʳ. Davies is appointed to agree with workmen to meet such addition.

Nicholas Davies	Robert McLaurine Minister
Alexander Trent	John Fleming }
Littleberry Mosby	Thompson Swann } Churchwardⁿ
Rhoderick Easley	George Carrington

In obedience to an order of vestry of Southam Parrish we the subscribers Possessioned the following Lines (viz) the lines between Thomas Turpin and Thomas Prosser, both Parties Present. the lines Betwen Thoˢ. Turpin and John Cannefax, the lines Between Thoˢ Turpin John Archer Thoˢ

Jefferson and Joseph Mayo, the said Mayo Jefferson and Archer fail[d] to attend. the Lines Between Tho[s] Prosser and John Pleasents, the said Pleasents failed to attend. the lines between John Baskervile, Richard Ligon, John Radford, Joseph Bundurent, George Radford, Walter Maxey, Robert Hughes, and James Holeman, all Parties Present. Certified under our hands this 30th Day of March 1760.

        Edward Parrott
        John Cannifax
        George Radford

[122] August 22nd 1760

February the 6th 1760 The lines Peaceable and Quietly Possessioned as Followeth. The line between Col[o]. William Randolph & Rich[d] Povall, Present Rich[d] Eggelston and Rich[d] Povall. The line Between Col[o]. William Randolph & William Elam, Present Rich[d] Eggelston & W[m] Elam. The line between Nicholas Giles and William Elam, Present Nicholas Giles And William Elam. The line between Nicholas Giles & William Archer, Present Nicholas Giles & William Archer. The line between William Archer and William Bailey, Present Nicholas Giles & William Archer. The line between Col[o]. William Randolph & William Bailey, Present Richard Eggleston & Nicholas Giles. The line between Col[o]. William Randolph And William Archer, Present William Archer & Richard Eggleston. The line between Nicholas Giles and Robert Williamson, Present John Gamon and Nicholas Giles. The line between William Archer & Rob[t]. Williamson, Present Osborn Locket & John Gamon. The line between W[m]. Archer and Phillip Thomas, Present Samuel Childres & Phillip Thomas. The line between Richard Williamson & Phillip Thomas, Present Samuel Childres & Phillip Thomas. The line between Nathaniel Maxey And Phillip Thomas, Present Samuel Childres & Phillip Thomas. The line between Richard Williamson & Nathaniel Maxey, Present Samuel Childres & Phillip Thomas. The line between Rich[d] Povall And Nathaniel Maxey, Present William Hudspeth & Phillip Thomas. The line between William Smith & Rich[d] Povall, Present. W[m]. Hudspeth And W[m]. Smith. The line between Richard Williamson and Robert Williamson, Present William Smith & John Gamon. The line between Richard Williamson & William Smith, Present John Gamon & William Smith. The line between William Smith and Col[o]. William Randolph, Present Rich Eggleston & W . Smith. The line between Col[o]. William Randolph & Robert Williamson, Present

Richd Eggleston & John Gamon. The line between Col^o. W^m. Randolph & William Elam, Present Richd Eggleston & William Elam. The line between Robert Williamson & Wm Ealam, Present W ^{m} Elam & John Gamon.

          Richard Povall
          Phillip Thomas Ju^r.

In obedients to an order of Vestry the 11th Day of August 1759. we the subscribers being appointed Possessioners gave our attendance but No one appeared.

To Capt. Thomas Davenport   Henry Macon
Clerk Vestry of Southam Parrish   William Womack
          Daniel Coleman Ju^r.
          John Noel

[123] August 22nd 1760
In compliance to an order of vestry of Southam Parrish Dated September 11th 1759. we the subscribers have Possessioned the several Lines Between Randolphs Road and Appamattox River the County Line and Clover Forrest Road (Viz), Ryland Randolphs Line & Leander Hughes, Ryland Randolph and Isham Richerson, Ryland Randolph and James Anderson, Ryland Randolph and John Woodson, Ryland Randolph and William Hall, John Woodson and William Hall, John Woodson and Robert Hall, John Woodson and Roger Williams, James Anderson and Roger Williams, Ryland Randolph and Roger Williams, Ryland Randolph and Saymore Scott, Isham Richerson and Saymore Scott, Charles Williams and Saymore Scott, Charles Anderson and Saymore Scott, Charles Anderson and Charles Williams, George Wright and Charles Williams, George Wright and Charles Anderson, Witness our Hands. Present

  John Woodson Sherieff   Charles Anderson
  Leander Hughes   John Woodson
  Roger Williams   Saymore Scott
  Powel Hughes

Pursuant to an order of Vestry for Possessioning the Lines Between Brookses Road Randolphs Road the County Line and the Clover Forrist Road and the Persons in the said Bounds not all attending to shew their Lines we have Possessioned the several Lines as followeth (to witt) March 1760.

128   VESTRY BOOK OF SOUTHAM PARISH

Between: George Wright & Alexander Trent
           Charles Williams & George Wright
           Thomas Williams & Alexander Trent
           Ryland Randolph & Thomas Williams
           Alexander Trent & Ryland Randolph
           Ryland Randolph & Isham Richerson
           Peterfield Trent & Alexander Trent
           Archibald Cary & Peterfield Trent
           Henry Bell & Alexander Trent
           Robert Johns & John Gannaway

The above Lines were Possessio[n]ed in the presents of Thomas Wright John Walker John Gilliam and Joseph Fuquay and Robert Pierson.

                    George Wright
                    Thomas Williams
                    John Wright
                    Charles Lee

[124]   August 22nd 1760
In obedience to an order of Vestry for Southam Parrish the 11th Day of August 1759. we the Subscribers Benjamin Harrison Benjamin Wilson And Drury Scruggs have Possessioned the following Lines. Possessioned: Beginning on Randolph Creek on the line Between Alexander Trent and Tucker Woodson. Present Capt. Allen
Also the Line between John Jude & Alexr. Trent do do
As Also the Line between Benja. Wilson John Jude & Alexr. Trent do
As also the Line between Alexr. Trent Drury Scruggs & Benja Wilson do
As also the Line Between Benja Wilson & Lenard Keeling
As also the Line Between the said Keeling & Drury Scruggs
As also the Lines Between the said Keeling Thos Tabb & Drury Scruggs
As also the Lines Between Thos Tabb Benja Harrison & Colo Archd Cary
As also the Lines between Benja Harrison Colo Archd Cary & Joseph Farrer
As also the Lines between the sd Farrer & Alexr Trent Present Capt Allen
As also the Lines between the sd Trent & Colo Archd Cary Present do

                    Benjamin Harrison
                    Benjamin Wilson
                    Drury Scruggs

In obedience to an order of vestry we the subscribers have Possessioned all the Lands and new Marked the several lines as followeth (Viz).
The line Between:

Richard Daniel	& Richard Weatherford	Present Joseph Hubburd
d⁰	& Joseph Jinkins	Present Joˢ. Hubburd
Richard Weatherford	& d⁰	d⁰
William Hambleton	& d⁰	d⁰
d⁰	& John Boles	Wᵐ Hambleton
George Slaughter	& d⁰	d⁰
d⁰	& William Arnold	John Boles
John Boles	& Stephen Davenport	Wᵐ Hambleton
d⁰	& Henry Davenport	d⁰
d⁰	& Joseph Davenport	John Boles
d⁰	& Phillemon Davenport	d⁰
d⁰	& Joseph Jinkins	d⁰
Phillemon Davenport	& d⁰	d⁰
d⁰	& Mary Jinkins	Joseph Jinkins
Thoˢ Davenport Juʳ	& Phillemon Davenport	d⁰
d⁰	& Mary Jinkins	d⁰
Joseph Jinkins	& d⁰	d⁰
Stephen Davenport	& Wᵐ Davenport	Wᵐ Arnold
William Arnold	& d⁰	Stepⁿ Davenport
d⁰	& Benjᵃ Sims	Wᵐ Arnold
Wᵐ Davenport	& d⁰	Stephen Davenport
d⁰	& Henry Davenport	Wᵐ Davenport
Joseph Davenport	& d⁰	d⁰
d⁰	& Phillemon Davenport	d⁰

[125]   August 22ⁿᵈ 1760
The lines Between

Joseph Davenport	& John Jones	Present Wᵐ Davenport
Thoˢ Davenport Juʳ	& Harrison Jones	d⁰
d⁰	& William Hambleton	d⁰
d⁰	& James Davenport	Wᵐ Watson
d⁰	& Henry Davenport	d⁰
Wᵐ Hambleton	& Wᵐ Watson	d⁰
James Davenport	& d⁰	d⁰
John Smith	& d⁰	d⁰
d⁰	& James Davenport	d⁰

dº	& Benjamin Sims	James Davenport
James Davenport	& dº	dº
dº	& Wᵐ Davenport	dº
Benjamin Sims	& Hodgeses Orphan	dº
John Smith	& dº	dº
dº	& Samuel Meridith	dº
William Watson	& dº	Christopher Watson
William Womack	& dº	dº
dº	& William Watson	dº
dº	& Henry Harman	dº
William Watson	& dº	dº
Maurice Langhorn	& dº	dº
dº	& William Watson	dº
dº	& Henry Farmer	dº
dº	& John Farmer	dº

Part of a Line between William Hambleton and Jinkinses orphans thought to Be Removed Or oltered [altered] by John Bostick now in Dispute And Not Possessioned.

Henry Davenport
Henry Harman
Richard Daniel
Richard Weatherford

Persuent to an order of vestry we the subscribers have possessioned and Renewed And Marked the several lines. Beginning at Henry Coxes line below Clements Mill and Runing Between Mʳˢ. Hughes to his Corner upon Wayleses Land. then Between Hall Coxes and Wayles to Pringles Corner. then between Pringle and Wayles to Wayleses Corner. Then between Hall Coxs & Pringle to Halls Corner. Then Between Hall Coxs Pringle & Burton. Then Between Pringle & Burton to Pringles Corner upon Wayleses line. Then between Pringle & Wayles to Wayleses Corner. Then from Burtons Corner upon Wayleses line to Richard Parker Senʳ. Then the line Between George Cox & Burton to George Coxes Corner. Then the line between Burton & Lawrance Smith to Benajah Thomson Corner. Then between Benjah Thomson & Burton to the Widow Parkers Burton stopt one line of Possession, Then the line between the Widow Parker and Richards To a Corner. Then along Parkers line to Burtons

Henry Cox. Tho[s] Oazeley and Allen Freeman Present, Then along the lines between Wayles Henry Hatcher and Josiah Thompson to Buckingham Road. Then along the lines Between Richard Parker and James Patteson to their Corner. To Bowles Then Between Bowles and Patteson to Littleguinea Road

[126]   August 22nd 1760
Thence from Guinea Road the line between Patteson Frank Allen & Cit Chalton to Pattesons Corner upon the River. Then the line between Cit Chalton & Richard Daniel to a Corner. Then along Daniels line to Littleguinea Bridge. then from Daniels Corner along Jinkinses line To Guinea Road. Then Begining from the Road the line between Bowles & Tho[s]. Merryman to Parkers Corner. Then between Richard Parker & Tho[s]. Merryman to a Corner. Then between F[r]ed Hatcher and Richard Parker to a Corner Between Henry Hatcher and Fed Hatcher to Buckingham Road. Then Begining at the Road The line Between Frederick Hatcher & Tho[s]. Merryman to a Corner Upon Richard Parkers line. Benajah Thompson Robert Scruggs and Francis Allen Present.

Lawrance Smith
George Cox
Richard Parker Sen[r].

We the subscribers have Renewed and Marked all the severall lines within the Mentioned bounds and also marked the line between Joel Lockitt & Edward Watkins both there, Present and agreed. also between Thomas Lockett & Joel Lockett, Present and agreed. & also marked the Line between William Aiken & Edward Watkins, both Presen[t] & agreed. Also marked the Line between Edward Watkins & Francis Cheatom, Both Present & agreed. & also Marked the Line Between Edward Watkins and John Watkins, both present & agreed. & also between Edward Watkins and Thomas Moseley, both agreed. & also Marked the Line Between John Watkins & Abraham Baugh, boath agreed. & also Marked the Line Between John Watkins & Benjamin Watkins, Present & agreed. and Also new Marked the Line Between John Wherley & Benjamin Watkins, Both Present & agreed. & also new marked the Line Between John Wherley and Charles Maxey, both Present & agreed. & also marked the Line Between Charles Maxey & William Wherley, both Present & agreed. And also new marked the Line between Edward Moseley and William Maxey, both Present & agreed. & also between Thomas Moseley & John Moseley, both

Present & agreed. & also Between Abraham Baugh & Joseph Baugh, both Present & agreed. and also Marked the Line Between Thomas Woldridge & Thomas Watkins present And agreed. & also marked the Line Between Thomas Watkins and Walter Scott, both Present and agreed. and also marked the Line Between Benjamin Watkins & Walter Scott, Present & agreed. & also Marked the Line between Edward Watkins & Isham Aikin, both Present & agreed. & also That is all the Lines that is within our Bounds according to the order that was sent to us, we

Isham Aiken
Edward Watkins
Abraham Baugh

[127]   August 22nd 1760

In obedience to an order of the vestry of Southam Parrish appointing Us Possessions we have Possessioned as follows February 20th 1760. The line between Jeremiah Cannon and Phenehas Glover, Present Benjamin Cannon and the said Glover. Between Jeremiah Cannon and David Reynolds, Present Benjamin Cannon. Between the said Phenehas Glover & David Reynolds, both Present. Between George Carrington & David Reynolds, both Present. Between the said George Carington & James Gilliam, Present the said Carrington & Samuel Tayler in behalf of Gilliam. Between the said George Carrington & Phinehas Glover, both Present. Between the said George Carington & Joseph Price, both Present. Between Paul Carington and Joseph Price, Present the said Price & George Carrington in behalf of The said Paul Carrington. Between Paul Carrington & Vallintine Martin, Present the said George Carrington. Between the said Paul Carrington and Alexander Trent, Present the said George Carrington in behalf of the said Paul Carrington and Job Thomas in the behalf of the said Trent. Between the said Paul Carrington & John Reynolds, Present the said Reynolds and the said George Carrington in behalf of the said Paul Carrington. Between John Reynolds & Alexander Trent, Present Job Thomas in behalf of Trent and Present also the said Reynolds. Between James Cunningham & John Reynolds, Present the said Reynolds & Job Thomas. Between James Cunningham & Alexander Trent, Present Job Thomas for Trent. Between James Cunningham & Drury Woodson, Present Job Thomas and Thomas Christian. February 21th. The Line between Joseph Price & Valentine Christian, both Present. Between Valentine Martin & Alex^r. Trent, Present the said Martin & Job

Thomas for Trent. Between Joseph Price & the said Trent, Present the said Price & Job Thomas for Trent. Between Alexander Trent & Maurice Langhorne, Present Job Thomas for Trent & Benjamin Walker overseer for Langhorne. Between Joseph Price & Maurice Langhorne, Present the said Price & Benjamin Walker For Langhorne. Between Gideon Martin & Joseph Price, both Present. Between Valentine Martin & Orson Martin, Present the said Orson and Gideon Martin for Valentine Martin. Between Joseph Price & Orson Martin, both Present. Between Orson Martin & Phenehas Glover, Present. The said Orson. Between Joseph Price and Phenehas Glover, Present Gideon Martin.

John Reynolds
Joseph Price

[128] August 22nd. 1760

In obedience to an order of the vestry wee the Possessioners Micajah Mosby John Stevenson & Charles Finch Begining at Deep Creek have Possessio[n]ed The line between John Pleasant & Micajah Mosby, Richard Pirkins Present. Also the lines between Micajah Mosby & John Scott, Thomas Tucker Present. Also the lines between Thomas Bedford & Micajah Mosby, John Scott Present. Also the lines between Charles Edwards & Micajah Mosby, John Scott Present. Also the lines between Thomas Bedford & John Scott, Abraham Womack Present. Also the lines between Thomas Bedford & Jane Randolph, John Scott Present. Also the line between Jane Randolph & Charles Edwards, Abraham Womack Present. Also the line between Thomas Bedford & Edward Morgan, John Scott Present. Also the lines between John Stevenson & Jane Randolph, James Barnes Pres^t. Also the lines between John Stevenson & Charles Finch, also the lines between William Stratton & John Stevenson, James Barnes Present. Also the Lines between William Stratton & Jane Randolph, Abraham Womack Present. Also the line between Abraham Womack & Robert Hughes, W^m. Stratton Present. Also the lines between Jane Randolph & Abraham Womack, William Stratton Present.

Micajah Mosby
Charles Finch
John Stevenson

In obedience to an order of vestry for Southam Parrish we being ordered to Possession, Begin the 21st. Day of February 1760 & Renewed the line between Col^o. George Carrington & James Gilliam, George Carrington

Present and for James Gilliam Thomas Fields Present. Also between Col°. George Carrington And Samuel Tayler, both parties present. Also between Col°. George Carrington And Phillip Mayo, George Carrington Present. Also Between Benjamin Cannon And Phenehas Glover, Glover & Cannon both Present. Also between Benjamin Cannon & John Prier, Benjamin Cannon Present & for John Prier Samuel Tayler Present. Also Between John Prier and William Rowland, said Rowland Present and for John Prier. Samuel Tayler Present. Also between William Rowland & James Gilliam, said Rowland Present and for James Gilliam Thomas Field Present. Also between David Reynolds and Jeremiah Cannon, both Perties Present. Also between James Gilliam and John Prier, for John Prier Samuel Tayler Present & for James Gilliam Thomas Fields Present. Also between James Gilliam & Samuel Tayler, The said Tayler Present & for James Gilliam Thomas Fields Present. Notis has bin given to all the rest that hold lands with our precincts or to the overseers of Those that Do not live within the bounds of our Precincts & they failed to attend. Therefore, no other Lands are Possessioned in the said Precincts but what is above Mentioned. Given under our Hands March 1760.

Benjamin Cannon
Samuel Tayler

[129]   August 22nd 1760

Whereas by an order of the vestry of Southam Parrish bearing Date 11th of August 1759 Edward Tabb James Moss & Henry Stratton is appointed to Possession Certain Lands Between Deep & Muddy Creeks. in obedience to the said order We the subscribers have Compleated the said Possessioning in manner Following (Viz).

Between:

Charles Scott & Bowler Cock	Present Jesse Miller
Jesse Miller & Charles Scott	Present Jesse Miller
Edward Tabb & Miller	Both Present
Francis Steger & Miller	Present Miller
Benjamin Mosby & Francis Steger	Present Mosby
Bowler Cock & Benjamin Mosby	Present Mosby & William Holland
Bowler Cock & John Moss	Present W^m. Holland & James Moss
Bowler Cock & James Moss	Present Moss & Holland

Jacob Mosby & James Moss	Present Moss
Edward Tabb & James Moss	both Present
Edward Tabb & Alexander Moss	Both Present
Alexander Moss & Jacob Mosby	Present Moss
Benjamin Bedford & John Pleasants	Present Micajah Mosby
John Pleasants & Micajah Mosby	Present Mosby
Jacob Mosby & Waddell	Present Micajah Mosby
Micajah Mosby & Waddell	Present Mosby
William Tucker & Waddell	Present Micajah Mosby
William Tucker & Micajah Mosby	Present Thomas Tucker
William Tucker & Richard Ligon	Present Thomas Tucker
Richard Ligon & Waddle	Present Tho[s] Tucker
Richard Ligon & Edward Morgain	Present Tho[s] Tucker
Henry Stratton & Waddell	Present Stratton
Edward Morgain & Henry Stratton	Present Stratton
Charles Finch & Thomas Stratton	
William Stratton & Thomas Stratton	
William Stratton & Abraham Womack	
William Stratton & Tho[s]. Randolph	Present Stratton
Nicholas Davies & Tho[s]. Randolph	Present Davies
Nicholas Davies & William Stratton	Both Present
Nicholas Davies & Robert Hughes	Present Davies
Edward Tabb & Abraham Womack	Present Tabb
Between:	
Nicholas Davies & Abraham Womack	both Parties Refus[d].
Nicholas Davies & Bowler Cock	both failed to attend
Nicholas Davies & Nicholas Speirs	d[o]
Nicholas Davies & Edward Tabb	Davies d[o]
Edward Tabb & James Aiken	Aiken d[o]
James Aiken & Francis Steger	Aiken d[o]

Edward Tabb
James Moss

[130]   August 22nd 1760

Pursuant to an order of the Vestry of Southam Parrish Dated August the 11th. 1759 we the subscribers began January 16th. 1760 to Possession the several Lines of the several Persons herein Mentioned (Viz) Begining at Fine Creek. a Line between John Pleasants & Bennet Goode, Pleasants failing To attend. A line between Daniel Wilmore & Bennet Goode, a line between John Railey & Bennet Goode, Then on the line between Daniel Stoner & Bennet Goode, on the line between Daniel Stoner & David Caesor, on the line between Daniel Stoner & John Hughes, on the line Between John Pleasants & Daniel Stoner, On the line between the said Pleasants & William Cox, Then on the line between the said Cox and Henry Bagby to Michaux Ferry Road, Then on the line between the said Bagby & John Pleasants, Then Between Pleasants & Robert Hughes, Then Between the said Henry Bagby & Elizabeth Cox to the above Road, Then Between Robert Hughes & Elizabeth Cox, on the line between Daniel Stoner & William Cox, on the Line between Paul Michaux & the said Stoner, on the line between John Fleming & John Pleasants, Then between John Fleming & Joseph Johns, Then between the said Johns & Pleasants, Then between the said Johns & Pleasants, Then between the said Johns & Daniel Wilmore, Then between the said Wilmore and Susannah Carner, Then between the said Wilmore & Pleasants, Then between Wilmore & John Railey, then between the said Railey & John Pleasants, Then Between the said Railey & Joseph Johns, Between the said Railey & William Reynolds Dec^d, Between the said Rayley & David Seizer, between the said Seizer and John Spurlock, Between Seizer & John Hughes, Between the said Hughes and Spurlock, Between the said Hughes & Silvater Alford, Between John Spurlock & William Reynolds Dec^d, between the said Reynolds & Alford, between the said Reynolds & Joseph Johns, Between Alford & John Fleming, Between the said Fleming & John Hughes, Between John Hughes & Robert Hughes Dec^d, between Robert Hughes & John Pleasants, Between Richard James & Robert Hughes, Between the said James & Jacob Michaux, Between Jacob Michaux & Nicholas Wilkinson to the Ferry Road, Then between the said Wilkinson & Richard James, Then between Bennet Goode & David Seizer.

Persons failing to attend (Viz) John Pleasants & Daniel Stoner, Daniel Stoner & Benjamin Netherland, Daniel Stoner & Charles Woodson, A Peace of a Line between John Pleasants and Susanna Carner not to be found, nor no attendance.

        John Rayley
        Bennet Goode
        Henry Hobson
        David his mark X Seizer

[131]   August 22nd 1760
Att a Court held for Cumberland County February 25th. 1760 on the Return of Humphrey Smith & John Maxey Possessioners. Produced in court by the Church wardens of Southam Parrish it is ordered that the surveyor of this County with a Jury Do lay out and Possession the lines Between Thomas Cock & Thomas Ballow and Return the survey Thereof with the Proceedings to the next Court after the survey Made.
A copy T Swann CCC

The Jury haveing met in company with the surveyor Thomas Cock & Thomas Ballow agreed to Poseession their lines Peaceably & Quietly without the Jury.
Francis Maccraw D. Sher.

Cumberland June Court 1760
The above Report was Returned and ordered to be Recorded
Test George Carrington Ju^r. D.CC
A copy George Carrington Ju^r. D.CC

In obedience to an order of the court of Cumberland County Dated February 25th 1760 We the subscribers being Mett and Duly sworn to examine the Lines in Dispute between Nathaniel Maxey & Thomas Cocks have accordingly Examined the same in company With the surveyor of this county & Do find the lines Run in the following Manner (to witt). From a corner Mentioned in the said Maxeys Patent in Cocks line south 45 degrees West to Pointers, south 70 degrees West to Pointers. both which courses agree with Both their Pattents as near as is common, and from thence south 45 Degrees West to a black oak which said Last Course Difers much from both their Patents. and it appears to us that the lines above mentioned are the lines that the said Maxey was Willing to have had Possessioned but the said Cocke Refused to have it Done. Witness Our hands and seals this second Day of June mdcclx.

Henry Clay	L.S.
John James Dupuy	L.S.
William Hudspeth	L.S.
George Owen	L.S.
William Smith	L.S.

Att a court held for Cumberland County June 23rd 1760. The above Report was Returned and ordered to be Recorded.
Test
Thompson Swann CC.

Benjamin Netherland	L.S.
Thomas Moseley	L.S.
George Cardwell	L.S.
Joseph Woodson	L.S.
Poindexter Mosby	L.S.
John Burch	L.S.
Rhoderick Easley	L.S.

A Copy   George Carrington D. CCC.

[132]   August 22nd. 1760
In obedience to an order of the court of Cumberland County Dated February The 25th 1760 we the subscribers being met and Duly sworn to Examine The lines in Dispute between John Radford and Walter Maxey have Accordingly Examined the same in company with the surveyor of this County and Do find that the Lines Runs in the following Manner (to witt) from a Corner Hickory in Thomas Ballows line, West to George Radfords line and have Possessioned the same and it appears to us that That is the line That John Radford Refused to have Possessioned. Witness our hands & seals June The second mdcclx.

	Henry Clay	L.S.
	Joseph Woodson	L.S.
	Poindexter Mosby	L.S.
Cumberland, July Court 1760	Benjamin Netherland	L.S.
The above Report was ordered to be Recorded		
	William Hudspeth	L.S.
Test	Thomas Moseley	L.S.
Geo Carrington Jr. D. CC	George Owen	L.S.
	William Smith	L.S.
	John James Dupuy	L.S.
	Rhoderick Easley	L.S.
	George Cardwell	L.S.
	John Burch	L.S.

A Copy   George Carrington Jr. D.CCC

In obedience to the within order we have given Publick Notis and No proper attendance.

Rhoderick Easley
Poindexter Moseby

Pursuant to an order of vestry the subscribers gave Publick notis and Gave their attendance and Possessioned Benjamin Mosbys and Francis George Stegers lines, Mosby & Steger Present. Mary Burtons and Francis George Stegers, John Cardwell her overseer and Steger Present. Bowler Cock & John Mayo failed to give their attendance tho. we have Possessioned their Lines.

Francis Geo. Steger
Littleberry Mosby
January 30th 1760

****

[133]   November 22nd 1760

Att a Vestry held for Southam Parrish at the Courthouse of Cumberland County November 22nd. 1760. Present the Reverend Robert McLaurine Minister, Thompson Swann Churchwarden, George Carrington, Thomas Turpin, Nicholas Davies, John Baskervile, Littleberry Mosby, and Rhoderick Easley Gent. Vestrymen.

Thomas Davenport is chosen & appointed Clerk of the Vestry.

Southam Parrish	D^r.	Neet. Tob^o.	Cask
To the Reverend Robert McLaurine Minister		16000	640
and six percent for scrinkage		960	
To John Cardwell Clerk of Petervile Church		1000	40
To Gideon Glen Clerk of Tarwallet Church		1000	40
To Thos. Freeman Fretwell Clerk of Ham Chappel		1000	40
To Silvanus Witt Clerk of South Chappel		1000	40
To Thomas Davenport Clerk of the vestry		500	20
To the Cask aded		820	820
To Roger Hill sexton of Petervile Church		500	
To Susanna Easley d^o. of Tarwallet d^o		500	
To Rachal Farris d^o of Ham d^o		500	
To Hester Wherley d^o of South d^o		500	

140 VESTRY BOOK OF SOUTHAM PARISH

To Avis Tayler for keeping Sanderses Child	1500
To Frances Epperson for keeping Reynoldses Child	500
To Vallintine Martin for keeping Joannah Parrish	600
To Daniel Wilmore for keeping Elizabeth Howel	800
To Poindexter Mosby for keeping George Dobbings	800
To Edward Parrott for keeping Catharine May	1000
To Elenor Sutlief a Pore Person	600
To Anne Eaton a Pore Person (now for the Parrish use)	500
To Col°. George Carrington for the support of Elizth Golliham	400
To Ditto for the support of Job Walker	500
To Thompson Swann for four coppys of acts of assembleys to be Read in Churches	112
To Henry Farmer for keeping Henry Farmer Senr.	600
To Alex^r. Trent for the support of Philemon Childres family	800
To William Dillion for being Duble Listed	17
To Murrel Allen for being Dubble Listed	17
To the Tob°. Levyed for the Use of the Parrish to Pay the Cash	7500
C^r.	40526
By Part of the last years Deposetom in the Coll^r. hands	1483
D^r.	39043
To the Collectors sallery at 6 p cent on 41871 lb Tobo.	2512
To a Deposetom in the Collectors hands	316
C^r.	41871
By 2463 Tiths at 17 lb Tob°. p pole	41871

[134] November 22nd 1760
Southam Parrish   D^r. in Cash

To William Terrel for Building an addition to Ham Chappel when finish & Recv^d	£ 49.19.6
To Amey Hill for Providing for Anne Eaton & in her sickness & burying her	3.15.0
To Benj^a. Mosby for supplying the several Churches in this Parrish with bread & wine	5. 8.0
To William Smith for takeing & burying a Poor Person	5. 0.0
	£ 64. 2.6

Francis Maccraw and Frederick Hatcher is appointed Collectors of the Above Levy for this Parrish for the Ensuing year they Giveing Bond and

Good security to the Church wardens according to Law.

Ordered that Nicholas Davies agree with workmen to Remove the two upper Pews in Ham Chappel and to Put wooden shetters to the new building windows.

Ordered that Thomas Turpin & John Baskervile agree with workmen To seeal South Chappel & furnish the same with Pews & under Pin the same.

Ordered that Nicholas Davies & Carter Henry Harrison Have Leave To build an addition in the North side of Ham Chappel for the use of their Familys Provided the same Do not hurt or Pregudice the said Chappel.

Possessioners Returns
Williams Daniel, Robert Kent, William Mills & John Seay Return to be Recorded. George Hancock, William Moseley & Richard Moseley to be Recorded. John Hobson, William Hobson, Field Robinson & Samuel Jones to be Recorded.

Littleberry Mosby & Rhoderick Easley are appointed Church Wardens for the Ensuing year.

Nicholas Davies	Robert McLaurine Min^r.
Thomas Turpin	Littleberry Mosby Ch warden
John Baskervile	Rhoderick Easley Ch Warden
Thompson Swann	George Carrington

[135]   November 22nd 1760
Pursuant to an order of vestry baring Date the 11th Day of August 1759 we the subscribers Have Possessioned the lands & Renewed the lines between Bollings Road the Main Road Buckingham Road & the County line as followeth Begining the 10th Day of November 1759 & Possessioned. Warham Easleys Land, himself Present & shewed the lines. William Daniels Land Possessioned, himself Present & shewed the lines. John Seays land Possessioned, himself Present & shewed the lines. the Church acre Possessioned, John Seay & Gideon Seay Preasent. one line of Henry Garrots between Him & Ralph Fliping Possessioned, Garrott Present & not knowing any more of his Lines. Thomas Gutterys land Possessioned, himself Present & shewed the lines. William Samsons land Possessioned, himself Present and shewed the lines. Robert Kents land

Possessioned, himself Present & shewed the lines. Benjamin Hendricks land Possessioned, himself Present and shewed the lines. William Daniels land Possessioned, Himself Present & shewed the lines. Daniel Coleman Senr. land Possessioned, himself Present & shewed the lines. Maurice Langhorns land Possessioned, himself Present and shewed the lines. James Daniels land Possessioned, Williams Daniel shewed the lines. William Mills land Possessioned, himself Present & shewed the lines. James Browns land Possessioned, John Hill showed the lines. The following lands have not bin Possessioned: Martin Burks land not Possessioned himself not being at home, Henry Scruggs Land not Possessioned his overseer not knowing the lines, John Bullocks land Not Possessioned his Tenant not knowing the Lines, Robert Hudgens land not Possessioned his Tenant being at home, William Hudgens land not Possessioned, himself not being at home, Thomas Johns Land not Possessioned Himself not being at home, Alexander Trents land not Possessioned his overseers not knowing his lines, James Wilkins land not Possessioned Himself not being at home, John Taylers land and Anthony Levillions land is not Possessioned there living no body on Either of there Lands to shew their lines, Given under our hands this Twenty sixth Day of March 1760.

       Williams Daniel
       Robert Kent
       William Mills
       John Seay

In obedience to an order of vestry we the subscribers have Possessioned The several lines as Followeth (Viz). The line Between Capt. Creed Haskins & George Hancock, Present Creed Haskins & George Hancock. The line between Creed Haskins & William Marshall, Present Creed Haskins & Wm Marshall. The line between Creed Haskins & Richd Moseley, Present Creed Haskins & Richd Moseley. The line between Wm Moseley & Richd Moseley, Present W^m. Moseley & Richd Moseley. The line between Arther Moseley & Wm Moseley, Present William Moseley. The line between Capt. Arther Moseley & Lodowick Elam, Present Lodowick Ealam. The line between Lodowick Elam & John Northcut, Present Lodowick Elam. The line between Gedion Locket & Lodowick Elam, Present Lodowick Elam.

[136] November 22nd 1760
The line between Gideon Locket & Capt Arther Moseley, Present Gideon Lockett. The line between Mark Tayler & John Northcut, Present Mark Tayler. The line between Capt Arther Moseley & Mark Tayler, Present Mark Tayler. The line between Lodowick Elam & John Northcut, Present Lodowick Elam & John Northcut. The line between Edward Watkins & Joel Lockett, Present Joel Lockett. The line between Joel Lockett & Thos Lockett, Present Joel Lockett & Thos Lockett. The line between W^m. Marshall & Francis Marshall, Present Francis Marshall. The Lands belonging to the orphans of George Williamson George Todd and Timson not Possessioned for want of somebody to shew lines.

George Hancock
William Moseley
Richard Moseley

Cumberland County Southam Parrish the 11th of August 1759 we John Hobson & William Hobson Field Robinson & Samuel Jones Possessioners begun at Francis George Stegers line & John Mayo & the line between Steger and Maddox, Steger Present. The line between Joseph Fuqua & Maddox and Fuqua Present. the line between Fuqua & Christopher Robinson, Fuqua Present. The line between William Clark & Robinson & Fuqua Present. The line between Christopher Robinson & John Robinson and John Robinson Present. The line between William Hobson & John Robinson, Both Parties Present. The line between John Robinson and Charles Bradshaw, Both Parties Present. The line between Charles Bradshaw & Field Bradshaw, both Parties Present. The line between Charles Bradshaw & Simon Gentrey, both Parties Present. The line Between Jentry & Grays, Jentry Present. The line between Gentry and Murrey, Jentry & John Brown Present. The line between Jentrey and Jonus Meador, both Parties Present. The line between Walter Keeble and John Burton, Keeble Present. The line between Gideon Patteson and Josiah Bradshaw, both Parties Present. The line between John Mayo & David Winneford, both Parties Present. The line between Frederick Hatcher & W^m. Hobson, Hobson Present. The line between Hobson & Randolph Johnson, both Present. The line between Thos Merryman and Johnson, Johnson & his son Present. The line of William Hudson Done Between him and Richd Alderson, both Present. The line between Alderson and Jacob Mackgehe, Alderson Present. Adcock Hobson line Done Between him & Joseph Hubburd, Hobson Present. The Line

Between John Hubburd & Walter Keeble, Keeble Present. The line Between Michal Jones & Gideon Patteson, Jones Present. M^r. Wayles overseer know Not his lines. William Battersby Tenant know not Battersbys line. Henry Hatcher Did not want his Done. Josiah Thomson Did not Want his Done. Jacob Mackgehe Did not want his Done. William Hobson Did not want his Done.

[137]   November 22nd 1760
Samuel Jones Did not want his Done. John Bradshaw Did not Want his Done. William Bradshaw Did not want his Done. John Hobson Did not want his Done. Field Robinson Did not want his Done. Given under our Hands.

John Hobson
Field Robinson
William Hobson
Samuel Jones

****

Att a Vestry held for Southam Parrish at the Courthouse of Cumberland County the 20th Day of September 1761. Present Littleberry Mosby, & Rhoderick Easley Churchwardens, George Carrington, Nicholas Davies, Wade Netherland, John Fleming, Alexander Trent, and Thompson Swann. Gent. Vestrymen.

Ordered that the Parrish collectors Pay all the Tobacco that is in their hands belonging To this Parrish to the Churchwardens.

Ordered that the churchwardens Pay William Terrell the sum of twentyfive Pounds In Part for the addition to Ham Chappel.

Nicholas Davies	Littleberry Mosby ⎫
Wade Netherland	Roderick Easley ⎬ CW
Alexander Trent	George Carrington
Thompson Swann	John Fleming

****

Att a vestry held for Southam Parrish the 29th. Day of December 1761 at Cumberland Courthouse: Present the Reverend Robert McLaurine Minister, Littleberry Mosby & Roderdick Easley Church Wardens, George Carrington, Thomas Turpin, John Fleming, Creed Haskins, Alexander Trent. Gent. Vestrymen.

Southam Parrish	Debtor	Neet Tob°	Cask
To the Reverend Robert McLaurine Minister		16000	640
and six p cent for scrinkage		960	
		16960	

[138]   December 29th 1761

Southam Parrish	Debtor.	Neet Tob°	Cask
To the sum brought forward		16960	640
To John Cardwell Clk of Petervile Church		1000	40
To Gideon Glenn Clk of Tarwallet Church		1000	40
To Thos. Freeman Fretwell Clk of Ham Chappel		1000	40
To Silvanus Witt Clk of South Chappel		1000	40
To Thomas Davenport Clk of the Vestry		500	20
To the Cask aded		820	820
To Roger Hill Sexton of Petervile Church		500	
To Susannah Easley d°. of Tarwallet d°.		500	
To Rachal Farris d°. of Ham Chappel		500	
To Esther Wherley d° of South d°		500	
To Avis Tayler for keeping Winkfield Sanders		1500	
To Francis Epperson for keeping Reynolds Child		500	
To Daniel Wilmore for keeping Elizabeth Howl		800	
To Poindexter Mosby for keeping George Dobings		800	
To Henry Farmer Jur. for keeping Henry Farmer Senr		600	
To Thompson Swann for Coppys List Tiths		98	
To John Mayo for two Tiths twice Listed at 17 lb Tob° p pole		34	
To Elenor Sutlief a Poor Person		600	
To Col°. Carrington for Elizabeth Golliham		400	
To d°. for the support of Job Walker		500	
To Alexr. Trent for the support of Phillemon Childres Jur family		800	

To d⁰. for the support of Nathan Hamptons family	800
To Elizabeth Wright for keeping Cannefaxes boy Two years the year 1760 & 1761	800
To Rhoderick Easley for 8 Insolvents at 17 lb Tob⁰ Each	136
To Elizabeth Yarbrough a Poor Person	500
To Tabitha Fiphs a Poor Person	600
To Edward Parrott for keeping Catharine May seven weaks & burying her	600
To the Tobacco Levyed for the use of the Parrish to Pay The Cash debt & the Defishencys for Last Year	8000
To the Collector for Collecting 46080 lb at 6 p cent	2764
To a Deposetom in the Collectors hands	968
Creditor	46080
By 2560 Tiths at 18 lb Tob⁰ p pole	46080

Debter in Cash	
To Benjamin Mosby for furnishing four Churches with Bread and Wine for Last Year	£5.14.6
To Roger Hill for Clearing the spring at Petervile Church 6/16 & Benches Blocks & steps 18/6	1. 5.0
To John Maxey for hooks for the windows of South Chappel	0.10.0
	7. 9.6

[139] December 29ᵗʰ 1761

To the sum Brought over	£ 7. 9.6
To Charles Maxey for fixing the hooks to South Chappel windows	0. 2.6
To John Alexander for Franklins Children	0.10.0
To Robert MͨLaurine for boxing the Eves of the kitchen at the [Glebe] and sealing the same	1. 0.0
To Joseph Epperson in Part for work to be Done at South Chappel	50. 0.0
Creditor	59. 2.0
By Cash in Col⁰. John Flemings hands	8.11.10
	£ 50.10.2

Thomas Davenport Sherieff is appointed Collector of the above Levy he giveing Bond and good security according to Law some time Betwixt now and the first Day of March next and it is ordered that he Collect of Every Tithable Person within This Parrish 18 lb of Tob°. & Pay the same to the several Creditors as above.

Ordered that John Mayo Gent. have Leve to build a gallery in the Southeast Corner of Petervile Church. Provided he Doth not lessen the Room nor Pregudice the said Church and that he give bond & good security to the Churchwardens for the same and to Remove the same when found Necessery by the Vestry and that he give the Said bond before he begins the said Work.

Ordered that Benjamin Mosby have Leve to build a gallery in the North East Corner of Petervile Church Provided he Doth not Lessen the Room nor Pregudice The said Church and that he give bond and good security to the Churchwardens For the same and to Remove the same when found Necessary by the Vestry and That he give the said bond before he begins the said work.

Ordered that Col°. Carrington agree with workmen to Remove the Pulpit and Communion Table in Ham Chappel and fix them in the Proper Places in the New Building.

Creed Haskins	Robert M°Laurine M
John Fleming	Littleberry Mosby
Alexander Trent	Rhoderick Easley } C W
	George Carrington
	Thomas Turpin

****

[140] June 28th 1762
Att a vestry held for Southam Parrish the 28th Day of June 1762. Present George Carrington, Nicholas Davies, John Fleming, Thomas Turpin, Wade Netherland, Thompson Swann, and Littleberry Mosby. Gent. Vestrymen. Order^d That Nicholas Davies Gent. Do view and Examine the Work Done by William Terrel on Ham Chappel and when The same is Compleated according to agreement that He the said Nicholas Davies Do Receive the same.

Nicholas Davies	George Carrington
Thompson Swann	John Fleming

Littleberry Mosby   Tho⁵. Turpin
                     Wade Netherland

****

Att a vestry held for Southam Parrish the 22ⁿᵈ. Day of December 1762. Present the Revᵈ Robert McLaurine Minister, Littleberry Mosby, Rhoderick Easley Church wardens, George Carrington, Thomas Turpin, Nicholas Davies, John Baskervile and Thompson Swann Gent. Vestrymen.

Southam Parrish Debtor	Neet Tobº.	Cask
To the Revᵈ. Robert McLaurine Minʳ.	16000	640
and 6 p cent for scrinkage	960	
To Jnº Cardwell Clk. Petervile Ch	1000	40
To Gideon Glen dº. Tarwallet dº.	1000	40
To Tho⁵. Freeman Fretwell dº Ham dº.	1000	40
To Silvanus Witt dº. of South dº.	1000	40
To Tho⁵. Davenport Clk. Vestry	500	20
The Cask aded	820	820
	22280	

[141]   December 22ⁿᵈ 1762

Southam Parrish Debtor	Neet Tobº.
The sum brought forward	22280
To Roger Hill Sexton of Petervile Church	500
To Susannah Easley Sexton Tarwallet dº	500
To Rachal Farris Sexton Ham dº	500
To Hester Wherley Sexton South dº	500
To Avis Tayler for keeping Winfield Sanders	1500
To Francis Epperson for keeping Reynoldses Child	500
To Poindexter Mosby for keeping George Dobings	800
To Francis Epperson one Levy twice Listed	18
To Anne Nuckels two Levys Dubel Listed	36
To Daniel Wilmore for keeping Elizᵗʰ Howl	800
To Elenor Sutlief a Poor Person	600
To Colº. Carrington for support of Elizᵗʰ. Golliham	400
To dº for support of Job Walker	500

To Wm Basham for support of Henry Farmer	800
To Richard Amis a poor Person of this Parrish	500
To William Cheatwood for takeing Care of Jn° Woods a poor orphan Child to this Day	500
To the Clerk of Cumberland County Court for Copys of four Acts of Assembly to be Read in The Churches	112
To Richard Pringlea for keeping Catharine May three months	250
To W^m. Maxey for keeping & Cloathing W^m. Elsom a Poor boy of this Parrish	600
To Rhod. Easley for 12 Insolvents at 18 lb Tob°.	216
To Thos. Davenport for 40 Insolvents at 18 lb Tob° Each	720
To Charles Maxey for Benches at South Church	100
To Tob°. Levyed for the use of the Parrish To Pay the Cash Debt of £79.9.0	12000
To the Collector his Sallery at 6 p cent	2970
To a Depossetum in the collectors hands	1312
	49514

Contra   Creditor

By 2606 Tiths at 19 lb Tob° p Pole	49514
Debtor in Cash	
To W^m. Terrel & Thos. Mountegue	£ 15. 6.6
To Benj^a. Mosby for furnishing four Churches with Bread & wine	5.17.0
To Rich^d. Epperson for work when finish^d. & Receiv^d at South Chapel	50. 0.0
To Thos. Davenport for the Cure of Tabitha Phips a Poor Person of this Parrish	8. 5.6
	£ 79. 9.0

[142] December 22nd 1762
Littleberry Mosby is appointed Collector of the above Levy he giveing Bond and good security according to Law and he Collect of Every Tithable Person in this Parrish 19 lb of Tob°. and Pay the same to the several Parrish Creditors.

Order^d. That Thomas Hall be appointed and he is hereby appointed Clerk of South Chappel in Room of Silvanus Witt as he hath Removed out of This Parrish.

Order^d. that M^r. Nicholas Davies have Leave to Build a Gallery or Pew in the North side of Ham Chappel Joining to the old Gallery so that he Do Not Pregudice the said Church for the use of his own Family.

Henry Macon and Nicholas Davies Gent. are appointed Church Wardens for the Ensuing Year.

Ordered that suit be brought against John Woodson and His Securitys for the Tobacco that is in his hands Due to This Parrish.

Ordered that Alexander Trent Pay the Eight hundred Pounds of Tobacco that is in his hands belonging to this Parrish to the support of Phillemon Childreses family.

Ordered that an addition be built to the middle of the North Side of Petervile Church thirty by Twenty four feet and Shingle the old building together with the new with good heart Shingles the same to be Done and Compleatly Finished in a good workman Like manner and Thompson Swann and John Baskervile Gent. agree With workmen to Build and finish the same.

Thos Turpin	Robert McLaurine Minister
John Baskervile	Nicholas Davies CW
Littleberry Mosby	George Carrington
Rhoderick Easley	Thompson Swann

****

[143]   July 23rd. 1763
Att a Vestry held for Southam Parrish att the Courthouse of Cumberland County for Laying off the said Parrish into small Precincts and appointing Posessioners to Possession the same the 23rd. Day of July 1763. Present Nicholas Davies Churchwarden, George Carrington, Creed Haskins, John Baskervile, Jno. Fleming, Thompson Swann, Littleberry Mosby & Rho^d. Easley Gent. Vestrymen. Pursuant to an order of Cumberland County Court Dated June 27th. 1763. The Church wardens have Laid off the said Parrish into small Precincts which are as followeth Viz.

Ordered That Charles Anderson Saymore Scott and James Anderson on the 10th Day of November Next begin and Possession all the Lands and Renew and Mark the several lines Between Randolphs Road the Clover Forrist Road and the county line and make their Return according to Law.

Ordered That George Wright Thomas Williams and Robert Johns on The 10th Day of November Next begin and Possession all the Lands and Renew and mark the several Lines Between Randolphs Road the Clover Forrist Road the County line and Brooksis Road and make Their Return according to Law.

Ordered That John Raine Joseph Michaux and John Chambers on The 10th Day of November Next begin and Possession all the Lands & Renew and mark the several lines Between Appamattox River Green Creek and Randolphs Road and make their Return according to Law.

Ordered That Thomas Johns Jarrott Ellison and William Hudgens Ju^r on the 10th Day of November Next Begin and Possession all the Lands and Renew and mark the several lines Between Brookses Road the County line Bollings Road and the Main Road and make their Return according to Law.

Ordered That Warren Walker James Brown John Wright & John Holeman on the 10th Day of November Next begin and Possession all the lands and Renew and mark the several lines Between Angoler Creek Appamattox River Green Creek and Randolphs Road & make their Return according to Law.

Ordered The Isaac Allen Matthew Nelson and John Nelson on The 10th Day of November Next begin and Possession all the lands and Renew and mark the several lines Between Greatguinea Creek Appamattox River Angoler Creek & Col^o. William Macons upper Lines and make their Return according to Law.

Ordered That Nathan Glen William Anglea Ju^r. & Charles Lee on the 10th. Day of November Next begin and Possession all the lands & Renew and Mark the several lines between begining at Col^o. Wm Macon upper lines on the same to Angoler Creek up the same to Randolphs Road Down the same to Glens Path on the same to Great Guinea Creek Down the same to the Begining and make their Return according to Law.

[144] July 23rd 1763

Ordered That William Womack Daniel Coleman Ju^r. Daniel Allen and Mark Andrews on the 10th Day of November Next begin and Possession all the lands and Renew and mark the several lines Between Tarwallet Run Greatguinea Creek as high as Glens Path and the Main Road and make their Return according to Law.

Ordered That Charles Ballow W^m. Hambleton W^m. Davenport and Henry Harmon on the 10th Day of November Next begin & Possession all the lands and Renew and Mark the several lines between Little Guinea Creek Appamattox River Greatguinea Creek Tarwallet Run and the Main Ridg Road and make their Return according to Law.

Ordered That John Jones Richard Sharp Henry Martin & Lewis Orrange on the 10th Day of November Next Begin and Possession all the Lands and Renew and mark the several lines Between Little Guinea Creek Buckingham Road Guinea Road Burtons Brook & Appamattox River and make their Return according to Law.

Ordered That Lawrence Smith Richard Parker Ju^r. Thomas Moody and George Cox on the 10th Day of November Next begin and Possession all the lands and Renew and mark the several lines Between Appamattox River Burtons Brook Guinea Road Buckingham Road and the Road to Clements & Coxes Mill & make their Return according to Law.

Ordered That Charles Clay Henry Clay Ju^r. & Jesse Carter on the 10th Day of November Next begin and Possession all the lands and Renew and mark the several lines Between Deep Creek the Middle Road to Salleys Path on that to Buckingham Road on that to Lyleses Road on that to Appamattox River to Clement Mill on the Road from Clement Mill to Buckingham Road Down the same to M^r. Harrises Path to John Mayos Mill and make their Return according to Law.

Ordered That William Bailey William Smith Joiner & Phillip Thomas Jr on the 10th Day of November Next begin and Possession all the land and Renew and mark the several lines Between Appamattox River Fighting Creek Buckingham Road and Lyleses Road & Make their Return according To Law.

Ordered the John Moseley Benjamin Hatcher & Henry Clay on the 10th Day of November next begin and Possession all the lands & Renew & mark the severall lines Between from the fork of Fighting Creek Randolphs Mill Creek to Buckingham Road Down the same to the Church Down the Creek To the fork and make their Return According to Law.

Ordered That John Cox James Ligon & Thomas Moseley on the 10th Day of November Next Begin and Possession all the Lands and Renew and mark the severall lines Between Genito Road the Church Road Fighting Creek and Appamattox River and make Their Return According to Law.

[145]   July 23rd. 1763
Ordered that Edward Watkins Francis Cheathem & Abraham Baugh on the 10th Day of November Next begin and Possession all the lands and Renew & mark The several lines between the New Road Buckingham Road the Church Road and Genito Road and make their Return according to Law.

Ordered That Israel Winfrey Joseph Baugh & Lodowick Elam on the 10th. Day of November Next Begin and Possession all the lands and Renew and mark the several lines Between King William Parrish the New Road Genito Road and the County line and make their Return according to Law.

Ordered That Wm Marshal Francis Marshal & Mark Tayler on the 10th. Day of November Next Begin and Possession all the Lands and Renew and mark the several lines Between The County line Appamattox River and Genito Road and make their Return according to Law.

Ordered that Williams Daniel John Seay William Mills and Henry Scruggs on the 10th Day of November Next begin and Possession all the lands and Renew and mark the several lines Between Bollings Road the Main Ridg Road Buckingham Road and the County line & make their Return according to Law.

Ordered that Capt Samuel Allen Thomas Guttery & Robert Hudgens on the 10th Day of November Next begin and Possession all the lands and Renew and mark the several lines between Willises River Soakass Creek to Daniels Old houses & Buckingham Road & make their Return according to Law.

Ordered That James Holloway John Bowden Isaac Beacham & W^m. Rowton on the 10th Day of November Next begin and Possession all the lands & Renew and Mark the several lines Between Harrisons Road the Road to John Burtons ordinary Buckingham Road to Daniels old houses & Soakass Creek and make Their Return according to Law.

Ordered that William Clerk Gideon Patteson W^m. Hobson Little Creek & Adcock Hobson on the 10th Day of November Next begin and Possession all the Lands and Renew and mark the several lines Between Buckingham Road the Road from Jno. Burtons To Murreys the Courthouse Road to the Path by Stegers to John Mayo Mill and the Mill Path to Benj^a Harrises and make their Return according to Law.

Ordered that George Owen John Burch & Benj^a Netherland on the 10th day of November Next Begin and Possession all the lands and Renew and Mark The several lines Between the Middle Road Randolphs Church Road Buckingham Road and M^r. Salleys Path and make their Return according to Law.

Ordered that Richard Ligon John Baskervile & W^m. Davis on the 10th Day of November Next Begin and Possession all the Lands and Renew and mark the several lines Between the Middle Road Randolphs Church Road Buckingham Road and the Road from the Negros Arm to M^{rs}. Mayo and make their Return according to Law.

Ordered that Nathaniel Maxey John Radford J^r. & Peter Furcrun on the 10th Day of November Next Begin and Possession all the Lands and Renew and mark the Several lines Between Joneses Creek King William Parrish lines & Buckingham Road and make their Return according to Law.

Ordered that Edward Parrott W^m. Watson and George Radford on the 10th Day of November next Begin and Possession all the lands and Renew and mark the several lines Between Joneses Creek King William Parrish lines James River Fine Creek to the Middle Road the Middle Road to M^{rs}.

Mayo. M^rs^. Mayo Road to Buckingham Road and make their Return according to Law.

[146]   July 23rd. 1763
Ordered that John Hughes Richard James Thomas Epperson and Capt. Bennet Goode on the 10th Day of November Next Begin & Possession all the Lands and Renew and Mark the several lines Between The Road from Michaux Ferry to Speires ordinary at the Courthouse or Middle Road Down the Middle Road to Fine Creek Down Fine Creek to James River and up James River to the said Ferry and make their Return according to Law.

Ordered that Jacob Michaux Daniel Johnson & James Bagby on The 10th Day of November Next Begin and Possession all the Lands and Renew and mark the several lines Between James River the Ferry Road to Paul Michaux the River Road and Solomans Creek and make their Return according to Law.

Ordered that James Tayler son of Wm Tayler William Howard Joseph Mosby and Edmond Toney on the 10th Day of November Next Begin and Possession all the Lands and Renew and mark the several lines Between Deep Creek the Middle Road the Road from Speirses to Paul Michaux The River Road to Solomons Creek Solomons Creek and James River And make their Return according to Law.

Ordered that Micajah Mosby Charles Finch & Robert Beck on the 10th Day of November Next Begin and Possession all the Lands & Renew and mark the several lines Between Deep Creek James River Muddy Creek and the River Road and make their Return according to Law.

Ordered That Abraham Womack Jesse Miller & William Stratton on the 10th Day of November Next Begin and Possession all the Lands & Renew and mark the several lines Between Muddy Creek as high as Scotts Mill Scotts Road to the Middle Road the Middle Road Deep Creek and the River Road and make their Return according to Law.

Ordered That John Cardwell Francis George Steger & Benj^a^ Mosby on the 10th Day of November Next Begin and Possession all the Lands and Renew and Mark the several lines Between Deep Creek the Path to John

Mayo Mill and the Middle Road and make their Return according to Law.

Ordered That Hezekiah Mosby David Parker and John Merryman on the 10th Day of November Next Begin and Possession all the Lands and Renew and mark the several Lines Between the Middle Road to Murreys ordinary Muddy Creek to Scotts Mill Scotts Road to the Middle Road and make their Return according to Law.

Ordered that John Woodson William Dillion & Henry Dillion on the 10th Day of November Next Begin and Possession all the Lands and Renew and mark The several lines Between Muddy Creek James River Willises River and the River Road and make their Return according to Law.

Ordered that John Murrey Drurey Hudgens and John Carter Deep Run on The 10th Day of November Begin and Possession all the Lands and Renew and mark the several lines Between Muddy Creek the River Road Carters Ferry Road and the Chapel Road to Scotts Mill and make Their Return according to Law.

Ordered That Leander Hughes Ju^r. Thomas Mountegu and William Flippen on the 10 Day of November Next Begin and Possession all the Lands and Renew and Mark the several lines Between Muddy Creek to Murreys ordinary to Middle Road Carters Ferry Road and the Chappel Road and make their Return according to Law.

Ordered That Thomas Tabb William Holland & John Holland on the 10th Day of November Next Begin and Possession all the Lands and Renew and Mark the several lines Between Barnards Road Horn Quarter Road And Willises River and make their Return according to Law.

[147]   July 23rd. 1763
Ordered That John Carter Ju^r. John Newton & Francis Amos Ju^r. on the 10th. Day of November Next Begin and Possession all the Lands and Renew & mark The several lines Between Carters Ferry Road Bernards Road Willises River and the River Road and make their Return according to Law.

Ordered That Benj^a Wilson Drurey Scruggs and Robert Brown on the

10th. Day of November Next Begin and Possession all the lands and Renew and Mark the several lines Between Willises River Buckingham Road the County Line and Randolphs Creek and make their Return according To Law.

Ordered That Phenehas Glover Isham Reynolds and Joseph Price on the 10th. Day of November Next Begin and Possession all the Lands and Renew and Mark the several lines between Willises River Randolphs Creek the County Line and the River Road and Make their Return according to Law.

Ordered That Samuel Tayler Drury Woodson and Hezekiah Daverson on The 10th Day of November Next begin and Possession all the Lands and Renew and mark the several lines Between Willises River James River the County Line and the River Road and make their Return according to Law.

Order That the Churchwardens agree with some Person to Grub and Clear one acre of Land Round Ham Chappel for the safety of the said Chappel.

Edward Parrott agrees to keep Anne Amoss Comager an orphan Child He Recieved in May Last Att the Rate of five hundred Pounds of Tob" p annum.

Order That Nicholas Davies Churchwarden Enquire into the state of the Stable at the Glebe of this Parrish wheather it is or was finished according to agreement or Not and make Report to the Next Vestry.

Order That the Churchwardens with the surveyor of this County and Samuel Oslin Settle and Lay off the Bounds of the Land bought for this Parrish att Ham Chappel according to the Deed made.

Order That the Collector of this Parrish sell the Tobacco Levyed for the Use of this Parrish and account for the same when Required.

    John Baskervile   Nicholas Davies Ch Warden
    John Fleming   George Carrington
    Littleberry Mosby   Creed Haskins
    Rhoderick Easley   Thompson Swann

[148] September 29th. 1763
Att a vestry held for Southam Parrish at the Courthouse of Cumberland County the 29th Day of September 1763. Present the Reverend Robert McLaurine Minister, Nicholas Davies and Henry Macon Ch. Wardens, George Carrington, Thomas Turpin, John Baskervile, Thompson Swann, and Littleberry Mosby, Gent. Vestrymen.

Southam Parrish Debtor	Neet Tob°.	Cask
To the Rev^d. Robert McLaurine Minister	16000	640
To 6 p cent for scrinkage	960	
To John Cardwell Clk Petervile Church	1000	40
To Gideon Glen d°. of Tarwallet Church	1000	40
To Thos Freeman Fretwell d°. of Ham Chappel	1000	40
To Thos Hall d°. of South Church	1000	40
To Thos Davenport Clk Vestry	500	820
To the Cask aded	820	
To Roger Hill Sexton of Petervile Church	500	
To Susanah Easley d°. of Tarwallet d°	500	
To Rachal Farris d°. of Ham Chappel	500	
To Hester Wherley d°. of South d°	500	
To Avis Tayler for keeping & Clothing Winfield Sanders	1500	
To Francis Epperson for keeping & Clothing Reynolds Child	500	
To Poindexter Mosby for keeping & Clothing Geo. Dobing	800	
To Daniel Wilmore for keeping & Clothing Elizth Howl	800	
To Elenor Sutlieft a Poor Person	600	
To Col°. Carrington for support of Elizth Golliham	400	
To Richd Amis a poor Person of this Parrish	600	
To W^m. Basham for keeping Henry Farmer from Chrismas untill the 29th. of Augt Last	452	
To Henry Farmer Ju^r. for the support of Henry Farmer Senr. from the 29 Augt to this Date	155	
To Thompson Swann for Listing the Glebe Land	11	
To the said Swann for Copy List Tiths	98	

To the Clk Vestry for Extraordinary servises as Possessioning year	520
To [?] Parker for being twice Listed one Levy	19
To Littleberry Mosby for Insolvents	437
To the Tob° Levyed for the use of the Parrish to Pay the Cash Debt	10000
To the Collector 6 p cent for Collecting the abov	2668
To a Deposetum in the Collectors hands	640
C^r	44480
By 2780 Tiths at 16 lb Tob° p pole	44480

Debtor in Cash

To Walter Keeble for work at Petervile Church when complyed with as agreed	£ 78. 0.0
To Roger Hill for setting up horseblocks at Petervile Church and one days work	11.3
To Col°. Thomas Turpin for advertiseing in the Gazette the work to be done at Petervile Church	7.0
To Thompson Swann for Expenses in Letting the work att Petervile Church	1. 7.0
To Richard Epperson for building a gallery in South Chappel when finished according to agreement	12. 5.0
To Thomas Mountague for work to be done at Ham Chappel	26.14.8
Contra Cre^d debt.	119.4.11

By Littleberry Mosby Paid Thos Mountague	£ 26.14.8	
By d°. Paid Richard Epperson	12.05.0	38.19.8
	Ball^e Due	80. 5.3

[149] September 29th. 1763
Littleberry Mosby is appointed Collector of the above Levy he giving bond and security To the Church wardens according to Law and he is to Collect of Every Tithable Person in this Parrish 16 lb of Tob° and Pay the same to the several Parrish Creditors.

Order That Nicholas Davies agree with workmen to Repair the stable at the Glebe of this Parrish.

Nicholas Davies and Henry Macon Gent. are Continued Churchwardens for the Ensuing Year.

  Thomas Turpin   Robert McLaurine
  John Baskervile   Nicholas Davies Ch. Warden
  Thompson Swann Henry Macon Ch. Warden
  Littleberry Mosby George Carrington

      ****

Att a Vestry held for Southam Parrish at the Courthouse of Cumberland County the 27th Day of February 1765 Present the Reverend Robt McLaurine Minister, Nicholas Davies and Henry Macon Churchwardens, George Carrington, Creed Haskins, John Baskervile, Thompson Swann, Littleberry Mosby, John Fleming, and Alexander Trent, Gent. Vestrymen.

The Returns of the several Possessioners are as followeth viz:
John Murrey Drury Hudgens and John Carter to be Registered.
Samuel Tayler Drury Woodson and Hezekiah Daverson to be Registered.
William Hudgeons Gerreard Ellison and Thomas Johns to be Registered.
James Holloway John Bowden and William Rowton to be Registered.
William Clerk and William Hobson to be Registered.
Joseph Price Charles Reynolds and John Reynolds to be Registered.
Edward Watkins Abraham Baugh and Francis Cheathem to be Registered.
William Marshal Francis Marshal and Mark Tayler to be Registered.
Israel Winfrey and Joseph Baugh to be Registered.
Thomas Tabb and William Holland to be Registered.
Charles Ballow W^m. Hambleton William Davenport and Henry Harman to be Registered.
Hezekiah Mosby and John Merryman to be Registered.
John Hughes Richd James Bennet Goode and Thomas Epperson to be Registered.
Nathan Glen W^m. Anglea Ju^r. and Charles Lee to be Registered.
John Radford Ju^r. and Peter Furcrun to be Registered.
Lawrance Smith George Cox Thos. Moody And Richd Parker Ju^r to be Registered.
John Jones Henry Martin Lewis Orrange and Richd Sharp to be Registered.
George Owen John Burch and Benj^a Netherland to be Registered.

Warren Walker and James Brown to be Registered.
John Wright and John Holeman to be Registered.
Williams Daniel John Seay Wm Mills and Henry Scruggs to be Registered.
Thos Moseley John Cox and James Ligon to be Registered.
Wm Womack Mark Andrews Daniel Allen & Daniel Coleman to be Registered.
Benj^a. Wilson Drury Scruggs and Robert Brown to be Registered.
Mathew Nelson Isaac Allen and John Nelson to be Registered.
John Raines Joseph Michaux and John Chambers to be Registered.
George Radford Edward Parrott & Wm Watson to be Registered.

[150]   February 27th. 1765
George Wright Thos Williams and Robert Johns to be Registered.
Micajah Mosby Charles Finch and Robert Beck to be Registered.
Charles Anderson James Anderson and Saymore Scott to be Registered.
John Carter John Newton and Francis Amos Ju^r to be Registered.
Benj^a Hatcher and John Moseley to be Registered.
Abraham Womack Jesse Miller and W^m. Stratton to be Registered.
Jacob Michaux James Bagby and Daniel Johnson to be Registered.
John Woodson William Dillion and Henry Dillion to be Registered.
James Tayler Joseph Mosby Wm Howard and Edmon Toney to be Registered.
Jesse Carter Charles Clay and Henry Clay to be Registered.
Leander Hughes W^m. Flippin and Thos Montague to be Registered.

Southam Parrish	D^r.	Neet Tob^o.	Cask
To the Reverend Robert McLaurine Minister		16000	640
To 6 p cent for scrinkage		960	
To John Cardwell Clk Petervile Church		1000	40
To Gideon Glen Clk Tarwallet Church		1000	40
To Thos. Freeman Fretwell Clk of Ham C[h]appel		1000	40
To Thos. Hall Clk South Chappel		1000	40
To Thos. Davenport Clk of the Vestry		500	20
To the Cask aded		820	820
To Roger Hill Sexton of Petervile Church		500	
To Susannah Easley Sexton Tarwallet Church		500	
To Rachel Farris Secton Ham Chappel		500	
To Hester Wherley Sexton South Chappel		500	

To Avis Tayler for keeping and Cloathing Winfield Sanders	1500
To Francis Epperson for keeping and Cloathing Reynoldses Child	500
To Poindexter Mosby for keeping and Clothing George Dobbins	800
To Daniel Wilmore for keeping and Clothing Elizabeth Howl	800
To Henry Farmer Ju^r. for keeping and Cloathing Henry Farmer	600
To Elenor Sutlief a Poor Person	600
To Richard Amis a poor Person	600
To Col^o. Carrington for the support of Elizabeth Golliham	400
To James Allen for seven Levys Dubble listed at 19 lb Tob^o p pole in the year 1762	133
To Thos Davenport Coroner for serving a writ The Parrish vs. John Woodson	21
To Edwd. Parrott for keeping Anne Comagers Child	500
To Elizth. Wright for keeping Cannefaxes Child two years	800
To W^m. Smith for Providing for Mary Williamson a poor Person with her Children	500
To John Harvey & his wife Poor People	500
To M^r. Swann for Clk fees vs. Woodson	82
To Henry Farmer Ju^r. a further allowance for Providing for his father	200
To George Carrington for surveying Ham Chap[el] Land	350
To Littleberry Mosby for Insolvents	816
To Joseph Chandler for the support of his Child	300
To Hester Wherley a Poor Person	200
To Rachel Farris a poor Person	100
To Charles Maxey for Cleaning South Chappel after the workmen	<u>100</u>
	34682

[151]   February 27th. 1765
Southam Parrish   Debtor   Neet Tob".
To the sum brought forward   34682

To Tob° to Pay the money Debts & for the use of the Parrish	38000
To the Collector 6 p cent for Collecting 78568 lb Tob°	4714
To a depositum in the Collectors hands	1172
C^r.	78568
By 2806 Tiths at 28 lb Tob° p pole	78568

Debt^r in Cash

To John Riddle for Repairing the stable at the Glebe of this Parrish	£ 5.12.6
To Thos Montegue for work to be done at Ham Chappel when finished and Received	67. 3.11
To John Welch for takeing Care of Alex^r Mullis in his Sickness and finding a sheet to bury him in	7.14.0
To M^r. Davies the ballance of his Accompt	14.2
To William Fleming for a fee vs John Woodson	15.0
To George Carrington Gent the Bal^c of his accompt	3. 6.4½
To Littleberry Mosby Bal^c his Accompt	16.10.1½
To M^r. McLaurine for servises Done at the Glebe	1. 0.0
To Walter Keeble for work Done at Petervile Church to be paid when the work is Received	77. 0.0
To Cash towards Paying for work to be done at Tarwallet Church	15. 0.0
To Creed Haskins his Accompt	3.15.0
	198.11.1
C^r.	
By Alex^r. Trent 800 lb Tob° at 2^d Paid in Part to Littleberry Mosby	6.13.4
By John Fleming	8.11.10
By the Collector for several Oaths	15.0
	16. 0.2

Ordered that George Carrington Joseph Carrington & Littleberry Mosby who are Appointed Collectors for this year to Collect of Every Tithable Person in this Parrish 28^{lb}. of Tob°. he giveing bond and security according to law and Pay the same To the several Creditors.

Mary Bell appointed Sexton of Tarwallet in the Room of Susannah Easley. Carter Henry Harrison Elected a Vestryman in the Room of Rhoderick

Easley Who has Removed. Nicholas Davies this day Resigned his seat in vestry and thereupon W^m. Fleming Is Elected in his Room. Creed Haskins this day Resigned his seat in Vestry & thereupon Arther Mosley is Elected in his Room. Thos. Turpin & Thompson Swann are appointed Churchwardens of this Parrish for The Ensuing year. The Gentmen who let the work at the several Churches to View and Receive the same when finished.

    John Fleming   Robert McLaurine
    Alex^r. Trent   Thompson Swann C.W.
    Henry Macon   George Carrington
    Littleberry Mosby   John Baskervile

[152]   February 27th. 1765

November the 10th 1763. According to the order we the Subscribers hath bin and Possessioned Thomas Mountegues Land, himself Present. Drury Hudgenses Land, himself Present. Thomas Turpins Land, John Murrey & Drury Hudgens Present. John Murreys land, himself Present. William Terrels land, himself Present. Nicholas Davies land, Charles Barker Present. William Palmers land, John Creasea Present. John Alexanders land, himself Present. Thomas Waltons land, Charles Barker and himself Present. John Rolands land, John Creasey Present. Peter Martins [land], John Creasea and Charles Barker Present. John Carters [land], himself Present. John Scotts land, the Parties Present. John Creasea land, himself Present. Part of William Dillions and Henry Dillions land, John Creasea Present. Part of Carter Harrisons Land, Charles Barker Present. Part of Orlando Hughes Land, Thomas Mountague Present. John Woodsons land, Drurey Hudgens & John Murrey Present. Boler Cocke and Richard Ligons their lands unpossessioned.

                            John Murrey
                            Drurey Hudgens
                            John Carter

In obedience to an order of Vestry for Southam Parrish being ordered To Possession Begin the 27th Day of February 1763 and Renew the line Between Drurey Woodson and Phenehas Glover, Both Parties Present. also Between Drurey Woodson and David Pryer, Present James Gilham. Also Between Drurey Woodson and Jerimiah Cannon, Present James Gilham. Also between David Reynolds and Jeremiah Cannon, Present

James Gilham. also between Jeremiah Cannon and W^m. Rowland, Present Jo^s Gilham. also between David Reynolds and W^m. Rowland, Present David Reynolds. Also between Jo^s Gilham and Wm Rowland, Present David Reynolds. Also between Saml Tayler and Daniel Jones, Present John Parrish. Also between Daniel Jones and John Meador, Present John Parrish and James Gilham. February 28th. Renewed the lines Between Hezekiah Daverson and Samuel Tayler, Both Parties Present. also between Hezekiah Daverson and John Meador, Present Jo^s Gilliam. also between Col^o. George Carrington and Samuel Tayler, Present Capt George Carrington. Also between Col^o Carrington and Phillip Mayo, Present Capt Carrington. Also between Robert Carter and Phillip Mayo, Present James Johnson. March the 3rd Day Renewed the line Between Phillip Mayo and Bennoni Boatwright, Present Joseph Grifin. also between Boatwright and Joseph Grifin, [Present] James Johnson. a[l]so between Joseph Grifen and Phillip Mayo, Present James Robinson. March the 16th Day Renewed the line between Phillip Mayo and John Wayles, Present Jo^s. Johnson and W^m. Austin. Also between Robert Carter and John Wayles, Present Jo^s. Johnson & Wm Austin. also between C.H. Harrison and Burton Newton, Present John Jones. Also between C. H. Harrison and John Wayles, Part of the line between them and was Desird by M^r. Harrison, also by W^m. Austin in the behalf of Jno Wayles not to Possession the line between them Near the River, John Jones Present.

           Sam^{ll}. Tayler
           Drury Woodson
           Hezekiah Daverson

[153] February 27th. 1765

Whereas we the Subscribers were appointed Possessioners of all the land between Brookses Road the County line Bollings Road and the Main Road after Haveing Given publick notis according to Law for the People to show their Lines we have Possessioned the line between Gerrard Ellison and Col^o. Cary, Present M^r. James Watkins Stuard. Also a line between Gerrard Ellison & Grisham, Present James Watkins. also a line between Julius Davenport and Gerrard Ellison, Present James Watkins. also a Peace of a line between William Hudgens and John Archer, Present Robert Hudgens. also a Peace of a line between Robert Hudgens and John Archer, Present Robert Hudgens. one line between Gresham and Robert Hudgens, Present Robert Hudgens. also a peace of a line between Robert Hudgens and Joseph Calland, Present Robert Hudgens. also one line

Between Cary & John Woodson, Present James Watkins. also one line between Cary and Joseph Calland, Present James Watkins. also one line between Cary and Thomas Davenport, Present James Watkins. also one line between Cary and James Wilkins, Present James Watkins and James Wilkins. also one line between M^r. Alex^r. Trent and James Wilkins, Present James Wilkins and James Watkins. Also one line between Alex^r. Trent and Cary, Present James Watkins & James Wilkins. Also one line between Cary & Julius Davenport, Present James Wilkins and James Watkins. also one line between Thomas Johns and John Archer, Present Joseph Johns & Thos Johns Ju^r. also a line between Thos. Johns and Julius Davenport, Present Joseph Johns and Thos. John.

The Reason that the other lands in our Precincts is not Possessioned is by Reason no other Person give their attendence to shew their lines.
March 10th. 1764   William Hudgens
                                 Gerrard Ellyson
                                 Thos. Johns

In obedience to the order of vestry we the subscribers we have Possessioned and Renewed the lines (to witt). The line between Jonus Meador & Richd Murrey, Present John Meador. a line between Jonus Meador and Charles Hutchison and Hutchison Present. a line between Hutcherson & Edward Tabb. between Tabb and Jonus Meador. a line between the orphan Holloways & James Anderson, Present John Bradley. two lines between the orphans and John Bradley. a line between Bradley and James Holloway. a line between Holloway and Mark Andrew. a line between Holloway and John Bowden. A Line between Holloway and Edward Tabb. a line between James Holloway and Samuel Holloway, William Holland Present. a line between Sam^{ll} Holloway and Tabb. a line between Sam^{ll} Holloway and William Holland. a line between W^m. Holland and Edward Tabb. a line between Sam^{ll} Melton and Wm Allen. a line between Wm Allen and Thos. Allen, Samuel Melton Present. a line between Thos. Allen and James Daniel. a line between William Hix and W^m. Allen. a line between W^m. Hix and Thos Allen. a Line between W^m. Hix and James Daniel. a line Between W^m. Hix and John Burton. a line between W^m. Hix and John Burton.

[154] February 27th. 1765
A line between William Hix and William Rowton. a line between William Hix and Samuel Melton. a line between William Rowton and William Allen, Charles Holland Present. A line between William Rowton and Charles Holland. a line between Charles Holland and Mark Andrews. a line between Charles Holland & Williams Daniel. a line between William Allen and Charles Holland. a line Between William Rowton and Mark Andrews, James Adams Present. a line between John Bradley and Williams Daniel, John Bradley Present. Two lines between John Bowden and Edward Tabb, Charles Holland Present. a line between John Bowden and M^r. Fuqua. a line between Bowden and Andrews Not Done because there was No one to shew the lines.

James Holloway
John Bowden
William Rowton

We W^m. Hobson and W^m. Clerk Met on the Land of Joseph Fuqua Possessioned The line between Christopher Robinson and Fuqua, Christopher Robinson and said Fuqua Present. the line between W^m. Clerk and Fuqua, Clerk and Fuqua Present. The line between Fuqua and W^m. Mattox, Fuqua Present. The line between Christopher Robinson and W^m. Hobson Dec^d, Christopher Robinson Present. The line between W^m. Hobson Dec^d. And W^m. Clerk, W^m. Hobson and W^m. Clerk Present. The line between Jacob Macgehe and W^m. Clerke, Jacob Macgehe and Clerke Present. The line between W^m. Hobson Dec^d. and Richd Alderson, Said Alderson Present. The line between Richd Alderson and John Hobson, Richd Alderson Present. The line between Richard Alderson and Thomas Nash, Alderson and Nash Present. the line between Alderson and Robert Scruggs, Alderson Present. The line between W^m. Meanley and Alderson, Alderson Present. the line between Meanley and Robt. Scruggs, Meanley and Scruggs Present. The line between Brumskil and Alderson, Alderson Present. The line between Clerk and Brumskil, Jacob Macgehe and Clerke Present. The line between Brumskil and W^m. Hobson, Hobson Present. The line between W^m. Hobson and Frederick Hatcher, Hobson and Hatcher Present. The line between John Brown and W^m. Hobson, Brown and Hobson Present. The Line between W^m. Hobson and Robert Scruggs, Hobson and Scruggs Present. The line between W^m. Hobson and William Battersby Dec^d, Hobson Present. The line between Fed Hatcher and Batersby Dec^d, Hatcher present. The line between John Robinson and W^m

Hobson Dec^d, Robinson Present. The line between John Robinson and the land in Dispute between Tabb and Chamberlin, Robinson Present. John Mayo Gent. No attendence. Francis George Steger No attendence. the Land in Dispute Between Tabb and Chamberlin no attendence.

[155]   February 27th. 1765

M^r. John Wayles No attendence. Henry Hatcher No Attendence. Brumskil no attendence. Josiah Thomson no attendence. no attendence on The Land of William Battersby Dec^d.

William Clarke
William Hobson

May the 29th. 1764

The Precincts in the order of Vestry. We The Possessioners Divided and this is a Return of our Part.

A Just Account of the lines Possessioned Between Willises Creek Randolphs Creek the County line and the River Road. The line between George Carrington and Joseph Price, Carrington Present. the line between Phenehas Glover & the said Carrington, Carrington Present. the line between James Gilliam & the said Carrington, Carrington Present. the line between James Gilham and David Reynolds, Carrington Present. the line between Phenehas Glover and Drury Woodson, said Reynolds and Woodson Present. the line between David Reynolds and Phenehas Glover, the said Reynolds & Woodson Present. The line between Orson Martin and the said Glover, John Glover Present. the Line between Joseph Price and Orson Martin, the Possessioners Present. The line between Gid Martin and Joseph Price, Said Martin & Melton Burford Present. The line between Gid Martin & Maurice Langhorne, Melton Burford [and] Daniel Boatwright Present. The line between Alex^r. Trent and the said Langhorne, Daniel Boatwright & Melton Burford Present. The line between Joseph Price and the said Trent, Daniel Boatwright Present. The line between Jane Martin and the said Trent, Daniel Boatwright Present. The line between Joseph Glover, John Glover Present. The line Between Joseph Price & Jane Martin, John Glover present. The line between John Lewis and the said Price, The Possessioners Present. The line between Alex^r. Trent and the said Lewis, Daniel Boatwright Present. The line between John Reynolds and the said Lewis, Daniel Boatwright Present. the line Between Alex^r. Trent & John

Reynolds, Daniel Boatwright Charles Reynolds Present. The line between Drury Woodson & the said Trent, Charles Reynolds Present. The line between William Sanderson and the said Woodson, Charles Reynolds Present. the line between John Reynolds and the said Sanderson, Charles Reynolds Present.

Test. Joseph Price
John Reynolds

Our Most Obedience to the Vestry of Southam Parrish we the subscribers Have new marked all the lines between the New Road Buckingham The Church Road and Geneto Road and also New marked the line Between Edward Watkins and William Mosley both Present & agreed and also New marked the line Between Joel Locket and Thomas Locket Both Present.

[156]   February 27th. 1765
Thence between Thomas Moseley and Edward Watkins and Edward Watkins and Francis Cheathem Present, and thence new marked the line between Edward Watkins and Francis Cheathem both Present and agreed, and thence New marked the line between Isham Akin and Edward Watkins both Present and agreed, thence new marked the line between Edward Watkins and John Watkins both Present and agreed, and thence new marked The line between John Watkins and Thomas Watkins both Present & agreed, Thence new marked the line between Thomas Watkins and John Wherley Both Present and agreed, thence new marked the line between Thomas Watkins and Walter Scott both Present and agreed, thence new marked The line Between Thomas Watkins and Thomas Wooldridge & Thomas Watkins Ju^r. Present, and thence new marked the line between Abraham Baugh and Joseph Baugh Both Present and agreed, and thence new Marked the line between John Watkins and Abraham Baugh both Present and agreed, and thence new marked the line between John Watkins and William Aikin both Present and agreed, thence new marked the lines Between Henry Clay and Walter Scott Henry Clay Present, thence new Marked the line between Charles Maxey and John Mosley both Present and agreed, thence New marked the line between John Whorley & Charles Maxey both Present and agreed, thence new marked the lines between William Whorley and Charles Maxey both Present and agreed, thence New marked the line between William Wherley and Peter Furkran both Present and agreed, also between John Mosley

and Peter Furkram Present and agreed, This being all the lines within the said Bounds.

Edward Watkins
Abraham Baugh
Francis Cheatham

In obedience to an Order of vestry Dated the 23rd. Day of July 1763. we the subscribers have Possessioned the several lines as followeth Viz. The line between Creed Haskins & W^m. Marshall, Present Creed Haskins. The line between Richard Moseley and William Marshall, Present Richard Moseley. the line between W^m. & Francis Marshalls, Present Francis Marshall. the line between Francis Marshall and John Todd, Present John Todd. the line between Arthur Moseley and John Todd, Present Arther Mosley. the line between Arther Moseley and Francis Marshall, Present Arther Moseley. the line between Arther Moseley & Thos. Lockett, Present Both. the line between Thos. Lockett & Joel Lockett, Present Both. The line between Joel Locket and Edward Watkins, Present both. the line Between Arther Moseley and Gideon Lockett, Present Both. the line between Arther Moseley and Lodowick Elam, Present Both. the line between Lodowick Elam and Mark Tayler, Present Both. the line between Mark Tayler and John Northcut, Present Both. The lines between The Orphans of William Hoseley dec^d. and others not Possessioned. The lines between the Orphans of George Williamson Dec^d and others not Possessioned.

William Marshall
Francis Marshall
Mark Tayler

[157]   February 27th. 1765

We the subscribers Pursuant to an order of Court for that Purpose to us Directed Have Processioned the lines between Arther Moseley & Gideon Lockett by Consent of both, said Lockett being Present. as also between said Moseley and Christopher Bass, Present Alex^r. Bass on behalf of said Christopher. as also between said Moseley and William Chetwood, Present Gideon Locket. as also between James Baugh and Joseph [Baugh], Present Henry Moore. as also between Benjamin Bailey and James Baugh, said Moore Present. as also between Joseph Baugh and Abraham Baugh, said Abraham Present. as also between said Abraham and John Watkins,

Said Abraham Present. as also between Joseph Jackson and Jeremiah Hatcher, both Present. as also between Arther Moseley and Israel Winfrey, said Moseley Present. as also between said Arther and Jeremiah Hatcher by Consent as also between said Arther and Joseph Jackson, said Jackson Present.

Israel Winfrey
Joseph Baugh

Pursuant to an order of vestry we the subscribers have seen the Lands as under Mentioned Possessioned the lines between William Holland and Samuel Brown, also between James and Samuel Brown, also between Samuel Holloway and William Holland, also between William Holland and Butlers orphans, also Between John Minter and William Holland, also between John Minter & John Hollands Orphans, also between John Minter & Charles Fleming, also between Edward Tabb and William Holland, Also between Samuel Holloway and Butlers Orphans, also between John Bradley and Samuel Holloway, also between John Bradley and Butlers orphans, also between John Bradley and John Holloways orphans, also between Charles Fleming and Leonard Keeling, also between John Hollands Orphans [and] Leonard Keeling, Also between John Hollands Orphans and Thos Tabb, also between Benjamin Harrisons Orphans and Thomas Tabb, Also Between James Anderson and Thomas Tabb.

Thomas Tabb
William Holland
March 1764

We the appointed Possessioners have advertised Mett and Possessioned the Following lines (Viz^t). Between Joseph Jinkins and Charles Ballow, Present John Boles. Between Charles Ballow and Richard Weatherford, Present John Boles and Joseph Jinkins. Between Joseph Jinkins & Mary Jinkins, Present John Boles. Between Joseph Jinkins & Richd Weatherford, Present John Boles. Between W^m. Hambleton & Joseph Jinkins, Some Part of the line in Dispute, Present John Boles. Between William Hambleton & John Boles, Present Joseph Jinkins. Between William Arnold & John Boles, Present Joseph Jinkins & William Arnold Ju^r. between Wm Arnold and Mary Davenport, Present W^m. Arnold Ju^r. & Joseph Jinkins. between John Boles and Joseph Davenport, Present Joseph Jinkins. between Thos. Davenport Senr and John Boles, Present

Joseph Jinkins. Between Thomas Davenport Senr and Joseph Davenport, Present John Boles.

For want of attendance we have not Possessioned The whole of our Precincts.

Charles Ballow
W^m. Hambleton
W^m. Davenport
Henry Harman

[158]   February 27th. 1765

We the Subscribers Could Not Possession any of the Within Lands For want Of attendance to shew the lines.

Hezekiah Mosby
John Merryman

Pursuant to an order of Vestry held for Southam Parrish we The subscribers have begun January the Ninth 1764 and Possessioned The lines within mentioned. Begining on a line between John Fleming and John Pleasants. thence on a line between John Fleming and Joseph Johns, also between. Joseph Johns & John Pleasants, also the line between Joseph Johns & William Reynol Orphan, thence On a line between John Pleasants & John Railey, thence on a line Between John Railey and Daniel Wilmore, thence on a line Between Daniel Wilmore and John Pleasants, A short line between John Plesasants and Bennet Goode No attendance, thence on a line between Daniel Wilmore and Bennet Goode, thence On a line between Bennit Goode and John Railey, thence on a line Joining Goode & David Seizer, thence on a line Joining Goode & John Hughes, thence on a line Joining Goode and Peter Stoner, thence on a line Joining John Hughes and Peter Stoner, thence on a line Joining John Hughes and Henry Hobson, thence on a line Joining Hobson & Peter Stoner, thence on a line Joining John Pleasants & Stoner, thence on a line Joining W^m. Cox and Stoner, thence on a line Joining Paul Michaux and Stoner, thence on a line Joining John Pleasants and Stoner, thence on a line between Benjamin Netherland and Stoner, line between Charles Woodson & Stoner No attendance, also between Stoner & Mayo No attendance, thence on a line between John Railey & W^m. Renold Orphan, thence on a Line Joining David Seizer & Railey, thence on a line Joining John

Fleming and Renold, thence on a line Joining David Seizer and Renolds, thence on a line Joining John Hughes & Renold, thence on a line Joining John Hughes & Seizer, thence on a line Joining John Fleming and Hughes, thence on a line Joining John Hughes and Martha Hughes, thence on a line Joining John Pleasants and Martha Hughes, thence on a line Joining Pleasants & Henry Bagby, thence on a line Joining Pleasants & William Cox, thence on a line Joining Cox and Henry Bagby, thence on a line Joining Bagby and John Cox, thence on a line Joining John Cox & Martha Hughes, Thence on a line Joining Cox and Nicholas Wilkinson, thence on a line Joining Wilkinson & Martha Hughes, thence on a line Joining Martha Hughes and Richard James, thence on a line Joining Richd James and Nicholas Wilkinson, also a line Joining Richd James and Jacob Michaux, Thence on a line Joining Jacob Michaux & John Wilkinson, thence on a line Joining John Wilkinson and Nicholas Wilkinson, also a Line Joining Henry Hobson & John Pleasants.

John Hughes
Richard James
Bennit Goode
Thomas Epperson

[159]   February 27th. 1765
Pursuant to an order of Vestry held for Southam Parrish the 23rd. Day of July 1763 We the subscribers hath Peaceably Possessioned the following lines. The line between Col^o. W^m. Macon and Thomas Wright, also between Col^o Macon & James Dorham, Between Col^o Macon and Christopher Chafin, Between Col^o. Macon & William Anglea Senr, Between Thomas Wright and James Dorham, Between James Dorham and Francis Epperson, between W^m. Anglea Senr. & James Dorham, Between Francis Epperson & Christopher Chafin, between Christopher Chafin & W^m. Anglea Senr, Between W^m. Anglea Senr. & Flemstead Ransone, Between W^m. Anglea Ju^r. & Francis Epperson, between W^m. Anglea Senr. and William Anglea Ju^r, between W^m. Anglea Senr. & John Pleasants, between W^m. Anglea Senr. and Francis Epperson, between Francis Epperson and Thos Wright, between Francis Epperson & Edward Macgehe, between Francis Epperson & John Pleasants, between Francis Epperson & John Brown, between Edward Macgehe & John Brown, between Edward Macgehe & Charles Lee, between John Brown & John Pleasants, between John Brown and Mad^m. Mayo, between John Brown & Charles Lee, between Charles Lee & Mayo, between Charles Lee &

Thomas Johns, between Charles Lee & Christopher Chalton, between Edward Magehe & Thomas Wright, between W^m. Anglea and John Pleasants, between Gideon Glenn & Edward Macgehe, Between Gideon Glen and Joseph Calland, between Gideon Glen & Capt. Davenport, Between Capt. Davenport & Joseph Calland, between Robert Johns and Gideon Glen, between Robert Johns and Charles Lee, between Robert Johns & John Brown, between John Brown & Capt. Davenport, Between Robert Johns & Capt. Davenport, between John Brown and Abraham Chalton, What is not Possessioned in our Precincts was For want of People to shew their lines.

Nathan Glenn
W^m. Anglea Ju^r.
Charles Lee

In obedience to an order of vestry of Southam Parrish Dated the 23rd. Day of July 1763 we the Subscribers have Processioned the lines (Viz). The lines between Creed Haskins and Thomas Ballow, Ballow Present. The lines between Sam Hatcher and John Maxey, Maxey Present & Benj^a. Hatcher for Sam Hatcher. the Lines between Peter Fercran and Sam Hatcher, Benj^a. Hatcher Present for Sam and Fercran Present for himself. The lines between John Pleasants And John Maxey and Maxey Present for both Parties. the lines between William Maxey and John Maxey, John Maxey Present for both Parties. The lines between John Maxey and Humphrey Smith both Parties Present. The lines between Humphrey Smith and Thomas Ballow Both Parties Present. The lines between Nat Maxey and Thos. Ballow both Parties Present. the lines between Thos. Ballow and Pleasants, both Parties Present. the lines between John Pleasants & Jno. Radford Ju^r. both Parties Present.

[160]   February 27th. 1765

The lines between Thomas Ballow and John Radford, Ballow Present and John Radford Ju^r. for his father. the lines between Creed Haskins and John Radford, Thomas Ballow and Richard Radford Present by agreement. The lines between John Pleasants and Susanah Epperson both Parties Present. The lines between John Pleasants and Nathaniel Maxey both Parties Present. The lines between John Pleasants and Thos. Turpin Ju^r. both Parties Present. The lines between Thomas Turpin Ju^r. & Nat Maxey both Parties Present. The lines between John Smith and Nat

Maxey, Maxey Present [and] Richard Blankinship for Smith. The lines between William Maxey and James Smith both Parties Present. The lines between W^m. Maxey and Easter Langsdon both Parties Present. The lines between John Pleasants and W^m. Maxey, W^m. Maxey Present for both. The lines between Peter Fercran and John Pleasants, Fercran Present and W^m. Maxey for Pleasants. the lines between John Pleasants & Easter Langsdon, Langsdon Present & W^m. Maxey for Pleasants. the lines between Easter Langsdon & W^m. Whirley both Parties Present.

All the above lines Quietly Possessioned Given under our hands This 26th Day of March 1764

John Radford Ju^r.
Peter Fercran

Pursuant at an order of the vestry we the Subscribers have Possessioned the Bounds following Viz^t. Begining at Henry Coxes line Runing to Richard Pringles Corner, thence along the line between Pringle & M^r. Wayles and the line between Pringle & William Burton, and thence between Pringle and Henry Cox, thence the line between Henry Cox & George Cox, Thence the line between George Cox & W^m. Burton, thence the line between George Cox and Lawrance Smith, thence the line between W^m. Burton and Richard Parker Senr, thence the line between W^m. Burton & Lawrance Smith, and thence the line between W^m. Burton and Thos. Moodys lines Possessioned, Present Henry Cox Abraham Baker & Archer Austin. The line Between Josiah Thomson and Richd Parker Senr. Not Shown, Thence the Line between Frederick Hatcher & Drusilla Parker, Thence along the line Between Frederick Hatcher & Richard Parker Senr. to John Browns Corner, Thence the line between Brown & Frederick Hatcher to the Road, thence the Line between Brown and Richd Parker Senr. to a Corner, thence the Line between Brown & Benj^a. Bowles to the Road, thence the line Between James Patteson & Benj^a Bowles to the Road lines Possession^d, Present Frederick Hatcher John Brown & Henry Cox Ju^r. The line between Richd Parker Senr. & James Patteson Not shewed, the Lines between Rich^d. Parker Senr. & Drusilla Parker Not shewed, the Line between Thos. Moody & Drusilla Parker Not shewed, The line between Drusilla Parker and W^m. Burton. Possessioned Henry Cox Ju^r. & Royston Present, thence the line between Thomas Moody and Lawrance Smith Possessioned.

Lawrance Smith

George Cox
Thos. Moody
Richard Parker Ju^r.

[161]   February 27th 1765
Pursuant to an order of vestry to us directed we the subscribers have Possessioned the lines after Mentioned which is as followeth.
The line between:

Williams Daniel	& John Farmer	Present John Farmer
Henry Farmer	& W^m. Davenport	d^o d^o
Sam^ll Meridith	& d^o	d^o W^m. Arnold
Wm Watson	& d^o	d^o & David Watson
d^o	& Susannah Martin	W^m. Watson & Wm Hambleton
d^o	& Wm Hambleton	d^o & d^o
Susanah Martin	& W^m. Davenport	d^o
James Arnold	& d^o	d^o
d^o	& John Burton	William Arnold
d^o	& Lewis Orange	the Parties
Susanah Martin	& d^o	W^m. Hambleton
Humphrey Keeble	& d^o	Walter Keeble
d^o	& Susanah Martin	Humphrey Keeble
d^o	& W^m. Hambleton	d^o
d^o	& Capt. Davenport	d^o
d^o	& John Jones	d^o

No other Persons attended to shew their lines within our Precincts for Which Reason Proceeded No further February 23rd. 1764.

John Jones
Henry Martin
Lewis Orrange
Richard Sharp

In submition to order of vestry held for Southam Parrish the 23rd July 1763 have begun and Possession as between John Hyde Sanders and Mayos orphans, Col^o. Carrington Ex^r. for Mayo [orphans] and Sanders [was] Present. also between Abraham Salley and William Smith, James Brian and Smith Present. between Dock Hix & Salley Hanson, McDuel

& Brian Present. and between Hix & Smith, McDowel & Smith Present. also Between Hix & John Barns, said Smith & McDowel Present. also between Smith & Barns, The said Smith & his son Robert Smith Present. And between the said Barns & S^d Netherland Barns and George Cardwell, Barns Present. Each line between Said Netherland and Cardwell, Said Barns Present. also between William Hudspith and John Burch, both Present. also between Burch and Major Richard Pouvaul, the aforesaid Burch and Hedspeth Present. also between Burch and Henry Macon, Ambrose Ransone and Burch Present. Also between Macon and George Owen, the said Ransone and Owen Present. also between Macon & John Hide Sanders, the said Ransone and Sanders Present. also Between Sanders and John Netherland, John Low [Law?] Present. also between John Netherland & George Owen and Netherland and John Burch, Burch and George Owen the three lines Possessioned. By the Possessioners No other Present. The Above Mentioned lines Quietly Possessiond as Witness our hands.

George Owen
John Burch
Benj^a. Netherland

All lines unposessioned is as followeth: as between John Barns and John Pleasants Senr, None attended for Pleasants. also between John Netherland & John Pleasants Senr, None attended for Pleasants. also between John Netherland & Francis Macraw, Macraw fail[ed] to attend. also between W^m. Hudspith & Thos Ozburn, None attended for Ozburn. also Between Henry Macon & Randolph Orphans Land, None attended for Randolph.

George Owen
John Burck
Benj^a Netherland

[162] February 27th 1765
Pursuant to an order of vestry of Southam Parrish Dated 23rd Day of July 1763 we the subscribers have Possessioned all the Lands in our Bounds in manner and form following to witt. Between Richard Ward and Matt Nelson, Present James Archdacon. Between Matt Nelson and John Nelson, Present Isaac Duffee. between John Nelson and Flemstead Ransone Present Isaac Duffee. between Matt Nelson and Flemstead Ransone, Present James Archdecon. between said Nelson and Joseph

Hammon, Present Isaac Duffe. between said Nelson and Warren Walker, Present James Archdecon. between said Walker and Joseph Hammon, Present Isaac Duffee. between said Walker and Richard Wards Entry, Present Isaac Duffee. between Flemstead Ransone and Joseph Hammon, Present Isaac Duffee. Between Warren Walker and Valintine Corley, Present Isaac Duffee. Between said Walker and Isaac Duffee, Present W^m. Owen. between said Walker and W^m. Owen, Present W^m. Walker. Between W^m. Walker and W^m. Owen, Present John Brown. between W^m. Owen and Isaac Duffee, Present William Walker. between W^m. Owen and James Towns, Present W^m. Walker. between W^m. Walker and said Towns, Present Thomas Webb. between said Walker and Jonus Reynolds, Present Valintine Corley. between Valintine Corley and Jonus Reynolds, Present W^m. Walker. between said Corley and W^m. Anglea, Not Possessioned for want of some one to shew the line. Between Valintine Corley & W^m. Anglea Ju^r, Present W^m. Walker. between James Reynolds and Valintine Corley, Present W^m. Walker. between said Reynolds and an Entry of Richd Wards, Present Valintine Corley. between said Entry of said Corley, Present Jonus Reynolds. between James Brown and said Entry, Present W^m. Walker. between James Brown and John Brown, Present W^m. Walker. between said John Brown and Col^o. Peter Randolph, Present W^m. Walker. between James Brown and said Randolph, Present W^m. Walker. between John Brown and Natt Watkins, Present Thos. Webb. between said Watkins and Col^o. Peter Randolph, Present Thos. Webb. between Col^o. Peter Randolph and James Towns, Present Thomas Webb. between said Towns and Natt Watkins, Present John Brown.

James Brown
Warren Walker
20th Day of March 1764

Conformable to an order of vestry held for Southam Parrish the Twenty third Day of July 1763, we the subscribers have Possessioned as follows. The line between Col^o. Peter Randolph and James Brown In Presence of Zechariah Brown. the line between the said James Brown and John Pleasants in Presence of Zechariah Brown. James Anglea and the line between Zechariah Brown & John Pleasants, Present James Anglea and Zechariah Brown. between Zechariah Brown and James Brown, Present James Anglea & Zechariah Brown. the line Between John Pleasants and John Mayo, Present Ja^s. Anglea & Zech^h. Brown.

[163]   February 27th 1765
The line between John Pleasants and John Cook, Present James Anglea. Between John Pleasants and John Holoman, Present James Anglea. the line Between John Pleasants and Col°. Peter Randolph, Present James Anglea. The line between Col°. Peter Randolph and John Holoman, Present Thoˢ. Webb. The line between Col°. Peter Randolph and John Raine, Present Thoˢ Webb. Between John Raine and John Holoman, Present Thoˢ Webb. the line Between John Raine and John Cook, Present John Cook. the line between John Cook & John Holeman, Present John Cook. the line between John Cook and John Wright, Present John Cook. the line between William Shepard and John Lee, Present John Lee. the line between John Lee & John Wright, Present John Lee. the line between John Wright & John Mayo, Present John Lee. the line between John Lee & John Mayo, Present John Lee. the line between John Wright and William Sheppard, Present John Lee. the line between John Wright and Thoˢ Carter, Present John Lee. the line between W . 'Sheppard and Ambrose Wright, Present Jn⁰. Lee.

John Wright
John Holoman

Pursuant to an order of vestry for Southam Parrish bearing Date 23ʳᵈ July 1763. We Williams Daniel John Seay William Mills and Henry Scruggs did on the Tenth of November begin and Renew the lines of the Church Land, Present Daniel Coleman and Henry Harman. The lines between James Daniel and Maurice Langhorn Renewed, Present Maurice Langhorn. the lines between the said Langhorn and Daniel Coleman Renewed, Daniel Coleman & Maurice Langhorn Present. the line between Benjᵃ. Hendrick & Maurice Langhorn Renewed, Maurice Langhorn Present. the line between the said Langhorn & Henry Harman Renewed, Maurice Langhorn & Henry Harman Present. the line between Benjᵃ Hendrick & Henry Harman Renewed, both Parties Present. the line Between Henry Harman and John Tayler Renewed, Henry Harman Present. The line between John Daniel and John Tayler Renewed, Present Jn⁰ Daniel. The line between Jn⁰ Daniel & Jn⁰ Seay, both Parties Present. the line Between John Seay and Warham Easley, both Parties Present. the line Between Warham Easley and William Mills Renewᵈ, both Parties Present. The lines between Benjᵃ Hendrick & Richᵈ Barker Renewᵈ, Benjᵃ Hendrick And Jn⁰ Telphra[?] Present. the line between Anthony Levillion & Benjᵃ Hendrick Renewᵈ, Present Jo ˢ Starkie. the line between James

Brown and Richd Barker Renew^d, Present Jo.^s Starkey. the line between James Brown and Thos Guttery Renew^d, Thos Guttery Present. the line between Wm Sampson and Thos Guttery, Present Thos Guttery. the line between Archabald Cary & William Samson, Present W^m. Sampson. the line between Archabald Cary and Robert Kent Renew^d, Present Robert Kent. the line between Robert Kent and Phillip Dunford Renew^d, Present Robert Kent. the line between Robert Kent and W^m. Mills Renew^d, both Parties Present. the line between William Mills and Anthony [Le]Villion, Present W^m. Mills. the line between W^m. Bates & Henry Scruggs Renew^d, Present Henry Scruggs. the line between Henry Scruggs and W^m. Daniel Renew^d, Henry Scruggs Present. the line between the said Scruggs & Robt Hudgens Renew^d, Henry Scruggs Present. the line between the said Scruggs & Jno Bullock, Henry Scruggs Present. the line between the said Scrugg & Henry Garret Renew^d, Henry Scruggs Present. the line between the said Scruggs and Archabald Cary Renew^d, Henry Scruggs Present. the line between the said Scruggs and Robt Kent Renew^d, Henry Scruggs Present. the line between The said Scruggs and W^m. Mills Renew^d, both Parties Present. the line Between the said Scruggs and Warham Easley, both Parties Present. the line Between Warham Easley & W^m. Bates Renew^d, Warham Easley Present. the line between Warham Easley & Jno Daniel Renew^d, Warham Easley Present.

[164]   February 27th 1765
The line Between William Daniel and Wharham Easley Renewed, Warham Easley Present. the line between James Wilkins and Peter Campbell from the County line Renewed, James Wilkins Present The line between the said Wilkins and Alex^r Trent Renewed, James Wilkins Present. the line between the said Wilkins and Peterfield Trent to Bollings Road Renew^d, James Wilkins Present. Given under our hands this 30th of April 1764.
                                    Williams Daniel
                                    John Seay
                                    William Mills
                                    Henry Scruggs

We the subscribers in obedience to an order of the Vestry of Southam Parrish Dated this 23rd Day of July 1763 Have Possessioned the following Lines (Viz). The lines between John Moseley and Thos Moseley, both Parties Present. The lines between W^m. Clay and Thos Moseley, Henry

Clay Present for W^m. Clay. The lines between Henry Clay and W^m. Clay, both Parties Present. The above said Lines Quietly Possessioned Given under our hands this 15th day of March 1764.

> Thomas Moseley
> John Cox
> James Ligon

Agreeable to an order of vestry of Southam Parrish we the Subscribers have Possessioned the following lines. Beginning Att Randolphs Creek at a line Between Alex^r Trent and Tucker Woodson. A line Between Trent and James Anderson. A line between Trent & George Walton. A line between Trent and Drurey Scruggs. a line between Trent & John Jude. A line Between Drury Scruggs & Benj^a Wilson. A line between the Said Wilson and Lennard Keeling, Daniel Boatwright And Bartholomew Field Present. A line between the said Keeling and Drurey Scruggs. A line between the Said Scruggs & Robt Brown. A line between the said Brown & Lennard Keeling. A line between The said Keeling & Thos. Tabb. A line between the Said Tabb and Cary Harrison. a line between the Said Harrison & Robt Brown, Present Cary Harrison. A line between the Said brown & Arch^d Cary. A line between the Said Cary and Cary Harrison. a line Between Alex^r Trent and Robert Anderson. a line between the Said Trent & James Southall, Cary Harrison and Natha^l Morris Present. a line between the said Southall & Robt. Anderson. a line Between the said Anderson and Archabald Cary.

[165]   February 27th 1765
A line between the Said Cary and James Southall, Alex^r Trent William Sampson Robert Anderson Nathaniel Morris & Cary Harrison Present. The following lines are not Possessioned: A line between Thomas Tabb and Robert Brown Not to be found. a line between Waltho Daniel and Alex^r. Trent. A line between Cary Harrison and Joseph Woodson. A line Between the Said Woodson and Archabald Cary. A line between the said Woodson and Alex^r. Trent. No Person to show the lines.
March the 26th 1764   Benjamin Wilson
                                 Drurey Scruggs
                                 Robert Brown

We the subscribers have advertised and met and for want of attendence Could not Possession the Bounds Laid of[f] for us.

March 24th 1764 Matthew Nelson
Isaac Allen
John Nelson

In obedience to the within order we have Possessioned all the Land between Green Creek Randolphs Road and the River, Beginning at Green Creek at the line Between John Woodson and John Cook, thence between Woodson and Thomas Cocks Estate, thence between Woodson & Johnson, thence between Johnson & Cottrell, thence Between Cottrell & Aron Butler, thence between Butler & Henry Pattillo, thence Between Cottrell & Warren Walker, thence between Walker & Butler, thence between Walker & Butler, thence between Walker & Col°. Peter Randolph, thence between Butler & Col°. Peter Randolph, thence between Col°. Peter & Pattillo, thence Col°. Peter & Cocks Estate, thence between Cocks Estate & Pittillo, thence between Patillo & Johnson, thence between Cocks Estate & Johnson, thence between Woodson & Michaux, then Cottrell & Michaux, thence between Woodson and Anderson, thence between Woodson & Ambrose Wright, thence between Wright & Anderson, thence between Woodson & Michaux, thence between Anderson & Matthias Williams, Thence between Williams and Lumpkin, thence between Lumkin & Hughes, thence Between Hughes & Williams, thence between Williams & Fretwell, thence between Williams [and] Michaux, thence between Michaux and Fretwell, thence between Michaux & Chambers, Thence between Ray & Walker, thence between Walker & Michaux, thence between Michaux & Ray, thence between Michaux & Chambers, thence between Chambers and Fretwell, thence between Walker & Col°. Richd Randolph, thence between Col°. Rich^d & Ray, thence between Col°. Rich^d and Chambers, thence between Riland and Chambers, thence between Hughes and Chambers, thence between Hughes [and] Fretwell, thence between Ryland Randolph & Hughes, in the Presence of John Woodson & Charles Cottrell.
To Capt Thomas Davenport in Cumberland
John Raine
Joseph Michaux
John Chambers

[166]   February 27th. 1765
In obedience to an order of Vestry of Southam Parrish We the

subscribers Have Possessioned the following lines (Viz). The lines between Thomas Turpin and Thomas Prosser, both Parties Present. The lines between Thomas Turpin John Archer Thos. Jefferson, the said Jefferson & John Archer failed to attend. the lines between Thos. Prosser & John Pleasants, the Said Pleasants fail to attend. the lines between John Baskervile Richard Ligon John Radford Ju^r George Radford Joseph Mayo James Davis for Mayo. Joseph Bundurant John Radford Present. Creed Haskins Robert Hughes and James Holman all Parties Present. the said Thomas Prosser in the Behalf of James Holman Dec^d. Certified under our hands This 2nd Day of March 1764. also a line between George Davis and John Radford Ju^r., Davis & George Radford [Present].

George Radford
Edward Parrott
William Watson

Pursuant to an order of Vestry held for Southam Parrish the 23rd. of July 1763. Appointing the subscribers to Possession the Lands between Randolph Road the Clover Forrist Road Brooks's Road and the County line and the Owners of the Said Lands not all giving their attendence to shew their Lines we have Possessioned the several lines as followeth Viz. Between George Wright & Alex^r Trent, Thos. William and Alex^r. Trent, Richd Randolph & Alex^r. Trent, Peterfield Trent & Alex^r. Trent, Henry Bell & Alex^r. Trent, Henry Bell and John Ganaway, Thos. Davenport & Robt Johns, George Wright & Charles Williams.

George Wright
Thos. Williams
Robert Johns

Pursuant to an order of Vestry We the subscribers have Possessioned and New Marked all the lines within this order.

Micajah Mosby
Robert Beck
Charles Finch

[167] February 27th. 1765
In obedience to an order of Vestry held for Southam Parrish the 23rd Day of July 1763. we the subscribers have Possessioned the Land between Randolph and Clover Forrist Roads and the County line and is as followeth: the Lines of George Wright, William Sheppard, Ambrose

Wright, Charles Anderson, Charles Williams, Saymore Scott, Mary Richerson, Col°. Richd Randolph, James Anderson, Roger Williams, John Woodson, and Samuel Phelps.

          Charles Anderson
          James Anderson
          Saymore Scott

March Court 1764
In obedience to an order to us directed 23rd. July 1763 that we John Carter Ju^r. John Newton and Francis Amoss Ju^r. Begun and Possessioned Renewed and marked The several lines between Carters Ferry Road Bernards Road Willises River and The River Road and make Return according to Law. Sam^{ll}. Brown Refuses to Show his lines. Possession ^{d} Edmon Clements's lines, Edmond Clement Present. Robert Smiths lines, Robert Smith Present. Robert Browns lines, Robt Brown Present. John Watts's lines, John Watts Present. Andrew Edwards lines, Andrew Edw^{ds}. Present. James Gardian lines, W^m. Mason Present. Thos. Dews lines, Thos Dew Present. Anne Hill Refuses to attend. Joel Meggs's lines, Joel Meggs Present. John Robinson lines, John Robinson Present. Sam^{ll} Atkinson lines, Samuel Atkinson Present. John Jefferson Refuses to attend. John Bernard Refuses To Attend. Job Thomas lines, Job Thomas Present. W^m. Sandersons Lines, W^m. Allen Present. Jonus Meador lines, Jonus Meador Present. Jacob Winfrey Refuses to attend. Sam^{ll} Oslin lines, Sam^{ll} Oslin Present. Sam^{ll}. Bridgwater lines, Saml Bridgwater Present. John Armsteeds Lines, John Armsted Present. John Burtons lines, John Burton Present. John Salmon lines, John Salmon Present. Rachal Farris's Lines, Benj^a. Farris Present. Daniel Russel Lines, Daniel Russel Present. John Lewis lines, John Burton Present. Edm^d Prices lines, Edmond Price Present. M^r. Carter Henry Harrison, M^r. Harrison Present.. Francis Amoss Senr. lines, Francis Amoss Present. W^m. Dillion lines, Benj^a Dillion Present. Thos Bollings orphans lines, Francis Amoss Present. John Carter Ju^r. lines, John Carter John Newton and Francis Amoss Ju^r. Present. John Newton his lines, John Newton John Carter and Francis Amoss Ju^r. Present. Witness Our Hands this 26th Day of March 1764.

          John Carter
          John Newton
          Francis Amoss Ju^r.

[168] February 27th. 1765
Whereas we the subscribers being appointed Possessioners by order of Vestry. And for want of attendence Could Not Possession the Land within Our Precinct.

Cumberland
March the 25th 1764

William Womack
Mark Andrews
Daniel Allen
Daniel Coleman

January the 24th Day 1764
Then Begun to Possession To one line between Ch. Hatcher & J. Moseley. To one line between C. Henry Clay & J. Moseley Present. to one line Between Brit Randolph Dec^d. & Ben. Hatcher, J. Marcum Present. To one line between the Widdow Blackbun & Ned Haskins, W^m. Maxey Present. to one line between the Widdow Blackbun [and] James Davis, Geo D[avis]. & B. Hatcher Present. to one line between John Radford & George Davis, [both] Present. To one line between John Radford & Samuel Hobson Present. to one Line between Rich^d. Ligon and Sam^{ll} Hobson & Ben. Hatcher Present. To one line between Brit Randolph Dec^d. and Maj^r. Povaul, J. Marcum Present. To one line between Brit Randolph Dec^d. & Henry Clay, J. Marcum Present. to one line Between the Widdow Blackbun & Ben Hatcher, W^m. Maxey Present. To all the Lines in our Precincts Possession^d in Peace.

Ben. Hatcher
John Moseley

Pursuant to an order of the Vestry we the Possessioners begining at Deep Creek have Possessioned the lines as followeth: the lines Between Micajah Mosby and John Pleasants, Thos. Tucker Present. Also between Micajah Mosby & John Poindexter, Thos Tucker Present. Also between Micajah Mosby & W^m. Tucker, Thos. Tucker Present. Also Between W^m. Tucker & Archabald Hix, Thos Tucker Present. also Between Archabald Hix & John Poindexter, Thos. Tucker Present. also Between Thos. Tucker and Edward Morgan. also between Thos. Tucker & John Poindexter. All other People in Our Precincts Say they would Not have their Lines Possessioned they are Plain Enough.

Abraham Womack
Jesse Miller
William Stratton

[169]   February 27th 1765

In obedience to an order of the Vestry of Southam Parrish we the Subscribers have Possessioned all the lands and new marked all the lines within the bounds to us Prescribed (Viz). we began the eight Day of December 1763 and marked the line Between John Franklin and Charles Woodson, then the line between John Franklin and Daniel Johnson, Present John Franklin. then the line between James Bagby and Charles Woodson, Present James Bagby. then the line between Daniel Johnson and James Bagby, Present Daniel Johnson. then the line Between Anthony Minter and James Bagby. then the line between William Cox and Anthony Minter, Present Anthony Minter. then the line between William Cox and Robert Bagby. then the line between W^m. Cox & John Cox, Present W^m. Cox. then the line between John Hide Sanders & James Bagby, Present John H. Sanders. then the line between John Johnson & James Bagby. Then the line between John Johnson and Elizth. Gay, Present John Johnson. Then the line between Jacob Michaux and John Wilkinson. then the line Between W^m. Wilkinson & John Wilkinson. then the line between Nicholas Wilkinson and John Wilkinson, Present John Wilkinson. then the line Between W^m. Wilkinson and Nicholas Wilkinson. then the line between Nicholas Wilkinson & John Cox, Present Nicholas Wilkinson. then the Line between James Meredith and W^m. Wilkinson. then the line Between Elizth Gay and W^m. Wilkinson. then the line between Wm Fleming and W^m. Wilkinson. then the line between Paul Michaux and W^m. Wilkinson, Present W^m. Wilkinson. then the line between Paul Michaux & Jacob Michaux. then the line between W^m. Fleming & Jacob Michaux, Present Jacob Michaux. then the line between John Minter and William Fleming. then the line between John Minter & Wade Netherland, Present John Minter. Then the line between W^m. Fleming & Wade Netherland. then the line between Wm Fleming and John Walton, Present Wm Fleming. Then the line between John Walton and Wade Netherland, Present Wade Netherland. then the line between Wm Fleming and Elizth Gay, Present W^m. Fleming. then the line [between] Elizth Gay and James Meredith, Present James Meredith. then the line between Edward Cox and W^m. Cox. then the line between W^m. Cox and Henry Bagby, Pres^t. Henry Bagby. then the line between John Cox and Henry Bagby, Present Henry Bagby. then the line between Jacob Michaux and Paul Michaux. then the Line betweeen Jacob Michaux & John Minter, Present Jacob Michaux and John Minter. being all the lines in our Precincts in Witness Whereof we

have hereunto Sett Our hands this 20th Day of April 1764.
To Capt Thos. Davenport C.V.   Jacob Michaux
　　　　　　　　　　　　　　　James Bagby
　　　　　　　　　　　　　　　Daniel Johnson

In obedience to an order of Vestry of Southam Parrish dated the 23rd day of July 1763. we the Subscribers have Possessioned between the 10th Day of November 1763 and the last day of March 1764 the lines of the Several Persons Land in our Precincts as follows to Witt: the line between Anne Hughes and Nicholas Davies, Present Edward Arms & Nicholas Davies. the line between John Woodson & Nicholas Davies, Both Parties Present. the line between Robert Furlong & Nicholas Davies, both Parties Present. the line between Robert Furlong & Peter Martin, Present Furlong. the Line between John Woodson & Robert Furlong, both Parties Present. the line between William Dillion & Robert Furlong, both Parties Present. the line between Carter Henry Harrison and W^m. Dillion, both Present. the line between W^m. Dillion and Henry Dillion, both Present. the line between Carter H. Harrison & Henry Dillion, both Present.

[170]   February 27th. 1765
The uper line between W^m. Dillion & Henry Dillion, both Present. the uper Line between Carter Henry Harrison & W^m. Dillion, both Present. the line Between Carter Henry Harrison & John Woodson, both Present. the line between Carter Henry Harrison and George Carrington, Present Carter Henry Harrison. And the line between Carter Henry Harrison and John Witch, Present Carter Henry Harrison. Given under Our hands the thirty first day of March 1764.
　　　　　　　　　　　　　　　John Woodson
　　　　　　　　　　　　　　　W^m. Dillion
　　　　　　　　　　　　　　　Henry Dillion

In obedience to an Order of Vestry we begun to mark the Line between Benj^a. Bedford and Joseph Mosby, Benj . Bedford Present. the line between Joseph Mosby and Abraham Salley, Benj^a. Bedford Present. the line between Benj^a. Bedford and Abraham Salley, Benj^a. Bedford Present. then the line between Abraham Salley and the Glebe, Benj^a. Bedford and James Bryant Present. Then the line between Abraham Salley and Roger Hill, Benj^a. Bedford and James Bryant Present. then the line between Benj^a. Bedford & Edmond Toney, Benj^a. Bedford Present. then the line between Benj^a. Bedford and James Tayler, Benj^a. Bedford Present. then the line between Benjamin Bedford and Dunkin Robinson, Benj^a. Bedford Present. then the line Between Benj^a. Bedford and John Pleasants, Benj^a. Bedford Present. Then the line between John Pleasants and Dunkin Robinson, Dunkin Robinson Present. then the line between John Pleasants and William Farguson. then the line between Thomas Randolph and John Pleasants. then the line between Thos. Randolph & W^m. Farguson. Then the line between Mary Mayo & Edmond Toney. then the line between Edmond Toney and James Tayler. then the line between Mary Mayo and Avis Tayler. then the line between William Taylor & Avis Tayler. then the line between W^m. Howard & Avis Tayler. then The line between W^m. Howard and Thos. Randolph. then the line Between W^m. Howard and John Hyde Sanders. then the line between James Tayler and Mary Mayo, Ben^j. Netherland Present. then the Line between James Tayler and George Tayler, Benj^a. Netherland Present. then the line between W^m. Howard and James Tayler, Benj^a. Netherland Present. then the line between James Tayler and Avis Tayler. then the line between W^m. Howard & George Tayler, Benj^a. Netherland Present. then the line between George Tayler and Mary Mayo, Benj^a. Netherland Present. then the line between Bartholomew Stovall Senr. and Mary Mayo, Benj.^{a} Netherland Pres^t. Then the line between Edmond Toney & Mary Mayo, Benj^a. Netherland Present. then the line between Edmond Toney & Robert Chandler, Benj^a. Netherland Present. then the line between Benj^a. Netherland and Charles Woodson, Benjamin Netherland Present.

[171]   February 27th. 1765
The line between Charles Woodson and David Chandler, Benj^a. Netherland & David Chandler Present. then the line between Robert Chandler & David Chandler, Benj^a Netherland & David Chandler Present. then the line between David Chandler and John Walton, Benj^a Netherland & David Chandler Present. then the line between David Chandler and & William Davis, David Chandler & Benj^a. Netherland Present. then the line between John Walton & W^m. Davis, David Chandler & Benj^a Netherland Present. then the line between Mary Mayo and Robert Chandler, Jesse Chandler Present. then the line between Mary Mayo & David Chandler, Benj^a Netherland [&] David Chandler Present. then the line between Mary Mayo & John Walton, Jesse Chandler Present. then the line between Edmond Toney & and Bartholomew Stovall Senr. then the line between

Benj^a Netherland and John Pleasants. then the line betwen John Peasants and Paul Michaux, W^m. Scott Present. then the line between John Pleasants and James Bagby, James Bagby Present. then the line between John Franklin & John Hyde Sanders, John Franklin Present. then Between John Franklin & Bat Stovall Ju^r, John Franklin Present. then Between John Hyde Sanders & Barthomew Stovall Ju^r., John Hyde Sanders present. then between John Hyde Sanders & George Gaddey, John Hyde Sanders Present. then Between George Gaddey & Bartholomew Stovall Ju^r, John Hyde Sanders & George Gaddey & Bartholomew Stovall Ju^r Present. then between Bartholomew Stovall Senr & Bartholomew Stovall Ju . 'Both Present. There is an old inn line in the lands belonging to Avis Tayler forbid being Possessioned by W^m. Farguson. Given under our hands This 2nd Day of March 1764.

         James Tayler
         Joseph Mosby
         William Howard
         Edmond Toney

January 9th. 1764
Charles Clay Henry Clay & Jesse Carter do Possession the lines between William Daniel and Henry Cox, George Cox & Jo. Cox Present. also between W^m. Daniel and Martha Hughes, Henry Cox & Joseph Cox Being Present. likewise between W^m. Daniel and Judith Cox, Henry Cox [&] W^m. Cox Present. also between Martha Hughes & Judith Cox, W^m. Daniel [&] Henry Cox Present. Charles Clay [and] Henry Clay do Possession Between Capt. Poindexter Mosby & John Phelps. also between John Netherland & Joseph Woodson, Capt. Mosby Present & John Netherland and John Phelps. Capt Mosby being Present also between Joseph Woodson & John Netherland. between Joseph Woodson & Henry Clay. Between Francis Macraw & John Phelps, Capt. Mosby Present. Between Capt Poind^r Mosby & Henry Clay in the Presence of John Phelphs Francis Macraw & Thos. Wilks.

         Jesse Carter
         Charles Clay
         Henry Clay

[172] February 27th. 1765
We the appointed Possessioners betwen Muddy Creek Carters Ferry Road and the Middle Road and Chappell Road have bin according To order and

Possessioned such lines as we found (to Witt.): the line between John Pleasants and Sampson Fleming, Sampson being Present. also Between the Said Sampson & Jacob Winfrey, Sampson being Present. also between W^m. Hughs Dec^d. and Sampson, the same Present. the line Between W^m. Hughes Dec^d & John Watts, Simon Hughes Present. the Line between d^o. & W^m. Hudgens Orphan, d.^{o} Present. the line between D. & John Merryman Ju^r, d^o. Present. the line between d. & Jacob Winfree, d. Present. also the line between Robert Duglass and W^m. Hudgens Orphan, Robert Duglas Present. the line between D^o. & W^m. Sampson, d^o. Present. the line between d^o. & James Hudgens Orphan, d. 'Present. the line between d^o. & W^m. Fleppin, D.^{o} Present. the line between d.^{o}& Ralph Flippin, d^o. Present. also the line between Ralph Flippin & John Merryman Ju^r, Ralph Flippin Present. the line between d^o. & W^m. Flippin, d^o Present. The line between d.^{o}& Tho. Walton, d Present. the line between W^m. Flippin and Tho 'Walton, W.^{m}Flippin Present. the line between d^o. & James Hudgens orphan, d^o. Present.. the line between d^o. & Thos. Montague, d^o. Present. also the line between Leander Hughes and Thos. Montague, Leander Hughes Present. the line between d'. & Orlando Hughes, D^o. Present. the lines between d^o & Boler Cocke, d^o Present. the line Between d^o. & Thos Walton, d^o. Present. also the line between Drurey Hudgens & W^m. Clerk, Drury Hudgens Present. the line between d.^{o} & James Drake, d^o Present. the line between d^o & Meador, d^o. Present. the line between D^o. & James Hudgens orphan, d^o. Present. the line between d^o & Thos. Montague, d.^{o} Present. the line between James Hudgens & Thos. Montague, Drurey Hudgens Present. The lines which are not Possessioned are as followeth (to Wit): the line between W^m. Holland and John Pleasants because Pleasants lives Out of the Precincts & Holland Refused To go. also between Edward Clements & Holland because they both Refused to go. also between Clements & Pleasants for the former Reason. also between Pleasants & Jacob Winfrey because both lives out of the Precincts & Did not know when we Possessioned. also between John Merryman Ju^r. [and] Jacob Winfrey because Merryman Refused to go. also Between John Merryman & W^m. Hudgens for the same Reason. also Between John Watts & William Hudgens because Watts lives out of the Precincts and there was None to shew Hudgens's line. also Between Watts and W^m. Sampson for the same Reason. also between James Hudgens and Meador Because both Parties were absent. Also Between Meador and James Drake for the same Reason. Also between James

Drake and William Clerk for the same Reason.

[173]   February 27th. 1765
And if there Rimains any More we dont Remember them.

Leander Hughes
William Flippin
Thomas Montague

****

Att a vestry held for Southam Parrish at Cumberland County Courthouse the 27th January 1766. Rev^d. Robert McLaurine Minister Present, Thomas Turpin & Thompson Swann Church Wardens, George Carrington, John Baskervile, Wade Netherland, Alexander Trent, John Fleming, Littleberry Mosby Gent Vestrymen. George Carrington Junr. is appointed Clerk of this Vestry. William Fleming Being Elected a Vestryman of this Parrish Subscribing according to Law, Present Mr Wm Fleming.

Southam Parrish Deb^r.	Neet Tob^o.
To the Rev^d M^r McLaurine Minister Sallery & Cask	17600
To John Cardwell Clk of Petervile Church	1040
To Gideon Glen Clk of Tarwallet Church	1040
To Thos Freeman Fretwell Clk Ham Chappel	1040
To Thomas Hall Clk South Church	1040
To Amey Hill Sexton of Petervile Church	500
To Rachal Farris Sexton of Ham Chappel	500
To d^o. for Clearing Round Ham Chappel	100
To d^o. a poor Person	100
To Mary Bell Sexton of Tarwallet Church	500
To Hester Wherley sexton of South Chappel	500
To d^o. a Poor Person	200
To Avis Tayler for keeping Winfield Sanders	1500
To Francis Epperson for keeping Reynolds's Child	500
To Poindexter Mosby for keeping George Dobings	800
To Daniel Wilmore for keeping Elizth Howl	800
To Henry Farmer Ju^r for keeping Henry Farmer	800
To Eleanur Sutlief a Poor Person	600
To Thos Turpin for Richd Amis a Poor person	600
To Edward Parrott for keeping Comagers Child 3 months	150

To Elizth Wright for keeping Cannefaxes Child	400
To John Harvey and wife Poor People	500
To Joseph Chandler for support of his Child	300
To Mary Bell a poor Person	100
To Mary Speirs a poor person	500
To John Franklin for 1 tithe wrong Listed last year	28
To Joseph Calland for the support of Mary Childres	500
To George Carrington Clk Vestry this Day	250
To Thos Davenport late Clerk	250
To Joseph Carrington for Insolvents	1574
To Littleberry Mosby for Insolvents	712
	35024

[174] January 27th. 1766
Southam Parrish Deb^r. Cash & Neet Tob°.

To the Sum due brought forward		35024
To John Watts Constable for Removing Judith May a poor Person to Antrim Parrish, Halifax County	4. 0.6	336
To James McDowel for a Table Cloth	1.18.0	
To W^m. Whorley for work Done at South Church in horse blocks steps &c.	10. 3.0	
To Thos Montague for work to be done at Tarwallet Church to be Paid when Done & Receiv^d	12.16.0	
To Thos Montague for bal^c Due for work Done at Ham Chappel to be Paid when work Received	2. 7.0	
To Amey Hill for Clearing Round Peterville Church & Eight Benches at said Church	1.10.0	
To Benj^a. Mosby for Bread & wine use Ch	4.14.6	
To 100£ in the Collectors hands to be Laid out as The Vestry shall Direct towards Lessening the Tob° Charge Supposed at 12000 lb Tob°	100. 0.0	
To the Collector for Collecting 25795 lb Tob°		1548
To the Depositom in the Collectors hands		887
Bal^c in money in he Collectors hands	21.18.4	
	159. 7.4	37795

Southam Parrish C^r.
By Cash in the Collectors hands	134. 5.6
By d°. in d°. for work to be done at Tarwallet Last year	15. 0.0

By George Carrington Ju^r. for fines Recv^d for 2 Oaths	10.0	
By Littleberry Mosby for fines Recv^d for 4 Oaths	1. 0.0	
By do for Cash Recv^d of Col^o. Fleming	8.11.10	
	159. 7.4	
By £100 Supposed in Tob^o		12000
By 2865 Tiths at 9 lb Tob^o p pole		25795
		37795
By Bal^c in money in the Collectors hands	£ 21.18.4	

George Carrington Littleberry Mosby & Joseph Carrington appointed Collectors and ordered that they give bond and security to the Churchwardens and that they Receive of Every Tith in this Parrish 9 lb of Tob^o. and Pay The Creditors above as far as the same will Pay.

Order^d That a 12 feet shed be made to one End of the Glebe house to be in length Equil to the Breadth of the house with one Chimney with two fire Places and that M^r. Swann M^r. Baskervile & M^r. Mosby or any Two of them Employ some Person to do the same.

Order^d That three Porches be built at Petervile Church and that Mr Baskervile M^r. Swann & M^r. Mosby or any two of them Employ some Person to Do The same.

The Vestry being infomed that Thos. Freeman Fretwell Clk of Ham is a Person of Disorderly by behavour it is ordered that he appear at the Next Vestry To answer the same.

M^r. Turpin and M^r. Swann Continued Church wardens the Ensuing year.

   John Fleming   John Baskervile
   Robt. McLaurine   Littleberry Mosby
   Wade Netherland   Thos. Turpin C. W
   W^m. Fleming   Alex^r. Trent
   Thompson Swann C W George Carrington

****

[175] May 26th. 1766

Att a Vestry held for Southam Parrish the 26th. Day of May 1766. Present Thomas Turpin and Thompson Swann Church wardens, George

Carrington, John Baskervile, Alex^r. Trent, John Fleming, Littleberry Mosby & W^m. Fleming Gent Vestrymen.

It appearing that the money alloted by the Vestry at the Laying the Last Levy for Discharging 12000 lb Tob^o. Part of the said Levy will fall short in Discharging the same the Collectors are Empowered to Purchase the Tob^o. to the Amount of the said 12000 lb of Tob^o. upon the best Terms he Can to be applyed In discharge of so much of the said Levy.

Thos. Turpin C. W	Thompson Swann C. W
George Carrington	John Fleming
John Baskervile	Alex^r. Trent
Littleberry Mosby	William Fleming

****

Att a Vestry held for Southam Parrish at Cumberland County Court House the 17th Day of March 1767 for Laying the Parrish Levy. Present Thos. Turpin and Thompson Swann Church Wardens, George Carrington, John Baskervile, John Fleming, Wade Netherland, Henry Macon, Littleberry Mosby & William Fleming Gent Vestrymen.

Thomas Davenport Ju^r is appointed Clerk of the Vestry.

Southam Parrish D^r.	lb Neet Tob^o.
To the Rev^d. Robert McLaurine Minister his Sallery	16000
To d^o. for Cask	640
To d^o. 4 p cent for scrinkage	640
To John Cardwell Clk of Petervile Church	1040
To Gideon Glen Clk Tarwallet d^o	1040
To Thos Freeman Fretwell Clk Ham d^o.	1040
To Thos Hall Clk of South d^o	1040
To Amey Hill Sexton of Petervile Church	500
To Hester Wherley d^o. of South d^o. 500 & as poor 200	700
To Mary Bell d^o. of Tarwallet d^o	500
To the adm^r. of Rachal Farris d^o. of Ham d^o	500
To Avis Tayler for keeping Winfield Sanders	1500
To Francis Epperson for keeping Reynoldses Child	500
To Poindexter Mosby for keeping George Dobings	800

To Daniel Wilmore for keeping Elizth Howl	800
To Henry Farmer Ju^r for keeping Henry Farmer	800
To Elenor Sutlief a Poor Person	600
Thos. Turpin for Richd Amis a Poor Person	600
To Elizth Wright for keeping Cannefaxes Child	400
John Harvey and wife poor people	500
To Joseph Chandler for support of his Child	300
To Mary Bell a Poor Person	100
To Mary Speirs a Poor person	500
	31040

[176] March 17th Day 1767.
Southam Parrish D^r.   Neet Tob^o.

To the sum brought forward	31040
To a further allowance to Col^o Turpin for keeping Richd Amis	200
To Benj^a Mosby for keeping Francis Porter two months	406
To Littleberry Mosby for 23 Insolvents	207
To Joseph Carrington for Insolvents	106
To Thomas Davenport Clk Vestry	800
To Tob^o Levyed to Pay the Cash Debt	8000
To the Collector his Sallery at 6 p cent	2445
To a Depositum in the Collectors hands	1616
	44820

C^r.

By 2988 Tiths at 15 lb Tob^o p pole	44820

D^r. in Cash

To Amey Hill for Railing under Petervile Church	£ 1.10.0
To Thomas Davenport his accompt for Mary Childres a poor Person	18.9
To d^o for the Cure of Elizth. Henderson a poor Person	5. 0.0
To Littleberry Mosby for the Difference between 2^d p pound and 18/ p hundred on 12000 lb Tob^o for the Parrish	8. 0.0
To d^o. for his Expenses in Doing the same	1. 0.0
To Thos. Walton Ju^r for keeping the Widdow Finch & her Children to this time	5. 0.0
To Benj^a. Mosby for supplying the Churches with Bread and wine and for the three Porches and some Other work Done at Petervile Church	20. 9.9

To Levyed for the use of this Parrish for Paying
Thos. Montague his Ballance for work at the Glebe
When finished he haveing Received he haveing Received
Twenty Pounds in Part of Littleberry Mosby late Coll^r. 26. 0.0
                                                        67.18.6

It apprearing to this Vestry that there is Levyed through Mistake To the Reverend Robert McLaurine four thousand four hundred & Eighty Pounds of Tob^o. he agrees to Pay for the same at twelve shillings & six Pence p hundred when Required.

John Barns is appointed Clerk of Petervile Church in the Room of John Cardwell.

Richard Crump and William Turpin is appointed Collectors For this Parrish of Southam and it is Ordered that they Give Bond and Security According to Law and that they Collect 15 lb. of Neet Tob^o. of Every Tithable Person in this said Parrish and Pay the Creditors Above as far as the same will Pay.

[177]   March 17th Day 1767
William Fleming and Alex^r. Trent are appointed Church Wardens for the Ensuing year.

Ordered That the Collectors Pay Henry Macon one thousand Pounds of Tob^o. out of the Depositum in His hands for the use and Support of Henry Harman and his Family.

Wade Netherland Gent Resigns his Seat in this Vestry and John Netherland Gent Is Elected Vestryman in the Room of the said Wade Netherland.

Henry Macon Gent Resigns his Seat in this Vestry and Maurice Langhorn Gent is Elected in his Room.

   Robert McLaurine W^m. Fleming C.W.
   George Carrington Thos. Turpin
   John Baskervile   John Fleming
   Thompson Swann Littleberry Mosby

****

Att a Vestry for Southam Parrish at the Courthouse of Cumberland County The 20th. Day of November 1767 for Laying the Parrish Levy.

Present the Rev^d. Robert McLaurine, W^m. Fleming and Alexander Trent C. W., George Carrington, Thos. Turpin, John Baskervile, Thompson Swann, Littleberry Mosby, John Netherland, Carter Henry Harrison & Arther Moseley Gent Vestrymen.

John Railey is Elected a Vestryman in the Room of Col^o. John Fleming Dec^d.

Southam Parrish Deb^r.	Neet Tob^o
To the Reverend Robert McLaurine Minister	16000
To d^o for Cask	640
To do. 4 p cent for scrinkage	640
To John Barns Clk Petervile Church	1040
To Gideon Glen d^o. of Tarwallet d^o	1040
To Thos Freeman Fretwell d^o. of Ham d^o	1040
To Thos. Hall d^o. of South d^o	1040
To Amey Hill Sexton Petervile Church	500
To Hester Wherley d^o. of South d^o. 500 & as poor 200	700
To Mary Bell d^o. of Tarwallet d^o 500 & as poor 100	600
To W^m. Palmer Sexton of Ham d^o	500
	23740

[178]   November 28th day 1767

Southam Parrish	Deb^r.	lb Neet Tob^o.
To the sum brought forward		23740
To Avis Tayler for keeping Winfield Sanders		1500
To Francis Epperson for keeping Reynoldses Child		500
To Daniel Willmore for keeping Elizth Howl		800
To Henry Farmer Ju^r for keeping Henry Farmer		800
To Elenor Sutlief a poor Person of this Parrish		600
To Col^o. Thos. Turpin [for Richd Amis] a Poor Person of this d^o		800
To Elizth Wright for keeping Canafaxes Child		400
To John Harvey and wife Poor People		500
To Joseph Chandler for the support of his Child		300

To Mary Speirs a Poor Person of this Parrish	500
To Francis Macraw for keeping & Cloathing George Dobings and the said Macraw agrees to keep and Cloath the Said Dobins for 400 lb Tob° p annum	400
To Arther Moseley for the support of John Bailey For the Ensuing year	600
To Amey Hill for the support of Marmaduke Hix and His wife for the Ensuing year	1500
To Alex^r Trent for keeping Francis Porter the year Past	1000
To W^m. Price for keeping and Clothing Francis Porter for the Ensuing year & Paying M^r. Trents accompt against the said Porter for some goods Received	1500
To W^m. Turpin for 29 Insolvents at 15 lb Tob°. p pole	435
To Thos Davenport Clk of the Vestry	1000
To Edward Parrott for keeping Ann Amis Comager for Last year and the Present year	1000
To Elizabeth Wright a poor Person of this Parrish	1000
To Tob°. Levyed to Pay the Cash Debt	2500
To the Collector for Collecting the above	2482
To a Depositum in the Collectors hands	1143
	45000

By 3000 Tiths at 15 lb Tob° p pole   45000

Deb^r in Cash

To Benj^a Mosby for supplying three Chruches with bread and Wine this Present year	£ 2. 5.0
To Arther Moseley for supporting John Bailey	1.19.11
To Robert Bisco for Makeing a Coffin for Mary Williamson a poor person	10.0
To Alex^r Trent for Glass Puttey & Nails for the use of the Churches	6. 4.0½
To Amey Hill for supporting Duke Hix and his wife to this Date and five Shillings for a fine for a per of shoes Paid by W^m. Smith brought in	3. 0.0
	19. 4.11½

[179] November 28th. day 1767
Ordered that the Rev^d. Robert McLaurine Purchase two Prayer books for the use of this Parrish.

William Turpin and Richard Crump are appointed Collectors for the Ensuing year on their giveing bond and security according to Law and ordered that they Collect of Every Tithable Person in this Parrish 15 lb. of Neet Tob°. and Pay the same to the Parrish Creditors.

William Fleming and Alex^r. Trent are Continued Church wardens for the Ensuing year.

Littleberry Mosby	Robert McLaurine
Arther Moseley	Alexander Trent C. W
Carter Henry Harri[s]on	William Fleming C. W
N[J]ohn Netherland	John Baskervile
	Thompson Swann

****

Att a Vestry held for Southam Parrish at the Courthouse of Cumberland County the 10th Day of February 1769. Present the Reverend Robert McLaurine Minister, Alex Trent and W . Fleming C.W. George Carrington, Thos. Turpin, Thompson Swann, Littleberry Mosby, John Netherland and Carter Henry Harrison Gent. Vestrymen.

Southam Parrish	Deb^r.	Neet Tob^o.
To the Reverend Robert McLaurine Minister		16000
To d°. for Cask		640
To d°. for Scrinkage 4 p cent		640
To John Cardwell Clk of Petervile Church		1040
To Gideon Glen Clk of Tarwallet Church		1040
To Thos. Freeman Fretwell Clk of Ham Church		1040
To Thomas Hall Clk of South Church		1040
To Amey Hill Sexton of Petervile Church		500
To Mary Bell Sexton of Tarwallet d°. 500 & as poor 100		600
To Hester Wherley. d°. of South d° 500 & as poor 200		700
To William Palmer d°. of Ham d°		500
To Avis Tayler for keeping Winkfield Sanders		1500
To Francis Epperson for keeping Reynoldses Child		500

To Daniel Wilmore for keeping Elizth Howl	800
To Henry Farmer Ju^r for keeping Henry Farmer	800
To Elenor Sutlief a Poor Person	600
To Col^o. Thos. Turpin for Richd Amis a poor Person	800
To Elizth Wright for keeping Cannefaxes Child	400
To the Widdow Harvey a poor Person	500
To Joseph Chandler for support of his Child	300
To Mary Speirs a Poor Person	500
	30440

[180]   February 10th Day 1769

Southam Parrish	Deb^r.	Neet Tob^o
To the Sum brought forward		30440
To Edward Parrott for keeping Ann Amis Comager		500
To Elizth Burnet a poor Person		200
To George Carrington Ju^r for John Witch a Poor Person		500
To Thomas Holland for keeping Jesse Holland twelve Months B[a]rsheba Holland five months & Stephen Holland three months orphans of Charles Holland Dec^d		1000
To James Hollaway for keeping Barsheba Holland Eight months orphan of Charles Holland Dec^d		200
To W^m. Turpin for insolvents		330
To Richd Crump for Insolvents		30
To Thos Davenport Clerk of the Vestry		1000
To Susannah Easley for being Sexton of Tarwallet Church in the year 1765		500
To W^m. Palmer for two setts of horse blocks at Ham Ch		100
To Tob^o Levyed to Pay the Cash debt		1000
		35800
To the Collector for Collecting the above		2148
To a Deposetum in the Collectors hands		2560
		40508

C^r.

By 3116 Tiths at 13 lb Tob^o p pole   40508

Debt[r] in Cash
To Alex[r]. Trent & C[o]. for W[m]. Price	£ 2.10.0
To Benj[a] Mosby for supplying the several Churches in the Parrish with bread & wine	3. 6.0
To Jinkins Jinkins for Carrying Hollands Orphan to Docter Cable	15.0
To George Carrington Ju[r] for sundrys for the use of John Witch	1. 2.4
To Col[o] Carrington for 3½ yards of cotton for John Witch	<u>7.4</u>
	8. 0.8

William Turpin & Jesse Thomas are appinted Collectors for the Ensuing year on their giveing bond and security to the Church wardens and Order[d]. That they Collect of Every Tithable Person in this Parrish 13 lb of Neet Tob[o]. and Pay the same to the Parrish Creditors.

John Netherland & Arther Mosely are appointed Church wardens for the Ensuing year.

Carter Henry Harrison Resigns his seat in this Vestry & George Carrington Ju[r]. is Elected a Vestryman in his Room.

Order[d]. That Col . [o]George Carrington & George Carrington Ju . settle with the Late Collectors for the two last years and Receive the ball[c] Due to this Parrish in their hands and also with the Present Collectors for this year.

Order[d]. That Thompson Swann & John Netherland Agree with workmen to fix benches in the New Building and stop the Leaks in Petervile Church.

George Carrington	Robert M[c]Laurine
Thompson Swann	Alex[r] Trent C.W
Littleberry Mosby	W[m]. Fleming C.W
John Netherland	Tho[s] Turpin

[181]   February 15th. Day 1770
Att a Vestry held for Southam Parrish at the Courthouse of Cumberland County the 15th Day of February 1770. Present John Netherland Churchwarden, George Carrington, Thos Turpin, John Baskervile, Littleberry Mosby, Thompson Swann & Wm Fleming Gent Vestrymen.

Southam Parrish	Debr. lb Neet Tobo.
To the Revd. Robert McLaurine Minister	16000
To do for Cask	640
To do. 4 p cent for scrinkage	640
To John Barns Clk of Petervile Church	1040
To Gideon Glen do. of Tarwallet do	1040
To Thos Hall Clerk of South Church	1040
To Amey Hill Sexton of Petervile Church	500
To Mary Bell do. of Tarwallet do. 500 & as poor 100	600
To Esther Whorley do. of South do. 500 & as poor 200	700
To William Palmer do. of Ham do	500
To Avis Tayler for keeping Winfield Sanders	1500
To Francis Epperson for keeping Reynoldses Child	300
To Daniel Wilmore for keeping Elizth Howl	800
To Henry Farmer Jur for keeping Henry Farmer	800
To Elenor Suitlief a Poor Person	600
To Colo. Turpin for Richd Amis a Poor person	800

John Railey & George Carrington Jur. this Day subscribed
   The Test in Vestry according to Law.
Present John Railey & George Carrington Jur Gent Vestrymen

To John Cook for keeping & Clothing Richd Tatum a Poor Person	800
To John Wright for keeping Cannefaxes Child	400
To the Widdow Harvey a Poor person	500
To Joseph Chandler for support of his Child till it died	150
To Littleberry Mosby towards defraying the Charges of Mary Speirs Decd	500
To John Minter for keeping Francis Porter	1500

To George Carrington Ju[r]. for Eliz[th] Burnet	200
To Jesse Thomas for 200 [20] Insolvents at 13 lb Tob[o] Each	260
To W[m]. Turpin for Insolvents	286
To Tho[s] Davenport Clk of the Vestry	1000
To William Dillion for the support of his mother	500
To the Estate of Tho[s] Freeman Fretwell late Clerk of Ham Church six months	520
To Joseph Palmer Present Clerk of Ham Church	520
To Tob[o] Levyed for the use of the Parrish	6765
To the Collectors 6 p cent for Collecting 44044 lb Tob[o]	2643
	44044

C[r].
By 3146 Tiths at 14 lb Tob[o] p pole   44044

Deb[r] in Cash
To Robert Murrey for Necessarys for Duke Hix	£ 1.17.6
To Benj[a] Mosby for Bread and wine for the several Churches	2.18.6
	4.16.0

[182]   February 15th. Day 1770
Southam Parrish   Deb[r]. in Cash
To the sum brought forward	£ 4.16.0
To Francis Amoss for sundeys supplyed his Fathers family in the time they had the small Pox	2.17.0
	7.13.0

Ordered That Col[o] George Carrington Pay the above Cash Debts out of the Money That is in his hands.

Ordered That Jesse Thomas and George Jude be appointed Collectors of the above Levy they giving Bond and Security to the Church wardens according to Law and that they Collect of Every Tithable Person in This Parrish 14 lb of Neet Tob[o] and Pay the same to the several Parrish Creditors.

Edward Haskins is Elected a Vestryman in the Room of Arther Moseley Dec[d].

John Railey is appointed Church Warden with John Netherland in The Room of Arther Moseley Dec^d.

Ordered That Littleberry Mosby W^m. Fleming & George Carrington Ju^r Purchase a Tract of Land Not Exceeding one hundred acres and to Employ Persons to Erect Necessary houses thereon for the Reception of the Poor of this Parrish and also to settle with the Collectors.

Thompson Swann	John Netherland C.W
W^m. Fleming	John Railey C.W
Littleberry Mosby	George Carrington
George Carrington Ju^r.	John Baskervile

****

Att a vestry held for Southam Parrish att the Courthouse of Cumberland County the 20th Day of March 1771. Present John Netherland Church warden, Thomas Turpin, John Baskervile, Littleberry Mosby, Thompson Swann, William Fleming, George Carrington Ju^r, & Alexander Trent Gent. Vestrymen.

Southam Parrish	D^r.	Neet Tob^o.
To the Rev^d. Robert McLaurine Minister		16000
To d^o. for Cask 640 & to d^o. for scrinkage 640		1280
To John Barns Clk Petervile Church		1040
To Gideon Glen Clk Tarwallet Church		1040
		19360

[183]   March 20th day 1771

Southam Parrish	Deb^r.	Neet Tob^o.
To the Sum brought forward		19360
To Joseph Palmer Clk of Ham Church		1040
To Thomas Hall Clk of South Church		1040
To Amey Hill Sexton of Petervile Church		500
To Mary Bell d^o. at Tarwallet 500 & as Poor 100		600
To William Palmer d^o. at Ham d^o.		500
To Easter Wherley d^o. at South d^o 500 and as Poor 200		700
To Thomas Davenport Clk of the Vestry		1000
To Avis Tayler for keeping & Clothing Winfield Sanders		1500

To Daniel Wilmore for keeping Elizabeth Howl	800
To Edward Parrott for keeping Richard Amis	800
To Henry Farmer Ju^r. for keeping Henry Farmer	800
To Elenor Sutlief a Poor Person of this Parrish	600
To Francis Macraw for keeping & Clothing George Dobins two years to this time	800
To Edward Jinkins for keeping Francis Porter	1500
To George Carrington Ju^r. for the support of Elizabeth Burnet a Poor person	350
To William Dillion for the Support of his Mother	800
To Edward Parrott for keeping Ann Amis [Comager] the two years past	1000
To Amey Hill for keeping Duke Hix the two years Past	1500
To John Netherland for the support of Letteshe Cardwells Children	800
To Thomas Strange for the support of his two unfortunate children	800
To William Tucker for one Levy Rong listed	14
To Thos Tucker for keeping Sarah Rogers to this time with a Child of three years old	350
To Thos Holland for keeping Charles Hollands orphans the two years past	1600
To W^m. Stratton for one Levy Rong Listed	13
To Thos Holland a further allowance for keeping Charles Hollands orphan	400
To Jesse Thomas for 17 Insolvents at 14 lb Tob^o Each	266
To the Collector for Collecting the above 6 p cent	2314
To a Depositum in the Collectors hands	1809
	43556

C^r.
By 3213 Tiths at 12 lb Tob^o p pole	38556	
By Bal^c Cash supposed to be sufficient To purchase Tob^o	5000	43556

Deb^r. in Cash
To Amey Hill for mending a Chest	£ 0. 2.6
To Doctor W^m. Cable for keeping and trying to Cure Stephen Holland for a cancer in his mouth	36. 9.4

To Alex.r Trent for providing Necessarys for Rebecca Goff as p accompt	1. 6.3
To Benj.a Mosby for supplying the several Churches with Bread and wine	3. 2.6
To George Carrington Ju.r for Necessarys for Elizabeth Burnet Last year	0.10.6¾
To Robert Smith for Six Benches and two hors blocks at Tarwallet Church	2.10.0
To Thomas Holland for keeping and Clothing Stephen Holland orphan of Charles Holland to this time	1.19.6
	46. 0.7¾
C.r	
By Bal.c of Cash	£ 50. 1.4¼
By Bal.c in the hands of L. Mosby for the Tob.o Levyed Last year for the use of the Parrish	76. 2.0
Supposed a bal.c of Cash in the Hands of Col.o Carrington	20. 0.0
	146. 3.4¼

[184] March the 20th Day 1771
Ordered That Jesse Thomas and William Hill is appointed Collectors of the Above Levy they Giveing Bond and Security to the Church wardens according To Law and that they Collect of Every Tithable in this parrish Twelve Pounds of Tob.o and Pay the same to the several parrish Creditors as far as the same will go.

M.r M.cLaurine Minister   C.r
By two prayer books for the use of the Churches out of the money in his hands   £ 3.13.0

Order.d That John Netherland and Littleberry Mosby agree with workmen To Repair the Garden at the Glebe M.r McLaurine Paying for the Same out of the money in his hands.

Order.d That the Collectors pay John Cook one thousand Pounds of Tob.' Out of the Depositum in his hands for the support of Tatum a poor Person.

Order^d That the Collectors pay Thomas Tucker 500 lb Tob ⁿout of the Depositum Towards the support of Sarah Rogers.

John Hughes is Elected a vestryman in the Room of John Railey Resigned.

Joseph Mayo is Elected a Vestryman in the Room of Col^o. Turpin He haveing Resigned.

Joseph Calland is Elected a Vestrymen in the Room of Maurice Langhorn he haveing Refused.

Arther Moseley is Elected a Vestryman in the Room of Edward Haskins he haveing Refused.

William Fleming and George Carrington Ju^r. is Elected Church wardens for the Ensuing year.

    William Fleming Churchwarden
    George Carrington Ju^r Churchwarden
    Robert McLaurine   John Baskervile
    Thompson Swann   John Netherland
    Alexander Trent   Littleberry Mosby

****

[185]   July the 29th. Day 1771

Att a vestry held for Southam parrish at the Courthouse of Cumberland County for Laying off the said parrish into Small precincts and appointing possessioners to possession the Same the 29th Day of July 1771. Present William Fleming & George Carrington Ju^r. Churchwardens, George Carrington, John Baskervile, John Netherland, Littleberry Mosby,. Thompson Swann And Alex^r. Trent Gent. Vestrymen.

Ordered That Isham Richerson Moor Lumkin and Saymore Scott or any two of them between The Last day of September and the Last day of March next begin and Possession all the lands and Renew and Mark the several lines between Randolphs Road Appamattox River The County line and the Clover Forrist Road and made their Return according to Law.

Ordered That George Wright and Thomas Williams some time between the Last day of September and The Last day of March next begin and Possession all the Lands and Renew and mark the several lines between Randolphs Road the Clover Forrist Road the County line and Brookses Road and make their Return according to Law.

Order^d That Joseph Michaux William Sheppard and John Chambers or any two of them Between the Last day of March and the Last day of September next begin and Possession all the Lands and Renew and mark the several lines between Appamattox River Green Creek and Randolphs Road and make their Return according to Law.

Order^d Thomas Word John Colquitt and Jarrett Ellison or any two the them between The Last day of September and the Last day of March next begin and Posession all the Lands and Renew and mark the several lines Between Brookses Road and County line Bollings Road and the Main Road and Make their Return according to Law.

Order^d That Warren Walker William Walker and John Holeman or any two of them Between the Last day of September and the Last day of March next begin and Possession all the Lands and Renew and mark the several lines Between Angoler Creek Appamattox River Green Creek & Randolphs Road and make their Return according to Law.

Order^d That Joshua Doss Joseph Allen and Henry Macon or any two of them Between the Last day of September and the Last day of March next Begin and Possession all the Lands and Renew and mark the Several lines between Great Guinea Creek Appamattox River Angoler Creek and Col^o William Macon Upper lines and make their Return according to Law.

Order^d That William Lee Joseph Lee and James Glen Senr. or any two of them Between the Last day of September and the Last day of March next begin and Possession all the Lands and Renew and mark the several lines between Col^o. William Macon upper lines Angoler Creek Randolphs Road Glens Path to Great Guinea Creek and the said Creek to the said Macon Line And make their Return according to Law.

[186] July the 29th Day 1771
Order'd That Mark Andrews Daniel Allen and John Noel or any two of them Between the Last day of September and the Last day of March next Begin and Possession all the Lands and Renew and Mark the several Lines between Tarwallet Run Greatguinea Creek as high as Glens Path and the Main Ridge Road and make their Return according to Law.

Order'd That William Davenport William Hambleton William Major and Benjamin Sims or any two of them Between the Last day of September and the Last Day of March next begin and Possession all the Lands and Renew and Mark the several Lines Between Littleguinea Creek Appamattox River Greatguinea Creek Tarwallet Run and the Main Ridge Road and make Their Return according to Law.

Order'd That John Jones Henry Martin and John Burton or any two of them Between The Last day of September and the Last day of March next begin and Possession all the Lands and Renew and Mark the several Lines Between Littleguinea Creek Buckingham Road Guinea Road Burtons Brook and Appamattox River and make their Return according to Law.

Order'd That William Allen Burton Thomas Moody & George Cox or any Two of them Between the Last day of September and the Last day of March next begin and Possession all the Lands and Renew and Mark the several lines Between Appamattox River Burtons Brook Guinea Road Buckingham Road and the Road to Clements and Coxes Mill and make their Return according to Law.

Order'd That Poindexter Mosby Jesse Carter and Robert Moor or any two of them Between the Last day of September and the Last day of March Next Begin and Possession all the Lands and Renew and Mark the several Lines between Appamattox River Clements Mills Path Buckingham Road The Cross Road by Mr. Swanns to the Middle Road on that to Salleys Path on That to Buckingham Road on that to Lyleses Road on that to Appamattox River and make their Return according to Law.

Order'd That William Smith Joiner William Ealam and Charles Lewis or any Two of them Between the Last day of September and the Last day of March Next begin and Possession all the Lands and Renew and mark The several Lines between Fighting Creek Buckingham Road Lyleses Road and

Appamattox River and make their Return according to Law.

Order^d That Richard Eggleston Samuel Hobson and George Davis or any Two of them Between the Last Day of September and the Last Day of March Begin and Possession all the Lands and Renew and mark The several lines Between from the fork of Fighting Creek Randolphs Mill Creek to Buckingham Road down the same to Church thence down the Creek to the fork and make their Return according to Law.

[187]   July the 29th Day 1771.
Order^d George Williamson John Moseley and Thomas Moseley or any two of them between the Last day of September and the Last day of March Next Begin and Possession all The Lands and Renew and mark the several lines between Geneto Road the Church Road Fighting Creek and Appamattox River and make their Return according to Law.

Order^d That Edward Watkins Abraham Baugh and Edward Watkins Ju^r. or any two of them between the Last day of September and the Last day of March Next Begin and Possession all the Lands and Renew and mark the several lines Between the New Road Geneto Road the Church Road and Buckingham Road and make their Return according to Law.

Order^d That Israel Winfrey Joseph Baugh and Lodowick Elam or any two of them Between the Last day of September and the Last day of March Next Begin and Possession all the Lands and Renew and mark the several [lines] Between King William Parrish the New Road Geneto Road and the County Line and make their Return according to Law.

Order^d That Arther Moseley Edward Haskins and John Todd or any two of Them between the Last day of September and the Last day of March Next begin and Possession all the Lands and Renew and Mark the several lines Between The County Line Appamattox River and Geneto Road and make their Return According to Law.

Order^d That Matthew Sims John Seay and Alex^r. Guttery or any two of them Between the Last day of September and the Last day of March Next begin and Possession all the Lands and Renew and mark the several lines Between Col°. Bollings Road the Main Ridge Road Buckingham Road and the County Line and make their Return According to Law.

Order^d That Moses Hudgens William Coleman and Charles Barker or any two of them Between the Last day of September and the Last day of March Next Begin and Possession all the Lands and Renew and mark the Several lines between Willises River Soakass Creek to Daniels Old Houses and Buckingham Road and make their Return according to Law.

Order^d That John Bradley Thomas Holland and Thomas Bartee or any two of Them between the Last day of September and the Last day of March Next begin and Possession all the Lands and Renew and Mark The several lines between Harrison Road the Road to John Burtons Ordinary Buckingham Road and Soakass Creek and make their Return according to Law.

Order^d That John Hobson Field Robinson and Edward Robinson or any two of them Between the Last day of September and the Last day of March Next begin and Possession all the Lands and Renew and mark the several Lines between Buckingham Road the Road from John Burtons to Overtons Ordinary The Courthouse Road to William Clerks Path thence by the said Clerks and Richd Alderson Hobsons Mill Path to Buckingham Road and make their Return according to Law.

[188]   July the 29th day 1771

Order^d that William Clerk Joseph Harris and John Steger or any two of them Between the Last day of September and the Last day of March Next begin and Possession all the Lands and Renew and mark the Several lines Between Buckingham Road Hobsons Mill Path by Richard Aldersons and William Clerks to the Courthouse Road the Courthouse Road and The Cross Road by M^r. Swanns to the said Buckingham Road and make Their Return according to Law.

Order^d. That Francis Macraw Hughes Woodson and John Hyde Sanders or any Two of them between Last day of September and the Last day of March Next Begin and Possession all the Lands and Renew and mark the several Lines between the Middle Road Randolphs Church Road Buckingham Road and Salleys Path and make their Return according to Law.

Order^d That Richard Ligon George Radford and Richard Radford or any two of them between the Last day of September and the Last day of March Next begin and Possession all the Lands and Renew and mark the Several Lines Between the Middle Road Lyleses Road Buckingham Road and the Road from the Negros Arm to M^{rs}. Mayos And make their Return according to Law.

Order^d That Thomas Ballow Thomas Haskins and Charles Hatcher or any two of them between the Last day of September and the Last day of March Next begin and Possession all the Lands and Renew and Mark The several Lines between Joneses Creek King William Parrish Lines and Buckingham Road and make their Return according To Law.

Order^d. That Joseph Bundron William Watson and Edward Parrott or any Two of them between the Last day of September and the Last day of March Next begin and Possession all the Lands and Renew and Mark the several lines between Joneses Creek King William Parrish Lines James River Fine Creek to the Middle Road the Middle Road to M^{rs}. Mayo M^{rs}. Mayos Road to Buckingham Road and Make their Return according to Law.

Order^d That Bennet Goode John Hughes and Peter Stoner or any two of them between the Last day of September and the Last day of March Next Begin and Possession all the Lands and Renew and mark the several Lines Between the Road from Michaux Ferry to Woodsons Plantation on the Middle Road down the same To Fine Creek down Fine Creek to James River up James River To the said Ferry and make their Return according to Law.

Order^d. That Anthony Minter John Cox and Edward Cox or any two of them Between the Last day of September and the Last day of March Next Begin and Possession all the Lands and Renew and Mark the several Lines between James River the Ferry Road to Stoners Ordinary the River Road and Solomon Creek and make their Return according to Law.

[189]   July the 29th. Day 1771
Order^d That Micajah Mosby Patrick Fitchsimmons and Richard Baskervile or any two of them Between the Last day of September and the Last day

of March next begin and Possession All the Lands and Renew and mark the several Lines between Deep Creek James River Muddy Creek and the River Road and make their Return according to Law.

Order[d] That Nicholas Speirs Charles Scott and Edmond Logwood or any two of them Begin and Possession all the Lands and Renew and mark the several Lines Between Muddy Creek as high as Scotts Mill Scotts Road to the Middle Road the Middle Road Deep Creek and The River Road and make their Return according to Law.

Order[d] That Hezekiah Daniel [?] Mosby and David Parker or any two of them between the Last Day of September and the Last day of March Next begin and Possession all the Lands and Renew and mark the several Lines Between the Middle Road to Overtons Ordinary Muddy Creek to Scotts Mill Scotts Road to the Middle Road and make their Return according to Law.

Order[d] That Carter Henry Harrison Henry Landon Davies and John Woodson or any two of them between the Last day of September and the Last day of March Next begin and Possession all the Lands and Renew and mark the several Lines between Muddy Creek James River Willises River and the River Road and make their Return according to Law.

Order[d] That Thomas Walton John Murrey and Nicholas Mosby or any two of them between The Last day of September and the Last day of March Next begin and Possession all The Lands and Renew and mark the several Lines Between Muddy Creek the River Road Carters Ferry Road and the Church Road to Scotts Mill and make their Return according to Law.

Order[d] That John Fliping Simon Hughes James Hudgens and Francis Fliping or any two of them Between the Last day of September and the Last day of March Next begin and Possession all the lands and Renew and mark the several lines Between Muddy Creek to John Overtons Ordinary the Middle Road Carters Ferry Road and the Church Road and make their Return according to Law.

Order[d] That George Keeling Samuel Powel and Thomas Smith or any two of them Between the Last day of September and the Last day of March

Next begin and Possession all the Lands and Renew and Mark the several lines Between Bernards Road Hornquarter Road and Willises River and make their Return according to Law.

Order^d That Benjamin Wilson Drurey Scruggs Daniel Bootwright and Robert Brown or any two of them Between the Last Day of September and the Last day of March Next begin and Possession all the Lands and Renew and mark the Several lines Between Willises River Buckingham Road the County line and Randolphs Creek and make their Return according to Law.

Order^d That John Newton Austin Martin and Phenehas Glover Ju^r. or any two of them Between the last day of September and the Last day of March next begin and Possession all the Lands and Renew and mark the several lines between Willises River Randolphs Creek the County line and the River Road and Make their Return according to Law.

Order^d That Drury Woodson James Gilham and Hezekiah Davison or any two of Them Between the Last day of September and the Last day of March Next begin and Possession all the Lands and Renew and mark the several lines between Willises River James River the County Line and the River Road and Make their Return according to Law.

[190]   July the 29th. day of 1771
Order^d. That Benjamin Bedford Joseph Mosby and Robert Scruggs or any two of them Between the Last day of September and the Last day of March next begin and Possession all the Lands and Renew and mark the several Lines between Deep Creek the Middle Road down to Stewarts the Road from Stewarts to the Widdow Chandlers the Road from the Widdow Chandlers to the River Road above Duncan Robinsons and the River Road and make their Return according To Law.

Order^d. That James Pleasants Bartholomew Stovaul Ju^r. and Edmond Toney or any Two of them Between the Last day of September and the Last day of March Begin and Possession all the Lands and Renew and mark the several Lines Between the Middle Road the Road from Charles Woodson Quarter to Stoners Ordinary the River Road Solomans Creek James River Deep Creek the River Road down the Road above Dunkin

Robinsons to the Widow Chandlers The said Road and the Road from the Widdow Chandlers to St[e]werts and make their Return according to Law.

Order^d That Martin Richerson Jonus Meador and William Sanderson or any two of Them Between the Last day of September and the Last day of March Next Begin and Possession all the Lands and Renew and mark the several lines between Willises River Bernards Road Carters Ferry Road the Church Road to the Church Down the Church Spring Branch and Turkey Cock Run to the Creek and Make their Return according to Law.

Order^d That Francis Amos John Armsteed and Simon Roland or any two of them Between the Last day of September and the Last day of March Next begin and Possession all the Lands and Renew and Mark the several Lines Between Willises River The River Road Carters Ferry Road the Church Upper Road to the Church and Down the Spring Branch to Willises and make Their Return according to Law.

    William Fleming   ⎫
    George Carington Ju^r. ⎭ Churchwardens
    George Carrington   Alexander Trent
    John Baskervile   John Netherland
    Thompson Swann   Littleberry Mosby

****

[191]   December the 23rd. Day 1771
Att a vestry held for Southam Parrish at the Courthouse of Cumberland County The 23rd. Day of December 1771. Present William Fleming and Georg Carrington Ju^r Church Wardens, George Carrington, Alexander Trent, Thomson Swann, John Baskervile and John Netherland Gent. Vestrymen.

Southam Parrish	Deb^r.	Neet Tob^o
To the Rev^d. Robert McLaurine Minster		16000
To d^o. for Cask 640 and for scrinkage 640		1280
To John Barns Clk of Petervile Church		1040
To Gideon Glen d^o. at Tarwallet d^o		1040
To Joseph Palmer d^o. Ham d^o		1040
To Thomas Hall d^o. South d^o		1040

To Thomas Davenport Clk Vestry	1000
To Amey Hill Sexton at Petervile Church	500
To Mary Bell d°. at Tarwallet d°. 500 & as poor 100	600
To William Palmer d°. at Ham d°	500
To Easter Wherley d°. South d° 500 & as poor 200	700
To Avis Tayler for keeping Winfield Sanders	1500
To Daniel Wilmore for keeping Elizth Howel	800
'To Henry Farmer Ju^r. for keeping Henry Farmer	800
To Elenor Sutlief a poor Person	600
To Francis Maccraw for keeping George Dobings	400
To George Carrington assignee of Andrew Edwards for keeping Francis Porter	1500
To George Carrington Ju^r for support of Elizth Burnet a poor person	350
To William Dillion for the support of his mother 6 months	400
To Thos Strange for the support of his two unfortunate children	800
To Edward Parrott for keeping Richd Amis	900
To d°. for keeping Ann Amis Comager	500
To Amey Hill for keeping Duke Hix one year	750
To Jn° Netherland for the support of Letishe Cardwells Children	800
To Thos. Tucker for the ball^c. of keeping Sarah Rogers Ending the 20th. of March next	1000
To John Netherland for the support of Sarah Harvey two years	1000
To Thos. Holland for the support of Charles Hollands orphans	1000
To John Pigg for keeping Richd Tatum a poor person	1000
To John Pigg for keeping Abraham Deshazer three Months and finding Cloaths	300
To Moor Lumkin for keeping Abraham Deshazer 6 months	300
To Alex^r. Trent for the support of Rebecca Goff	600
To the Collectors 6 p ct. for Collecting 49320 lb Tob°	2959
To Tob°. To Pay the money Debts and a Depositum In the Collectors hands	6345
	49344

Deb^r in Money

To Littleberry Mosby for bread & wine	£ 3. 0.0
To Thos Montague for puting blocks to Ham Church and mending the Chest	2.19.8

To W^m. Allen for Cloths & board of Step^n. Holland Eight months	4.18.9
To John Netherland for ballance Due him For the garden at the Glebe	2.15.0
To Francis Maccraw for a coffin for Mary Dobings	0.10.0
	£14. 3.5

C^r.

By Jesse Thomas his bal^c. for Levys Rec^d. of tiths Not Listed	24
By 3288 Tiths at 15 lb Tob^o. p pole	49320
	49344

[192] December the 23rd. Day 1771
Jesse Thomas and William Cortilo Hill appointed Collectors of the above Levy Giving security to the Churchwardens.

David Coupland Elected a vestryman of this Parrish in the Room of John Hughes Refused.

Joseph Carrington Elected a Vestryman of this Parrish in the Room of Joseph Mayo Refused.

Benj^a. Wilson Elected a Vestryman of this Parrish in the Room of Arther Mosely Refused.

William Fleming and George Carrington Ju^r. Continued Church wardens The Ensuing year.

Order^d. That the Collector Pay the Church wardens Eight hundred Pounds of Tob^o. For the support of Humphrey Smiths widow and Children.

William Fleming } Church
George Carrington Ju^r. } wardens
Robert McLaurine   George Carrington
John Baskervile   Thompson Swann
Alex^r. Trent   John Netherland

****

[193]   Southam Parish August the first 1772
We the Subscribers being elected to serve as Vestrymen of the parish of Southam do promise to be conformable to the doctrine of the Church of the Church of England as by Law established.

Thomas Turpin, William Fleming, John Netherland, John Mosely, Littleberry Mosby, John Hughes, Edmond Logwood.

Thomas Turpin, W^m. Fleming, John Mosely, John Hughes and Edmond Logwood, Gentlemen begin duly elected Vestrymen of the said parish of Southam in pursuance of an act of Assembly pass'd in the 12th year of the reign of his present Majesty George the third, King of Great Britain &c. who having in the County Court of Cumberland taken and Subscrib'd the Oath of Abjuration and repeated and Subscribed the Test and also Subscribed to be conformable to the Doctrine and Discipline y^e. Church of England, proceed to business.

Ordered that Francis M.Craw be appointed Clerk of the said Vestry during pleasure.

Ordered that Thomas Turpin and Littleberry Mosby be appointed Church Wardens for the ensuing year.

Ordered that Littleberry Mosby and John Netherland Gent. receive from the Collectors of the last Leveys for Southam Parish the Depositum in their hands due to the said parish to sell the same and settle with the Vestry of Littleton Parish their proportion thereof.

Ordered that Francis McCraw apply to Thomas Davenport late Clerk of the Vestry of Southam parish for the vestry Books and Records of the same.

The returns of Thomas Word, Gerrard Ellison and John Colquett, of Matthew Sims, John Sea, and Alexander Guthery, of George Wright and Thomas Williams, of William Lea, Joseph Lea and James Glenn, of Josep[h] Bondurant and William Watson, and of Martin Richardson, Jonas

Meadows, and Willaim Saunders, processioners appointed by the Vestry of the said Parish of Southam the 29th day of July 1771 are received and ordered to be rejestered according to Law.

    Thomas Turpin ⎫
    LBerry Mosby ⎭ C. Wardens
    John Hughes   W^m. Fleming
    John Mosley   John Netherland
    Edmond Logwood

[194]   Processioners returns August the first 1772

24th Jany 1772. According to an Order of the Vestry for Southam Parish the 29th day of July 1771 We the Subscribers have after Sufficient notice given possessioned the Line betwixt Thomas Word and John Colquett, both parties present. also between Joseph Calland and Thomas Word, both parties present. also between the said Calland and Colquett. also betwixt the s^d Calland and Gerrard Ellison. also the Line betwixt Calland and Charles Lee. also between Calland and Thos. Davenport. also between Arch^d. Cary and s^d. Davenport. Also between s^d. Cary and Peter Field Trent. also between s^d. Cary and Alexander Stinson, to the County Line. also between s^d. Cary and James Wilkins. also between Alex^r. Trent and the said Wilkins. also between s^d. Cary and Trent. also between s^d. John Colquett. also betwixt s^d. Cary & Ellison. also betwixt s^d. Lee and Ellison. also betwixt the s^d. Ellison & Colquett.

                                    Thomas Word
                                    Gerrard Ellison
                                    John Colquitt

In obedience to an Order of the Vestrey held for Southam Parish, the 29th day of July One thousand seven hundred and seventy one, We Matthew Sims, John Seay and Alex^r. Guthery did begin and possession the line from Bowling Old Road between Thomas Johns and Peter Field Trent. then the Line between Thomas John and James Garrott, Thomas John Senr. present. the line between Matthew Sims and Thomas Johns, both parties present. The line between Thomas Johns and Joseph Calland, Thos Johns present. The line between Joseph Calland and Matthew Sims, Matthew Sims present. The line between Matthew Sims and William Dunge, Matthew Sims present. The line between Matthew Sims and Henry Scrugs possessioned, both parties present. The Line between Matthew Sims and John Seay possessioned, both parties present. The line between John Seay and James Garrott possessioned, Henry Garrott present. The line between James Garrott and Archibald Cary possessioned, Henry Garrott present. The Line between A. Trent and James Garrott possessioned, Henry Garrott present. The line between Matthew Sims and James Garrott poss^d, John M.Kinney present. The line between John Seay and Cary possessioned, John Seay present. The line between Jonathan Colquett and Cary possessioned, Jonathan Colquett present. The line between Jonathan Colquett and Benjamin Weaver possessioned, Jonathan Colquett present. The line between Jonathan Colquett and Warham Easley, both parties present. The line between H. Scruggs and Zach. Hendrick possessioned, Hendrick present. The line between Zach Henrick and W^m. Dunge possession'd, Hendrick present. The line between Hendrake and W^{hm} Easley, both parties present. The line between Hendrake and Darbey Tarlyle,

[195]   August the first 1773 [1772] Processioners Returns
Hendrake present. The line between Jonathan Colquett & Thomas Guthery, Colquitt present. The line between W^{hm} Easley and Thomas Calwell, Easley present. The line between W^{ham} Easley and Benj^a Weaver possessioned, Easley pres^t. The line between Jno Hill and Thomas Guthery possessioned, John Hill pres^t. The line between Faris and Amus possessioned, Daniel Coleman present. The line between John Hill and Cary possesisoned, John Hill present. The line between Thomas Hill and James Southall possess^d, Dennitt Hill present. The line between Thomas Hill and James Brown poss^d, Dennitt Hill present. The line between Thos. Hill and Jo^s. Calland possessioned, Dennitt Hill present. The line between John Hill and Thomas Hill Possessioned, John Hill present, The line between Danl. Coleman [and] Dar 'Tarlyle possessioned, Coleman present. The line between Daniel Coleman and Faris possessioned, Daniel Coleman present. The line between Jesse Sanders and Thomas Guthery possess^d, John Starkey present. The line between Jesse Sanders and John Hill possessioned, John Hill present. The line between Sanders and Joseph Calland possessioned, John Starkey present. The line between Jesse Sanders and James Brown possess^d, John Starkey and Jo^n. Spearman pres^t. The line between Jesse Sanders and Charles Barker poss . John Starkey pres^t. The line between Jesse Sanders and Williams Daniel poss^d, John Starkey pres^t. The line between Jesse Sanders and Calwell possessioned, John Starkey pres^t. The line between Jesse Sanders and

Benjamin Weaver poss[d], John Starkey Present. The line between James Southall and James Brown poss[d], William Edwards present. The line between James Brown [and] Joseph Calland possessioned, Jn°. Spearman pres[t]. The line between James Brown and Charles Barker poss[d], Jn° Spearman pres[t]. The line between Charles Barker and W[m]. Coleman, Charles Barker W[ms] Daniel present. The line between Charles Barker and Stephan Woodson poss[d], C. Barker present. The line between Charles Barker and Williams Daniel poss[d], both parties present. The line between Williams Daniel and Stephen Woodson poss[d], Williams Daniel present. The line between Williams Daniel and Amus possessioned, W[ms] Daniel pres[t]. The line between Williams Daniel and Faris poss[d], Williams Daniel present. The line between Williams Daniel [and] Thomas Calwell poss[d], W[ms] Daniel pres[t]. The line between Williams Daniel [and] Jesse Sanders poss[d], Will[m] Daniel pres[t]. The line between William Coleman and Stephen Woodson poss[d], William Coleman present. The line between William Coleman and Morriss Langhorn poss[d], W[m]. Coleman John Farmer present. The line between Morris Langhorn and Benj[a]. Mosby poss[d], John Farmer present. The line between Stephen Woodson and Morris Langhorn poss[d], John Farmer present. The line between Stephen Woodson and Amus poss[d], Jn°. Farmer present. The line between Alex Guthery and Amus poss[d], John Farmer pres[t]. The line between Alex. Guthery and Morris Langhorn poss[d], Jn°. Farmer pres[t].

[196] Processioners returns August the first 1772
The line between Thomas Culwell and Farris possessioned, Thomas Cullwell present. The line between Thomas Guthery and Benjamin Weaver poss[d], W[m] Guthery present. The line between Thomas Guthery and Carry possessioned, William Guthrey present.

Pursuant to an Order of the Vestrey of Southam parish dated the 23 day of July 1771. We the Subscribers have markt and renew'd the Several lines within the bounds within mentioned as followeth Viz. The lines between Samuel William and George Wright, between Alexander Trent and Thomas Williams, Between Saymer Scott Coll°. Richard Randolph, Between Alexander Trent [and] Coll°. Richard Randolph, between Alex[r]. Trent and John Gannaway Sen[r], Between Henry Bell and John Ganaway, Between Alexander Trent and Henry Bell no corner Tree to be found, Between Henry Bell and Cap[t]. Thomas Davenport, Between Cap[t]. Thomas Davenport and Col°. Arch[d]. Cary, between Robert Johns and

Capt. Thomas Davenport.

The above Lines were peacabley possessioned in presence of Charles Lee Senr, Robert Johns, Roger Williams and John Goss.

Georg Wright
Thomas Williams

In obedience to an order of Vestrey, we the subscribers have processioned the following lines: Begining on Coll^o. Macons Upper Line, between the said Macons and Nehemiah Glenn, Bernard Guthery and Hartwell Macon present. Between Coll^o. Macon and McGehee's Estate, Hartwell Macon Nathan Glenn & William McGehee present. Between Coll^o. Macon and Thomas Right, Hartwell Macon & Thomas Wright present. Between Nathan Glen and McGehee's Estate, Nath Glen and William M.Gehee present. Between Nathan Glen and James Glenn, both present. Between Nehemiah and James Glenn, Nathan Glen & James Glen present. Between Nathan Glen & James Glen, both present. Between James Glenn and Jeremiah Basham, Nathan Glen and James Glen pres^t. Between McGehees Estate and James Glenn, James Glenn & W^m McGehee present. Between Nathan Womack and Jeremiah Basham, William McGehee present. Between Nathan Womack and Thomas Johns, W^m. McGehee present.. Between Coll^o. Macon and James Durham, Hartwell Macon present & Thomas Wright. Between Coll^o. Macon and David Dickerson, Hartwell Macon and Thomas Wright present. Between Coll^o. Macon and Stanley Chaffin, Hartwell Macon and Joseph Chafin present. Between Coll^o. Macon and Nathan Chafin, Hartwell Macon & Joseph Chaffin present. Between William Angeley Senr. and Nathan Chafin,

[197]   August the first 1772
William Angely and Joseph Chaffin present. Between William Angely and Stanley Chaffin, both present. Between Stanley Chaffin and Francis Epperson, Stanley Chaffin present. Between David Dickerson and Francis Epperson, Francis Epperson present. Between William Angeley Junr. and Francis Epperson, Francis Epperson present. Between James Durham and Thomas Wright, Thomas Wright present. Between Joseph Angeley and Thomas Wright, Thomas Wright present. Between John Pleasants Dec^d. and Joseph Angeley, Francis Epperson and Joseph Angely present.

Between Francis Epperson and William Lee, both present. Between Tho⁵. Wright and Francis Epperson, both present. between John Brown and Francis Epperson, Thomas Wright present. between Thomas Wright and John Brown, Thomas Wright present. Between Charles Lee and Thomas Wright, both present. Between Gideon Glenn and Charles Lee, both present. Between Gideon Glenn & Tho⁵. Wright, both present. Between Nathan Womack and Tho⁵. Wright, Thomas Wright present. Between Gideon Glenn and Nathan Womack, Gideon Glenn present. between Gideon Glenn and Joseph Calland, Gideon Glenn present. Between Thomas Davenport and Joseph Calland, Gideon Glenn present. Between Robert Johns and Thomas Davenport, Robert Johns present. between Gideon Glenn and Robert Johns, both present. between Robert Johns and Charles Lee, both present. between Robert Johns and John Brown, Robert Johns presᵗ. Between Robert Johns and Richard Lee, both present. between Richard Lee and Thomas Davenport, Richard Lee present. between Richard Lee and Joseph Lee, both present. between John Brown and William Lee, both present. Between John Brown and Richard Lee, both present. Between John Brown & William Lee, both present. Between Davis Brown and William Lee, both present. Between Joseph Lee and John Wright, Joseph Lee present. Between Joseph Lee and John Lee, both present. Between Joseph Lee and Thomas Johns, Robert Johns present. Between John Lee and William Shapard, John Lee present. Between Thomas Johns and William Shapard, George Wright and Robert Johns present. Between William Shapard and George Wright, George Wright present. Between Thomas Johns and George Wright, George Wright and Robert Johns present. Between Alexander Trent & Thomas Johns, Robert Johns and George Wright present. Between Thomas Johns and John Gannaway, Robert Johns present. Between Thomas Johns and Joseph Lee, Robert Johns & Joseph Lee present. Between Davis Brown and John Wright, Davis Brown present. Between Davis Brown and Griffin Wright, both present. Between Griffin Wright and William Lee, both present. Between Griffin Wright & Wᵐ. Lee, both present. Between Griffin Wright & John Pleasants Estate, Griffin Wright present. The above Lines in quiet and peacable possession 22ᵈ January 1772. The Lines

[198] Processioners returns August the first 1772
between Charles Lee and John Brown Objected against being processioned by John Brown in presence of John Raine & Thomas Wright & Gerrard Ellison.

William Lee
Joseph Lee
James Glenn

March the 17, 1772. We Jo^s. Bondurant and William Watson, being appointed processioners, have processioned the several Lines Viz. A line between George Radford and Anthony Christian, both parties present. A line between Anthony Christian and Richard Ligon, both parties present. A line between Richard Ligon and George Radford, both parties present. A line between John Baskervile and George Radford, Samuel Baskervile [present]. A line between George Radford and Richard Radford, both parties present. A line between John Baskervile and Richard Radford, Samuel Baskervile and Richard Radford present. A line between John Baskervile and John Radford, Samuel Baskervile and John Radford present. A line between John Baskerfield [Baskerville] and Jo^s. Bondurant, Samuel Baskerfield and Jo^s. Bondurant present. A line between John Baskervile and Joseph Mayo, Samuel Baskervile and Joseph Mayo present. All peacabely possessioned, The rest of the Lines in our precincts Joins the Lines of M^r. John Pleasants decest, no attendance.

Joseph Bondurant
W^m. Watson

We Martin Richardson Jonas Meador and William Sanderson, being appointed possessione[r]s by a Vestrey held for Southam Parish the 29th day of July 1771. To possession all the Lands and View and mark the several Lines between Willisses Creek, Randolphs Road, Carters Ferry Road the Church Road to the Church Spring, down the said Spring Branch and Turkey Cook [Cock] Creek to Willisses. In pursuance to the said Order we have possessioned the lines as follows: Begining on a Line between Martin Richardson & James Austin, James Hudson present. Thence between Martin Richardson and Samuel Osline Dec^d, Jesse Oslin present. Thence between Martin Richardson and Danl. Bootwright, James Hudgeons present. Thence between James Meadors and James Austin, James Hudgens present. Thence between James Meador and W^m. Sanderson. Thence between W^m. Sanderson and Samuel Bridgwater. Thence between Joel Meggs and John Robertson, Jarrott Lyol and Jno. Robertson present. Thence between Joel Meggs and Parson Garden, Jarrot Lyal present.

[199]   August the first 1772
Thence between Samuel Oslin and John Hix, John Hix present. Thence between s^d. Hix and W^m. C. Hill, John Hix present. Thence between Jno. Hix & Ja^s. Daniel, Jno. Hix present. Thence between James Daniel and Allin Cridle, Allin Cridle present. Thence between Page Bond dec^d. and Allin Cridle, Allin Cridle present. Thence between Henry Wade and Parson Garden, Henry Wade Thomas Smith H^y Wade present. Thence between Thomas Smith and Parson Garden, Thomas Smith present. Thence between Edward Colemans and Thomas Smith, Thomas Smith present. Thence between James Brown and Edward Clemons, Edward Clemons present. Thence between Andrew Edwards and Parson Garden, Andrew Edwards Junr. present. Thence between James Brown and Samuel Brown, James Brown present. Thence between Andrew Edwards and James Brown, James Brown present. Thence between Andrew Edwards and William Edwards, W^m. Edwards present. Thence between Andrew Edwards and James Minter, John Minter present. Thence Between John Minter and Archibald Allin, James Minter present. Thence between William Edwards and Archibald Allin, James Minter present. Thence between William Edwards and Archibald Allin, James Minter present. Thence between W^m. Edwards and $Arch^d$. Allin, W^m. Edwards present. Thence between John Robertson & $Arch^d$. Allin, John Robertson present. Thence between John Jefferson and Archer Allin, John Roberson present. Thence between Alexander Trent and Archer Allin, James Foster & John Roberson present. Thence between Job Thomas & John Jefferson, Job Thomas present. Thence between John Jefferson and $Alex^r$. Trent, James Foster present. Thence between $Alex^r$. Trent and Job Thomas, Job Thomas present. Thence between Job Thomas and W^m. Sanderson, Job Thomas present. Thence between John Jefferson & W^m. Sanderson, John Robertson present. There is Lines between W^m. C. Hill & James Daniel. also between Page Bond Dec^d. and Parson Garden. also between William C. Hill & Page Bond dec^d. which is not possession'd for want to being showed the Lines.

Martin Richardson
Jonas Meador
William Sanderson

****

[200] November 28th 1772
At a vestry held for Southam Parish the 28th. day of November 1772 at the plantation of Robert Murrays in Cumberland County. Present Thomas Turpin and Littleberry Mosby Gent. Church Wardens. William Fleming, John Hughes, John Mosely, Edmond Logwood, John Netherland Gentlemen Vestry Men.

Southam Parish	D^r.	lb. Tobacco
To the Reverend Robert McLaurine		16000
To ditto for Cask 640 for Shrinkage 640		1280
To John Barnes Clerk of Petersvile		1040
To Thomas Hall Clerk of South Chappel		1040
To Amy Hill Sexton of Petersvile		500
To William Whorley Sexton of South Chappel		500
To Avies Taylor for keeping Winkfield Sanders		1500
To Daniel Wilmore for keeping Elizabeth Howl		800
To Ellenor Sutliff a pore person		600
To Edward Parrott for burying Richard Amos		130
To Thomas Strange for support of his unfortunate Children		800
To Amy Hill for keeping M. Duke Hix		750
To John Netherland for the Support of Latisia Cardwells Children		800
To Henry Honeybus for keeping Sarah Harvey		500
To John Fuquay for burying &c. Robert Dinwiddie		250
To Francis Mcraw for keeping George Dobins		400
To Georg Radford for one Levie over paid last Year		15
To Francis Epperson a poor person		800
To John Mosely for the use of James Bailey		500
To Francis Mcraw Clerk of the Vestry		800
To Tobacco to pay the Cash Account		10000
By Littleton Parish	[minus]	9460
		29545
To the Collector 6 p cent for Collecting the above Tobacco		1773
To a Depositum in the hands of the Collector to pay Co. Carington		1442
	D^r.	32760

Southam Parish in Money
To Littleton parish	£ 89.14.2¼
To the Reverend M‹Laurine	1.18.0
To John Maxey	0. 9.0
To the Reverend M‹Laurine for a Surplice	5. 0.0
To Littleberry Mosby for bread and Wine	2. 8.0
To William Low for Services done to Petersvile Church	0.14.0
To Coll⁰. Carrington for runing the Parish Line	5.1.11½
	105. 5.1¾
By a depositum in the late Collectors hands	20. 7.7½
	84.17.6¼
To M‹. John Netherland for finding a Coffin for Sarah Harvey	10.0
	£ 85. 7.6¼

[201]   November 28th. 1772
Southam Parish   Cr.
By 1638 Tithes at 20 pounds of Tobacco p poll   32760

John Jefferson appointed parish Collector on giving Bond and Security to the Church Wardens and he is authorised to demand the receive 20 pounds of Tobacco p. poll from every Tithable in the said parish.

Ordered that the church Wardens receive of the Vestry of Littleton Parish 9460 pounds of Tobacco and pay the same to the several Creditors.

       Thomas Turpin }
       L. Mosby   }   C. Wardens
       John Hughes   William Fleming
       Edmond Logwood   John Mosely
                            John Netherland

****

[202]   November the 12th. 1773
At a vestry held for Southam Parish at the House of Robert Murray's the 12th day of November 1773. For laying the parish Levey present Thomas Turpin, Littleberry Mosby, Thompson Swan, John Mayo, John Mosely, Edward Haskins, John Hughes, John Netherland, Edmund Logwood and William Fleming, Gentlemen Vestry Men.

Southam Parish　　　　　　　　　　D^r.	
To John Barnes Clerk of Petersvile Church	1040
To Thomas Hall Clerk of South Chappell	1040
To Amy Hill Sexton of Petersvile	500
To William Whorley Clerk of South Chappell	500
To Avies Taylor for keeping Winkfield Saunders	1500
To Daniel Wilmore for keeping Elizabeth Howl	800
To Thomas Strange for his unfortunate Children	800
To John Netherland for 'Tishea Cardwells Children	800
To Francis McCraw for keeping Geo. Dobbins	600
To Francis Epperson a poor person	800
To John Moseley for James Bailey	600
To Francis M^c.Craw Clerk of the Vestry his Sallery	800
To Ann Johnson a poor person, to be laid out by John Cox	600
For the use of Mary Pools Family to be laid out by the descretion of John Mosely	600
To Gideon Glenn 520 To Joseph Palmer 520	1040
To Thomas Davenport 500 Mary Bell 300	800
To W^m. Palmer 250 Henry Farmer 400	650
To George Carrington Assignee of Andrew Edwards	750
To Thomas Hollond 500 John Pigg 500	1000
To Moore Lumkin 150. Alexander Trent 300	450
To Avies Taylor for Support of Mary Rogers	500
To Susanna Epperson for keeping Mary Rogers to this date	100
To William Carr a poor person	600
To the Estate of the late Reverend Robert McLaurine Dec^d. for seven monthes Services as Minister of the said Parish	10033
To the Rev^d. John Hy[d]e Saunders 3000　Rever^d. Jesse Carter 3000	6000
	32903

[203]　November the 12th. 1773　　　　　　lb. Tobacco

Brought forward	32903
To the reverend James Oglesby	1167
To Tobacco to pay the money Debt	17000
To 6 p Cent for Collecting the above Tobacco	3064
	54134

Southam Parish in Money D^r.	
To Littleton parish	£ 89.14.2½
To a further Sum to Littleton Parish for arrears	27. 4.2
To Robert Bagby for Support of Ann Johnson	1. 7.9
To W^m. Whorley for Benches Racks & Blocks for South Chappel	1. 5.0
To Richard Eggleston for Benches at Petersvile	1.10.0
	121. 1.1½
C^r. By Mr John Netherland	15. 3.0
	105.18.1½
By a further Sum in Mr John Netherlands h^d.	2.15.0
	£ 103. 3.1½
C^r.	
By 1628 Tithes at 33 lb Tob^o p poll	53724
By a depositum in the hands of the Collector	410
	54134

Ordered that the Collectors receive of every Tithable person in the said parish 33^l of Tobacco, or in Lieu thereof Money at Seven Farthings p. pound, at the option of the payer, And pay the same over to the Several Creditors.

Ordered that Francis McCraw be appointed parish Collector, giving Bond to the Church Wardens, according to Law.

John Baskervile has resigned his Seat in the Vestry.

Richard Ligon chosen Vestryman in the room of John Baskervile.

Ordered that Edmund Logwood & John Mosley be Church Wardens the ensuing year.

Thompson Swann	Thomas Turpin
Edward Haskins	Littleberry Mosby
Wm Fleming	John Mosley ⎫
John Hughes	Edm^d. Logwood ⎬ Ch War
John Mayo	John Netherland

[204]   November the 23ᵈ. 1773
At a Vestry held for Southam Parish at Petersvile Church the 23ᵈ. day of November 1773. Present John Mosely, Littleberry Mosely [Mosby], John Netherland, John Hughes, Richard Ligon, William Fleming, Thomas Turpin, John Mayo, Edmund Logwood, Thomspon Swann, Samuel Hobson, Gent. Vestrymen. The Reverend John Hide Saunders is Elected Rector of the said Parish in the room of the late Reverend Robert MᶜLaurine Deceased.

John Netherland	John Mosely
Richard Ligon	Edmund Logwood
Thompson Swann	John Mayo
Samuel Hobson	Thomas Turpin
John Hughes	L. Mosby
	William Fleming

****

At a vestry held for Southam Parish at the Courthouse August the 22ᵈ. 1774 Present John Mosely, Churchwarden, John Netherland, John Mayo, Samuel Hobson, Richard Ligon and William Fleming Gent. Vestrymen.

Ordered that John Mosely sell the parish Tobacco in his hands, amounting to 2299 pounds of Tobacco.

Wᵐ. Fleming	John Mosely
Richᵈ. Ligon	John Mayo
John Netherland	Samuel Hobson

****

[205]   August the 19ᵗʰ 1775
At a vestry held for Southam Parish at Petersvile Church August 19ᵗʰ 1775 for laying the said parish off into small precincts and for appointing processioners to procession the same. Present John Mosely, Edmund Logwood, Thomspon Swann, John Netherland, Richard Liggon, Samuel Hobson, Edward Haskins and Littleberry Mosby Gent. Vestry Men.

Ordered That Philip Thomas William Elam and Charles Lewis, or any two of them between the last day of September next and the last day of March begin and procession all the Lands and renew and mark the several Lines between Fighting Creek Buckingham Road Lyles's Road and Appomattox River and make their return according to Law.

Ordered that George Williamson John Moseley Jun[r] & Thomas Moseley or any two of them between the last day of September & the last day of March next Begin & Procession all the Land and renew and mark the several Lines between Geneto R[o]ad, the Church Road to Fighting Creek & Appomattox River & Make their return according to Law.

Ordered that Richard Eggleston Samuel Hopson and George Davis or any two of them Between the last day of September and the last day of March next begin and procession all the Lands and renew and mark the several Lines between from the Fork of Fighting Creek, Randolphs Mill Creek to Buckingham Road down the same to the Church, thence down the Creek to the Fork and make their return according to Law.

Ordered that Edward Watkins Abram Baugh and Edward Watkins Jun[r]. or any two of them Between the last day of September and the last day of March next begin and procession all the Lands and renew and mark the several Lines between the New Road Genetoe Road the Church Road and Buckingham Road and make their return according to Law.

Ordered that Israel Winfrey Joseph Baugh and Lodowick Elam or any two of them Between the last day of September and the last day of March next begin and Procession all the Lands and renew and mark the several Lines between King W[m]. Parish the New Road Genetoe Road and the County Line and make their return according to Law.

Ordered that Arthur Mosley, Robert Williamson, Edward Haskins and John Cox or any two of them Between the last day of September and the last day of March next begin and procession all the Lands and renew and mark the several Lines between the County Line Appomattox River and Genetoe Road & make their Return according to Law.

Ordered that Hughes Woodson David Owen and John Barnes or any two of them Between the last day of September and the last day of March next

Begin and Procession all the Lands and renew and Mark the several Lines between the Middle Road, Randolph's Church Road, Buckingham Road and the Road from Salley's Plantation to Buckingham Road & make their Return According to Law.

Ordered that Joseph Mayo George Radford and John Liggon or any two of them between the last day of September & the last day of March next begin and procession all the lands and renew and mark the several Lines Between the Middle Road, Lyles's Road, Buckingham Road and the Road from the Negroes Arm to M^r. Joseph Mayos and make their Return according to Law.

[206]   August the 19th 1775
Ordered that Thomas Ballow Charles Hatcher Tho. Haskins and John Maxy or any two, Between the last day of September and the last day of March next begin and procession all the Lands and renew and mark the several Lines Between Jones's Creek, King W^m. Parish Line and Buckingham Road and to the lower end of the parish and make their return according to Law.

Ordered that Nathaniel Maxey W^m. Watson Edwd. Parrott and Aaron Haskins or any two Between the last Day of September and the last Day of March next, begin and procession all the Lands and renew and mark the several Lines, between Jones's Creek, King W^m. Parish Line and James River, Fine Creek to the Middle Road, Middle Road to M^r. Joseph Mayo's, M^r. Joseph Mayo's Road to Buckingham Road And make their Return according to Law.

Ordered that Bennett Goode Edmund Vaughan John Goode & Peter Stoner or any two, Between the last Day of September and the last Day of March next begin and procession all the Lands and renew and mark the several Lines between the Road from Michaux Ferry to Charles Woodson's Plantation on the Middle Road down the same to Fine Creek, down Fine Creek to James River up James River to the said Ferry and make their Return according to Law.

Ordered that Anthony Minter John Cox and Edward Cox or any two of them Between the last Day of September and the last Day of March next begin and procession all the Lands and renew and mark the several Lines between James River the Ferry Road to Robert Murray's Store and Solomons Creek and make their Return according to Law.

Ordered that Jesse Mosby Daniel Hix and Robert Murray or any two of them between the last day of September & the last day of March next begin and procession all the Lands and renew & mark the several Lines between Deep Creek, James River the Parish Line and the River Road and make their Return According to Law.

Ordered that William Mayo, James Drake and Edmund Toney Junr. or any two Between the last Day of September and the last Day of March next begin and procession all the Lands and renew and mark the several Lines between Deep Creek the Middle Road down to Loyd's the Road from Loyd's to Edmund Toney's The Road from Edmund Toney's to the River Road above Duncan Robertson's and the River Road, and make their Return according to Law.

Ordered that James Pleasants Bartholomew Stovall Junr. & Charles Woodson Junr. or any two of them between the last Day of September and the last Day of March next begin & procession all the Lands and renew and mark the several Lines Between the Middle Road the Road from Charles Woodson's to Robert Murrays' Store the River Road, Solomon's Creek, James River, Deep Creek the River Road down the road above Duncan Robinson's to Edmund Toney's and the said Road from Edmund Toney's to Loyd's and make their Return according to Law.

Ordered that George Cox Henry Cox and William Daniel or any two of them between the last Day of September and the last Day of March next

[207]   August 19th 1775
Begin and procession all the Lands and renew and mark the several Lines between Thomas Mooday's the Parish Line on Appamattox River to Swan's Creek and so to Buckingham Road and up the said Road to the Parish Line, the Parish Line to the Beginning and make their Return according to Law.

Ordered that Poindexter Mosby Jesse Carter & Robert Biscoe or any two of them between the last Day of September and the Last Day of March next begin and procession all the Lands and renew & mark the several Lines between Swann's Creek and Appamattox River down the said River to Lyles's Ford along Lyles's Road to Buckingham Road up the said Road to Swann's Creek and make their Return according to Law.

Ordered that Joseph Harris John Stegar Thomas Stegar and Hans Stegar or any two of them between the last Day of September and the last Day of March next begin and procession all the Lands and renew and mark the several Lines between the Parish Line on Buckingham Road to the Middle Road down the Middle Road to Salleys Path from thence to Buckingham Road & up Buckingham Road to the Parish Line along that to the Beginning and make their Return according to Law.

Ordered that Jesse Miller William Tucker John Stratton & William Stratton Junr. between the last Day of September and the last Day of March next begin & procession all the Lands and renew & mark the several Lines between Muddy Creek the Parish Line to the Middle Road, Deep Creek and the River Road and make their return according to Law.

On the Motion of sundry Inhabitants at the upper end of this Parish representing that they are at great Distance from their Parish Churches it is recommended to the present incumbent of this Parish that he preach one Sunday in three weeks at such place as shall be made convenient for him between Jesse Carters & M^{rs}. Ann Harris's on Buckingham Road.

Ordered that M^r. John Netherland make new Shutters to Petervile Church Windows put in Glass where it is missing and make new Steps to the Doors and other necessary Repairs that are wanting to the said Church.

From the Information of some of the Members of this Vestry that Thomas Hall Clerk of South Chappel neglects his Duty it is therefore ordered that the said Thomas Hall be summoned to appear before the next Vestry to be held for this Parish at Petersvile Church on the first Saturday in November next to answer Such Things as shall be objected against him.

   John Moseley   }
   Edmond Logwood } C Wardens
   Richard Liggon   Thompson Swann

John Netherland   Littleberry Mosby
Edward Haskins   Samuel Hobson

****

[208]
At a Vestry held for Southam Parish the second Day of March 1776. Present John Moseley, Edmund Logwood Church Wardens, John Mayo, William Fleming, Littleberry Mosby, John Netherland, Richard Liggon and Samuel Hobson Gent. Vestry Men.

Southam Parish D^r.	lbs Nett Tobacco
To the reverend John H Sanders	17280
To ditto for the Ballance his last years Sallery	5184
To John Barnes Clerk of Petersvile	1040
To Amy Hill Sexton of Ditto	500
To Thomas Hall Clerk of South Chappel	1040
To William Whorley Sexton of Ditto	500
To Avis Taylor for keeping Winkfield Sanders	1500
To Thomas Strange for Support of his unfortunate Children	800
To John Netherland for Tishia Cardwells Children	800
To Francis McCraw for Keeping George Dobins	600
To Ditto for Clerk of the Vestry	800
To John Mosley for Polls Family	1000
To Francis Epperson a poor Person	800
To John Mosby for James Bailey Senr.	400
To John Netherland for the Widow Nix'es Children	500
To Jane Johns for Keeping Elizabeth Howle	500
To Avis Taylor for keeping Mary Rogers	320
	33544
To 6 pr. Cent for Collecting the above Tobacco	2014
	35558
Southam Parish C^r.	
By 1755 Tithes at 20 lb p^r. Poll	35100
By Ballance due to the Collector	458
	35558

Creed Haskins is appointed Parish Collector on giving Bond and security to the Church Wardens according to Law and he is authorised and impowered to demand and receive of every Tithable Person of the said Parish two Shillings & Six Pence in the Lieu of 20 lb of Tobacco and that he pay the same to the several Creditors.

Southam Parish in Money	D^r.	
To M^r. John Netherland's Account for Repair done to Petersvile Church to be paid by Creed Haskins		£ 9.18.8
Southam Parish in Money	C^r.	
By a Depositum in Creed Haskins the late Collectors Hands		12. 3.9

Ordered that the Church Wardens agree with a Person to Keep and indeavour to cure Hannah Williams a Poor Person.

[209]
Thompson Swann has resigned his Seat in the Vestry.
Bennett Goode has resigned his seat in the Vestry.
Samuel Hobson has resigned his Seat in the Vestry.

Richard Eggleston appointed Vestry Man in the Room of Thompson Swann.
William Gay is Appointed Vestry Man in the Room of Bennett Goode.
Thomas Mosley is Appointed Vestry Man in the Room of Samuel Hobson.
Richard Ligon & Edward Haskins is appointed C[h]urch Wardens the ensuing Year.

Ordered that John Netherland and Littleberry Mosby View the Glebe and Cause such necessary repairs to be done as shall be found wanting.

Richard Liggon Church Warden	John Netherland
John Moseley	Littleberry Mosby
Samuel Hobson	William Fleming
Edmund Logwood	John Mayo

****

[210] March 8th, 1777
At a Vestry held for southam at William Prossers March the 8th 1778 [1777] for laying the Parish Levey. present Richard Ligon, John Mosely,

John Netherland, Edward Haskins, Thomas Moseley, William Gay, Edmund Logwood, Benjamin Mosby Gent. Vestry Men.

Southam Parish D^r.	neat Tobacco
To the Reverend John Hide Sanders his Sallery	17280
To Ditto for one Month and seven Days	1771
To John Barnes Clerk of Petersvile Church	1040
To Amy Hill sexton of Ditto	500
To Matthew Farley Junr. Clerk of Southam Chappel	1040
To William Whorley Sexton of the Same	500
To Avis Taylor for Keeping Winkfield Sanders	1500
To Thomas Strange for his unfortunate Children	800
To John Netherland for Littishea Cardwells Children	800
To Francis McCraw for keeping George Dobins	600
To Ditto for Clerk of the Vestry	800
To John Moseley for Pools Family	1000
To Ditto for James Bailey Senr.	400
To Francis Epperson a poor Person	800
To Elizabeth Nix for the support of herself and Children	500
To Jane Johns for keeping Elizabeth Howl	500
To Tobacco to pay the Money Debts	4792
To 6 percent for Collecting the above Tobacco	2077
	36700
Southam Parish C^r.	
By 1742 Tithes at 21 lb of Tobacco p poll	36582
Ballance due the Collector	118
	36700

Southam Parish in Money D^r.	
To Avis Taylor for keeping Mary Rogers	£ 1. 0.0
To William Taylor for doctring Hannah Williams	4.17.6
To the Reverend John Hide Saunders's Account	14. 3.1
To Luke Kent his Accou[n]t for Work done the Glebe By M^r. Sanders's Directions	11.11.3
To Littlebery Mosby for Wine	1. 4.0
To George Carrington Junr. for a Coppy List of Tithes	10.0
	33.5.10
To a further account to Luke Kent	10. 1.0
	£ 43. 6.0

Ordered That Thomas Thompson Swann be appointed to Collect the present parish Levey on his giving Bond and Security to the Church Wardens According to Law And that he receive of every Tithable person in the said Parish Twenty one pounds

[211]
of Tobacco. He is also appointed to Collect the last years Levey which lies yet unpaid and that he receive of every Tithable person in the Said Parish Twenty pound of Tobacco or in Lieu thereof two Shillings & Six pence and pay the same over to the several Creditors.

Edmund Logwood has Resigned his Seat in the Vestry.

Vincent Markham is appointed Vestryman in the Room of Edmond Logwood who has Resigned.

William Fleming	Richard Ligon
William Gay	Edward Haskins
Littleberry Mosby	John Moseley
Thomas Moseley	John Netherland

****

At a vestry held for Southam Parish at William Prossers the 12th day of February 1778 for laying the parish Levey. Present Richard Ligon, John Moseley, John Netherland, Littleberry Mosby, William Fleming, William Gay, Thomas Moseley Gent. Vestrymen.

Southam Parish	D^r.	lb Nett Tobacco
To Thomas Strange for his unfortunate Children		800
To John Netherland for Letishea Cardwell's Children		800
To Robert Pool a poor person		600
To Avis Taylor for keeping Wingfield Saunders		1500
To George Radford as Adm^r. of Joseph Johns for keeping Elizabeth Howl		500
To Francis McCraw as Clerk of the Vestry		800
To Francis McCraw for keeping George Dobins		600
		5600

To 6 p Cent for Collecting the above Tobacco	336
	5936
Southam parish C^r.	
By 1841 Tithes at 3 pound of Tobacco p poll	5523
By Ballance due the Collector	413
	5936

Richard Eggleston has resigned his Seat in the Vestry.

Richard Crump is elected Vestryman in the room of Richard Eggleston who has resigned.

Ordered that Francis McCraw Settle with Creed Haskins and Thomas Thompson Swann two late Collectors and receive the ballance of their accounts and account with the Vestry.

William Gay and Thomas Moseley is appointed Church Wardens the ensuing year.

Thomas Thompson Swann is appointed parish Collector to collect the above Tobacco and is authorised to demand and receive of every Titheable person in the said Parish three pounds of Tobacco on his giving Bond and Security to the Church Wardens according to Law and that he pay the same to the several Creditors.

Vincent Markham	W^m. Gay
L. Berry Mosby	Thomas Moseley
John Netherland	Richard Ligon
W^m. Fleming	John Moseley

****

[212]   January 2^d. 1779

At a Vestry held for Southam parish at Scottville Jany. 2^d. 1779. Present

Thomas Moseley	Church Warden
John Netherland	L. Berry Mosby
John Moseley	Richard Ligon
Vincent Markham &	W^m. Fleming
Gen^t. members of the Vestry.	

Wm Clarke is elected Clerk of the Vestry in the room of Francis McCraw dec^d.

Southam Parish	D^r.	lb nett Tobacco
To Thomas Strange for his unfortunate Children		800
To John Netherland for Letishea Cardwell's Children		300
To Robert Pool a poor person		600
To Wm Johns for Keeping Elizabeth Howl		500
To M^rs. Mary McCraw for keeping George Dobbins		600
To James Bagbey for Keeping Sarah Wright and her children		600
To John Moseley for Keeping Mary Jennings		200
		3600
To 6 p ct. for collecting the above Tobacco		216
		3816
Southam Parish	C^r	
By 1803 Tithes at 2 pounds Tobacco p poll		3606
By ballance due the Collector		210
		3816

Ordered that John Netherland settle with Creed Haskins, Thos. T. Swann two late Collectors, and the Ex^rs. of Francis M^c.Craw dec^d. and receive the ballance of their Acco^t. and acco^t. with the Vestry.

Thos. T. Swann is appointed parish Collector to Collect the above Tobacco and is hereby authorised to demand and receive of every Titheable person in the said parish two pounds of Tobacco on is giving Bond and security to the Church Wardens according to Law and that he pay the same to the several Creditors.

William Mayo Junr. is elected Vestryman in the room of Thos. Turpin who has resign'd. Rich^d. Crump is elected Church-warden in the room of Wm Gay who has resign^d.

   Thos. Moseley Ch warden
   L. Berry Mosby John Netherland
   John Moseley Rich^d. Ligon
   Vincent Markham Wm Fleming

****

[213]   September 24th. 1779
At a Vestry held for Southam Parish at the Courthouse for Laying off the Said parish into Small Districts & for appointing Processioners to procession the Lands in the Same. Present
>   Thos. Moseley & Richard Crump Church Wardens
>   L. Berry Mosby, Edward Haskins
>   John Moseley, Vincent Markham
>   And John Netherland, Gent. Vestrymen.

Ordered that John Povall Charles Lewis & Wm Elam or any two of them between the last Day of September & the last Day of March next, begin & procession all the Lands & renew and mark the Several lines between Fighting Creek, Buckingame Road, Lyle's Road & Appomattox River, & make their Return according to Law.

Ordered that George Williamson Robert Williamson & John Moseley Junr. or any two of them between the last Day of September & the last Day of March next begin & procession all the Lands & renew & mark the Several Lines between Geneto Road the Church Road to Fighting Creek & Appomattox River And make their return according to Law.

Ordered the Samuel Hobson George Davis & Charles Povall or any two of them between the last Day of September & the last Day of March next begin & procession all the Lands & renew & mark the Several lines between from the fork of Fighting Creek, Randolphs Mill Creek to Buckingame Road down the Same to the Church, thence down the Creek to the fork, & make their return according to Law.

Ordered that Edward Watkins J^r. Abraham Baugh & Henry Watkins or any two of them between the last Day of September & the last Day of March next begin & procession all the Lands & renew & mark the Several Lines between the New Road, Geneto Road, the Church Road & Buckingame Road & make their Return According to Law.

Ordered that John Pankey Arthur Moseley Senr. & Henry Moore or any two of them between the last Day of September & the last Day of March next begin & procession all the Lands & renew & mark the Several lines between King W^m. Parish Line the New Road, Geneto Road & the County line And make their return according to Law.

[214]   September 24th. 1779
Ordered that Gideon Lockitt Arthur Moseley & Francis Marshall or any two of them between the last Day of September & the last Day of March next begin & procession all the Lands & renew & mark the Several lines between the County line Appomattox River & Geneto Road & make their return according to Law.

Ordered that Chuchea Baugh John Baugh & Rich^d. Eggleston Senr. or any two of them, between the last Day of September & the last Day of March next begin & procession all the lands & renew & mark the several lines between the Middle Road, Randolphs Church Road, Buckingame Road, & the Road from Abr^m. Salle's Plantation to Buckingame Road & make their return according to Law.

Ordered that John Ligon Thomas Colwell & Charles Woodson Senr. or any two of them between the last Day of September & the last Day of March next begin & procession all the Lands & renew & mark the Several lines between the Middle Road, Lyles Road, Buckingame Road & the Road from the Negroes Arm to Joseph Mayo's & make their Return according to Law.

Ordered that Richard Radford Jn^r. Maxey & Charles Hatcher or any two of them between the last Day of September & the last day of March next begin & procession all the Lands & renew & mark the Several lines between Jone's Creek, King W^m. Parish Line Buckingame Road & the lo[w]er end of the parish & make their Return according to Law.

Ordered that William Watson George Radford & Aron Haskins or any two of them between the last Day of September & the last Day of March next begin & procession all the Lands & renew & mark the Several lines between Jones Creek King W^m. Parish Line & James River, Fine Creek to the Middle Road, Middle Road to Joseph Mayo's, Joseph Mayo's Road to Buckingame Road & make their return according to Law.

Ordered that Edmund Vaughn Bennet Goode, William Rennold & Joseph

Mayo or any two of them between the last day of September & the last day of March next begin & procession all the Lands & renew & mark the several lines between the Road from Michaux Ferry to Charles Woodson plantation on the Middle Road, down the Same to Fine Creek, down Fine Creek to James River, up James River to the Said Ferry, & make their Return according to Law.

Ordered that Edward Cox, Samuel H. Saunders, & James Bagbey or any two of them between the last day of September & the last day of March next begin & procession all the lands & renew & mark the Several lines between James River, the Ferry Road to Prossers Ordinary, the River Road & Solomon's Creek & make their Return according to Law.

[215]   Sepr. 24th 1779
Ordered that Robert Hughes, Robert Murry & Daniel Hix or any two of them between the last Day of September & the last Day of March next begin & procession all the Lands & renew & mark the Several lines between Deep Creek, James River the Parish Line & the River Road & make their Return according to Law.

Ordered that James Drake, Edmond Toney Junr. & Robert Taylor or any two of them between the last Day of September & the last Day of March next begin & procession all the Lands & renew & mark the Several lines between Deep Creek, the Middle Road, down to Loyd's, the Road from Loyds to Edmond Toneys, the Road from Edm^d. Toneys to the River Road above Duncan Robertsons, & the River Road, & make their return according to Law.

Ordered that Charles Woodson Junr. Batt^w. Stovall & Edmond Toney or any two of them between the last Day of September & the last Day of March next, begin & procession all the Lands & Renew & mark the Several lines between the Middle Road, the Road from Charles Woodsons to Prossers Orindary, the River Road, Solomon Creek, James River, Deep Creek, the River Road, down the Road above Duncan Robertsons to Edmond Toneys & the said Road from Edm^d Toneys to Loyds, & make their return according to Law.

Ordered that Langhorn Tabb, Archelus Nunnally & Henry Cox Senr. or any of them between the last day of September & the last Day of March next begin & procession all the Lands & renew & mark the Several lines between Thos. Mooday's, the Parish Line on Appomattox River to Swanns Creek & so to Buckingame Road, & up the Said Road to the Parish Line, the Parish Line to the Begining & make their return according to Law.

Ordered that Francis E. Harris Robert Bisco & Poindexter Mosby or any two of them between the last Day of September & the last Day of March next begin & procession all the Lands & renew & mark the Several lines between Swanns Creek & Appomattox River, Down the Said River to Lyle's Ford along Lyle's Road to Buckingame Road, up the Said Road to Swanns Creek & make their Return according to Law.

Ordered that Thomas Stegar, Hans Stegar, Francis Stegar & Joseph Harris or any two of them between the last Day of September & the last Day of March next begin & procession all the Lands & renew & mark the Several lines between the Parish Line on Buckingame Road, to the Middle Road, down the Middle Road to Sallee's Path, from thence to Buckingame Road, up Buckingame Road to the Parish Line, along that to the begining & make their Return according to Law.

[216]   September 24th, 1779
Ordered that Edmond Logwood Jno. Moss & Nicholas Speers or any two of them between the last Day of September & the last Day of March next begin & procession all the Lands & Renew & mark the Several lines between Muddy Creek the Parish Line to the Middle Road Deep Creek & the River Road & make their return according to Law.

Ordered that Edmund Vaughn be appointed vestryman in the Room of William Gay who has resign'd.

Ordered that George Williamson be appointed vestryman in the Room of Richard Eggleston who has resign'd.

Thomas Moseley	} Church Wardens
Richard Crump	
John Moseley	John Netherland
Littleberry Mosby	Edward Haskins
	Vincent Markham

****

At a vestry held for Southam parish at the Courthouse for Laying the Parish Levy January 31st. 1780. Present
    Richard Crump &   Thomas Moseley Ch. Wardens
    John Netherland   Wm Fleming
    John Moseley   Littleberry Mosby
    Vincent Markham & George Williamson Gen^t. Vestrymen

Southam Parish The pre[se]nt year D^r.	lb Nett Tobacco
To Thomas Strange for his unfortunate Children	800
To Robert Pool a poor Person	600
To Mary McCraw for keeping George Dobbins	600
To Ditto for keeping Betsey Hopper 2 years	1000
To John Moseley for keeping Mary Jennings	200
Carried Forw^d	3200

[217] January 31st 1780

Brought Forward 3200 lb nett Tob^o	
To Paul Wright for keeping Sarah Wright's 2 Children	1000
To Ditto for keeping Ditto one month last year	100
To Patrick Fitsimmons for his unfortunate Child	500
To Thos. Wilkinson for his Ditto	500
To W^m. Clarke, Clerke of the Vestry	800
To 6 p C^t. for Collecting the above Tobacco	366
	6466
To a Depositum in the hands of the Collector	734
	7200
Southam Parish C^r.	
By 1800 Tithes at 4 pounds Tob^o. p poll	7200

Ordered that George Williamson be appointed Church Warden in the room of Richard Crump who has Resign'd.

Ordered that William Mayo Ju^r. be appointed Church Warden in the Room of Thomas Moseley who has Resign'd.

Ordered that Joseph Harris be appointed vestryman in the room of W^m. Fleming who has resign'd.

Ordered that Francis E. Harris be appointed Vestryman in the room of John Mayo who has Resign'd.

Ordered that the 500 lb. Tobacco levy'd the last year for William Johns for keeping Eliz^a. Howl be paid unto David Ciezar, it appearing to the vestry that he the Said Ciezar perform'd the Services.

Ordered that Vincent Markham be appointed Parish Collector to collect the parish Levy for the present & the last year on giving Bond & Security to the Church Wardens according to Law.

Ordered that the Collector be authorised to Demand evry Titheable person two pounds Tobacco for the last year & four pounds Ditto for the present year or in lieu thereof 6/ p pound at the Option of the payer & pay the Same to the Several Creditors.

    Richd Crump & Thos. Moseley Ch. Wardens
    John Netherland W^m. Fleming
    John Moseley   L. Berry Mosby
    Vincent Markham George Williamson

[218] Processioning Returns October 10th. 1780
In obedience to an order of Vestry held for Southam Parish We the Subscribers have procession'd the following Lines Viz^t. the Line between Peyton Randolph & William Macon, present Richard Eggleston & William Macon. Line Between Peyton Randolph & Seth Ligon, Present Richard Eggleston & Seth Ligon. Line Between Peyton Randolph & Samuel Hobson, Present Charles Harris & Samuel Hobson. Line between Peyton Randolph & Est^a of Brett Randolph, Present John Pitman & Charles Harris. Line between Peyton Randolph & Charles Povall, Present Charles Povall. Line between Seth Ligon & Samuel Hobson, Present Seth Ligon & Samuel Hobson. Line between Seth Ligon & Anthony Christian, Present Seth Ligon. Line between Samuel Hobson & Anthony Christian, Present Samuel Hobson. Line between George Davis & Anthony Christian, Present George Davis & Anthony Christian Ju^r. Line between George Davis & George Radford, Present George Davis & George Radford. Line between George Davis and William Blackburn, Present George Davis & William Blackburn. Line between Brett Randolph & George Davis, Present John Pitman & George Davis. Line between Brett

Randolph & William Blackburn, Present John Pitman & William Blackburn. Line between William Blackburn & Benj^a. Hatcher, Present William & Benjamin Hatcher. Line Between William Moseley & William Blackburn, Present Joiles Fuquay & William Blackburn. Line between Brett Randolph & Benjamin Hatcher, Present John Pitman & Benjamin Hatcher. Line Between Charles Hatcher & James Bransford, Present Charles Hatcher & James Bransford. Line between James Bransford & John Moseley Ju^r, Present James Bransford. Line between Benjamin Hatcher & Jesse Roper, Present Thos Ballow & Benjamin Hatcher. Line Between Brett Randolph & Elijah Clay, Present John Pitman & Elijah Clay. Line Between Brett Randolph & Charles Povall, Present Charles Povall & Peter Wilkinson. Line Between Brett Randolph & Samuel Hobson, Present Samuel Hobson & John Pitman.

Samuel Hobson
George Davis
Chas. Povall

Agreable to an Order of the Vestry of Southam Parish we the Subscribers have procession'd all the lines in our precincts the people all present or Consenting.

Gideon Lockitt
Arthur Moseley

[219]   Processioning Returns October 10th. 1780
In obedience to an Order of the Vestry of Southam parish we have procession'd the following Lines Vizt. Line Between William Moseley & George Radford, Present Joiles Fuquay for Moseley. Between Anthony Christian & George Radford, Both present. Between John Jude & Miriam Pleasants, Present Benjamin Jude & William Bagbey. Between S^d. Pleasants & Robert Pleasants, Present William Bagbey for both. Between Thos. Turpin & Robert Pleasants, Present William Bagbey & Rich^d. Cumpton. Between S^d. Turpin & William Archer, Present Richd Cumpton for both. Between Samuel Pleasants & Robert Pleasants, Present William Bagbey for Both. Between Thos. Turpin & Henry Archer, Present Richard Cumpton for both. Between Thos. Turpin & Samuel Pleasants, Present Richard Cumpton & William Bagbey. Between Anthony Christian & Seth Ligon, Present George Radford.

George Radford
William Watson

We Robert Hughes & Robert Murry being appointed processioners of the Land lying between Deep Creek & Muddy Creek, James River & the Road have mark'd the lines as follows, March 14th 1780,

Between
Robert Hughes & David Hughes	Dav^d Hughes & Wm Tucker present
David Hughes & Thos Tucker Ju^r	Dav^d Hughes & Jno. Beck present
Thos. Tucker Ju^r. & Thos. Bolling	D^o. & D^o. present
Thos. Bolling & Robt. Hughes	D^o. present
John Steuard & Ditto	both present
Thos. Bolling & Jno Stewart	Jno. Steuart present
W^m. Stratton & John Stewart	Both present
Ditto & Thos. Bolling	Wm Stratton & D^d Hughes present
Ditto & Robert Murry	Jesse Tucker present
Thos. Bolling & D^o.	Ditto present
Danl Hix & Thos. Bolling	Danl. Hix present
Arch^d Hix & D^o.	D^o. present
Danl. Hix & Robt Murray	Both present
Arch^d Hix & W^m. Tucker	Both present
D^o. & Jno Swann	Arch^d Hix & Jno. King present
Ditto & Richd Minter	Both present
Richd Minter & Jno. Swann	Minter & Jno. King present
D^o. & Chas. Logan	Ri^d Minter & D^o present
Jno. Swann & D^o.	D^o present
D^o. & Jesse Mosby	D^o present
D^o. & Chas. Logan	D^o present

          Robert Hughes
          Robert Murry

[220] Processioning Returns October 18th 1780
Agreable to an Order of Vestry of Southam Parish we the Subscribers have processioned the following Lines March 1780 Viz^t

Between
Abram. Baugh	& Wm Ronolds	Abra^m & Joseph Baugh present
D^o	& Wm Chitwood ⎫	
D^o	& Rachel Baugh ⎭	D^o D^o

Between
W^m. Chitwood	& W^m. Marshall	parties present
Wm Marshal	& Henry Moore	D^o D^o
Henry Moore	& Rachel Baugh	Wm Marshall D^o
Wm Chitwood	& Christopher Bass	Wm Chitwood D^o
D^o	& Benj^a Moseley	D^o D^o
D^o	& Matt^w Farley ⎫	
D^o	& Wm Ronold ⎭	D^o D^o
Matt^w Farley	& D^o	Abram Baugh & Matt Farley Ju^r D^o
Edwd Watkins	& Matt^w Farley	Edwd Watkins & D^o D^o
D^o	& Benj^a Moseley	D^o & D^o D^o
Matt^w Farley	& Edwd Watkins ⎫	
D^o	& Benj^a Moseley ⎭	D^o & D^o D^o
Benj^a Moseley	& Gid^n Lockett ⎫	
D^o	& Mark Taylor ⎭	Matt^w Farley & Ja^s Flowers D^o
D^o	& Chris^r Bass	D^o D^o
Jno. Pankey	& Alex^r Trent	Jno. Pankey D^o
Wm Johnson	& Peter Depp	
D^o	& Edm^d Wooldridge	
D^o	& Wm Wooldridge	Wm Johnson & Wm Woold^r D^o
Wm Wooldridg	& Jno Burton ⎫	
D^o	& Eleazer Clay ⎭	Jno. Burton & D^o
Arthur Moseley	& Henry Hatcher	
D^o	& Eleaz^r. Clay	
D^o	& Jo^s. Jackson ⎫	Arthur Mosley & Henry Hatcher Ju^r
D^o	& John Fowler Ju^r ⎭	

Chesterfield & Powhatan County
The line from Buckingham to Geneto Road

Jno. Pankey	& Jno. Fowler Ju^r.	Wm Wooldridge & Ja^s Hill D^o
John Fowler	& Jo^s. Jackson	D^o D^o
W^m. Wooldridge	& Eleazar Clay	
W^m. Marshall	& Henry Moore Senr	

John Pankey
Henry Moore
Arthur Moseley

In pursuance of an Order of Vestry of Southam parish we the Subscribers have processioned all the Lands contained in our Respective bounds according to Law.

Rih^d. Radford
Jno. Maxey
Chas. Hatcher

[221] Processioning Returns October 18th 1780
March 4th 1780 In Obedience to an Order of the vestry of Southam Parish We the Subscribers have procession'd all the Lands Within Our Bounds according to Law.

Edm^d Toney Ju^r
Robert Taylor

Pursuant to an Order of Vestry to us directed we have procession'd the Lands & Mark'd the Several lines contain[ed] in our Respective Bounds according to Law Viz^t.
Between

Chas Lewis & Thos Howlett		Chas Lewis & Francis Barbee	present
Hughes Woodson	& Richd Povall	D^o & D^o	D^o
Thos Howlett	& D^o	J. Drake & D^o	D^o
Chas Lewis	& Phill Thomas	Chas Lewis & Vincent Markham	D^o
D^o	& Vincent Mark^m	parties	D^o
Thos Howlett	& D^o	D^o	D^o
Poindexter Mosby	& D^o	D^o	D^o
D^o	& Thos Howlett	D^o	D^o
D^o	& Mary McCraw	Francis Barbee	D^o
D^o	& Patteson's Est^a	Richd Crump	D^o
	& Richd Crump	parties	D^o
Richd Crump	& Wm Mayo	Richd Crump	D^o
D^o	& Robt Biscoe	parties	D^o
D^o	& Saml Hobson	D^o	D^o
D^o	& Patteson Est^a	Richd Crump	D^o
Robt Smith & Poindexter Mosby		Poind^r Mosby & Bartlett Colley	D^o
Joseph Woodson	& D^o	D^o	D^o
Saml Hobson	& Robt Biscoe	parties	D^o
D^o	& Chas Clay	D^o	D^o
	& Ja^s. R. Bradley's Est^a	Chas Clay	D^o
Robt Biscoe	& William Mayo	Robt Biscoe	D^o
Ja^s R. Bradley's Est^a	& D^o	Charles Clay	D^o
D^o	& Francis E. Harris	Francis E Harris	D^o

Ann Harris	& Wm Mayo	Chas Clay	D^o
D^o	& Robt Moore	D^o	D^o

Francis E. Harris
Robert Biscoe
15th March 1780

[222] Processioning Returns October 20th 1780
In Conformity to an Order of the Vestry of Southam Parish held September 24th 1779. We the Subscribers have procession'd the Lands in our appointed bounds according to Law &c Viz^t.

The line Between Edwd Watkins & Arthur Moseley, Both parties consenting.
The line between Edwd Watkins & one M$^{rs.}$ Jones, Edwd Watkins present.
Between Thomas Moseley & Edwd Watkins Ju^r, both present.
Between Edwd Watkins Junr & Edwd Watkins Senr, Both Consenting.
Between Thos Moseley & Edwd Watkins Senr, Both present.
Between John Moseley & Thos Moseley, Thos Moseley present.
Between John Moseley & Alex^r Trent, Jno Moseley present.
Between John Moseley & James Bransford, Both present.
Between Alex^r Trent & John Dean, Dean present.
Between Abraham Baugh & Alex^r Trent, John Vest present.
Between Abraham Baugh & Wm Ronold, John Vest present.
Between Wm Ronold & Matt^w Farley, John Vest present.
Between Alex^r Trent & John Pankey, Peter Day present.
Between Edwd Watkins & John Watkins, Matt^w Farly present.
Between Alex^r Trent & John Watkins, John Vest present.
Between James Bransford & John Dean, both present.

Edward Watkins
Abraham Baugh

In Obedience to an Order of vestry held for Southam Parish Sep 24 1779 We the Subscribers have processiond the following lines Viz^t:

Between Peyton Randolph & John Baugh, John Baugh present.
Between

Peyton Randolph & Wm Elam		Thos Rice & Wm Elam	D^o
D^o	& Wm Archer	D^o	D^o

D⁰	& Jn⁰. Povall	D⁰ & Jn⁰. Povall	D⁰
Wᵐ Elam	& Stoaks McCaul	Davᵈ Thomson & Wᵐ Elam	D⁰
D⁰	& Wᵐ Archer	Wᵐ Archer & D⁰	D⁰
Stoaks McCaul	& Phil Thomas	Davᵈ Thomson & Phil Thomas	D⁰
Philip Thomas	& Chaˢ Lewis	D⁰	D⁰
Stoaks McCaul	& D⁰	D⁰	D⁰
D⁰	& Chaˢ Povall	D⁰	D⁰
Chaˢ Lewis	& Richᵈ Povall	John Povall	D⁰
Stoaks McCaul	& J. P. Baugh	Davᵈ Thomson & Jn⁰ Baugh	D⁰
Chaˢ Povall	& D⁰	Jn⁰ Povall & D⁰	D⁰

John Povall
Chaˢ Lewis
William Elam

[223]   Processioning Returns Octʳ 20ᵗʰ. 1780
Agreable to an Order of the Vestry to us Directed we the Subscribers have procession'd all the lines in our precincts the people all present or Consenting.

       Robert Williamson
       John Moseley Juʳ

Agreable to an Order of the Vestry of Southam Parish to us directed we the Subscribers have procession'd all the following lines Vizᵗ: The lines round Anthony Minters Land, Anthony Minter present. the lines around James Bagbey Land, Anthony Minter present. The lines around Samuel H. Saunders Land, William Carr present. the lines around Robert Bagbey's Land, William Clarke present. the lines around William Kerrs Land, William Kerr present. The lines around William Cox's Land, Henry Bagbey present. The lines around John Cox, Jn⁰. Cox present. The lines around Edward Coxes Land, Edward Cox present. The lines around Edmund Vaughn, Edward Cox present. The lines around William Gays Land, William Gay present. The lines around John Wilkinson Land, John Wilkinson present. The lines around William Fleming's Land, Wᵐ. Gay present. The lines around Burrell Baughs Land, Wᵐ. Gay present. The lines around Joseph Ligons Land, Wᵐ. Gay present. the lines between Paul Wright & Thoˢ. Wilkinson, Samuel Woodson present. The lines around James Wilkinsons Land, Paul Wrigh[t] present. The lines around Joel Owens land, Joel Owen present.

James Bagbey
Samuel H. Saunders

Agreable to an Order of Southam Parish to us Directed Sep 24th 1779 We the Subscribers have processioned all the lines in our appointed Bounds Viz^t: line Between James Bradley and William Cox, present William Clements & Edward Harris. the line Between Edward Harris and William Cox, present Edward Harris and William Clements. the line Between Edward Harris and William Daniel, parties present. the line Between Henry Skipwith & Francis E. Harris. the lines between Francis E. Harris and James Bradley's Estate. the line Between Henry Cox and William Daniel, Edwd. Munford present. Between William Daniel and Edward Munford. Between Henry Skipwith and Edwd Munford, present Edward Munford. Between Henry Skipwith and the land Henry Hatcher liv'd upon, Present Edward Munford. Between the said Hatchers Land and Robert Gordin, Present Robert Gordin and Edward Munford. Between Henry Skipwith and Robert Gordin, Pres^t Robert Gordin and Edward Munford. Between William A. Burton and Langhorn Tabb, Pres^t. Edwd Munford and Robert Gordin. Between William A. Burton and Robert Gordin, Pres^t. Edw Munford.

[224]
the line between Thomas Moody and William A. Burton, parties present. Between Langhorn Tabb and George Cox, present Edward Munford and Langhorn Tabb. Between Archelus Nunnally and George Cox, parties present. Between Henry Cox and George Cox, parties present. Between Henry Cox and Edward Munford, parties present. Between Henry Skipwith and William Daniel, Edward Munford present.

Archelus Nunnally
Henry Cox

****

At a vestry held for Southam Parish at the Courthouse for Laying the Parish Levy 28th Febuary 1781. Present William Mayo Ch. Warden, Litt^y Mosby, John Netherland, Vincent Markham, Edwd. Haskins, Thos. Moseley & Edm^d Vaughn Gent Vestry^n.

Southam Parish the present year D^r		nett Tob^o.
To Thos. Strange for his unfortunate Children		800
To Robert Pool a poor person		600
To Mary McCraw for keeping George Dobbins		600
To Ditto for keeping Betsey Hopper		600
To Paul Wright for Keeping Sarah Wrights two Child^n.		1200
To Patrick Fitsimmons for his unfortunate Child		600
To Thos. Wilkinson for his Ditto		600
To Jno. P. Bondurant for keeping John Hopper two years terminateing in Augt next		1200
To William Mayo and George Williamson for the Support of Lodwick Elam		3000
To Jean Elam for keeping said Loddowick Elam four Months in the last year		600
To W^m. Clarke as Clk to the Vestry (for last year)		800
To 6 p C^t. for Collecting the above Tob^o.		636
		11236
Cr. By 1800 Tithes at Six pounds Tob^o. p poll		10800
To Balla Due the Collector		436
		11236

[225]
Ordered that Vincent Markham be appointed Collector to Collect the above Tob^o. on giving Bond and Security to the Church wardens According to Law.

Ordered that the Collector be authorized to Demand of evry Titheable person in this parish Six pounds Tob^o. or in Lieu thereof two Dollars p pound at the Option of payer and pay the Same to the Several Creditors.

Ordered that John Swann be appointed vestryman in the room of Francis E. Harris who refuses to serve.

Ordered that Wm Ronold be appointed vestryman in the room of Joseph Harris who refuses to serve.

      W^m. Mayo Ju^r.   Vincent Markham
      Edwd. Haskins   Edm^d. Vaughn

Lit.ʸ Mosby   Thoˢ. Moseley
John Netherland

****

At a Vestry held for Southam Parish at the Courthouse Oct.ʳ 17. 1781. Present William Mayo Ju.ʳ & George Williamson Ch wardens, Edw.ᵈ Haskins, Vincent Markham, Edm.ᵈ Vaughn, Thoˢ. Moseley and John Moseley Gent Vestrymen.

Ordered that Churchwardens of this paris[h] let the keeping of Mary Smith and her Child Susannah upon the best terms they can and that provision for the paying of the Same be made at the Laying the next parish Levy.

W.ᵐ Mayo Ju.ʳ   George Williamson
Thoˢ. Moseley   Edw.ᵈ Haskins
Edm.ᵈ Vaughn   Vincent Markham
                                     John Moseley

****

[226]   25ᵗʰ May 1782
At a Vestry held for Southam Parish at Petersville Church for laying the parish Levy 25ᵗʰ May 1782. Present. George Williamson & William Mayo Ju.ʳ Ch Wardens, John Netherland, Thoˢ. Moseley, John Moseley, Edmund Vaughn, Vincent Markham & Rich.ᵈ Crump Vestrymen.

Southam Parish the present year	D.ʳ	nett Tob.ᵒ
To Thoˢ. Strange for his unfortunate Children		800
To Rob.ᵗ Pool & wife poor Persons		600
To Mary M.ᶜCraw for support of George Dobbins		600
To Ditto for Keeping Betsey Hopper		600
To Paul Wright for Keeping Sarah Wrights Two Children		1200
To Patrick Fitsimmons for his unfortunate Child		600
To Jn.ᵒ Peter Bondurant for keeping John Hopper		600
To William Ronald & Edmund Vaughn for support of Mary Smith & her Child Susannah till the laying the next Levy		1200
To William Clarke as Clerk to the Vestry for the last and present year		1200

To 6 p C⁺. for Collecting the above Tobº.	192
	8692
To a Depositum in the hands of the Collector	308
	9000

Southam parish	Cʳ	
By 1800 Tithes at five pounds Tobo p poll		9000
By Vincent Markham Collector for the year 1779 & 1780	} 3/4 Specie	

Ordered that the Collector be authorized to Demand and receive of evry Titheable person in this parish Six pounds Tobº. for the last year and five pounds Tobº. for the present year, or in lieu thereof 20/ p hundred at the Option of the payer and pay the same to the several Creditors.

[227]
Ordered that Benjamin Mosby be appointed Collector to Collect the aforementioned Tobº. on Giving Bond & Security to the Church Wardens According to Law.

Ordered that William Ronald & Edmund Vaughn be appointed Church Wardens in the Room of William Mayo & George Williamson who has Resign'd.

Sign'd   William Mayo Jʳ, George Williamson, Vincent Markham, John Netherland, Edmᵈ. Vaughn, John Moseley, Thomas Moseley, Richᵈ Crump

****

At a vestry held for Southam Parish at the Courthouse for Laying the Parish Levy February 27ᵗʰ 1783. Present William Ronald & Edmund Vaughn Ch. Wardens, Vincent Markham, Thoˢ. Moseley, John Moseley, George Williamson, John Netherland & Richᵈ Crump. Vestrymen.

Southam Parish the present year	Dʳ	nett Tobº.
To Thoˢ. Strange for his unfortunate Children		1200
Robert Pool & wife poor persons		600

Mary McCraw for keeping George Dobbins	600
Ditto for keeping Betsey Hopper	600
Jacob Wright keeping Sarah Wright's Two Children	1200
Patrick Fitsimmons for his unfortunate Child	600
Jn° Peter Bondurant for keeping John Hopper	600
William Ronald & Edmund Vaughn for Support of Mary Smith & her Child Susannah	3000
William Clarke Clerk to the Vestry	500
To 6 p C^t. for Collecting the above Tob°.	534
	9434
C^r. By a Depositum in the Collectors hands	1366
	10800
By 1800 Tithes at 6 lb Tob°. p poll	10800

Ordered that the Collector shall settle with the Chur[c]h Wardens for the Depositum the last & present year in his hands.

[228]   February 27th. 1783

Ordered that the collector be authorized to Demand of evry Titheable person in this Parish Six pounds of Tobacco for the present year or in lieu thereof at the rate of twenty Shillings p hundred at the Option of the payer and that the said Collector pay to the several Creditors the Several Sums of Tob° to them Levy'd or if the same be Collected in money at the said rate of twenty Shillings p hundred in full Discharge of such Tob°.

Ordered that Benjamin Mosby be appointed to Collect the above mentioned Tob° on giving Bond and Security to the Church Wardens according to Law.

Signed   Wm Ronald   Edm^d Vaughn
          John Netherland   John Moseley
          George Williamson   V. Markham
          Thos. Moseley   Richd Crump

****

At a vestry held for Southam Parish at the Courthouse Novr. 6th 1783 for Laying the parish off into Districts and for Appointing persons to procession the Lands in the Same and for other purposes. Present Edm[d] Vaughn Ch Warden, Littleberry Mosby, Rich[d] Crump, Vinc[t] Markham, John Moseley, Tho[s]. Moseley & George Williamson Vestrymen.

Ordered that John Povall William Elam & Field Archer or any two of them between the last Day of Sep[t] & the last day of March next begin and procession all the lands and renew and mark the Several lines between Fighting Creek, Buckingame Road, Lyles Road and Appomattox River and make their Return according to Law.

[229]   Nov[r]. 6th, 1783
Ordered that John Moseley Jun[r]. Benj[a] Moseley and Edw[d] Watkins Sen[r] or any two of them between the last Day of Sep[r] and the last Day of March next begin and procession all the Lands and renew and mark the Several lines Between Geneto Road, the Church Road to Fighting Creek & Appomattox River and make their Return according to Law.

Ordered that Sam[l]. Hobson, George Davis & Cha[s]. Povall or any two of them between the last Day of Sep[r] and the last Day of March next begin & procession all the Lands and renew and mark the Several lines Between from the fork of Fighting Creek, Randolphs Mill Creek to Buckingame Road thence down the Same to the Church thence down the Creek to the Fork and make their Return according to Law.

Ordered the Edw[d]. Watkins Jun[r] Abra[m]. Baugh, & Matt[w]. Farley Sen[r]. or any two of them between the last Day of Sep[r]. & the last day of March Next, begin and procession all the lands and renew and mark the Several lines between the New Road, Geneto Road, the Ch[h]. Road and Buckingame Road and make their Return according to Law

Ordered that Seth Hatcher, Arthur Moseley Sen[r] & Henry Moore or any two of them between the last Day of Sep[t] and the last Day of March next begin & procession all the lands & renew and mark the Several lines between King W[m] Parish, the New Road, Geneto Road and the county line and make their Return according to Law.

Ordered that Gideon Lockitt, Arthur Moseley and W[m]. Moseley or any two of them between the last Day of Sep[r]. and the last Day of March next begin and procession all the lands and renew and mark the Several lines between the County Line, Appomatox River and Geneto Road and make their Return according to Law.

Ordered that Crutcher Baugh John Eggleston & Jacob Williamson or any two of them between the last day of Sepr and the last day of March next begin and procession all the lands and renew & mark the Several lines between the Middle Road, Randolphs Chur[c]h Road, Buckingame Road and the Road that leads from Salles Plantation to Buckingame Road & make their return according to Law.

[230]   Novr. 6th. 1783.
Ordered that John Ligon Seth Ligon & William Macon or any two of them Between the last day of Sepr. and the last day of March next begin and procession all the lands and renew and mark the several lines between the Middle Road, Lyles Road, Buckingame Road and the Road from the Negroes Arm to Joseph Mayo's and make their return according to Law.

Ordered that Peter Pollock John Maxey and Chas. Hatcher or any two of them between the last day of Sepr. and the last day of March next begin and procession all the lands and renew and mark the Several lines between John's's Creek, King Wm Parish line and Buckingame Road and the lower end of the parish and make their Return according to law.

Ordered that George Radford Gideon Flournoy and Benjamin Jude or any two of them between the last day of Sepr. and the last day of March next begin and procession all the lands and renew and mark the Several lines between Jones's Creek, King W^m. Parish line and James River, Fine Creek to the Middle Road, Middle Road to Joseph Mayo's, Joseph Mayo's Road to Buckingame Road and make their return according to Law.

Ordered that Bennit Goode Joseph Mayo and John Good or any two of them between the last day of Sepr. and the last day of March next begin and procession all the lands and renew and mark the Several lines between the Road from Michaux Ferry to Chas. Woodsons Plantation on the Middle Road down the Same to Fine Creek down Fine Creek to James River, up the Same to the said Ferry and make their return according to Law.

Ordered that John Cox John Baugh and James Bagbey or any two of them between the last Day of Sepr and the last Day of March next begin and procession all the Lands and renew and mark the Several lines between James River the Ferry Road to Prossers Ordinary and Solomons Creek and make their Return according to Law.

Ordered that Robert Hughes Daniel Hix and Edward Hix or any two of them between the last Day of Sepr. and the last day of March next begin and procession all the lands and renew and mark the Several lines between Deep Creek, James River, the Parish line and the River Road and make their return according to Law.

[231] Novr. 6th. 1783
Ordered that Edm^d Toney Junr Robt. Taylor & James Taylor or any two of them between the last Day of Sep^r. & the last Day of March next begin and procession all the lands and renew and mark the Several lines between Deep Creek the Middle Road down to Loyds the Road from Loyds to Edm^d Toneys the Road from E^d. Toneys to the River Road above Duncan Robertsons and the River Road and make their Return according to Law.

Ordered that Edm^d Toney Senr, Chas Woodson Ju^r and Batt Stovall or any two of them between the last Day of Sepr and the last Day of March next begin and procession all the lands and renew and mark the Several lines between the Middle Road the Road from Chas. Woodsons to Prossers Ordinary, the River Road, Solomons Creek, James River, Deep Creek the River Road down to the Road above Duncan Robertsons to Edm^d Toneys and the Said Road from Edm^d Toneys to Loyds and make their return according to Law.

Ordered that Langhorn Tabb Archelus Nunnally and Edwd Munford or any two of them between the last Day of Sepr. and the last Day of March next begin and procession all the lands and renew and mark the Several lines between Thos. Moody's, the Parish line on Appomattox River to Swans Creek and so to Buckingame Road, up the Said Road to the Parish lines, the paris[h] line to the Beginning and make their return according to Law.

Ordered that Francis E Harris Robt. Bisco & Edwd Harris or any two of them Between the last Day of Sepr and the last Day of Mark [March] next begin and procession all the lands and renew and mark the Several lines between Swans Creek and Appomattox River down the River to Lyles Ford, along Lyles Road to Buckingame Road up the said Road to Swans Creek and make their return according to Law.

Ordered that Thos. Stegar Hans Stegar and Joseph Harris or any two of them between the last of Sepr and the last Day of March next begin and procession all the lands and renew and mark the Several lines between the Parish line on Buckingame Road to the Middle Road down the Middle Road to Salle's Path from thence to Buckingame Road up Buck^{me}. Road to the Paris[h] line along that to Begining and make their Return according to Law.

[232]   6th. Novr. 1783.

Ordered that Edm^d Logwood Robt. Mosby and Nicholas Speers or any two of them between the last day of Sepr. and the last Day of Mar. next begin and procession all the Lands and renew and mark the Several lines between Muddy Creek the Parish line to the Middle Road, Deep Creek and the River Road and make their Return according to Law.

	D^r.	nett Tob^o.
Southam Parish the ensuing year		
To Thos. Stranges two Children and Esther Stranges Child		1800
To Robt. Pool & wife Poor persons		1000
To Mary McCraw for keeping George Dobins		700
To Betsey Hopper		600
To Jacob Wright for keeping Colman Wright		600
To Jno. P. Bondurant for keeping Jno. Hopper		600
To Edm^d Logwood for keeping Mary Smith and her Child Susannah		2500
To W^m. Johns for keeping Eliz^a. Howl in the year 1778		500
To W^m. Clarke, Clerk of the Vestry		600
To 6 p C^t. for Collecting the above Tob^o.		<u>534</u>
		9434
To a Depositum in the Collectors hands		<u>1366</u>
C^r. By 1800 Tithes at 6 pounds Tob^o p poll		10800

Ordered that evry Titheable person in this Parish pay to the Collector Six pounds Tob° or Money at two pence half penny p pound at the Option of the payer and pay off the parish Creditors according to Law.

Ordered that Vincent Markham lay out the Tob°. Levyed for Stranges Children and that the parish Collector for the last Collection pay the Tob°. Levy'd for Thos. Strange last ~~year~~ Collection to Vincent Markham.

[233]   6th. Novr. 1783.
Ordered that Littlebery Mosby Senr and John Netherland be appointed Church Wardens in the Room of W^m. Ronald and Edm^d Vaughn who has resign'd.

Ordered that Vincent Markham be appointed Collector to Collect the Parish Levy for the ensuing year.
Sign'd   John Moseley, Littleberry Mosby, Richd Crump,
            Thos Moseley, George Williamson, Edm^d. Vaughn

****

At a vestry held for Southam Parish at the Courthouse January 31st. 1785 for Laying the Parish Levy &c. Present Littleberry Mosby & John Netherland Ch. W^s, Thos. Moseley, Richd Crump, George Williamson, Edm^d. Vaughn and William Ronald Vestrymen.

Southam Parish the present year	D^r. lb Tob°.
To Vincent Markham for Support of Thos. Stranges Children and Esther Stranges Child	1800
To Robt. Pool and wife Poor Persons	1000
To Mary M^c.Craw for Support of George Dobbins	700
Ro Rich^d. Crump for Support of Tabitha Hopper's three youngest Children	1200
To John. P. Bondurant for John Hopper	600
To George Mosby for Sarah Whalens two Children, Twelve Months from the time he receiv'd them	1000
To William Clarke Clerk of the Vestry	600
To 6 p C^t. for Collecting the above Tob°	414
	7314

		C^r.
By 1800 Tithes at four pounds Tob^o. p poll		7200
By a Depositum in the Collector's hands		114
		7314
Carr^d. Forw^d		Ordered

[234]   Jany. 31st. 1785

Ordered that evry titheable person in this parish pay to the Collector four pounds Tob^o. or money at three pence p pound at the option of the payer and pay off the Parish Creditors according to Law.

Ordered that William Smith be appointed Collector to Collect the fore mention'd Tob^o. on giving Bond and Security to the Church wardens for the Same.

Ordered that Littleberry Mosby, Rich^d. Crump, & John Netherland or any two of them be appointed to Settle with the Parish Collectors for all Arrears.

Sign'd   Jno. Netherland, Littleberry Mosby, Thos. Moseley, Rich^d. Crump, Edm^d. Vaughn, George Williamson, And W^m. Ronald.

****

At the meeting of the Vestry of Southam Parish Powhatan County, at the Courthouse of the said County on Saturday the 30th day of April 1791. Present, the Reverend John H. Saunders, Richard Crump, Edward Carrington, George Williamson, William Bentley, William Mayo and Peter F^d. Archer who having subscribed severally to the articles prescribed by the convention proceeded to the choice of Church Wardens.

When Richard Crump and William Mayo Gentlemen, were unanimously elected to that office.

Ordered that Thomas Turpin Junr. be appointed Clerk to the Vestry.

The following Members paid each six shillings in conformity to an order of the Committee of the Convention (To Wit.). Edward Carrington, Vincent Markham, William Bentley, William Ronald, Peter F^d. Archer,

Richard Crump, William Mayo, William Moseley, John Macon, Brett Randolph, George Williamson and Littleberry Mosby Jun'.

Ordered that Edward Carrington, with the present Minister John H. Saunders, be a Deputation from this Parish, to the Convention to be holden in the City of Richmond on the First Tuesday in next month.

Ordered That the Clerk transmit to the Rev^d. M^r. Buchanan agreeably to an order of the Standing Committee of the Convention, a list of the property belonging to the church of this parish, which consists of the following articles (To Wit.) The Glebe land estimated at £300, a half worn surplice 20/, a half worn damast Table cloth 5/, a prayer Book and Bible Damaged 15/, a Table & chest 10/.

[235] April 30th 1791
Ordered That the Clerk give due notice agreeably to an ordinance of the Convention to all the members of the vestry to be punctual in their attendance at the next meeting.
Ordered That the vestry be adjourned.
   Signed
   Jno. H. Saunders Min^r.
   Rich^d. Crump   ⎫
Teste William Mayo   ⎭ Church Wardens
   Ed. Carrington
   Thomas Turpin Junr. Clk.

   W. Bentley
   George Williamson ⎫
   Peter F^d. Archer   ⎭ Ves^y. Men.

****

Agreeable to an order of the Overseers of the poore for Powhatan County, we the Subscribers have processioned the hereafter mentioned lines:

The lines between William Harris & Peter Sublet. between William Harris & Anthony Martin. between William Harris & Daniel Branch. between

Thomas Harris & Daniel Branch. Between William Forsee & Anthony Martin, Pr^t. J^s. Martin. between Philip Gatch & William Forsee, Pre^t. Jas Martin. between Philip Gatch & Willaim Forsee, Prct. Jas Martin. Between Philip Gatch & George Smith, Pret Philip Gatch. Between Anthony Martin & George Smith, Prt Jas. Martin. Between Anthony Martin & David Patterson, Pret. Anthony Martin. Between David Patterson & George Smith, Pret George Smith. Between David Patterson & Stephen Forsee, Pret George Smith. Between James Brient estate & David Patterson, Pret George Smith. Between Jas. Brient Estate Deceased & James Brient, Pret George Smith. Between Widow Harris & James Brient estate, Prt George Smith. Between James Brient & Widdow Harris, Prt George Smith. Between William S Smith & John Depp, Pret George Smith. Between William S Smith & Samuel Pankey, Pret George Smith. Between William S Smith & Benjamin Sublett, Pret George Smith. Between William S Smith & William Street, Pret George Smith. Between William Forsee & M^{rs}. Bingley, Prt George Smith. Between Stephen Forsee & James Brient. Between John Harris Junr & Thomas Porter. Between Thomas Porter & Isaac Porter. The lines Between John Harris Junr & Anthony Martin. Between Anthony Martin & John Scott, Pres^t. An^y. Martin. Between Anthony Martin & Benjamin Harris, Pres^t. Thos. Porter.

[236]   Processioners Returns April 1792
Between Benjamin Harris & Hanna Porter. Between Between Benjamin Harris & James Brients Estate, Pres^t. Anthony Martin. Between the Widow Harris & James Brient Estate, Pres^t. James Brient. Between Anthony Martin & Isaac Porter, Pres^t. Thomas Porter. Between Hanna Porter & James Brients Estate. Between William Street & M^{rs}. Bingley. Between John Howard & William Golden. Between William Golden & Isaac Lookado. Between Peter Dean & William Golden. Between William Street & Peter Dean. Between Benjamin Sublet & Peter Dean. Between Benjamin Sublet & Samuel Roper. Between John Sublett & Samuel Roper. Between Samuel Roper & William Johnson. Between Samuel Roper & Peter Dean. Between John Sublett & William Johnson. Between William Johnson & Alex^r Trent. Between Alex^r Trent & M^{rs}. Tinsley. Between Alex^r. Trent & John Sublet. Between Alex^r. Trent & Seath Hatcher. Between John Sublet & Seth Hatcher. Between John Sublet & David Trabue. Between David Trabue & Benjamin Sublet. Between Benjamin & John Sublett. Between William Johnson & M^{rs}. Bingley. Between Seth

Hatcher & William Hopkins. Between Seth Hatcher & Robert Jordans Estate. Between Isaac Porter & Hanna Porter. the lines between Robert Jordans Estate & Samuel Pankey. Between Robert Jordans Estate & William Hopkins. Between William Hopkins & John Dep. Between Philip Gatch & M^{rs}. Bingley. Between John Howard & Joseph Meridith. Between Joseph Meridith & Isaac Lucadoe. Between Joseph Meridith & Peter Lucadoe. Between Thomas Golden & Peter Sublett. Between Peter Sublett & Philip Gatch. Between Philip Gatch & Silas Flournoy. Between Peter Sublett & Peter Lucado. Between James Bryant & Stephen Forsee. Between Stephen Forsee & Sterling Smith.

John Harris Junr.

Thomas Harris

In obedience of an order of the oversears of the poor made October the twenty ninth one thousand seven hundred and ninety one we the subscribers have processioned the lines between Jenito Road and the Church Road down to Fighting Creeak to Appomattox beginning on the line between Capt W^{m}son & Joseph Lewis, both preasant. and the line betweean Capt Williamson & Samuel Seldin, both preasant. & the line beatweean Capt W^{m}son & Thomas Goode, both preasant. & the line betweean Capt W^{m}son & Ligons Estate, Capt W^{m}son & Jos Lewis preasant. & the line betweean Thos Goode & Ligons Estate, Thos Goode & Edward Sims overseear preasant. and the line betweean Edward Wadkings & Jos Lewis, & Jos Lewis present

[237]   Processioners Returns April 1792
by the Consent of Wadkings. & the line betweean John Forlines & William Strattons, Jas Hix Overseear preasant. and the line betweean William Stratton & William Moseley, James Hix preasant. and the line betweean Thos Moseley & William Stratton, Jas Hix preasant. & the line betweean William Stratton and Edward Wadkings, Jas Hix preasant. and the line betweean Thos Moseley & Edward Wadkings, Jas Hix preasant. & the line betweean Thos Moseley & William Moseley, Jas Hix preasant. and the line betweean William Moseley & Jno Forline, Josiah Forlines preasant. given under our hands this twenty seventh day of March one thousand seven hundred and ninety two.

Jno Forlines

Thomas Moseley

Appendices

APPENDIX A

PARISH OFFICIALS

MINISTERS

1746-1751	John Robertson
1751-1773	Robert McLaurine
1773-1801	John Hyde Saunders

VESTRYMEN

The following men served as vestrymen for Southam Parish. The years in which they served are listed though the years of service may not be continuous.

Charles Anderson	1745-1749	Richard Ligon	1773-1780
Peter Field Archer	1791	Edmond Logwood	1772-1778
James Barnes	1745-1749	Henry Macon	1759-1767
John Baskerville	1749-1771	Vincent Markham	1780-1784
Stephen Bedford	1747-1757	John Mayo	1773-1776
William Bentley	1791	William Mayo	1791
Edward Carrington	1791	Littleberry Mosby	1758-1783
George Carrington	1745-1771	Arthur Moseley	1767
Richard Crump	1782-1791	John Moseley	1772-1783
Thomas Davenport	1751-1759	Thomas Moseley	1778-1785
Nicholas Davies	1745-1762	John Netherland	1776-1784
Roderick Easley	1760-1763	Wade Netherland	1752-1775
John Fleming	1756-1767	William Randolph	1746-1748
William Fleming	1767-1781	William Ronald	1785
William Gay	1778-1779	Abraham Salley	1751-1752
Benjamin Harris	1749-1756	Samuel Scott	1745-1752
Benjamin Harrison	1745-1747	Thompson Swann	1756-1775
Carter H Harrison	1767-1770	James Terry	1745-1751
Creed Haskins	1745-1766	Alexander Trent	1745-1771
Edward Haskins	1773-1782	Thomas Turpin	1745-1773
Samuel Hobson	1773-1776	Edmund Vaughn	1781-1785
John Hughes	1772-1773	George Williamson	1781-1791

CHURCH WARDENS

1745	George Carrington, William Randolph
1746	Nicholas Davies, Thomas Turpin
1747	Nicholas Davies, Thomas Turpin
1748	Nicholas Davies, Thomas Turpin
1749	Stephen Bedford, James Barnes
1750	Stephen Bedford
1751	Benjamin Harris, Creed Haskins
1752	Benjamin Harris, Creed Haskins
1753	John Baskerville, Abraham Salley
1754	John Baskerville, Wade Netherland
1755	John Baskerville, Wade Netherland
1756	John Baskerville, Wade Netherland
1757	Thomas Davenport, Alexander Trent
1758	Thomas Davenport, Alexander Trent
1759	John Fleming, Thompson Swann
1760	John Fleming, Thompson Swann
1761	Roderick Easley, Littleberry Mosby
1762	Roderick Easley, Littleberry Mosby
1763	Nicholas Davies, Henry Macon
1764	Nicholas Davies, Henry Macon
1765	Thompson Swann, Thomas Turpin
1766	Thompson Swann, Thomas Turpin
1767	William Fleming, Alexander Trent
1768	William Fleming, Alexander Trent
1769	William Fleming, Alexander Trent
1770	John Netherland, John Railey
1771	George Carrington Jr, William Fleming
1772	Littleberry Mosby, Thomas Turpin
1773	Littleberry Mosby, Thomas Turpin
1774	Edmond Logwood, John Moseley
1775	Edmond Logwood, John Moseley
1776	Richard Ligon, John Moseley
1777	Richard Ligon, John Moseley
1778	Richard Crump, Thomas Moseley
1779	Richard Crump, Thomas Moseley
1780	William Mayo, George Williamson
1781	William Mayo, George Williamson

1782 William Ronald, Edmund Vaughn
1783 Littleberry Mosby Sr, John Netherland
1785 Littleberry Mosby, John Netherland
1791 Richard Crump, William Mayo

CLERKS OF THE VESTRY

These are the men whose handwriting is found in the vestry book. Fortunately, they all wrote with very legible handwriting. Spelling, however, varied greatly, from clerk to clerk, and even from line to line.

1745-1749 Robert Walton
1749-1751 James Terry
1752-1772 Thomas Davenport Jr
1765   George Carrington (partial year)
1772-1778 Francis McCraw
1779-1785 William Clarke
1791   Thomas Turpin Jr

CLERKS OF THE CHURCHES

The clerks, sometimes called readers, were literate men who conducted services in the churches and chapels when the parish minister was unavailable.

Peterville Church
1745-1746 Robert Walton
1747-1769 John Cardwell
1770-1775 John Barnes

Tear Wallet Church
1745-1747 James Terry
1748-1749 John Hubbard
1750-1751 James Terry
1752   John Hubbard
1753-1772 Gideon Glenn
after 1772 Littleton Parish

Ham Chapel
1745-1770 T. F. Fretwell
1770-1772 Joseph Palmer
after 1772 Littleton Parish

South Chapel (Worley's Chapel)
1745-1762 Sylvanus Witt
1763-1774 Thomas Hall
1775   Matthew Farley

SEXTONS

The sextons were responsible for keeping the church buildings clean and doing other work assigned by the vestry. Sometimes, the sexton was a poor person and their work as sexton provided them with a small income.

Peterville Church
1745-1749 John Legrand
1750-1757 Amy Low (Loe)
1758-1764 Roger Hill
1765-1775 Amy Hill

Ham Chapel
1745-1746 not yet built
1747-1751 Michael Johnson
1752-1767 Rachel Farris
1768-1772 William Palmer
after 1772 Littleton Parish

Tar Wallet Church
1745-1746 not yet built
1747-1749 William Easley
1750-1764 Susannah Easley
1765-1772 Mary Bell
after 1772 Littleton Parish

South Chapel
1745-1747 not yet built
1748-1757 John Worley
1758-1772 Esther Worley
1773-1775 William Worley

PARISH COLLECTORS

1745-1746	none recorded	1770	Jesse Thomas
1747	John Smith		George Jude
1748-1754	none recorded	1771-1772	Jesse Thomas
1755-1759	John Woodson		William Hill
1760	Francis McCraw	1773	John Jefferson
	Frederick Hatcher	1774	Francis McCraw
1761	Thomas Davenport	1775	Creed Haskins
1762-1764	Littleberry Mosby	1776-1777	Creed Haskins
1765-1766	Littleberry Mosby		Thomas T. Swann
	George Carrington	1778-1779	Thomas T. Swann
	Joseph Carrington	1780-1781	Vincent Markham
1767-1768	Richard Crump	1782	Benjamin Mosby
	William Turpin	1783	Vincent Markham
1769	William Turpin	1784	William Smith
	Jesse Thomas		

APPENDIX B

VESTRY MEETINGS

The date for each vestry meeting is listed here with the general purpose of the meeting. Meetings which authorized the laying of the levy and the paying of creditors are noted as accounts and the year for which the payments were being made. Each four years, land boundaries were processioned. The vestry divided the parish into precincts and assigned several men to supervise the processioning for that precinct. The orders for processioning and the returns were recorded in the vestry minutes.

1745	[date?]	orders	1755	2/8	orders
	8/22	orders		8/11	proc. orders
	11/?	1745 accounts		12/2	1755 accounts
1746	6/30	orders	1756	4/19	proc. returns
1747	1/12	1746 accounts		11/29	1756 accounts
	2/25	orders	1757	12/15	1757 accounts
	6/15	orders	1758	12/21	1758 accounts
	7/27	proc. orders	1759	8/11	proc. orders
	11/27	1747 accounts		12/15	1759 accounts
1748	1/26	orders	1760	8/22	proc. returns
	5/21	proc. returns		11/22	1760 accounts
	9/16	orders			proc. returns
1749	1/26	1748 accounts	1761	9/20	orders
	12/16	orders		12/29	1761 accounts
	12/20	1749 accounts	1762	6/20	orders
1750	4/24	orders		12/22	1762 accounts
1751	1/8	orders	1763	7/23	proc. orders
	1/29	1750 accounts		9/29	1763 accounts
	9/10	proc. orders	1765	2/27	1764 accounts
	12/16	1751 accounts			proc. returns
1752	5/16	orders,	1766	1/27	1765 accounts
		proc. returns		5/26	orders
	12/9	1752 accounts	1767	3/17	1766 accounts
1754	1/30	1753 accounts		11/20	1767 accounts
	12/2	1754 accounts	1769	2/10	1768 accounts

1770	2/15	1769 accounts	1779	1/2	1778 accounts
1771	3/20	1770 accounts		9/24	proc. orders
	7/29	proc. orders	1780	1/31	1779 accounts
	12/23	1771 accounts		10/18	proc. returns
1772	8/1	proc. returns	1781	2/28	1780 accounts
	11/28	1772 accounts		10/17	orders
1773	11/12	1773 accounts	1782	5/25	1781 accounts
	11/23	orders	1783	2/27	1782 accounts
1774	8/22	orders		11/6	1783 accounts
1775	8/19	proc. orders			proc. orders
1776	3/2	1775 accounts	1785	1/31	1784 accounts
1777	3/8	1776 accounts	1791	4/30	orders
1778	2/12	1777 accounts			

APPENDIX C

VESTRY LEVY

Each year the vestry laid a levy in pounds of tobacco on the taxable persons in the parish in order to pay creditors.

Year	Titheables/Tobacco	Levy	Year	Titheables/Tobacco	Levy
1745	1207 @ 33	39831	1766	2988 @ 15	44820
1746	1267 @ 27	34209	1767	3000 @ 15	45000
1747	1306 @ 35	47600	1768	3116 @ 13	40508
1748	1325 @ 35	46375	1769	3146 @ 14	44044
1749	1428 @ 37	52836	1770	3213 @ 12	38556
1750	1517 @ 30	45510	1771	3288 @ 15	49320
1751	1579 @ 27	43033	Littleton Parish formed		
1752	1609 @ 29	47465	1772	1638 @ 20	32760
1753	1725 @ 25	43125	1773	1628 @ 33	53724
1754	1872 @ 23	43056	1774	no records	
1755	1947 @ 16	31152	1775	1755 @ 20	35100
1756	2013 @ 20	40260	1776	1742 @ 21	36582
1757	2098 @ 19	39862	1777	1841 @ 3	5520
1758	2145 @ 19	40755	1778	1803 @ 2	3606
1759	2310 @ 17	39270	1779	1800 @ 4	7200
1760	2463 @ 17	41871	1780	1800 @ 6	10800
1761	2560 @ 18	46080	1781	1800 @ 5	9000
1762	2606 @ 19	49514	1782	1800 @ 6	10800
1763	2780 @ 16	44480	1783	1800 @ 6	10800
1764	2806 @ 28	78568	1784	1800 @ 4	7200
1765	2865 @ 9	25795			

APPENDIX D

GLOSSARY and ABBREVIATIONS

accompt	account
alfins	oalfins, archaic word for orphans
cask	the casks which contained the tobacco
Clk	clerk
contra	used in "contra credit" meaning amounts collected or taken in
C^r	creditor, one who is owed
C.V.	clerk of the vestry
CW	churchwarden; variety of abbreviations used
dec'd	deceased
depositum	deposit
D^o	ditto
D^r	debtor, one who owes
&c	etcetera, etc.
insolvents	those unable to pay their tithes
inst.	instant, meaning of this month
L.S.	legal signature
moiety	one of two equal parts
neet tobacco	tobacco which has been processed and prepared
p	per
p annum	per annum, yearly
p cent	percent
p pound	per pound
possession	word used for procession, various spellings
tobo	tobacco
vizt	videlicet, meaning 'that is to say,' or 'namely'

BIBLIOGRAPHY

Agee, Helene B. *Facets of Goochland (Virginia) County's History*. Richmond, VA: Dietz Press, 1962.

Bicentennial and Homecoming, Rocky Oak Methodist Church, July 1949.

Brydon, George. *The Clergy of the Established Church in Virginia and the Revolution*. Richmond VA, 1933.

Cabell, Priscilla H. *Turff & Twigg, Volume One, The French Lands*. Richmond, VA., 1988.

Clark, Jewell and Elizabeth T. Long. *A Guide to Church Records in the Archives Branch, Virginia State Library*. Richmond, Virginia: Virginia State Library, 1981.

Cocke, Charles F. *Parish Lines, Diocese of Southern Virginia*. Richmond, VA: Library of Virginia, 1964.

Couture, Richard. *Powhatan, A Bicentennial History*. Richmond, VA: Dietz Press, 1980.

Cumberland County VA Historical Society. *Cumberland County, Virginia, and its People*. Marceline, MO: Walsworth Publishing, 1983.

Cumberland County VA Historical Society. *Cumberland County, Virginia, Historical Bulletin*, December 1987; September 1989; October 1993.

Davis, Vernon and James Rawlings. *The Colonial Churches of Virginia, Maryland, and North Carolina*. Richmond, VA: The Dietz Press, 1985.

Douglas, William. *The Douglas Register*. Baltimore, MD: Genealogical Publishing Company, 1966.

"Excerpts of History of Tar Wallet Baptist Church, Cumberland County, Virginia," *The Farmville Herald*, August 15, 1930.

Farmville Herald. *Today and Yesterday in the Heart of Virginia, A Reprint of the Edition of the Farmville Herald*, March 29, 1935.

Genealogies of Virginia Families, from the William and Mary College Quarterly Historical Magazine, 1982, Vol. IV, p 345.

Goodwin, Rev. Edward. *The Colonial Church in Virginia*. Milwaukee, Wisconsin: Morehouse Publishing Co., c1927.

Grundset, Eric. *Historical Boundary Atlas of Central Virginia*. Fairfax, VA: Grundset, 1999.

Gwathmey, John H. *Twelve Virginia Counties Where the Western Migration Began*, 1937.

Hening, William. *The Statutes at Large, Being A Collection of All the Laws of Virginia*. 132 volumes. Richmond, 1809-1823.

"Historic Places, Rocky Oak Church," *Powhatan Today Weekender*, August 28, 1999, page 4.

Hopewell, John S. "Handle with Care: County Loose Papers: A Petition to Clear Willis River in Cumberland County, 1774," *Magazine of Virginia Genealogy*, Vol. 39, No. 3, p 207.

Hopkins, Garland E. *The Story of Cumberland County, Virginia.* Privately Issued, Winchester, Virginia, 1942.

Kolbe, J. C. "Cumberland County Tithable Lists for 1759," *Southside Virginian*, Vol. 2, April 1984; Vol 3, October 1984.

Lurvey, A. Jean. *Goochland County Tithe Lists 1735-1747.* Springfield, MO: Lurvey Publications, 1985.

Lurvey, A. Jean. *Goochland County Tithe Lists 1748-1749.* Springfield, MO: Lurvey Publications, 1979.

Meade, William. *Old Churches, Ministers and Families of Virginia.* 1857.

Nugent, Nell. *Cavaliers and Pioneers, Abstracts of Virginia Land Patents and Grants.* Richmond VA: Virginia State Library.

Powhatan County Independence Bicentennial Committee. *Powhatan's Heritage 1977.* Powhatan, Virginia, 1977.

Powhatan County Independence Bicentennial Committee. *Powhatan's Heritage 1700-1978.* Powhatan, Virginia, 1978.

Putney, Dorothy R. *Tar Wallet Church, A History.* October 1993.

"Restoration Hopes High for Old Peterville Church," *Richmond News Leader*, May 12, 1953.

Saunders, James E. *Early Settlers of Alabama.* New Orleans, LA.: Graham & Son, 1899.

Stewart, Charles E. Address at Peterville Baptist Church, Powhatan County, Virginia, 1928.

Vaughan, Michael K. *Crucible and Cornerstone, A History of Cumberland County, Virginia.* Atlanta, GA: Resource Development Internship Project, 1969.

Winfree, Waverly K. *The Laws of Virginia, Being a Supplement to Hening's 1700-1750.* Richmond, VA: The Virginia State Library, 1971.

MAPS

Cumberland County
    dated 1777; size: 15 5/8 x 12 1/4"; restored in April 1947; LVA.

Powhatan County
    1858 map: "Drawn by Cadets M. B. Hardin and L. W. Reed, VMI cadets, class of 1858"
    1880 map: "Map of Powhatan County, VA, by J. E. LaPrade, 1880."

INDEX

Acin, see Akin
Acts of Assembly 21,140
Adams, James 167
Adams, Patrick 25
Advertising in newspaper 159
Agee (Age), Matt 26
Aiken, Aikin, Akins, see Akin
Akin, Isham 79,86,94,116,124,132, 169
Akin, James 135
Akin, William 25,26,131
Albemarle County i,iii
Alderson, Richard 143,167,211
Alexander 68,93
Alexander, John 14,35,146,164
Alford, Silvater 31,108,136
Allday, Perrin 30
Allen 55
Allen, Archer 225
Allen, Archibald 225
Allen, Capt. 128
Allen, Daniel 152,161,185,209
Allen, Francis 88,116,131
Allen, Isaac 64,77,151,161,182
Allen, James 64,76,162
Allen, James Sr 92
Allen, John 68
Allen, Joseph 208
Allen, Julius 88,104
Allen, Murrel 140
Allen, Samuel 54,69,79,86,98,99,117, 153
Allen, Samuel Jr 17
Allen, Thomas 166
Allen, William 101,166,167,184,217
Amis, Richard 149,158,162,191,195, 197,200,202,205,216
Amos (Amoss) 220,221
Amos, Richard 226

Amoss, Francis xiv,46,51,60,98,184, 203,215
Amoss, Francis Sr 184
Amoss, Francis Jr 156,161,184
Anderson, Charles iii,1,6,47,48,54, 76,86,87,114,124,127,150,161, 184
Anderson, James viii,8,19,68,76,93, 99,127,150,161,166,171,181,184
Anderson, Robert 181
Andrews, Mark 152,161,166,167, 185,209
Angela, William 55,87
Anglea, James 178,179
Anglea, Joseph 222
Anglea, William 174,178
Anglea, William Sr 173,222
Anglea, William Jr 115,151,160,173, 174,178,222
Angles, William 89
Angola Creek 55,77,115,151,208
Antrim Parish 192
Appomattox River iii,9,17,18,19,25, 56,76,77,78,79,101,114,115,116, 117,121,127,151,152,153,207, 208,209,210,231,233,234,241, 242,244,258,259,261,266
Archdeacon, James 177,178
Archer, Field 258
Archer, Henry 247
Archer, John 29,33,126,165,166,183
Archer, Peter Field 263,264,268
Archer, William 126,251,252
Arms, Edward 187
Arms, Margaret 50,63
Armsteed (Armsted), John 98,120, 184,215
Arnold, Henry 64
Arnold, Thomas 87

INDEX 279

Arnold, William 54,64,69,88,90,92, 129,171,176
Arnold, William Jr 171
Ashby vii
Askew's Path v,viii,12
Atchison, Mr. 38,39
Atkins, Joseph 97
Atkins, Samuel 98
Atkinson, Samuel 98,184
Attorney fees 43
Austin, Archer 175
Austin, James 224
Austin, William 165

Bacon 51
Bagby, Harry 86
Bagby, Henry 32,80,96,136,173,252
Bagby, James 155,161,186,187,189, 240,243,252,253,260
Bagby, Robert 58,80,86,96,118,186, 229
Bagby, William 247
Bailey, Benjamin 170
Bailey, James 226,228
Bailey, James Sr 235,237
Bailey, John 198
Bailey, William 56,78,89,104,115, 126,152
Baker, Abraham 56,68,69,175
Baker, Hannah 110
Baker, Mrs. 109
Baley, see Bailey
Ballew, William 4,5
Ballow, Charles 152,160,171,172
Ballow, Thomas 118,137,138,174, 212,232,247
Bandy, Richard 92
Banely, Colonel 35
Baptists v,vii
Barbee, Francis 250
Barclay, Andrew 44
Barker, Charles 164,211,220,221

Barker, Richard 179,180
Barksdail, see Barksdale
Barksdale, Higginson 77,115
Barksdale, John 65
Barn at glebe 111,125
Barnard, William 73
Barnard's (Bernard's) Road 57,58, 82,98,120,156,184,214,215
Barnes, Capt. 36
Barnes, James 1,2,4,5,7,8,9,19,22,40, 41,43,45,47,48,53,133,268,269
Barnes, John 177,196,197,202,204, 215,226,228,231,235,237,270
Barnes, Widow 97
Barnet's Fork 17
Barnet's Road 15
Barnett, William 53
Barns, see Barnes
Bartee, John 92
Bartee, Thomas 211
Basdale, Coyller 97
Basham, Jeremiah 222
Basham, William 87,92,149,158
Basham, William Sr 64,84,92,106
Basham, William Jr 64
Baskerville, George 29
Baskerville, John ix,12,25,33,41,43, 45,47,48,50,52,53,54,59,62,69, 70,71,73,74,75,76,83,85,87,105, 107,108,111,114,118,121,124, 126,139,141,148,150,154,157, 158,160,164,183,191,194,196, 197,199,202,204,207,215,217, 224,229,268,269
Baskerville, Mr. 1,193
Baskerville, Richard 212
Baskerville, Samuel 224
Bass, Alexander 170
Bass, Christopher 100,170,249
Bass, William 26,30
Bassett 87
Bassett, Thomas 24,27,30,31,66

Bates 12,13
Bates, Charles 24
Bates, Isaac 5,31,34
Bates, James 29,32
Bates, John 13,24,27,28
Bates, William 180
Battersby, William 104,144,167,168
Baugh, Abraham 55,66,69,79,86,94,
 116,124,131,132,153,160,169,
 170,171,210,231,241,248,251,
 258
Baugh, Burrell 252
Baugh, Chuchea/Cruther 242,259
Baugh, J P 252
Baugh, James 25,26,170
Baugh, John 86,242,251,260
Baugh, Joseph 10,25,26,55,66,69,79,
 102,117,132,153,160,169,170,
 210,231,248
Baugh, Rachel 248,249
Baugh, Thomas 25,26
Bayley, Abraham 99
Bayly, see Bailey 56
Beacham, Isaac 117,154
Beck, John 248
Beck, Robert 155,161,183
Bedford 93
Bedford, Benjamin 135,187,188,214
Bedford, Capt. 28,52
Bedford, Col. 84,94,95
Bedford, Stephen iv,1,2,3,7,8,9,19,
 21,22,36,37,40,41,45,47,48,50,
 52,53,54,59,61,62,63,69,70,71,
 73,74,75,76,83,85,87,105,107,
 108,111,113,268,269
Bedford, Thomas 47,51,66,68,94,
 133
Bell, David 69
Bell, Henry 87,128,183,221
Bell, Mary 163,191,192,194,195,197,
 199,202,204,216,228,271
Bell, Mr. 31

Bell, Widow 50
Benches 46,70,71,74,113,122,146,
 149,192,201,206,229
Bentley, Rachel x
Bentley, William 263,264,268
Bernard, John 184
Bible 44,60,264
Bingley, Mrs. 265,266
Biscoe (Bisco), Robert 198,233,244,
 250,251,261
Blackbon, Blackbun, see Blackburn
Blackburn, John 65
Blackburn, Widow 185
Blackburn, William 246,247
Blaikley, Elizabeth x
Blaikley, William x
Blankenship, Richard 175
Blevins (Blevings), John vii,2,9,36,
 43,67
Blocks 146,216,229
Blunt, Alexander 42,43,46,51,60,70
Boatwright, Benoni 165
Boatwright, Daniel 168,169,181,214,
 224
Boles, John 84,90,106,129,171,172
Bolling, Maj. 31
Bolling, orphans 184
Bolling, Thomas 184,248
Bolling, William 97,98
Bolling's Old Road 219
Bolling's Pt. 38
Bolling's Road 54,77,79,115,117,
 141,151,153,165,180,208,210
Bolton, John 99
Bond, Page 225
Bond, William 15,23,84,98
Bondron, see Bondurant
Bondurant, John 26
Bondurant, John Peter 254,255,257,
 261,262
Bondurant, Joseph 33,34,80,126,
 183,212,218,224

INDEX

Bondurant, Peter 26
Books
  carrying books 44
  parish book 45
  prayer books 44,199,206,264
  record book 43
  vestry book 218
Borrow money 43
Bostick, Charles 19,37,64
Bostick, John 55,77,91,130
Bostick, William 72,73,74,84
Bowden, John 117,154,160,166,167
Bowker, Achillis 78,86,91,97
Bowker, Peter 112
Bowles 131
Bowles, Benjamin 175
Bowling, see Bolling
Bowls 44
Bracket, Thomas 31,34
Bradley, David 64
Bradley, James 253
Bradley, James R 250
Bradley, John 35,57,68,99,166,167, 171,211
Bradley, Thomas 27
Bradshaw, Charles 103,143
Bradshaw, Field 103,143
Bradshaw, John 103,144
Bradshaw, Josiah 103,143
Bradshaw, Judith 20,21,42,46,60,70
Bradshaw, William 104,144
Branch, Daniel 264,265
Bransford, James 247,251
Braseal, Breazeal, see Brazeal
Brazeal, Henry 11,31,56,104,105
Bread & wine 46,47,106,109,113, 123,140,146,149,192,195,198, 201,203,206,216,227
Brian, Brient, see Bryant
Bridgwater, Samuel 15,30,39,42,57, 60,82,86,98,184,224
Brooks Mill 18

Brooks Road 18,54,76,77,114,127, 151,165,183,208
Brown, Davis 223
Brown, Elizabeth 60,109,110
Brown, James 90,93,115,142,151, 161,171,178,180,220,221,225
Brown, John 18,60,89,90,143,167, 173,174,175,178,223
Brown, Robert 156,161,181,184,214
Brown, Samuel 93,98,171,184,225
Brown, Zechariah 90,178
Brown's cornfield 87
Brumskil 167,168
Brumskil, John 104
Bryant, James 176,177,187,265,266
Buchanan, Rev. Mr. 264
Buckingham County iii
Buckingham Road vii,10,11,12,16, 17,18,26,36,54,55,56,57,58,59, 78,79,80,98,101,116,117,118, 120,121,131,141,152,153,154, 155,157,169,209,210,211,212, 214,231,232,233,234,241,242, 244,249,258,259,261
Buckingame Road, see Buckingham Road
Build a chapel 1,2,4,7,8,22,39,43
Build quarter 73
Bullock, John 89,142,180
Bunn 65
Burch, John 117,138,154,160,177
Burford, Melton 168
Burks, Martin 142
Burnet, Elizabeth 200,203,205,206, 216
Burnet, John 34,103
Burton 101,130
Burton, Hutchins 17,25,29,31
Burton, John 79,88,98,99,104,117, 143,154,166,176,184,209,211, 249
Burton, Josiah 17

Burton, Mary 139
Burton, Richard 17
Burton, Robert 17,31,92
Burton, Samuel 16,20,25,101
Burton, William 175
Burton, William A 253
Burton, William Allen 209
Burton's Brook 152,209
Burton's Ordinary 154,211
Burton's Path 17,18
Burton's Road 152
Burying poor 3,20,60,70,112,140, 146,163,226
Butler, Aaron 114,182
Butler, John 93
Butler, orphans 171
Butterwood Creek 10

Cable, Doctor xiv,201,205
Caesor, see Seizer
Calland, Joseph 165,166,174,192, 207,219,220,221,223
Calwell, Thomas 220,221
Campbell, Peter 180
Cancer of the mouth 205
Cannefax, boys 112,122,146
Cannefax, child 162,192,195,197, 200,202
Cannefax, Edward 74
Cannefax, Francis 72,73,74,84,106
Cannefax, John 11,33,34,58,118, 124,126
Cannon, Benjamin 82,86,103,120, 124,134
Cannon, Jeremiah 132,134,164,165
Cannon, John 32
Cardwell, George 59,65,69,80,86,96, 97,138,177
Cardwell, John 7,16,19,36,42,46,51, 57,59,63,69,70,72,74,83,105,108, 112,122,139,145,148,155,158, 161,191,194,199,270

Cardwell, Letitia 205,216,226,228, 235,237,238,240
Cardwell, Richard 57,63,69
Carner, Susannah 136
Carr, William 93,228,252
Carrington, Edward 263,264,268
Carrington, George (Colonel) viii,1, 2,4,5,6,7,8,9,19,21,30,31,33,34, 38,39,40,41,43,45,47,48,50,52, 53,54,59,61,70,71,73,74,75,76, 85,97,102,103,108,110,111,114, 121,122,123,124,132,133,134, 138,139,140,141,144,145,147, 148,150,157,158,160,162,163, 164,165,168,176,187,191,192, 193,194,196,197,201,202,203, 215,216,226,227,228,268,269, 270,271
Carrington, George Jr xiv,124,137, 138,191,193,200,201,202,203, 204,205,206,207,215,216,217, 237,269
Carrington, Joseph 163,192,193,195, 217,271
Carrington, Mr. 44
Carrington, Paul 132
Carter, Charles 119
Carter, Daniel 97
Carter, Jesse x,152,161,189,209,228, 233,234
Carter, John 56,81,97,156,160,161, 164,184
Carter, John Jr 156,184
Carter, Robert 14,31,34,103,165
Carter, Robert Jr 31,56,81,103
Carter, Thomas 2,23,179
Carter's Ferry 156
Carter's Ferry Road 119,156,184, 189,213,215,224
Cary 166
Cary, Archibald 29,47,50,69,92,128, 180,181,219,220,221

Cary, Col. 165
Ceizar, see Seizer
Chactune, see Cheatham
Chaffin, Stanley 222
Chafin, Christopher 87,173
Chafin, John 63,64,92
Chafin, Joseph 222
Chafin, Nathan 222
Chair Road 16,17,57,81,119
Chalton, Abraham 174
Chalton, Christopher (Cit) 88,101, 131,174
Chamberlin 168
Chambers 182
Chambers, George 57,81,86,104,119
Chambers, John 114,151,161,182
Chambers, Joseph 208
Chandler 12,24
Chandler, David 118,188
Chandler, Jesse 188
Chandler, Joel 12,24,28,36,37,58,66,
Chandler, Joseph 24,162,192,195, 197,200,202
Chandler, Mrs. 95
Chandler, Robert 81,86,96,188
Chandler, Timothy 95
Chandler, Widow 214,215
Chandler, William 12,24,28
Chapel Road v,viii,12,14,16,17,57, 58,82,98,120,156,189
Charton, Major 28
Cheatham, Francis 23,26,131,153, 160,169,170
Cheatham, Thomas 26
Cheatwood, James 25,26
Cheatwood, Matthew 25,26
Cheatwood, William 149,170,248, 249
Cheetum, see Cheatham
Chest 43,84,205,216,264
Chesterfield County ii,iii,249
Chetwood, see Cheatwood

Chew, Larkin 102
Children 50,85,146,162,195,205,216, 217,226,228,235,237,238,240, 245,254,255,256,257,261,262
Childres, Mary 192,195
Childres, Philemon 109,112,140,150
Childres, Philemon Jr 122,145
Childres, Samuel 126
Childress, Lemmy 85
Childrey, Benjamin xi,7,11,12,16,21, 24,29,31,56,78,86,97,105
Chitwood, see Cheatwood
Christian 57
Christian, Anthony 224,246,247
Christian, Anthony Jr 246
Christian, Thomas 82,98,132
Christian, Valentine 132
Chsot, see Scott
Chumley, William 29,64
Church 55,56,78,153,210,215,231, 241,258
Church acre 141
Church addition 61,141
Church land 179
Church Road 55,59,78,79,81,116, 153,169,210,213,215,224,231, 241,258,266
Church spring 224
Church spring branch 215
Church Upper Road 215
Clark, see Clerk
Clarke (Clark), William 98,104,113, 143,240,245,252,254,255,261, 262,270
Clay, C. Henry 185
Clay, Charles 152,161,189,250,251
Clay, Eleazer 249
Clay, Elijah 247
Clay, Henry 10,23,25,33,55,64,65, 69,78,86,93,102,116,137,138, 153,161,169,181,185,189
Clay, William 10,23,55,64,65,69,101,

180,181
Clay's Fork 10
Clay's Path 10
Cleaning church 162
Cleaning church yard 60
Clearing ground 8,20,46,157,191,192
Clearing spring 146
Clements, Edmond 184
Clements, Edward 98,190
Clements, William 253
Clement's Mill 55,56,78,101,116, 121,130,209
Clement's Mill Path 209
Clement's Road 152
Clemons, Edward 225
Clerk of vestry 42,47,48,51,59,61,71, 72,74,83,105,108,112,122,123, 124,127,139,145,148,158,159, 161,191,192,194,195,198,200, 203,204,216,218,226,228,235, 237,238,240,245,254,255,261, 262,263
Clerk summoned by vestry 234
Clerk, William 154,160,167,190,191, 211
Clover Forest Road 114,127,151, 183,207,208
Cockaham 37,95
Cocke, Bowler 36,67,94,134,135, 139,164,190
Cocke, James 27,29,104
Cocke, Thomas 55,76,90,137,182
Cockerham, Philip 36
Coffin 47,198,217,227
Coleman, Daniel vi,1,13,29,37,58,65, 69,89,91,92,161,179,185,220
Coleman, Daniel Sr 68,99,142
Coleman, Daniel Jr vi,19,51,54,63, 64,77,86,92,115,124,127,152
Coleman, Edward 225
Coleman, Thomas 54,69,99
Coleman, William 211,221

Collector 3,6,38,43,47,52,62,71,73, 76,84,85,106,107,109,110,112, 113,140,144,146,149,157,159, 163,192,193,196,198,199,201, 203,205,206,207,216,217,218, 227,229,235,238,239,240,246, 254,256,257,262,263
Colley, Bartlett 250
Colquitt 29
Colquitt, Anthony 104
Colquitt, John 208,218
Colquitt, Jonathan 220
Colquitt, Thomas 219
Colwell, Thomas 242
Comager, Ann Amis 157,162,198, 200,205,216
Comager, child 191
Communion table 1,9,147
Constable 46,192
Convention 264
Cook (Cooke), John 18,55,77,86,90. 115,179,182,202,206
Cooper, John Brown 87
Copy list 46,145,158,237
Copy of acts 140,149
Corley, Valentine 89,178
Corn crib 62
Corn house 59
Coroner 162
Cotterell (Cottrell), Charles 76,114, 182
Cotton 201
County line 10,15,17,18,34,54,57,58, 76,77,79,82,83,98,114,117,120, 127,141,151,153,157,165,168, 180,183,207,208,210,211,214, 219,231,242,258,259
Coupland, David 217
Courthouse 52,59,61,70,71,74,83, 85,98,105,111,114,121,139,144, 150,155,158,160,191,194,197, 199,202,204,207,215,230,241,

245,253,255,256,257,262,263
Courthouse Road 12,16,58,65,79,81, 96,117,154,211
Cox, Edward 186,212,232,243,252
Cox, Elizabeth 136
Cox, Frederick 13,29,32,58,65,69
Cox, George 25,55,101,112,116,124, 130,131,152,160,175,176,189, 209,233,253
Cox, Hall 101,130
Cox, Henry 25,130,131,175,189,233, 235
Cox, Henry Sr 243
Cox, Henry Jr 175
Cox, John 32,98,116,153,161,173, 181,186,189,212,228,231,232, 252,260
Cox, Judith 189
Cox, Nicholas 36,37,104
Cox, Stephen 17,25,29,56
Cox, William 23,80,86,96,118,136, 172,173,186,252,253
Cox's Mill 152,209
Crafford, James 95
Creasy (Creacey), John 14,119,164
Cridle, Allen 225
Cross Road 209,211
Crump, Richard 196,199,200,239, 240,241,244,245,246,250,255, 256,257,258,262,263,264,268, 269,270,271
Cumberland County i,ii,iii,x,67,92, 98,105,108,111,114,121,137,138, 139,143,144,150,158,160,197, 199,202,204,207,215,226
Cumberland County Court 54,76, 149,194,218
Cumberland County Courthouse 124,145,191
Cumberland Courthouse vi
Cumpton, Richard 247
Cunningham, Alexander 98

Cunningham, James 15,30,82,86, 103,132
Cunningham, James Jr 57
Cunningham, Jonathan 57,82,86,98
Cunningham, William 30

Dairy 49
Daniel, Edward 57
Daniel, Hezekiah 213
Daniel, James 34,68,77,88,166,179, 225
Daniel, John 179,180
Daniel, Richard 90,101,115,124,129, 130,131
Daniel, Walter 31
Daniel, Waltho 181
Daniel, Watt 92
Daniel, Williams 18,29,54,68,69,79, 86,89,92,99,101,117,141,142, 153,161,167,176,179,189,220, 221,223,253
Daniels 17,18
Daniels, James 29,142
Daniel's old houses 117,154,211
Davenport, Capt. 174
Davenport, Henry 72,77,86,91,115, 124,129,130
Davenport, James 91,129
Davenport, Joseph 129,171,172
Davenport, Julius 115,165,166
Davenport, Mary 171
Davenport, Philemon 129
Davenport, Stephen 129
Davenport, Thomas 18,37,50,52,53, 59,61,62,69,70,71,72,73,74,75, 76,83,84,88,105,107,108,110, 111,112,114,121,123,127,139 145,146,148,149,158,161,162, 166,183,187,192,195,198,200, 203,204,216,218,219,221,222, 223,228,268,269,271
Davenport, Thomas Sr 88,90,91,

171,172
Davenport, Thomas Jr 61,85,86,87,
  90,91,129,270
Davenport, William 129,130,152,
  160,172,176,209
Daverson, Hezekiah 157,160,165
Davidson, Edward 55
Davies, Henry Landon 213
Davies, Mr. 163
Davies, Nicholas viii,ix,1,2,4,5,6,7,8,
  9,19,21,22,31,35,36,40,41,43,45,
  47,48,50,51,53,63,66,67,70,71,
  72,73,74,75,76,83,85,87,94,105,
  108,110,111,113,121,123,124,
  135,139,141,144,147,148,150,
  157,158,159,160,164,187,268,
  269
Davis, Charles 65
Davis, George 183,185,210,231,241,
  246,247,258
Davis, James 24,25,32,33,34,59,65,
  80,183,185
Davis, William 64,118,154,188
Davison, David 89
Davison, Hezekiah 214
Dawson, William x,4
Day, Peter 251
Dean, John 251
Dean, Peter 265
Deed for land 9
Deep Creek 12,36,56,57,58,81,94,
  119,121,133,134,152,155,185,
  213,214,233,234,243,248,260,
  261
Deep Creek Bridge 12,14
Deep Run 156
Deep Run Road vii
Dellon, see Dillion
Demand parish book 45
Depp, John 265,266
Depp, Peter 249
Deshazer, Abraham 216

Devonport, see Davenport
Dew, Thomas 184
Dickens, Christopher 82,86,94,98
Dickens, Thomas 27,28,29
Dickerson, David 222
Dickerson, John 73
Diggs, Dudley 28,29
Dillion, Benjamin 184
Dillion, Henry 31,56,81,119,156,
  161,164,187
Dillion, Mary 123
Dillion, Mrs. 203
Dillion, Widow vii,14,15,56,82
Dillion, William 14,31,98,119,140,
  156,161,164,184,187,203,205,
  216
Dinwiddie, Robert 226
Disorderly behavior 193
Dobbings, Dobings, Dobins, see
  Dobbins
Dobbins, George 3,5,20,21,42,46,
  47,60,70,72,73,74,84,106,108,
  112,122,123,140,145,148,158,
  162,191,194,198,205,216,226,
  228,235,237,238,240,245,254,
  255,257,261,262
Dobings, Mary 217
Doors 39,40,49,109,234
Dorham, James 173
Doss, Joshua 55,77,208
Doudy, James 29
Douglas, Robert 23,34,120,190
Drake, J 250
Drake, James 190,191,233,243
Dudley, William 32
Duffee, Isaac 177,178
Duglass, Duglis, see Douglas
Dumas, Ben 36,67
Dunford, Phillip 180
Dunge, William 219,220
Dunkin, John 32
Dupuy, John James 137,138

Durham, James 222

Easely, see Easley
Easley, Mary 52,113
Easley, Mrs. 61,60
Easley, Roderick 121,123,124,138, 139,141,144,145,146,147,148, 149,150,157,164,268,269
Easley, Susannah 51,52,70,72,74,84, 105,108,112,122,139,145,148, 158,161,163,200,271
Easley, Warham 47,52,89,141,179, 180,220
Easley, William 6,8,20,29,42,46,52, 271
Eaton, Anne 109,112,122,140
Edwards, Andrew 93,98,184,216, 225,228
Edwards, Andrew Jr 225
Edwards, Charles 133
Edwards, William 225
Eggleston, John 64,259
Eggleston, Richard 126,127,210,229, 231,236,239,244,246
Eggleston, Richard Sr 242
Elam, Jean 254
Elam, Lodowick 25,30,100,142,143, 153,170,210,231,254
Elam, William 104,105,126,127,209, 231,241,251,252,258
Eleam, see Elam
Ellison, Gerard 160,165,166,218, 219,223
Ellison, Jarrett 151,208
Elsom, William 149
Epperson, Francis 58,77,87,106,112, 115,122,140,145,148,158,162, 173,191,194,197,199,202,222, 223,226,228,235,237
Epperson, Joseph v,vii,84,107,109, 111,113,146
Epperson, Richard 27,58,90,149,159

Epperson, Susannah 174,228
Epperson, Thomas 155,160,173
Evans, George 104
Evans, William 102
Expenses for a suit 20
Expenses for traveling 44

Failure to comply with contract 51
Fain, Joel 23
Fain, Richard 22,23
Farguson, William 188
Faris, see Farris
Farley, Matthew 249,251,270
Farley, Matthew Sr 258
Farley, Matthew Jr 237,249
Farmer, Henry 72,74,84,106,116, 130,140,149,158,162,176,191, 195,197,200,202,205,216,228
Farmer, Henry Sr 108,140,145,158
Farmer, Henry Jr 108,145,158,162, 191,195,197,200,202,205,216
Farmer, John 23,25,88,91,130,176, 221
Farrar 69
Farrar, Joseph 31,92,99,128
Farrar, Rachel 36
Farrer, see Farrar
Farris 220,221
Farris, Benjamin 184
Farris, Rachel 62,67,70,72,74,84, 105,108,112,122,139,145,148, 158,161,162,184,191,194,271
Fees
   attorney fee 43
   clerk fee 20,42,162,163
   patent fee 44
Felps, see Phelps
Fercran, see Furcran
Fermer, see Farmer
Ferry Road 13,81,96,118,136,155, 212,233,243,260
Field, Bartholomew 181

Fields, Thomas 134
Fighting Creek 10,11,55,56,78,116,
    152,153,209,210,231,241,258,
    266
Finch, Charles 94,119,124,133,135,
    155,161,183
Finch, Widow 195
Fine Creek 11,12,13,58,67,80,96,
    118,135,154,155,212,232,242,
    243,259
Fines for oaths 193
Finney, William 31
Fitsimmons, Patrick 212,245,254,
    255,257
Flat Rock vii
Fleming, Charles 171
Fleming, Col. 193
Fleming, John 31,75,83,85,98,105,
    108,111,113,114,121,124,136,
    144,145,146,147,150,157,160,
    163,164,172,173,191,194,197,
    268,269
Fleming, John Jr 31
Fleming, Sampson 23,106,190
Fleming, William xiv,163,164,186,
    191,194,196,197,199,201,202,
    204,215,217,218,219,226,227,
    229,230,235,236,238,239,240,
    245,246,252,268,269
Flippen, Francis 213
Flippen, John 213
Flippen, Ralph 22,23,29,56,67,69,81,
    89,120,141,190
Flippen, Thomas 22
Flippen, William 156,161,190,191
Flipping, see Flippen
Flournoy, Gideon 259
Flournoy, Silas 266
Flowers, James 249
Ford, Culverine 115
Ford, Nathaniel 78,104,109
Forlines, John 266

Forlines, Josiah 266
Forsee, Stephen 265,266
Forsee, William 265
Forster, Dr. Thomas 92
Foster, James 225
Fowler, John 249
Fowler, John Jr 249
Franklin, children 146
Franklin, John 28,81,86,96,186,189,
    192
Freeman 88,101
Freeman, Allen 131
Freeman, Holman 25,104
Freeman, Mrs. 44
Freeman, Thomas xiii
French line ii,11,26,59,80
Fretwell 182
Fretwell, Thomas 2,5,19,42,46,53,
    59,70,72,74,83,105,108,112,122,
    139,145148,158,161,191,193,
    194,197,199,203,270
Fuqua, John 226
Fuqua, Joiles 247
Fuqua, Joseph 104,128,143,167
Furcrun, Peter 154,160,169,170,174,
    175
Furlong, Robert 187

Gaddey, George 189
Gallery 62,76,107,111,121,147,150,
    159
Gamon, John 126,127
Gannaway, John 128,183,223
Gannaway, John Sr 221
Garden 49,87,107,109,206,217
Garden, Parson 224,225
Gardian, James 184
Garret, Garrot, Garrott, see Garrett
Garrett, Henry 89,141,180,220
Garrett, James 219,220
Gasper, Susanna 31,67
Gatch, Philip 265,266

Gathwrite, Miles 14,35,37
Gay, Elizabeth 186
Gay, William 236,237,238,239,240, 244,252,268
Geneto, see Genito
Genito Bridge 55
Genito Road 9,10,78,79,116,117, 153,169,210,231,241,242,249, 258,259,266
Gentry, Simon 143
Gerratt, see Garrett
Giles, Nicholas 31,104,105,126
Gilham, see Gilliam
Gilham, Joseph 165
Gilliam, James 132,133,134,164,165, 168,214
Gilliam, John 128
Ginnito, see Genito
Gladoe, Samuel 99
Glass 106,123,198,234
Glass, James 24
Glaze windows 61,107,110,113
Glebe ix,xi,7,20,21,22,37,42,45,47, 48,50,52,59,60,62,63,73,75,83, 84,87,95,107,109,111,114,121, 123,146,157,159,163,187,193, 196,206,217,236,237,264
Glebe buildings 49
Glebe, former 24
Glebe garden 49
Glebe house 39,50,51,53,71
Glebe land 21,158
Glebe work 113
Glen, see Glenn
Glenn, Gideon 19,37,51,71,72,74, 83,87,105,108,112,115,122,139, 145,148,158,161,174,191,194, 197,199,202,204,215,223,228, 270
Glenn, James 87,218,222,224
Glenn, James Sr 208
Glenn, Nathaniel 115,151,160,172, 222
Glenn, Nehemiah 55,77,86,88,222
Glen's Path 77,115,151,208,209
Glover, John 168
Glover, Joseph 168
Glover, Phineas 15,30,34,35,57,82, 102,103,120,132,133,134,157, 164,168
Glover, Phineas Jr 214
Goff, Rebecca 206,216
Going, George 35,68
Golden, Thomas 266
Golden, William 265
Golliham, Elizabeth 122,123,140, 145,148,158,162
Gooch, William x,4
Goochland County i,ii,31,33
Goochland Court 9
Good, see Goode
Goode, Bennett 11,34,58,80,118, 135,136,155,160,172,173,212, 232,236,242,259
Goode, John 232,259
Goode, Thomas 266
Gordin, Edward 253
Goss, John 222
Gray 143
Gray, Edmund 41
Gray, William 38,39
Great Deep Creek 12
Great Deep Creek Bridge 16
Great Guinea Creek 54,55,77,115, 116,151,152,208,209
Great Guinea 18,19,87
Green Creek 18,19,76,77,89,115, 151,182,208
Griffin, Joseph 165
Grisham 165
Guinea Road 55,78,131,152,209
Guthery, see Guttery
Guttery, Alexander 210,218,219,221
Guttery, Bernard 222

Guttery, Thomas 69,79,86,89,98,99,
  117,141,153,180,220,221
Guttery, William 221

Hadaway, David 25
Hail, Hale, see Hall
Hale, John 32,65
Halifax County 192
Hall 65
Hall, Robert 127
Hall, Thomas xiii,32,33,35,56,64,66,
  69,149,158,191,194,197,199,202,
  204,215,226,228,234,235,270
Hall, William 127
Ham Chapel vii,xiii,6,8,9,14,15,19,
  20,42,43,44,51,52,53,57,61,62,
  70,72,74,75,76,82,83,84,85,105,
  106,108,109,112,113,122,124,
  139,140,141,144,145,147,148,
  150,157,158,159,161,162,163,
  191,192,193,194,197,199,200,
  202,203,204,215,216,270,271
Hamblet, Thomas 102
Hambleton, Edward 30,102
Hambleton, William 78,86,88,89,90,
  91,129,130,152,160,171,172,176,
  209
Hammon, Ambrose 89
Hammon, Joseph 178
Hammon, John Sr 89
Hampton, Nathan 146
Hancock, George 79,86,100,117,
  141,142,143
Hancock, Margaret 29
Hanson, Sally 176
Harman, Henry 63,64,77,86,91,115,
  130,160,172,179,196
Harmon, Henry 124,152
Harrelson, John 89
Harris, Ann 234,251
Harris, Benjamin 16,17,25,36,41,43,
  45,47,48,50,52,53,59,60,61,62,
  69,71,73,79,83,84,85,86,87,107,
  108,117,123,154,265,268,269
Harris, Charles 246
Harris, Edward 253,261
Harris, Francis E 244,246,250,251,
  253,254,261
Harris, Joseph 211,234,244,245,254,
  261
Harris, John Jr 265,266
Harris Mill 36
Harris Mill Path 121
Harris Path 57,152
Harris, Thomas 64,265,266
Harris, Widow 265
Harris, William 264
Harrison, Benjamin 1,2,3,4,5,6,7,9,
  19,31,34,36,41,57,59,67,69,82,
  86,92,99,120,124,128,171,268
Harrison, Carter Henry 141,163,
  165,184,187,197,199,201,213,
  268
Harrison, Carter 98,164
Harrison, Cary 181
Harrison's Road 54,79,98,117,154,
  211
Harvey, John 162,192,195,197
Harvey, Sarah 216,226,227
Harvey, Thomas v,vi,vii,2,7,8,9,18,
  29,38,39,48
Harvey, Widow 200,202
Haskins, Aaron 232,242
Haskins, Creed 1,2,4,7,8,9,19,21,22,
  29,40,41,43,47,52,53,54,59,61,
  62,69,70,71,73,75,76,83, 85,100,
  108,111,114,121,124,142,145,
  147,150,157,160,163,164,170,
  174,183,235,236,239,240,268,
  269,271
Haskins, Edward 203,207,210,227,
  229,231,235,236,237,238,241,
  244,253,254,255,268
Haskins, Mr. 60

INDEX

Haskins, Ned 185
Haskins, Thomas 212,232
Hatch, John 6,20,42,46,51,60,70
Hatch, wife 6,20,42,46,51,60,70
Hatcher 66,100
Hatcher, Benjamin 153,161,174,185, 247
Hatcher, Charles 185,212,232,242, 247,250,259
Hatcher, Frederick 72,74,84,104, 106,109,131,140,143,167,175, 271
Hatcher, Henry 25,26,131,144,168, 249,253
Hatcher, Jeremiah 171
Hatcher, Josiah 26
Hatcher, Samuel 26,27,33,65,174
Hatcher, Sean 265
Hatcher, Seth 258,266
Headspeth, see Hudspeth
Henderson, Elizabeth 195
Henderson, Richard 4,5,20,39
Hendrick, see Hendricks
Hendricks, Adolphus 17,29,85,88, 89,103
Hendricks, Benjamin 29,142,179
Hendricks, Zach 220
Henhouse 49
Henrico 37
Henrico County ii,35
Henrico Parish ii
Henry, Henry Jr 152
Hidesanders, see Saunders
Hill, Amy 140,191,194,195,197,198, 199,202,204,205,216,226,228, 235,237,271
Hill, Anne 184
Hill, Dennitt 220
Hill, James 249
Hill, John 98,142,220
Hill, May 192
Hill, Roger v,112,113,122,123,139, 145,146,148,158,159,161,187, 271
Hill, Thomas 220
Hill, William 206, 271
Hill, William C. 225
Hill, William Cortilo 217
Hinges 9,40,49,50,109
Hix 177
Hix, Archelus 185,248
Hix, Daniel 233,243,248,260
Hix, Dock 176
Hix, Duke (Marmaduke) 97,203, 205,216
Hix, Edward 260
Hix, James 266
Hix, John 225
Hix, Marmaduke 198,226
Hix, William 166,167
Hix, William Sr 99
Hopson, Adcock 143,154
Hobson, Henry 118,136,172,173
Hobson, John 17,79,86,104,117,143, 144,167,211
Hobson, Samuel 185,210,230,231, 235,236,241,246,250,258,268
Hobson, William 79,86,104,117,143, 144,154,160,167,168
Hobson's Mill Path 211
Hodges, orphan 91,130
Hodges, Thomas 87
Holcomb, Phillip 77
Holeman, James 126
Holeman, John 151,161,208
Holland fabric 44
Holland, Barsheba 200
Holland, Charles 106,167,200,205, 206,216
Holland, James 64,92
Holland, Jesse 200
Holland, John 72,120,156,171
Holland, orphans 171,201,205
Holland, Peter 23

Holland, Stephen xiv,200,205,206, 217
Holland, Thomas 99,200,205,206, 211,216,228
Holland, William 82,86,93,94,99, 120,134,156,160,166,171,190
Hollaway, see Holloway
Holloway, James 99,117,154,160, 166,167,200
Holloway, James Sr 68,93,99
Holloway, James Jr 68,99
Holloway, John 58,93,171
Holloway, John Sr 99
Holloway, John Jr 68
Holloway, orphan 166,171
Holloway, Samuel 166,171
Holloway, William 58,68,93,104
Holman, see Holeman
Holman, James 183
Holoman, John 179
Honeybus, Henry 226
Hooper, Elizabeth 103
Hooper, Joseph 15,34,35
Hopkins, William 266
Hopper, Betsy 245,254,255,257,261
Hopper, John 254,255,257,261,262
Hopper, Tabitha 262
Hopson, see Hobson
Hornquarter Road 17,58,82,120,156, 214
Horse blocks 8,19,42,46,84,85,106, 159,192,200,206
Horton, John Blan 101
Hoseley, William 170
Hount [Hunt?], William 28
Howard 95
Howard, Allen 36
Howard, John 265,266
Howard, Major 28
Howard, William 155,161,188,189
Howard's Quarter 58
Howel, Howle, see Howl

Howl, Elizabeth 21,42,46,51,60,71, 72,73,74,84,106,109,110,112, 122,140,145,148,158,162,191, 195,197,200,202,205,216,226, 228,235,237,238,240,246,261
Howlet, John 97
Howlett, Thomas 250
Hubbard, John 22,42,46,50,52,53, 71,90,104,144,270
Hubbard, Joseph 88,104,129,143
Huckaby, Thomas 64
Hudgens 106
Hudgens, Drury 156,160,164,190
Hudgens, James 190,213,224
Hudgens, Moses 211
Hudgens, orphan 190
Hudgens, Robert 69,89,99,142,153, 165,180
Hudgens, William 142,160,165,166, 190
Hudgens, William Jr 151
Hudgins, John 23
Hudgins, Philip 23
Hudson, James 224
Hudson, John 23
Hudson, William 143
Hudspeth, William 97,104,126,137, 177
Hughes 68,93,182
Hughes, Anne 187
Hughes, Anthony 12,24,28
Hughes, Ashford 23
Hughes, David 248
Hughes, Eleander 23
Hughes, Isaac 14,25,31,101
Hughes, John 36,79,86,102,121,136, 155,160,172,173,207,212,217, 218,219,226,227,229,230,268
Hughes, Joseph 31,32,80
Hughes, Leander 127,161,190,191
Hughes, Leander Jr 156
Hughes, Martha 173,189

Hughes, Mrs. 130
Hughes, Orlando 56,67,69,81,84,
    107,109,119,164,190
Hughes, Powel 127
Hughes, Robert 13,31,32,35,58,66,
    67,68,69,81,86,93,94,126,133,
    135,136,183,243,248,260
Hughes, Robert Jr 35,56
Hughes, Simon 190,213
Hughes, Stephen 30,31,32,58,67,69
Hughes, Thomas 69
Hughes, William 190
Huguenots ii
Hunt, see Hount
Hunt, William 36
Hutchison, Charles 166
Hutson, William 104
Hydesanders, see Saunders

Jackson, Gervas 36
Jackson, Joseph 171,249
James River i,ii,iii,14,15,34,56,57,58,
    65,80,81,83,96,118,119,154,156,
    157,212,213,214,232,233,242,
    243,248,259,260
James, Francis 32
James, Richard 155,160,173
James, Robert 136
Jefferson, John 184,225,227,271
Jefferson, Peter 33,34
Jefferson, Thomas 126,183
Jeffries, Thomas 115
Jeneto Road, see Genito Road
Jenkins 131
Jenkins, Edward 205
Jenkins, Jenkins 201
Jenkins, Joseph 88,91,129,171,172
Jenkins, Mary 88,90,129,171
Jenkins, orphans 90,91,130
Jennings, Mary 240,245
John, see Johns
Johns, Jane 235,237

Johns, John 152
Johns, Joseph 31,32,60,136,166,172,
    238
Johns, Robert 128,151,161,174,183,
    221,222,223
Johns, Thomas 29,89,142,151,160,
    166,174,219,222,223
Johns, Thomas Sr 219
Johns, Thomas Jr 166
Johns, William 17,240,246,261
John's Creek 259
John's Road 54
Johnson 182
Johnson, Ann 228,229
Johnson, Daniel 12,28,58,66,81,95,
    96,155,161,186,187
Johnson, James 165
Johnson, John 186
Johnson, Joseph 13,165
Johnson, Michael vii,8,20,40,42,46,
    51,60,62,70,271
Johnson, Randolph 143
Johnson, William 249,265
Joiner, William Smith 116,152,209
Jonas, John 116
Jones Creek 11,58,59,80,118,154,
    212,232,242
Jones, Daniel 103,165
Jones, Harrison 88,90,129
Jones, John 88,129,160,165,176,209
Jones, Michael 144
Jones, Mrs. 251
Jones, Samuel 99,103,117,141,143,
    144
Jordan, Abraham 66
Jordan, Robert 266
Jude, Benjamin 247,259
Jude, George 203,271
Jude, John 92,128,181,247
Jug 44
Jurden, see Jordan
Jury 137

Keeble, Humphrey vi,55,78,86,88,
    89,104,106,111,176
Keeble, Walter v,143,144,159,163,
    176
Keeling, George 213
Keeling, Lenard 92,128,171,181
Kendall, John 89
Kent, Anne 3,20
Kent, Luke 237
Kent, Robert 29,89,117,141,142,180
Kent, Widow 3,5,6,20,46,51,60,70,
    72,74,84,106,108,112
Kerr, William 252
Kibble, see Keeble
King George III 218
King, John 248
King William Parish i,iii,118,153,
    154,210,212,231,232,242,258,
    259
Kitchen at glebe 48,114,121,123,146

Lack of glebe 47,53
Laffoon, Thomas 20
Lake, John 28,36
Langhorn, Maurice 102,130,133,142,
    168,179,196,207,221
Langsdon, Easter 175
Lansdon, Esther 26
Law, John 177
Lax 12,13
Lax, William 12,28,36,37
Lea, see Lee
Leak, see Lake
Lee, Charles 77,86,87,88,114,124,
    128,151,160,173,174,219,223
Lee, Charles Sr 222
Lee, John 179
Lee, Joseph 208,218,223,224
Lee, Richard 223
Lee, William 208,218,223,224
Legrand, John 3,5,12,19,42,46,271
Legrand, Pierre v

Legrand, Widow 45
Levillion, Anthony 89,142,179,180
Lewis, Charles 209,231,241,250,252
Lewis, John 168,184
Lewis, Joseph 266
Lightfoot 44,87
Lightfoot, Dr. 22
Lightfoot, John viii,8,21
Ligon 266
Ligon, James 24,59,80,153,161,181
Ligon, John 232,242,259
Ligon, Joseph 252
Ligon, Matthew 24,25
Ligon, Richard 24,32,33,59,65,80,
    118,126,135,154,164,183,185,
    212,224,229,230,234,235,236,
    238,239,240,268,269
Ligon, Seth 246,247,259
Lile, see Lyle
Little Creek 154
Little Deep Creek 12
Little Guinea Bridge 101,131
Little Guinea Creek 77,78,116,152,
    209
Little Guinea Road 131
Littleton Parish iii,vi,vii,xii,xiv,218,
    226,227,229,270,271
Locker, Osburn 126
Locket, see Lockett
Lockett, Gideon 30,100,142,143,
    170,242,247,249,258
Lockett, Jacob 35
Lockett, Joel 25,30,35,78,86,100,
    102,116,131,143,169,170
Lockett, Thomas 10,30,35,78,86,
    100,102,116,131,143,169,170
Loe, see Low
Logan, Charles 248
Logwood, Edmond 213,218,219,
    226,227,229,230,234,236,237,
    238,244,261,268,269
Lokitt, see Locket

Lookado, Isaac 265,266
Lookado, Peter 266
Low 70,95
Low, Amy 45,51,59,71,72,74,84,105, 108,271
Low, John 177
Low, Thomas 37
Low, William 227
Lower Chapel 8,19
Lower Creek 55
Lower end of parish 232,242,259
Lowery (Lowry), Robert 64,68,69,99
Loyds 233,243
Lucadoe, see Lookado
Lumkin, Moore 207,216,228
Lumpkin 182
Lyle, Jarrott 224
Lyle's Ford 11,16,56,234,244,261
Lyle's Road 78,116,121,152,209,212, 231,232,234,241,242,258,259
Lyol, see Lyle

Macon, Col. 87,222
Macon, Hartwell 222
Macon, Henry 63,64,77,86,92,115, 123,124,127,150,158,160,164, 177,194,196,208,268,269
Macon, John 264
Macon, William 55,77,115,151,173, 208,246,259
Macon's upper lines 55,77,115,151, 208,222
Maddox 143
Madock, John 104
Maggehee 43
Maggehee, see McGehee
Main Road 10,14,54,55,77,78,79, 115,117,141,151,165,208
Main Ridge Road 152,153,209,210
Major, William 209
Making fires 71
Making lists 46

Mallet, Stephen 23,104
Manakintown ii
Manksfield, Samuel 24
Marchel, see Marshall
Marcum, J 185
Markham, Vincent 238,239,240,241, 244,245,246,250,253,254,255, 256,257,258,262,263,268,271
Marr, Gideon 88,90,91
Marshall, Francis 10,30,35,78,86, 100,102,143,153,160,170,242
Marshall, William 9,29,30,55,67,69, 72,100,142,143,153,160,170,249
Martin, Abraham vii,2,8,38
Martin, Anthony 264,265
Martin, Austin 214
Martin, Gideon 30,133,168
Martin, Henry 152,160,209
Martin, James 265
Martin, Jane 168
Martin, John 29,89
Martin, Orson 133,168
Martin, Paul 164
Martin, Peter 187
Martin, Susannah 88,176
Martin, Valentine 15,30,102,112, 122,132,133,140
Martin, Will 88
Mason family ix
Mason, William 184
Matthis, William 104
Mattox, William 167
Maxey, Charles 131,146,149,162,169
Maxey, John 27,118,137,146,174, 227,232,242,250,259
Maxey, Nathaniel 11,26,27,29,34,58, 80,104,126,137,154,174,175,232
Maxey, Radford 27
Maxey, Sill [Sylvanus] 27
Maxey, Sylvanus 11
Maxey, Walter 27,33,126
Maxey, William 11,26,27,58,66,80,

86,94,138,149,174,175,185
May, Catherine 106,109,122,123, 140,146,149
May, Henry 38
May, Judith xiv,192
Mayo 87,95,172
Mayo, Ann 24,36,37,63
Mayo, Daniel 24,34,95,96
Mayo, John v,90,104,112,139,143, 145,147,152,154,156,168,178, 179,229,230,235,236,246,268
Mayo, Joseph 126,183,207,217,224, 232,242,243,259
Mayo, Madam 96
Mayo, May 188
Mayo, Miss 24
Mayo, Mrs. 16,17,28,33,34,57,59, 80,81,118,119,154,155,173,212
Mayo, orphans 176
Mayo, Phillip 34,103,134,165
Mayo, William 233,250,251,253,254, 256,263,264,268,269,270
Mayo, William Jr 240,245,254,256
Mayo line 95
Mayo Mill 16,152,154,156
Mayo Mill Path 117
Mayo Old Mill 36,79,121
McCaul, Stoaks 252
McComack, David 92
McCoy 17,18
McCraw, Francis 71,72,74,80,96,97, 137,140,177,189,198,205,211, 216,217,218,226,228,229,235, 237,238,239,240,270,271
McCraw, Mary 240,245,250,254, 255,257,261,262
McDowel 177
McDowel, James 192
McDowel, see McDuel
McDuel 176
McGehee, Edward 55,77,86,87,88, 92,115,173,174

McGehee, Jacob 143,144,167
McGehee 222
McGehee, William 222
McGuire, John 98
McKinney, John 220
Mcklearing, see McLaurine
McLaurine 85
McLaurine, Robert ix,x,61,62,69,70, 71,72,73,75,76,83,87,105,108, 109,111,114,121,122,124, 139, 141,145,146,147,148,150,158, 160,161,163,164,191,193,194, 196,197,199,201,202,204,206, 207,215,217,226,227,228,230, 268
Mead, William x
Meador 190
Meador, James 190,224
Meador, John 165
Meador, Jonas 68,98,103,143,166, 184,215,219,224,225
Meador, Jonas Sr 99
Meadow, Joel 23
Meadows, see Meador
Meanley, John 95
Meanley, William 167
Meat 51
Medder, see Meador
Meggs, Joel 184,224
Melton, Samuel 99,166,167
Meredith, James 43,186
Meredith, Samuel 88,91,130,176
Meridith, Joseph 266
Merriman, see Merryman
Merriweather's Warehouse 38
Merryman, John 15,23,57,82,86,98, 156,160,172
Merryman, John Jr 190
Merryman, Thomas 57,77,87,131, 143
Methodists vii
Michaux 58,81,136,182

Michaux Ferry 58,65,118,155,212, 232,243,259
Michaux Ferry Road 80,136
Michaux, Jacob 13,32,58,65,98,155, 161,173,186,187
Michaux, James 136
Michaux, Joseph 151,161,182,208
Michaux, orphans 32
Michaux, Paul 13,29,42,58,65,69,70, 80,81,86,96,119,136,155,172, 186,189
Middle Creek 233
Middle Road 56,57,58,59,79,80,81, 118,119,121,152,154,155,156, 189,209,212,213,214,232,234, 242,243,244,259,261
Mill Creek 56
Mill Path 36,154
Miller, Jesse 134,155,161,185,234
Mills, William 29,54,69,79,86,89,117, 141,142,153,161,179,180
Minter, Anthony 186,212,232,252
Minter, James 225
Minter, John 58,82,86,93,94,171, 186,202
Minter, Richard 248
Mishshow, see Michaux
Montague, Thomas 149,156,159, 161,163,164,190,191,192,196, 216
Moody, Thomas 152,160,175,176, 209,233,234,244,253
Moore, Henry 170,241,249,258
Moore, Henry Sr 249
Moore, John 69
Moore, Robert 99,209,251
Morgan, Edward 133,135,185
Morris, Nathaniel 181
Mosby 93,213
Mosby, Benjamin v,35,52,113,119, 123,134,139,140,146,147,149, 155,192,195,198,201,203,206, 221,237,256,257,271
Mosby, George 262
Mosby, Hezekiah 16,36,119,156, 160,172
Mosby, Jacob 36,37,57,66,68,72,81, 86,94,95,104,135
Mosby, Jesse 233,248
Mosby, John 86,235
Mosby, Joseph 66,81,93,155,161, 187,189,214
Mosby, Littleberry xiv,57,81,86,104, 113,114,119,121,124,139,141, 144,145,147,148,150 157,158, 159,160,162,163,164,191,192, 193,194,195,196,197,199,201, 202,204,206,207,215,216,218, 219,226,227,229,230,235,236, 237,238,239,240,241,244,245, 246,253,255,258,262,263,268, 269,270
Mosby, Littleberry Sr 262,270
Mosby, Littleberry Jr 264
Mosby, Micajah 35,56,60,66,67,68, 69,81,86,93,94,119,124,133,135, 155,161,183,185,212
Mosby, Mr. 193
Mosby, Nicholas 213
Mosby, Poindexter 79,86,102,121, 123,138,139,140,145,148,158, 162,189,191,194,209,233,244, 250
Mosby, Robert 261
Mosby, Stephen 119
Moseley, Arthur 9,25,26,29,30,100, 142,143,164,170,171,197,198, 199,201,203,204,207,210,217, 231,242,247,249,251,258,268
Moseley, Arthur Sr 241,258
Moseley, Benjamin 26,30,100,249, 258
Moseley, Edward 65,66,78,86,93, 116,131

Moseley, J 185
Moseley, John 10,23,25,33,56,64,65,
    66,69,78,86,93,101,116,131,153,
    161,169,180,210,218,219,226,
    227,228,229,230,234,235,236,
    237,238,239,240,241,244,245,
    246,251,255,256,257,258,262,
    268,269
Moseley, John Jr 231,231,241,247,
    252,258
Moseley, Richard 10,29,30,35,55,67,
    69,79,86,100,117,142,143,170
Moseley, Thomas 64,101,102,131,
    138,153,161,169,180,181,210,
    231,236,237,238,239,240,241,
    244,245,246,251,253,255,256,
    257,258,262,263,266,268,269
Moseley, William 9,29,30,55,67,69,
    79,86,100,117,141,142,143,169,
    247,258,264,266
Mosham, see Mossom
Mosley, see Moseley
Moss 44,68
Moss, Alexander 14,35,66,94,135
Moss, James 94,119,124,134,135
Moss, John 134,244
Moss, Thomas 35,66,67,93,94
Moss, William 20,44,45,56,66,67,81,
    86,94,95
Moss, William Sr 14,47
Mossom 65
Mossom, John 10,27,32,33,56,66,69
Muddy Creek 14,22,56,57,66,81,82,
    98,119,120,134,155,156,189,213,
    234,244,248,261
Muddy Creek Bridge 66
Mullins, William 23
Mullis, Alexander 163
Munford, Edward 253
Murray, Robert xi,226,227,233,243,
    248
Murray's Road 79

Murray's Store 233
Murrey 98,100,101,117,143,154
Murrey, James 25,156,160,164,213
Murrey, Richard 68,82,85,86,98,99,
    103,106,109,111,166,203
Murry, see Murray, Murrey
Murry's Ordinary 119,156

Napkins 43
Nash, Thomas 167
Needlework 113
Negro's Arm Road 59,80,118,154,
    212,232,242,259
Nelson 178
Nelson, John 77,86,89,90,151,161,
    177,182
Nelson, Matthew 89,151,161,177,
    182
Netherland 3,177
Netherland, Benjamin 136,138,154,
    160,172,188,189
Netherland, John v,52,61,63,97,117,
    177,189,196,197,199,201,202,
    204,205,206,207,215,216,217,
    218,219,226,227,228,229,230,
    234,235,236,237,238,239,240,
    241,244,245,246,253,255,256,
    257,262,263,268,269,270
Netherland, Wade v,62,70,71,73,74,
    75,76,83,85,105,106,107,108,
    111,114,121,124,144,147,148,
    186,191,193,196,268,269
Nevil, Cornelius 34
Nevil, James 34,103
New Kent County 35
New Road 12,15,17,79,101,116,117,
    153,169,210,231,241,242,258
Newton, Burton 165
Newton, John 156,161,184,214
Nicholas, George 46
Nix, Elizabeth 237
Nix, Widow 235

Noel, John 115,124,127,209
Nordin, Chris 24
Norris, Nathaniel 181
Northcote, see Northcut
Northcut, John 30,100,142,143,170
Nuckels, Anne 148
Nuckels, Samuel 103
Nunnally, Archelus 243,253
Nunns thread 44

Oaths 3,6,7,41,53,75,163,193,218
Oazeley, Thomas 131
Office building 49
Oglesby, James x,228
Old inn line 189
Old mill 57
Orange, Lewis 152,160,176
Orphan child 149
Osburn, Thomas 177
Oslen, see Oslin
Oslin, Jesse 224
Oslin, Samuel 97,120,157,184,224, 225
Oven at glebe 52
Overseer 97,142,144,266
Overseer of poor 264,266
Overton's Ordinary 211,213
Owen 97
Owen, David 231
Owen, George 23,35,59,65,69,80,86, 96,97,117,137,138,154,160,177
Owen, Joel 252
Owen, William 178
Owle, see Howl
Ozburn 97

Paint glebe 83
Palmer, Joseph 203,204,215,228,270
Palmer, William 14,164,197,199,200, 202,204,216,228,271
Palmore, William 36
Panes of glass 46,106

Pankey, John 241,249,251
Pankey, Samuel 265,266
Parish line 233,234,243,244,260,261
Parish vs Woodson 162
Parish, see Parrish
Parker 101,159
Parker, David 156,213
Parker, Drusilla 175
Parker, Mrs. 72,73,84
Parker, Richard 17,25,55,86,101, 112,116,124,131
Parker, Richard Sr 130,131,175
Parker, Richard Jr 101,152,160,176
Parker, Robert 78
Parker, Widow 74,84,106,112,130
Parker, William 25,101
Parks, William 43
Parret, see Parrott
Parrish, Joannah 39,42,46,60,70,72, 74,84,106,108,112,122,140
Parrish, John 165
Parrott, Edward 80,109,118,122, 123,124,126,140,154,157,161, 162,183,191,198,200,205,212, 216,226,232
Patent fee 44
Patent for glebe 44
Patrolers 74
Patson, John 35
Patterson, David 265
Patteson 250
Patteson, Gideon 104,143,144,154
Patteson, James 131,175
Patteson Road 119
Pattillo, Henry 182
Payne, Josiah 29,64
Pendleton 23
Perkins, Richard 133
Peterville Church v,vi,viii,x,xi,1,2,5, 7,9,19,40,41,45,46,51,59,70,72, 74,76,83,84,85,105,106,107,108, 109,112,113,122,123,139,145,

146,147,148,150,158,159,161,
163,191,193,194,195,196,197,
199,201,202,204,215,216,226,
227,228,229,230,234,235,236,
237,255,270,271
Pews 61,111,141,150
Phelps, John 36,97,189
Phelps, Samuel 57,63,69,184
Phips, Tabitha 146,149
Pierson, Robert 128
Pigg, John 216,228
Pigg, Paul 64
Pitman, John 246,247
Pleasant, see Pleasants
Pleasants 68,87,93,95
Pleasants, James 214
Pleasants, John 24,28,31,32,34,35,
 66,67,94,97,104,109,126,133,
 135,136,172,174,175,179,183,
 185,188,189,190,222,233
Pleasants, John Sr 177
Pleasants, Miriam 247
Pleasants, Mr. 90
Pleasants, Robert 247
Pleasants, Samuel 247
Poindexter, John 185
Poindexter, Philip 16,23,36
Pollock, Peter 259
Pool 235,237
Pool, Mary 228
Pool, Robert 238,240,245,254,255,
 256,261,262
Poorhouse xiv,204
Porches 193,195
Porter, Francis 195,198,202,205,216
Porter, Hannah 265
Porter, Isaac 265
Porter, Thomas 265
Potter, Thomas 57,82
Pouval, see Povall
Povall, Charles 241,246,247,252,258
Povall, John 241,252,258

Povall, Maj. 185
Povall, Richard 10,32,33,78,86,105,
 116,124,126,127,177,250,252
Povall, William 65
Powel, Samuel 213
Powers, Toliac 36
Powhatan County ii,iii,249,263,264
Prayer books 44,199,206,264
Preaching 2,5,234
Presbyterians iii,vi
Prewit, see Pruit
Price, Edmond 184
Price, Joseph 15,30,70,98,102,103,
 120,124,132,133,157,160,168,
 169
Price, William 198,201
Prier, see Prior
Pringle 101,130
Pringle corner 130
Pringle, Edward 122
Pringle, Richard 149,175
Prior, David 34,103,164
Prior, John 134
Priyo, see Prior
Property of parish 264
Prosser, Thomas 126,183
Prosser, William xi,118,236,238
Prosser's Ordinary 243,260
Pruet, see Pruit
Pruit, Hugh 57,82,98
Pruit's Path vii,15,82
Pryer, see Prior
Pulpit 62,147

Quarters 90
Quit rents 60,63,111

Racks 109,229
Radford, George 118,124,126,138,
 154,161,183,212,224,226,232,
 238,242,246,247,249
Radford, John 11,27,32,33,34,58,65,

80,86,94,126,138,183,185
Radford, John Jr 154,160,174,175,
 183
Radford, Richard 174,212,224,242,
 250
Railey, Charles 13,32
Railey, John 67,69,80,118,136,172,
 197,202,204,207,269
Railing under church 195
Rails 9,49,107
Raine, John 151,161,179,182,223
Raley, see Railey, Riley
Randolph 68,95
Randolph, Brett 102,185,246,247,
 264
Randolph, Col. 56,59
Randolph, Jane 35,94,133
Randolph, Madam 95
Randolph Mill Creek 78,116,153
Randolph, Mr. 68
Randolph, Mrs. 28,93
Randolph, orphan 177
Randolph, Peter 90,178,179,182
Randolph, Peyton 246,251
Randolph, Richard 32,33,35,64,65,
 182,183,184,221
Randolph, Ryland 127,128,182
Randolph, Thomas 135,188
Randolph, William viii,1,2,3,4,6,7,8,
 19,21,22,24,32,33,34,41,44,45,
 64,65,97,102,105,126,127,268,
 269
Randolph's Church Road 59,80,118,
 154,211,232,242,259
Randolph's Creek iii,17,57,58,82,
 120,128,157,168,181,214
Randolph's Fork 10
Randolph's Mill Creek 210,231,241,
 258
Randolph's Road 18,19,54,55,76,77,
 114,127,151,182,183,207,208,
 224

Ranson, Ambrose 55,89,177
Ranson, Ambrose Jr 89
Ranson, Flamstead 173,177
Ray 182
Rayley, see Railey
Reading place 4,10
Realy, see Railey
Rediford, see Retterford
Removing glass 123
Rennals, Rennels, Rennolds, see
 Reynolds
Repairs 48,60,75,87,113,114,121,
 159,163,206,236
Retterford, John 29,36,54,67,69,77
Retterford, John Sr 115
Retterford, William 54
Reynolds 173
Reynolds, Charles 160,169
Reynolds, child 106,108,110,112,
 122,140,145,148,158,162,191,
 194,197,199,202
Reynolds, David 102,103,132,134,
 164,165,168
Reynolds, Isham 157
Reynolds, John 30,57,72,86,103,106,
 108,120,124,132,160,169
Reynolds, Jonas 89,178
Reynolds, orphan 172
Reynolds, William 31,136,172,242
Rice, Ann 44
Rice, Thomas 251
Richards 130
Richardson, Isham 87,127,128,208
Richardson, John 54
Richardson, Martin 215,218,224
Richardson, Mary 184
Richardson, Randolph 99
Richason, Richerson, see
 Richardson
Richmond 264
Riddle, John 163
Riddle, Thomas 88

Ridge Path 12,16,36,59
Ridge Road 116
Rigen, see Riggin
Riggin, William 23,26,33
Right, see Wright
Right, George 76
Riley, see Railey
Riley, Charles 31
Riley, James 31
Riley, John 31
Rinalds, see Reynolds
River Road 12,14,15,56,57,81,82,83, 96,118,119,120,155,156,157,168, 184,212,213,214,215,233,234, 243,260,261
Robards, see Roberts
Robert, Merry 23
Roberts, David 23
Roberts, James 35
Roberts, Morris 23,26
Roberts, William 4,5,16,35,36
Robertson, Christopher 104,143,167
Robertson, Duncan 188,214,215, 233,243,
Robertson, Edward 103,211
Robertson, Field 79,86,104,117,141, 143,144,211
Robertson, John viii,ix,x,4,5,7,9,17, 19,20,21,22,31,40,41,42,43,45, 46,47,48,50,51,52,53,54,59,70, 72,98,103,143,167,168,184,224, 225,268
Robinson, see Robertson
Robinson, James 33,165
Robusson, John 31
Rocky Oak Church viii
Rogers, Mary 228,235,237
Rogers, Sarah 205,207,216
Roland, John 164
Roland, Simon 215
Ronald, William 248,249,251,254, 255,256,257,262,263,268,270

Ronold, see Ronald
Roper, Jesse 247
Roper, Samuel 265
Routon, William 99
Rowland, John 44,46,67
Rowland, Michal 67,103
Rowland, William 134,165
Rowntree, Dudley 115
Rowton, William 117,154,160,167
Royston 175
Runalds, see Reynolds
Runnals, John 60,74,82,84
Russel, Daniel 184
Russell, Stephen 25
Russell, Thomas 26

Salley 37,95
Salley, Abraham ix,53,59,61,62,70, 71,75,97,176,187,242,268,269
Salley's Path 57,59,79,80,118,209, 211,234,244
Salley's Plantation 121,152,154,232, 242,259
Salmon 14
Salmon, John 15,57,67,82,120,184
Salmon, William 2
Sammon (Salmon), William 23
Sampson (Samson), William 141, 180,181,190
Sanders, see Saunders
Sanderson, William 169,184,215, 224,225
Saunders, child 3,5,6,20,40,42,46,60, 70,72,74,84,105,108,112,122,140
Saunders, Jesse 220,221
Saunders, John Hyde ix,x,12,27,28, 36,58,66,81,86,95,96,97,176,177, 186,188,189,211,228,230,235, 237,263,264,268
Saunders, Robert 3,5,6,20,40,42,46, 60
Saunders, Samuel Hyde 243,252,253

Saunders, Winfield 51,145,148,158, 162,191,194,197,199,202,204, 216,226,228,235,237,238
Saunders, William 219
Scales, Hendrick 3,5,20
Scales, Widow 3
Sceasor, see Seizer
Scott, Charles 134,213
Scott, John 28,36,133,164,265
Scott, Mr. 14,15
Scott, Samuel 1,2,3,4,5,6,7,8,19,20, 21,22,40,50,52,53,56,59,61,70, 83,94,268
Scott, Saymore 114,124,127,150,161, 184,207,221
Scott, Walter 132,169
Scott, William 189
Soctt's line 87
Scott's Mill 13,24,119,120,155,156, 213
Scott's Mill Road 213
Scott's Path 14
Scott's Road 155,156
Scottville 239
Scrugg, Tom 95
Scruggs, Drury 31,35,92,120,124, 128,156,161,181,214
Scruggs, Edward 68,93,95
Scruggs, H 220
Scruggs, Henry 142,153,161,179, 180,219
Scruggs, John 17,79
Scruggs, Robert 131,167,214
Sea, John 218
Seal church 141
Seay, Gideon 84,109,113,141
Seay, John 117,141,142,153,161,179, 210,219,220
Seizer, David 118,136,172,173,246
Seldin, Samuel 266
Sell glebe land 7
Sexton 8,19,20,40,42,45,46,47,51,52, 59,62,70,72,74,84,105,108,110, 112,122,139,148,158,161,163, 191,194,197,199,200,202,204, 216,226,235,237
Sharp, Richard 88,152,160
Shays, William 25,29
Shed at glebe 193
Shees, see Shays
Shepard, William 179,183,208,223
Sheriff 5
Sheriff, sub 20
Sheys, see Shays
Shockoe 44
Shoes 198
Shsot, see Scott
Shutters 9,121,141,234
Sims, Benjamin 129,130,209
Sims, Edward 266
Sims, Matthew 210,218,219,220
Skelton 34
Skelton, Reuben 103
Skinquarter Creek iii
Skipwith, Henry 253
Slaughter, George 129
Slaughter, Martin 64,72,90
Smallpox 203
Smith, William 16
Smith 101,177
Smith, Booker (Bowker) 42,47,56, 78,86,97
Smith, George 265
Smith, Guy 60
Smith, Humphrey 118,137,174,217
Smith, James 175
Smith, John 20,26,27,64,91,129,130, 174,175,271
Smith, John Jr 20,42
Smith, Lawrence 78,86,101,116,124, 130,131,152,160,175
Smith, Mary 255,257,261
Smith, Robert 98,177,184,206,250
Smith, Sterling 266

Smith, Susannah 255,257,261
Smith, Thomas 213,225
Smith, William viii,36,43,45,47,63,
 97,104,126,137,138,140,162,176,
 198,263,271
Smith, William S 265
Smoke house 49
Soakass Creek 117,153,154,211
Solomon's Creek 12,13,58,65,81,96,
 118,119,155,212,214,233,243,
 260
South Chapel vii,viii,40,46,51,61,62,
 70,72,74,83,84,105,108,109,110,
 112,113,122,139,141,145,146,
 148,149,158,159,161,191,192,
 194,197,199,202,204,215,216,
 226,228,229,234,235,270,271
Southall, James 181,220,221
Spaulding, John 32
Spearman, John 220,221
Spears, Speers, see Speirs
Speirs 81,118,119
Speirs, Alexander 29,69,89,92,99
Speirs, Mary 192,195,198,200,202
Speirs, Nicholas 44,68,94,99,135,
 213,244,261
Speirs Ordinary 155
Speirs, William 17,31,58,66,80,81,96
Spiers, see Speirs
Spring branch 215,224
Spurlock, John 31,136
St.. Anne's Parish i
St. James Northam i
St. James Parish i,ii,20
St. James Southam i
Stable 49,157,159,163
Standing Comm. of Convention 264
Starkey, John 220,221
Starkey, Joseph 179,180
Starkie, see Starkey
Stegar, see Steger
Steger 154

Steger, Francis 35,36,63,134,135,244
Steger, Francis George 104,119,139,
 143,155,168
Steger, Hans 234,244,261
Steger, John 211,234
Steger, Thomas 234,244,261
Stephenson 68
Stephenson, John 93,119
Steps 8,106,146,192,234
Stevenson, John 124,133
Steward, John 64,248
Stewarts 214,215
Still, William 29
Stinson, Alexander 219
Stith, Mr. 38
Stith, William 2,5
Stone, William 16,29,36,56
Stoner, Col. 96
Stoner, Danie l 32,136
Stoner, Maj. 24
Stoner, Peter 172,212,232
Stoner's Ordinary 212,214
Stort (Stourt), John 35,102
Stort, Randolph 35
Stovall 95
Stovall, Bartholomew 13,27,28,72,
 95,96,243
Stovall, Bartholomew Sr 188,189
Stovall, Bartholomew Jr 118,189,
 214,233
Stovall, George 16,35
Stovall, Thomas 12,46
Strange, children 205,216,226,228,
 235,237,238,240,245,254,255,
 256,261,262
Strange, Esther 261,262
Strange, Thomas xiv,205,216,226,
 228,235,237,238,240,245,254,
 255,256,261,262
Stratton 11,12,24,93
Stratton, Henry 66,67,94,119,134,
 135

Stratton, John 234
Stratton, Thomas 135
Stratton, William 56,66,68,69,81,86, 94,95,112,133,135,155,161,185, 205,248,266
Stratton, William Jr 234
Street, William 265
Sublett, Benjamin 265
Sublett, John 265
Sublett, Peter 264,266
Suinne, Joseph 27
Suit by parish 162
Surplice 44,227,264
Surveyor 137,138,157
Sutlief, Elenor 73,75,109,112,122, 140,145,148,158,162,191,195, 197,200,202,205,216,226
Swann, John 248,254
Swann, Mr. 162,193,209,211
Swann, T 137
Swann, Thomas Thompson 238, 239,240,271
Swann, Thompson 83,105,108,111, 112,113,114,121,124,138,139, 140,141,144,145,147,148,150, 157,158,159,160,164,191,194, 196,197,199,201,202,204,207, 215,217,227,229,230,234,236, 268,269
Swann's Creek 233,234,244,261

Tabb 168
Tabb, Edward 66,67,94,119,124,134, 135,166,167,171
Tabb, Langhorn 243,253
Tabb, Thomas 57,69,82,86,89,92, 99,104,120,128,156,160,171,181
Table 1,9,147,264
Table cloth 43,192,264
Tar the church 9
Tar Wallet Church vi,2,5,6,8,9,19, 22,39, 42,43,44,46,47,50,51,52, 53,61,62,70,71,72,73,74,75,83, 84,89,105,106,108,109,112,113, 121,122,124,139,145,148,158, 161,163,191,192,194,197,199, 200,202,204,206,215,216,270, 271
Tarlyle, Darby 220
Tatum 206
Tatum, John 98
Tatum, Richard 202,216
Taylor, Avis 112,122,140,145,148, 158,162,188,191,194,197,199, 202,204,216,226,228,235,237, 238
Taylor, George 188
Taylor, James 95,119,155,161,188, 189
Taylor, John 3,5,6,12,20,28,36,37, 40,42,46,51,58,60,66,70,72,74, 81,84,86,91,95,96,105,108,110, 119,142,179
Taylor, Mark 100,143,153,160,170, 249
Taylor, Richard 34
Taylor, Robert 243,250
Taylor, Samuel 15,34,35,57,82,86, 103,120,124,132,134,157,160, 165
Taylor, William 12,28,37,42,43,46, 51,58,60,66,69,70,81,85,86,96, 155,188,237
Tear Wallet Bridge 19
Tear Wallet Creek 18,54,55
Tear Wallet Hill 1
Tear Wallet Run 77,115,116,152,209
Telphra, John 179
Tenham, Robert 90
Terpin, see Turpin
Terrell, William 56,81,119,144,147, 149,164
Terrill, see Terrell
Terry, Daniel 25,55

Terry, Henry 29
Terry, James 1,2,3,4,5,6,7,8,9,19,22,
   39,40,45,47,48,50,51,52,53,54,
   59,61,62,64,70,268,270
Terry, Joseph 3,5,18,37,60
Terry, Zach 89
Thomas, Jesse 201,203,205,206,217,
   271
Thomas, Job 57,82,86,92,93,98,102,
   103,132,133,184,225
Thomas, Philip 11,24,29,31,32,104,
   126,231,250,252
Thomas, Phillip Jr 116,124,127,152
Thompson, see Thomson
Thomson 100,101
Thomson, Benajah 130,131
Thomson, David 92,99,103,252
Thomson, Josiah 131,144,168,175
Thomson, Robert 20,25,54,78,86,
   104,116
Three Bridges 12,13,58,80,96
Tilman, Thomas 69,99
Timson 23,24,35,64,65,100,101,102,
   143
Timson, John 30
Tinsley, Mrs. 265
Todd 100
Todd, George 30,67,143
Todd, John 170,210
Tomson, see Thomson
Toney, Edmond 28,81,95,96,118,
   155,161,187,188,189,214,243
Toney, Edmond Jr 233,243,250
Townes (Towns), James 89,178
Trabue, David 265
Trent, Alexander 1,2,3,4,5,6,7,8,9,
   19,21,29,40,45,48,50,53,54,68,
   69,73,79,86,87,89,99,105,107,
   108,109,110,111,112,114,117,
   121,122,124,128,132,133,140,
   142,144,145,147,150,160,163,
   164,166,168,180,181,183,191,
   193,194,196,197,198,199,201,
   204,206,207,215,216,217,220,
   221,223,225,228,249,251,265,
   268,269
Trent, Field 92
Trent, Henry 34
Trent, Peterfield 128,180,183,219
Tribeu, Jacob 26
Trigg, William 18,29,54,63,69,79,
   86,89,91
Tucker, Jesse 248
Tucker, Thomas 68,133,135,185,
   205,207,216,248
Tucker, Thomas Jr 248
Tucker, William 135,185,205,234
Turkey Cock Run 215,224
Turnbull, Charles 43,44
Turner, Ezekiel 4,5
Turpin 3
Turpin, Capt. 26
Turpin, Col. 202,207
Turpin, Thomas viii,1,2,4,6,7,8,9,19,
   20,21,22,26,27,33,40,41,43,47,
   48,50,54,59,60,71,73,75,76,105,
   108,111,114,121,139,141,145,
   147,148,150,158,159,160,164,
   183,191,193,194,195,196,197,
   200,201,202,204,218,219,226,
   227,229,230,247,268,269
Turpin, Thomas Jr 174,263,270
Turpin, William 196,198,199,200,
   201,203,271
Two Blazed Path 16,17,25

Upper end of the parish 234

Vaughn, Edmond 232,242,244,252,
   253,254,255,256,257,258,262,
   263,268,270
Vest, John 251
Vestry books 218
Vestry clerk 19,46

Vestry records 218

Waddell 135
Wade, Henry 225
Wadel, Noel 66,67,94
Wadkins, see Watkins
Walker, Benjamin 133
Walker, James 89
Walker, Job 75,140,145,148
Walker, Joel 89
Walker, John 128
Walker, Thomas 12,97
Walker, Warren 77,86,89,90,115,
   151,161,178,182,208
Walker, William 178,208
Walthoe, Mr. 44
Walton 12,95
Walton, George 181
Walton, John 186,188
Walton, Robert iv,2,3,5,19,23,28,37,
   38,42,45,46,270
Walton, Thomas 14,22,36,57,82,86,
   98,164,190,213
Walton, Thomas Jr 195
Wamack, see Womack
Ward, Richard 18,89,177,178
Warwick 45
Washing surplice 44
Watkins 90
Watkins, Benjamin 131,132
Watkins, Edward 10,23,26,35,79,86,
   94,100,116,124,131,132,143,153,
   160,169,170,210,231,249,251,
   266
Watkins, Edward Sr 251,258
Watkins, Edward Jr 210,231,241,
   251,258
Watkins, Henry 241
Watkins, James 165,166
Watkins, John 10,25,26,55,66,69,79,
   117,131,169,170,251
Watkins, Natt 178

Watkins, Thomas 10,23,132,169
Watkins, Thomas Jr 169
Watson 22
Watson, Christopher 91,130
Watson, David 176
Watson, William 55,78,86,88,89,91,
   116,129,130,154,161,176,183,
   212,218,224,232,242,247
Watts, John xiv,184,190,192
Watts, Thomas 15
Wayles, John 104,130,131,165,168
Wayles, Mr. 144,175
Weatherford, Richard 77,86,90,91,
   115,124,129,130,171
Weaver, Benjamin 220,221
Webb, Merry 15,70
Webb, Mrs. 44
Webb, Thomas 178,179
Welch, John 106,109,163
Weldon, Catherine x
Wett, see Witt
Whalen, Sarah 262
Wherley, Whirley, see Worley
Whitewash 40,49,83
Whiting, Matthew 63
Whitton, Thomas 88
Whorley, see Worley
Wilkins, James 89,142,166,180,219
Wilkinson, James 252
Wilkinson, John 186,252
Wilkinson, Nicholas 32,136,173,186
Wilkinson, Peter 247
Wilkinson, Thomas 189,245,252,254
Wilkinson, William 186
Wilks[inson?], Thomas 189
William, Samuel 221
Williams, Charles 127,128,183,184
Williams, Hannah 236,237
Williams, Matthias 114,182
Williams, Roger 127,184,222
Williams, Thomas 55,76,86,87,114,
   124,128,151,161,183,208,218,

221,222
Williamson, Capt. 266
Williamson, George 10,30,33,35,55,
  64,65,67,100,143,170,210,231,
  241,244,245,246,254,255,256,
  257,258,262,263,264,268,269
Williamson, Jacob 259
Williamson, Mary 162,198
Williamson, Richard 104,126
Williamson, Robert 126,127,213,
  241,252
Willis Bridge 15
Willis Creek 56,57,58,81,82,83,120,
  168,213,224
Willis River 14,15,17,18,34,117,119,
  153,156,157,184,211,214,215
Willis Chapel vii,2,5
Willis, William 36
Wilmore, Daniel 13,21,24,31,32,42,
  46,58,71,80,109,110,112,122,
  136,140,145,148,158,162,172,
  191,195,197,200,202,205,216,
  226,228
Wilson, Benjamin 82,92,120,124,
  128,156,161,181,214,217
Windows 124,141,146,234
Wine 43,44,46,51,60,63,85,106,109,
  113,123,140,146
Winfree, see Winfrey
Winfrey, Israel 10,25,26,79,86,102,
  117,153,160,171,210,231
Winfrey, Jacob 23,120,184,190
Winifred, see Winneford
Winneford, David 36,104,143
Winneford, George 79,86
Witch, John 200,201
Witt, Sylvanus 2,5,19,23,42,46,51,
  59,70,72,74,83,105,108,112,122,
  139,145,148,149,270
William Clerk's Path 211
Woldridge, see Wooldridge
Womack 93

Womack, Abraham 32,33,35,37,56,
  66,68,69,81,86,94,95,112,133,
  135,155,161,185
Womack, Abraham Sr 14
Womack, Abraham Jr 14
Womack, Nathan 222,223
Womack, Richard 94
Womack, W 37
Womack, William 6,19,20,46,51,54,
  63,64,69,77,86,91,92,115,124,
  127,130,152,161,185
Wood, Ambrose 68,69,99
Wood, Hannah 61
Wood, Henry 20,42
Wooding, Robert 31
Woods, John 149
Woods, Mr. 44
Woodson 97
Woodson, Charity 96
Woodson, Charles 24,28,136,172,
  186,188,214,232,243,259
Woodson, Charles Sr 242
Woodson, Charles Jr 233,243
Woodson, Drury 132,157,160,164,
  165,168,169,214
Woodson, Elizabeth 24
Woodson, Hughes 211,231,250
Woodson, Jacob 102
Woodson, John 18,20,29,36,37,54,
  60,64,69,71,73,74,76,85,86,87,
  88,99,106,109,110,111,113,114,
  122,124,127,150,156,161,163,
  164,166,182,184,187,213,271
Woodson, Joseph 16,29,56,69,72,
  78,84,86,97,106,108,112,121,
  122,138,181,189,250
Woodson, orphans 31
Woodson, Samuel 252
Woodson, Sanburn 59,65,69,80,96
Woodson, Stephen 31,221
Woodson, Tucker 92,128,181
Woodson's Plantation 212

Woodson's Quarter 214
Wooldridge, Edmund 249
Wooldridge, John 26
Wooldridge, Thomas 26,132,169
Wooldridge, William 249
Word, Thomas 208,218,219
Worley, Esther (Easter,Hester)
   109,110,112,122,139,145,148,
   158,161,162,191,194,197,199,
   202,204,216,271
Worley, John 23,40,42,46,51,60,70,
   72,74,84,105,108,110,131,169,
   271
Worley, William 23,26,131,169,175,
   192,226,228,229,235,237,271
Worley's Chapel 2,4,5,7,19,42
Wriggin, see Riggin
Wright, Ambrose 179,182,184

Wright, Colman 261
Wright, Elizabeth 122,146,162,192,
   195,197,198,200
Wright, George 54,86,87,90,114,
   124,127,128,151,161,183,208,
   218,221,222,223
Wright, Griffin 223
Wright, Jacob 257,261
Wright, John iii,29,90,112,114,124,
   128,151,161,179,202,223
Wright, Paul 245,252,254,255
Wright, Sarah 240,245,254,255,257
Wright, Thomas 128,173,174,222,
   223

Yarborough 101
Yarbrough, Edward 42,46
Yarbrough, Elizabeth 146

www.ingramcontent.com/pod-product-compliance
Lightning Source LLC
Chambersburg PA
CBHW052051230426
43671CB00011B/1866